The Social Consequences and Challenges of New Agricultural Technologies

Other Titles in This Series

The Impact of Population Change on Business Activity in Rural America, Kenneth M. Johnson

Rural Public Services: International Comparisons, edited by Richard E. Lonsdale and György Enyedi

*Science, Agriculture, and the Politics of Research, Lawrence Busch and William B. Lacy

*Rural Society in the U.S.: Issues for the 1980s, edited by Don A. Dillman and Daryl J. Hobbs

Technology and Social Change in Rural Areas: A Festschrift for Eugene A. Wilkening, edited by Gene F. Summers

*Available in hardcover and paperback.

Rural Studies Series

The Social Consequences and Challenges of New Agricultural Technologies
edited by Gigi M. Berardi and Charles C. Geisler

Although formal social impact assessment of changing technologies in U.S. agriculture is still in its infancy, scholars have
been documenting the effects of new technology throughout the
twentieth century. In this collection, Professors Berardi and
Geisler bring together historically relevant research and a carefully chosen cross section of contemporary work. Their review of
the literature is followed by an evaluation of the effects of
mechanization on labor and production, written in 1904, which provides a backdrop for papers from the 1940s and 1950s examining the
mechanization of agriculture in the South, in the Midwest, and in
rural areas in general. Subsequent chapters offer present-day insights on such topics as the socioeconomic consequences of automated
vegetable and tobacco harvesting, center-pivot irrigation, and organic and no-till cultivation. The authors also look at compensation and adjustment programs for displaced labor, the relationship
between technology and agribusiness growth, and the effectiveness
of university programs that prepare students to perform social
impact assessments in agriculture. The edited proceedings of a
spirited roundtable discussion on new directions for the study of
the social impacts of farm technology and the political economy of
agriculture provide the thought-provoking conclusion to this overview of the field.

Gigi M. Berardi is assistant professor of environmental science
at Allegheny College in Meadville, Pennsylvania. She is a contributor to several volumes, including *Food and Energy Resources* (Hall
and Pimental, eds.; 1983) and *The Tobacco Industry in Transition:
Policies for the Eighties* (Finger, ed.; 1981). Charles C. Geisler
is assistant professor of rural sociology at Cornell University
and a research associate with COACT Research, Inc., in Madison,
Wisconsin. He is coeditor of and contributor to *Land Reform,
American Style* (Popper; 1984), *Labor and the Environment: An Analysis
of and Annotated Bibliography on Workplace and Environment Quality
in the U.S.* (Buttel and Wiswall; 1984), and *Indian SIA: The Social
Impact Assessment of Rapid Resource Development* (Green, Usner, and
West; 1982).

The Social Consequences and Challenges of New Agricultural Technologies

edited by Gigi M. Berardi and Charles C. Geisler

Westview Press / Boulder and London

The paper used in this publication meets the minimum
requirements of the American National Standard for
Permanence of Paper for Printed Library Materials
Z39.48-1984.

Rural Studies Series, Sponsored by the Rural Sociological Society

Westview softcover editions are manufactured on our own premises using the
highest quality materials. They are printed on acid-free paper and bound into
softcovers that carry the highest rating of NASTA in consultation with the
AAP and the BMI.

Published in 1984 in the United States of America by Westview Press, Inc.,
5500 Central Avenue, Boulder, Colorado 80301; Frederick A. Praeger, President
and Publisher

Library of Congress Catalog Card Number: 84-50648
ISBN: 0-86531-666-X

Composition for this book was provided by the editors
Printed and bound in the United States of America

10   9   8   7   6   5   4   3

Contents

Tables

xiv

Figures

Foreword

We are indebted to Gigi Berardi and Charles Geisler for bringing together in one volume a substantial part of the major work by social scientists on the social and economic impacts of new agricultural technologies. The compilation provides perspective on the scope and nature of the accumulated research into commodities, commodity systems, and agricultural regions given the most attention by investigators. It serves as an introduction to the methods which have been used in assessing the impacts of new technologies in farm production. And it offers access to classic pioneering studies, to contemporary work not generally known or widely available, and to new material prepared specifically for this volume.

The selections pertain to studies of the consequences of new farming technologies in the United States, with the exception of the papers by Newby and Utting on agribusiness in the United Kingdom and by Kloppenburg on biotechnology. The editors caution that even for the United States the selections are not all-inclusive of the research-based literature available since publication of the historically important but little-known work in 1904 by H. W. Quaintance, The Influence of Farm Machinery on Production and Labor.

Agricultural technology with significant economic and social consequences was being adopted by American farmers long before the advent of the rural social sciences. McCormick's grain reaper (1831), Deere's steel share plow (1837), the horse-drawn sulky and gangplow, barbed wire fencing, and the windmill are a few examples of such innovations. By the time the rural social sciences had gained a place in the nation's land-grant colleges, in the United

States Department of Agriculture, and elsewhere, the continuing stream of new technologies had become an important factor in the drastic adjustments in American agriculture associated with the reduction in farm workers. Reorganization in the structure of agriculture had already had adverse impacts on many farming-based communities and on the living patterns of farm families.

Technology has continued to outstrip social scientists' ability to assess its impacts. A review of the relatively limited amount of empirical investigations to date into the impacts of technology in agriculture suggests that the research has been highly selective as to the types of technology and the agricultural regions studied. Mechanization in the South, especially in cotton production and in flue-cured tobacco harvesting, and mechanization of vegetable harvesting in California's irrigated farming areas have been well studied, but their conspicuousness points to the selectivity of the research. Why have the social impacts—positive and negative—of so many other important technological developments received so little research attention? Possible reasons include the relatively low concentration of labor in the production of commodities other than tomatoes and tobacco and institutional and funding constraints on research at various land-grant colleges.

With certain early exceptions, the initial scholarly social impact research was conducted during the 1930s and focused on mechanization in the Cotton Belt. The severe economic and social adjustment problems facing rural America at that time stimulated numerous studies of rural life conditions, many designed to aid in formulating or evaluating public policies and programs for agriculture and rural people. It was the political and social environment of the period which led to the United States Department of Agriculture's wide-ranging survey of major technological developments in agriculture, published in 1940 as Technology on the Farm. The report ventured to propose public-policy measures to minimize or cushion the negative consequences of technological change for the groups in agriculture most adversely affected. Written over forty years ago, the excerpt in this volume serves as a reminder of the ineffectiveness of public policies in this area and of the inability or unwillingness to develop effective policies.

For those with scholarly and policy interests in agriculture and rural life, this book is a valuable resource. It increases our understanding of the consequences of new farm technologies as well as our understanding of past policy attempts to mitigate technology's adverse impacts.

Olaf Larson
Ithaca, New York

PAUL S. TAYLOR

To his memory and his vision

Acknowledgments

The editors wish to thank the many individuals and organizations who assisted in the preparation of this volume. Foremost among these, in terms of encouragement and material support, is the Rural Sociological Society and its Rural Studies Series Editor, David Brown. We are honored that the work is appearing among the first in this series. Financial support was also generously provided by the New York State Agricultural Experiment Station of Cornell University; the Department of Geography at the University of Maryland, Baltimore County; the Department of Environmental Science at Allegheny College; and the Department of Rural Sociology at Cornell University.

Many people provided invaluable commentary, feedback, and technical assistance on preliminary materials and as the project matured. These people included Elaine Emling, Lillian Kirk, Raymond Jussaume, Ronald Vlieger, Catherine Tardiff, Francene Signor, and Kathleen Kotila. We are especially indebted to Olaf F. Larson for his careful review of the manuscript. Merging historical and contemporary manuscripts was a prodigious editorial task demanding skill, judgment, and patience, for which we thank Helene Moran Vigorita.

We extend thanks as well to the numerous authors and copyright holders for allowing the inclusion of their materials. Without their cooperation, this volume would not have been possible.

Gigi M. Berardi
Charles C. Geisler

Part 1
Introduction and
Literature Overview

1
A Time of
Research Synthesis

Gigi M. Berardi
Charles C. Geisler

Many generations of social scientists have conducted research on technological change in agriculture. Socioeconomic consequences resulting from the
substitution of machine power for human power have
been identified and debated. With few exceptions,
however, the value orientations of investigators have
been supportive of technological change, and have
allowed for little discussion of its assorted impacts
on more than one segment of the population and even
less on the possible adjustments or compensations for
those negatively affected by such change. Indeed,
new technology has usually been associated with progress. Such progress has been measured by increases
in standards of living for farm families and decreases in the use of child labor. But amid this
progress has also surfaced a variety of problems resulting from labor displacement and transfer of ownership, labor, and managerial functions from farm to
off-farm entities. Broad changes in the structure of
agriculture have also occurred, resulting in further
concentration of wealth and power.

Where scholars have studied socioeconomic
changes, the dominant conceptual model has been the
diffusion of technological innovations in agriculture. Herein, cultural background, psychological motivations, and social characteristics such as income
and education typically were treated as independent
variables influencing rates of adoption. Rarely was
the social realm viewed as an interesting dependent
variable in its own right. Historians, for example,
presented the biographies of inventors or grouped
farm technologies in evolving "family trees." Economists were more likely to study changes in the incidence of tractors or in accounting techniques thought
necessary to accommodate new field practices and to

3

4

increase yields. Sociologists and anthropologists
researched standard-of-living changes accompanying
new technologies and the personal-achievement motivations of technology adoptors. Critical commentators
investigated assorted consequences of agricultural
technology in the context of an evolving political
economy. Their results were often reported in dramatic and sensational prose.

There is, however, an emerging trend of scholar-
ship purposefully focused on social impacts and dat-
ing back at least to the turn of the century. Such
work examines institutional barriers in the land-
grant college system to research on the social impact
assessment (SIA) of new farming technologies. It
investigates certain socioeconomic consequences of
technological change within and across farm generations, the compensation mechanisms for those negatively affected by farm technologies, and the relationship between the concentration and centralization
of agricultural capital and the changing structure of
agriculture. It documents social-political factors
in the development of farm technologies as well as
socioeconomic effects associated with their adoption.

The chapters presented here represent an extensive though not exhaustive survey of this scholar-
ship. As one reviews the selections, it is obvious
that certain technologies, commodity areas, and farming systems have received most of the research attention on social impacts. For example, four of the
authors studied mechanization impacts on the rural
population in the South (Hamilton, Williams) or, more
specifically, Oklahoma (McMillan) and Louisiana
(Bertrand). Yet each of the four contributions is
unique in its insights or methodologies and warrants
attention as a benchmark in a changing state of the
art. Several excellent review articles (Goss and
Rodefeld, 1977, and Stockdale, 1969 and 1977)[1] have
been omitted due to space limitations. Contributions
focus almost entirely on the United States though, as
several authors note, the social impacts of changing
farm technologies in developing nations are oftentimes better understood than those at home.

Among the more recent research is the work of
Perkinson and Hoover, who have written on the probable impact of tobacco mechanization. The objectives
of their study (or, rather, series of studies, com-
piled for this volume) included simulation of the
distribution of changes in employment and income in
response to mechanization, estimation of the potential income lost from mechanization, and identification of the potential demand for retraining and other

social services during the period of rapid adjustment. Their study is in part a response to
criticisms of SIA such as those posed by another contributor, William Friedland; in their concluding
remarks, the authors raise important questions regarding the widely held belief that cotton mechanization was responsible for the large rural-urban
migrations of thirty to forty years ago.

The Berardi study of North Carolina tobacco
farmers provides a follow-up to the work by Perkinson
and Hoover. Berardi also studied tobacco, specifically in two North Carolina counties where tobacco
production is concentrated. However, Berardi's
objective was to determine how successful people
were, once displacement had occurred, in making the
transition out of agriculture. The work indicates
that because of the income transfers from the lease
and transfer provisions of the federal tobacco program, allotment holders adjust to displacement more
easily than people who have no equity in land.

Five articles deal with mechanization of commodities produced in California (Schmitz and Seckler,
Thompson and Scheuring, Friedland, Fredricks) and in
Oregon (Hussen). Here again, each study is unique in
its orientation and/or methodology. Schmitz and
Seckler attempt to determine social costs and benefits associated with the mechanical tomato harvester,
which, Thompson and Scheuring note, has become a symbol of "progress" in agriculture. To compute the
gross social rate of returns, Schmitz and Seckler employ the conceptual framework used by Griliches
(1958) and Peterson (1967), who estimated the benefit
to society from the introduction of hybrid corn and
from poultry research. Hussen takes this analysis
one step further by including a more detailed discussion of other factors which might affect estimates of
social returns.

Thompson and Scheuring also study tomato mechanization, focusing on the impact of the electronic
tomato sorter on seasonal farm employment. They use
a case-study approach, presenting detailed interviews
with processing-tomato growers as well as two-year
work histories for farm workers. They estimate the
possible increase in demand for social services as
labor displacement occurs. Thompson and Scheuring's
article is noteworthy for the careful introductory
discussion of why agricultural mechanization has become such a controversial topic, given that the number of workers affected is relatively small compared
with worker displacement in other industries.

Friedland studied technologies for tomato production as well as for lettuce, grapes, and citrus.

He is quick to point out, however, that the focus of his study is <u>agricultural commodity systems</u>. Friedland and his colleagues follow the approach of the inventors of mechanized harvesting systems by treating tomato production systematically from beginning to end through a programmatic approach to SIA. Unique to his study is the role of students in assisting in this research as part of an undergraduate teaching program at the University of California, Santa Cruz. Although critical of the structure and motivation of agricultural experiment station (AES) research at the land-grant colleges, Friedland also acknowledges the AES as a funding source for his own work (as it was for many other contributors to the volume). He argues for more anticipatory or projective, <u>ante-factum</u> studies, a model further discussed by Kloppenburg in chapter 19. Funding from the National Science Foundation program in Ethics and Values in Science and Technology (EVIST) provided adequate resources to complete Friedland's projective studies and to develop ideas on a political economy of agriculture. He concludes by emphasizing the need for a <u>gestaltist</u> approach in research rather than considering singular phenomena in isolation as is typical in positivistic science.

Anne Fredricks, a student of Friedland, further develops a political-economy approach to SIA. Utilizing a case-study methodology, she convincingly develops the relationship between technological change and the growth of agribusiness. She discusses how choosing Bud Antle, Inc., one of the most important U.S. and international shippers of iceberg lettuce, for a case study of corporate agribusiness was not arbitrary. Through new technologies such as vacuum cooling and field wrapping, as well as union contracts with the International Brotherhood of Teamsters, Bud Antle has succeeded in reducing uncertainty in the production process, gaining greater control over labor, and concentrating capital necessary for the company's internal growth.

Newby and Utting also deal with agribusiness, but in more general terms than Fredricks's work. Looking at agribusiness in both the United Kingdom and the United States, the authors contend that agribusiness is among the most important forces of social change and restructuring in rural society. This is accomplished through advisory and consultative services to farmer-adoptors and by controlling technological options available to farmers through agroengineering, agrochemical, and feedstuff firms.

Vertical integration, characteristic of American agribusiness, is not yet common in Britain. As in the
United States, however, agribusiness abroad is influencing nutrition, the economic sovereignty of small
producers, and interest in public accountability surrounding food production and consumption.

A third treatment of the social impacts of agri-
business--particularly those firms advancing biotech-
nology--is presented by Kloppenburg. As a means of
demystifying biotechnology, the author reviews the
American experience with hybrid corn in years past
and recalls the social impacts known to accompany the
Green Revolution abroad. Kloppenburg then turns to
the "gene revolution" at home. He contends that genetic engineering will result in extensive control
over the production process in agriculture. He
argues that we must understand the structure of the
industry, and the concentration of power inherent in
it, before we can attempt to monitor and control the
manner in which the world's gene pool will be ex-
ploited.

Other articles in the book include the overview
provided by Berardi; the historical insights provided
in the little-known work of H. W. Quaintance; the
1940 USDA report, "Technology on the Farm," which
surveys major technological developments in agriculture; the work undertaken by James Copp and numerous
collaborators for the Council for Agricultural and
Science Technology (CAST); and the report on sustained land productivity and equity consequences of
alternative agricultural technologies provided by
Geisler and his colleagues. Like Friedland, Geisler
and colleagues argue that technology does not simply
refer to a mechanical device such as a tractor or
harvester, but rather to an entire complex or system
of production. Systems of production analyzed in
their work include center-pivot irrigation, no-till
agriculture, and organic farming.

Although many of the articles presented here review the social impacts of mechanical devices such as
tractors and tobacco harvesters, the editors recognize the important social impacts of other technological developments, ranging from electricity and
milking machines to computer applications in agriculture. In part, space constraints prohibit inclusion
of research on these topics. But more to the point,
much valuable research on the social impacts of
changing agricultural technologies remains to be
done.

The research surveyed prompts numerous basic
questions. What methodological insights can be

8

gathered from the studies presented here for other
areas of SIA? Conversely, what lessons are there
from SIA in other domains that would enhance the
sophistication of SIA in agriculture? Do they provide guidelines and agendas for research in the 1980s
and beyond? Who will fund such research in the
future? How will recommendations for adjustment and
mitigation be implemented amid fiscal austerity, new
federalism, and their sequels? And how will analysts
working in the present assign weight to social impacts deferred to future generations in the name of
satisfying demands of present constituencies?

Adjustment and compensation programs are one
area of inquiry needing attention. Another is the
narrow range of production-technology options from
which farmers have to choose. These options reflect
the specific value systems of research institutions,
land-grant colleges, and private firms, for whom family farms, farm communities, and environmental well-
being are often secondary concerns. Beyond specific
technologies, impact assessment must graduate to the
more integrated level of agricultural commodity systems. Analyses offered in the present volume are but
a first step in this direction.

Perhaps now more than ever before, the importance of coordinating agrotechnology impact-assess-
ment efforts across disciplines must be recognized.
To report the toxicity of all pest-control chemicals
in a journal read exclusively by toxicologists, as
opposed to the larger body of entomologists, ecolo-
gists, and agronomists, would be an important oversight. Likewise, the academic isolation of social
scientists involved in social-impact reporting and
discovery must be bridged. The 1981 Rural Sociological Society's annual meetings in Guelph, Canada,
provided a setting for further roundtable, interdis-
ciplinary discussion of technology-impact issues.
Part 4 of this volume contains edited transcripts of
that discussion. It presents the views of various
scholars, some of whose work is included here. The
discussion extends the dialogue on many questions
that are treated in this book regarding technology
and socioeconomic change.

NOTE

1. References for all chapters appear in the
Integrated Reference List at the end of the book.

2
Socioeconomic Consequences of Agricultural Mechanization in the United States: Needed Redirections for Mechanization Research

Gigi M. Berardi

Despite the substantial impact of mechanization on society, this literature review revealed not only a paucity of empirical studies on socioeconomic consequences of mechanization but, among published studies, a high percentage of ex post facto research designs. Rarely have the direction and rate of the mechanization process been questioned. Future research should include ex ante facto research designs, guard against prevalent "social darwinist" orientations, and address technology policy issues. Compensation and agricultural adjustment programs need to be formulated and evaluated, especially with respect to the actual ability of the rural populations to adjust to new vocations and social environments.

INTRODUCTION

Mechanization of U.S. agriculture[1] has been considered a major factor of social, economic, and environmental change in rural areas (Donaldson and McInerney, 1973; Friedland, 1973a; Goss and Rodefeld, 1977; Rodefeld et al., 1978; and Williams, 1939). While the direction and degree of association between mechanization and such socioeconomic variables as number of farms and size of farms have been fairly well established, causal relationships have not. One of the reasons for this is that it is difficult to

Edited and excerpted from Rural Sociology 46 (3), 1981, pp. 483-504. Reprinted by permission.

control for the effect of extraneous variables such as urban/rural wage differentials.[2]

The treatment of consequences of mechanization has thus been both comprehensive and deficient. The studies are comprehensive in that there are many publications available on the mechanization of agriculture,[3] deficient in that very few are based on the empirical research needed to test hypotheses (Hoover, 1976). Most studies discussing socioeconomic consequences of agricultural mechanization between 1935 and 1975 were based on trend data analysis, mere speculation, or independent variables other than mechanization (Goss and Rodefeld, 1977). These articles basically were derived from four disciplines: (1) agricultural engineering, (2) agricultural economics, (3) environmental studies, and (4) rural sociology. For each of these disciplines, the characteristic value orientation has almost stereotypically influenced interpretation of the consequences. Thus, agricultural engineering and economics have tended to view consequences of agricultural mechanization as positive,[4] environmental studies as negative, with rural sociology somewhere in between.

It is ironic that, despite the extensiveness of this literature, most studies did not include any rigorous testing of hypotheses. Perhaps what is more surprising is that very few discussed the implications of their results, although often these results indicated major changes in the structure of agriculture due to concentration and centralization of capital.

More recently, however, there has been research interest in socioeconomic consequences of agricultural mechanization and other agricultural technologies (such as chemical fertilizers). This is due not so much to a desire to return to the days of the horse-drawn plow or widespread use of stoop labor, but to a concern for the environmental impact and high-energy use of modern agricultural technology, as well as political-economic concerns about changes in the structure of agriculture. It is in this context that the directions of mechanization research and policy are being questioned and examined more critically.

The purpose of this paper is twofold: (1) to review the literature on socioeconomic consequences of mechanization,[5] and (2) to suggest directions for future research--in particular, research on labor adjustments in the production of crops rapidly being mechanized (such as flue-cured tobacco).

CONSEQUENCES OF MECHANIZATION[6]

Numbers and Characteristics of Farm Work Force

One of the major direct effects of agricultural mechanization has been labor displacement; as agricultural operations are mechanized, the total agricultural work force has decreased (Friedland and Barton, 1976; Friedland and Nelkin, 1972; Fusfield, 1970; Hamilton, 1939; McMillan, 1949; Schmitz and Seckler, 1970), reducing the numbers of hired farm workers (Bertrand, 1951) and seasonally hired farm workers (Metzler, 1964; Rasmussen, 1968) as well as farm family workers (Tolley and Farmer, 1967). One notable exception to this, however, has been the development and adoption of the cotton gin, which resulted in greatly increased cotton production in the South and which led to the expansion of the plantation system, with its use of slave labor (Genovese, 1967; Hambidge, 1940; and Rasmussen, 1977). The burden of adjustment of the labor force usually fell to the least educated and skilled workers (Hamilton, 1939; Lianos and Paris, 1972; Martin and Johnson, 1978; Mellor, 1954; and Raper, 1946). This transition was especially difficult if the displaced workers were minority group members (Bryant and Leung, 1967; Dillingham and Sly, 1966), in which case discrimination also prevented them from entering the urban work force (Ponder, 1971).

For the remaining farm work force, however, working conditions in general became better; the working day was shorter, and there was less "drudgery" associated with farm work (Bertrand, 1951), although certain dangers to health and safety were noted with increased use of machinery (Donaldson and McInerney, 1973).

Usually associated with farm mechanization were increased sales per farm and increased net operator income (Bonnen and Magee, 1938; Constandse et al., 1968; Heady, 1960; Rasmussen, 1962; Tweeten, 1965; and Woolf, 1971). However, these increases in income and, to a certain extent, standard of living, were more pronounced for farm owners and farm operators than for hired farm labor. According to Lianos and Paris (1972), labor's share of farm income decreased from 72 percent in 1949 to 33 percent in 1968.

In terms of changes in characteristics of the farm work force, indirect consequences of mechanization included a shift in values, life styles, and farm skills (as agriculture assumed a more industrial character) and a decrease in family ties (Bertrand,

12

1951; Donaldson and McInerney, 1973); a shift in the
age of farm operators (McMillan, 1949); an increase
in women in the farm work force (Friedland and Barton, 1976; Quaintance, 1904); a decrease in the use
of child labor (Street, 1957); and changes in the occupational composition (that is, increased structural
differentiation of management and labor roles) of the
farm work force (Rodefeld, 1974, 1979).

Numbers and Characteristics of Farms

As the capital costs of farm production increased, the numbers and characteristics of farms
changed markedly. Many of the effects are well documented and can be directly related to mechanization
[for example, changes in the size of farms (Goss and
Rodefeld, 1977)], whereas other effects (such as increased economic concentration in the production of
certain commodities) cannot. However, all of these
effects, whether direct or indirect, have facilitated
the changes in the structure of agriculture discussed
below.

The most well documented effects[7] of mechanization on farm numbers and characteristics have been
that farms are decreasing in number (Bertrand, 1951;
Gardner and Pope, 1978; Guither, 1972; and Rodefeld,
1974), and increasing in size (Bertrand et al., 1956;
Kyle et al., 1972; McMillan, 1949; Perelman, 1972;
Saville, 1941; and Taylor, 1938). As a corollary of
this, productive assets are being concentrated on the
largest-sized farms (Ball and Heady, 1972; Breimyer
and Barr, 1972; Krause and Kyle, 1970; and Rodefeld,
1974, 1979). Farms with sales exceeding $100,000 or
operating 1,000 acres or more have been increasing
their numbers and sales in both absolute and relative
terms since 1964 (Rodefeld, 1979). Farms have also
become more specialized in the commodities they produce (Field and Dimit, 1970; White and Irwin, 1972)
and have assumed a more industrial/commercial character (Donaldson and McInerney, 1973; McMillan, 1949),
especially as greater interdependence with the nonfarm sector such as bankers and equipment dealers has
developed (Gates, 1960; Hamilton, 1939; McConnell,
1953).

As the capital costs of farm production have increased, it has become increasingly difficult to enter farming (Field and Dimit, 1970; Gates, 1960;
Perelman, 1972; and Rasmussen, 1977), especially for
minority groups (Ponder, 1971), and for farm operators to maintain high levels of capital ownership.
Increasingly, there is a transfer of ownership,

labor, and managerial functions from farm to off-farm
entities (Goss et al., 1979).[8] The transfer mechanisms here include provision of credit, off-farm ownership of land and nonland resources, vertical
integration, and off-farm ownership of farm businesses (Goss et al., 1979; Kyle et al., 1972). These
changes have facilitated the movement towards a more
concentrated (Ball and Heady, 1972; Breimyer and
Barr, 1972) and differentiated (LeVeen, 1978) agriculture, with the major farm organizational types
becoming tenant, larger-than-family, and industrial
(Rodefeld, 1979), an issue which is receiving more
attention by agricultural researchers (Flinn and
Buttel, 1980).

Other effects of mechanization on farm characteristics include an increase in labor productivity
(Kendrick, 1964; Pederson, 1954), an increase in
timeliness of field operations (Carleton and
Vanden Berg, 1970; Donaldson and McInerney, 1973),
and a decrease in hillside farming (Raper, 1946).[9]

Effects of Mechanization on Rural Society

One major effect of mechanization on rural society has been labor displacement. Though it was
frequently assumed by policy makers as well as agricultural academicians that displaced farm workers
went on welfare in the cities, this was not necessarily the case (Hamilton, 1939). Many people moved to
poorer farms or remained in the open countryside. Of
course, other displaced workers migrated from rural
areas (Anderson, 1961; Chittick, 1955; Flora and
Rodefeld, 1978; Hamilton, 1939; Hennessey, 1970;
Hill, 1962; McMillan, 1949; Reeder and LeRay, 1970;
and Smith, 1974). Usually, it was the better educated, younger members of the community who
migrated. Such selective migration is well documented (Goss and Rodefeld, 1977). Agricultural adjustment for people remaining in rural areas was thus
all the more difficult due to constraints related to
their education, vocational training, and age.

Those who did move from rural to urban areas
took more than their belongings with them. They also
took their patronage of local businesses, resulting
in a loss of community functions (Anderson and
Miller, 1953; Brunn, 1968; Folse and Riffe, 1969;
Fuguitt and Deeley, 1966; and Heady, 1974). Churches
and schools closed (Bertrand, 1958; Kolb, 1959), local businesses were boarded up, property values declined resulting in a reduced tax base (Bills and
Barkley, 1973; Raup, 1961), housing was abandoned.

Not all establishments were negatively affected, however; certain businesses prospered, such as those involved in selling and transporting agricultural inputs and outputs (Quaintance, 1904). In certain areas school attendance increased, since child labor was no longer needed in the fields (Bertrand, 1951; Street, 1957).

Effects of Mechanization on Urban Society

One of the most dramatic effects of rural outmigration (due in part to labor displacement resulting from agricultural mechanization) was increased racial tension, ghetto riots, and other uprisings of the 1960s (Fujimoto, 1969; President's National Advisory Commission on Rural Poverty, 1967; Vandiver, 1966). Concurrent with this increase in racial tensions in urban areas was a decrease in such tensions in rural areas (Street, 1957). This was due not so much to a change in the attitudes of rural people, but merely to a decrease in the rural minority population. Outmigration of rural poor to urban areas also resulted in increased demands on urban social services, such as welfare and unemployment, by those who could qualify for it (Hamilton, 1939). Effects of mechanization on urban society also included changes in the cost, quality, and variety of our food supply. While some researchers agree that mechanization has given us specialized foods at low cost (Lorenzen and Fridley, 1966), others disagree (Belden and Forte, 1976; Hightower, 1975; Robbins, 1974). As discussed in Consumer Reports (1975), the concern is that with increasing concentration (facilitated by mechanization) in food production and food processing, less competition and higher food prices result.

Increases in the price of energy have also resulted in food-price increases. Steinhart and Steinhart (1974) predicted that a quadrupling of energy prices would result in a sixfold increase in food prices within the next forty years, whereas Pimentel and Pimentel (1979) acknowledged that the relative prices of both fossil energy and labor affect the price of food. If the price of labor is cheap relative to the price of energy, fossil energy-intensive agricultural technologies do not seem a wise investment, particularly if these high production costs are passed on to consumers.

Concern for the quality of our food supply was debated as early as 1904 when Quaintance wrote, "The use of machinery is not without some influence on the

quality of the product . . . grain cut . . . before
it is thoroughly ripened, becomes shrunken and of
less value" (1904:28).[10] More recently, questions
have been raised about the quality of vegetables and
fruits, and in particular the ripeness, taste, and
appearance of tomatoes (Consumer Reports, 1973;
Friedland and Barton, 1976; Hightower, 1972). Robbins (1974) and Hennessey (1970) also argue that the
variety of our food supply has decreased, particularly for fruits such as apples, although others have
argued that our mechanized agriculture does provide
us with a varied, nutritious diet (Lorenzen and Fridley, 1966; Rasmussen, 1975).

Mechanized agriculture has also impacted on the
environment itself; for example, soil compaction has
resulted in the need for heavier tillage equipment
(Allison, 1973; Berardi, 1976) which, in turn, has
been a causative factor in soil erosion (Carter,
1977).[11] Increased mechanization has also resulted
in an increase in fossil energy use (Cottrell, 1955;
Perelman, 1973; Carter and Youde, 1974; Stockdale,
1977) and, in particular, fuels needed to operate the
machinery (Pimentel et al., 1973).

DISCUSSION

Status of Agricultural Mechanization Research
in the United States

According to Bishop (1967a), much of the
research emphasis in agricultural economics in the
1940s and 1950s was placed on improvements in
technology as a means of decreasing production costs
and increasing various production efficiencies. Surpluses (Bishop, 1967a) and labor displacement (Day,
1967) were rarely discussed. In a review of more
recent articles of the American Journal of Agricultural Economics, 1963 to 1973 (excluding proceedings
of the summer and winter meetings), only 6.7 percent
were found to deal with such domestic issues as income distribution, minimum wages, rural services,
farm laborers, or minority groups (Bawden, 1973).[12]
Bawden concluded that agricultural economists: (1)
too often have not given enough attention to who
benefits from their work, and (2) should focus research efforts and resources into more nontraditional
areas of inquiry.

According to Wade (1973), one reason why the social consequences of the technological revolution in
agriculture have been so neglected is that Congress
does not have a primary interest in social-science

research. The agricultural committees in Congress
have long been dominated by Southerners, who, according to sociologists, have not encouraged federally
funded research that would reflect negatively on the
socioeconomic conditions or race relations in their
states.

Other critics charge the land-grant college system, more generally, with narrowly focused research
(Barnett, 1975; Hightower, 1972) guided primarily by
"efficiency" (labor rather than fossil-energy) considerations and by a values orientation aimed at capital intensity (U.S. Department of Agriculture and
National Research Council, 1973; Wade, 1975) and economic concentration (Friedland and Kappel, 1979).
However, some researchers in the land-grant college
system are critically examining changes in the size,
scale, and organization of U.S. agriculture (Flinn
and Buttel, 1980; Gregor, 1979b; Rodefeld, 1979,
1975). Such research has otherwise been meager
(Doering, 1978), particularly research on the impact
of large farms on communities and trade areas. One
landmark study in this area was that of Goldschmidt
(1946).[13] Although criticized for theoretical and
methodological limitations (Goss, 1979), the study
continues to generate research interest in size and
scale issues in agriculture.

The results of the literature review (documented
above) revealed not only a paucity of empirical studies on the socioeconomic consequences of mechanization, but of those published, a high percentage of ex
post facto research designs and strong similarity in
the value orientation of the research itself. This
observation has also been made by other researchers
(Goss and Rodefeld, 1977). These orientations
(which, for the most part, reflect the stereotypic
value orientations of the researcher's discipline)
included: (1) favorable attitudes toward mechanization,[14] (2) emphasis on profit maximization (as discussed by Perelman, 1977), and (3) little emphasis on
labor displacement and other labor issues, perhaps
assuming that the country has a policy of full employment to absorb displaced agricultural workers
(Dorner, 1971).

Even those articles that examined the negative
impact of mechanization on rural farm people (for example, labor displacement) almost unanimously[15] had
the same ideology--people should be moved out of agriculture, perhaps being aided financially in the
"adjustment" process. The research has been based on
an acceptance of the status quo, rather than a ques-
tioning of the direction and rate of the mechanization process itself.

Redirections for the Future

The difficulty of controlling for the effects of extraneous variables precludes definitive statements regarding causality between mechanization and much of the socioeconomic change in rural areas, although agricultural researchers biased both for and against mechanization have often made statements based on speculation alone (Goss and Rodefeld, 1977). It is conceivable that further mechanization studies could have a quasi-experimental research design [Gold-schmidt's (1946) study, despite its shortcomings, is a good example of this], and an ex ante facto research design, and that many of the variables involved in agricultural innovations and socioeconomic change in rural areas could be quantified and rigorously analyzed (see Gregor, 1963, 1964, 1970, 1979b; Heffernan, 1972; Rodefeld, 1979). However, most studies are typically based on census data, with the data treatment being more descriptive than quantitative. Yet even with these data, causal relationships between mechanization and change in rural areas can be analyzed. Examples of such research include McMillan's (1949) study of social aspects of farm mechanization in Oklahoma and Bertrand's (1951) study of Louisiana agriculture and the socioeconomic changes which were attributable to adoption of mechanical power.

More recently, considerable work has been done on the socioeconomic consequences resulting from further mechanization of tobacco production (Economic Research Service, 1969; Grise et al., 1975; Hoff et al., 1977; Hoover and Perkinson, 1977b; Martin and Johnson, 1978; McElroy, 1969; Smith, 1975; United States Senate, 1975). The objective of many of these studies was to evaluate various human-resource adjustment programs as well as to study the impact of flue-cured tobacco mechanization on changes in the structure of tobacco production.

It is important to note that many of these tobacco studies were ex ante facto. Typically, we rely on history to give us perspective on the import and impact of mechanization (Friedland and Barton, 1976). However, once laborers are displaced and farms sold, there is little that can be done to reverse this trend, should it be viewed as socially undesirable or untenable. Indeed, research findings on the mechanization of flue-cured tobacco production in North Carolina (Berardi, 1979b) showed that significantly fewer displaced agricultural workers were "adjusting"--that is, finding off-farm employment, participating in income transfer programs, or migrating

from economically depressed areas--than commonly
thought. Although it is relatively easy for researchers to recommend agricultural adjustment assistance or "compensation," the logistics of the adjustment process are usually neither carefully planned
nor successfully executed. Thus, from a social-
policy perspective, this trend towards ex ante facto
research, as exemplified in studies on flue-cured
tobacco mechanization as well as fruits and vegetables (Cargill and Rossmiller, 1969; Carleton, 1963;
Friedland et al., 1978; Johnson and Zahara, 1976),
should be firmly established in future research
designs.

In addition to changes in research design,
changes in the orientations of the researchers themselves are needed. Much of the previous research has
been dominated by a "social darwinist" orientation
(Goldschmidt, 1978) which assumes that there is one
inevitable course of social change (concentration of
capital, increase in the size of farms, decrease in
the number of farms) which yields the greatest level
of societal benefits (through increased production
efficiencies). This perspective has been put forth
and debated in the American Journal of Agricultural
Economics (Brewster, 1958; Sinclair, 1958) as well as
other journals. Such debate and comment (Carleton
and Vanden Berg, 1970; Hennessey, 1970; Loftsgard and
Voelker, 1963; Parsons, 1963) is important for the
critical examination of the orientations and goals of
past and present mechanization research.

Other needed redirections for research include
more emphasis on technology assessment and "miniatur-
ization of technology" (Madden, 1978), or "appropriate technology" (Bossung, 1976; Schumacher, 1973),
on systems analysis (Fridley and Holtzman, 1974), and
on designing technology policy (Uhl, 1969). Policies
regarding the direction and degree of mechanization
should include the setting of goals and priorities[16]
to guide the rate of development and dissemination of
new technology. Uhl (1969) further suggests the possibility of "technological orders" similar to fruit-
and vegetable-market orders which would regulate
technological change and adoption. Such regulation
and policy articulation is also important in the
interest of conserving fossil fuels in agriculture.
In this respect, more studies of low fossil-energy
farming systems--for example, organic (Berardi, 1978;
Oelhaf, 1978), Old-Order Amish (Erickson et al.,
1980; Stoltzfus, 1973), and other extensive livestock
and cropping systems (Berardi, 1979a)--are needed.

Lastly, agricultural adjustment programs must
also be examined more critically (Berardi, 1979b;

United States Senate, 1978). In evaluating these adjustment programs, the actual ability of the rural
population (especially those members most vulnerable
to technological change) to adjust to a new vocation
and a new environment must systematically and compre-
hensively be examined, especially through much-needed
longitudinal studies. Previous researchers (many of
whom themselves have had guaranteed job security in
the form of academic tenure) have glibly suggested
various adjustment programs as a solution to the
labor-displacement problem (Fulco, 1969; Raper, 1946;
Schmitz and Seckler, 1970) when such adjustment may
have been very difficult (Bagdikian, 1967; Black Economic Research Center, 1973; McMillan, 1949; Milk,
1972).

CONCLUDING COMMENTS

The mechanization of agriculture in the United
States has resulted in a highly productive food system: the United States now dominates the world's
grain exports, and in fiscal 1980, U.S. agricultural
exports [used not only to generate foreign exchange,
but as a tool of diplomacy (Sisler, 1977)] are expected to increase to a record $38 billion (Eco-
nomics, Statistics, and Cooperatives Service, 1980).
This high level of productivity in the United States
is sustained more by biological than mechanical
advances. Nevertheless, researchers are quick to
highlight the production accomplishments of mechanized agriculture such as increases in labor productivity (Bainer, 1977; U.S. Department of Agriculture,
1975b), while research on the socioeconomic consequences of mechanization for all segments of society
often has been neglected (Bonnen, 1969).

The recommendations for redirections in mechanization research discussed in the previous section of
this paper include more emphasis on ex ante facto research designs, technology assessment, and technology
policy, as well as changes in the value orientations
implicit in the research itself. Although it is important to recognize that it is the individual farmer
who decides whether or not to adopt a new technology
and that this decision is based largely on relative
prices of labor and machinery, it is also important
to note that the range of options for various production technologies from which farmers must choose are
neither limitless nor random. Various technologies
are developed (or not developed) by the land-grant
colleges[17] and by private firms for specific reasons;
thus they reflect researchers' and funding agencies'

specific value orientations [see, for example, the
discussion of the suppression of development of the
long-handled hoe, as discussed in Perelman (1977) and
the development of a mechanization research budget as
a response to the end of the bracero program in 1964
(Friedland and Kappel, 1979)].

Producing change in research orientation is not
simple and yet, as Friedland and Kappel (1979) argue,
institutions are capable of being changed, especially
if the reward structure is consciously linked to a
change strategy. This process involves the articulation and prioritization of social goals and research
objectives, such that technology development occurs
under certain social and ecological constraints--that
is, with more foresight of socioeconomic and ecological consequences of the technology. Perhaps then we
can affirm the words of researchers Donaldson and Mc-
Inerney (1973:832): "There is evidence that progress
in machine technology could be even more beneficial
if its development and introduction were negotiated
in a more conscious fashion."

NOTES

I thank the following specialists for reading
an earlier draft and for their many helpful sugges-
tions: William H. Friedland, Department of Community
Studies and Sociology, University of California,
Santa Cruz; Kevin Goss, Division of Regional Ser-
vices, Department of Agriculture, Western Australia;
Howard F. Gregor, Department of Geography, University
of California, Davis; Michael Heiman, Department of
Geography, University of California, Berkeley;
Michael Perelman, Department of Economics, California
State University, Chico; Carville V. Earle, Depart-
ment of Geography, University of Maryland, Baltimore
County; Richard Rodefeld, Department of Agricultural
Economics and Rural Sociology, Pennsylvania State
University; Michael Schulman, Department of Sociology
and Anthropology, North Carolina State University;
Ingolf Vogeler, Department of Geography, University
of Wisconsin-Eau Claire; and, at Cornell University:
Pierre Borgoltz, Kenneth Robinson, Department of
Agricultural Economics; Antoinette Wilkinson, Depart-
ment of Communication Arts; David Pimentel, Depart-
ment of Entomology; Richard McNeil, Department of
Natural Resources; Frederick H. Buttel, Department of
Rural Sociology; Gould Colman, University Archives.
Any errors or omissions are the author's responsi-
bility.

This article was researched and written while
the author held an appointment in the College of

Agriculture and Life Sciences, Cornell University,
Ithaca, New York.

1. Mechanization is defined here as the substitution of machine power for human or animal power, and does not include other components of technological change such as biochemical advances.

2. Other reasons range from the lack of conceptual frameworks, although this is changing (see, for example, Goss et al., 1979), to the institutional obstacles to such research (Friedland and Kappel, 1979).

3. Particularly as it relates to the high level of production and productivity of U.S. agriculture, which in turn gives us a unique position in world food economics and politics (Butz, 1975; Frundt, 1975).

4. Exceptions do exist, of course (Hennessey, 1970; Schmitz and Seckler, 1970).

5. Sources used for the literature review include COMPASS (computer-assisted search service) at Cornell University (Ithaca, N.Y.); Indexing and Abstracting Journals other than those in the COMPASS system (Bibliography of Agriculture, Dissertation Abstracts), including: Agricultural and Horticultural Engineering Abstracts; Biological and Agricultural Index; Business Periodicals Index; Index of Economic Articles; International Bibliography of the Social Sciences; Journal of Economic Literature; Poverty and Human Resources Abstracts; Readers' Guide to Periodical Literature; Social Sciences Index; Sociological Abstracts; The Engineering Index; World Agricultural Economics and Engineering Abstracts; as well as bibliographies from numerous articles.

Although the review was extensive, it was not exhaustive--not all relevant studies have been included as documentation (for example, articles documenting six or seven consequences of mechanization may only be cited once in the text of the paper; where possible, only articles with some empirical analysis are cited). Otherwise, reading of the paper would be tedious. A more complete bibliography may be obtained from the author upon request. For other bibliographies on mechanization of agriculture, see Goss and Rodefeld (1977); Hall (1968); Kramer (1976); Scheiffer and Fujimoto (1969).

6. Except for consequences such as changes in the size of the agricultural work force, most of the consequences outlined and documented below are indirectly related to mechanization; mechanization was a critical enabling (rather than causative) factor of socioeconomic change.

7. Most of these studies were based on trend analysis of census data.

8. As this transfer occurs, there is reduced control over farm resources and a decrease in the extent to which productive effort of the manager is rewarded (Rodefeld, 1979).

9. One further effect, from a historical perspective, was the raising of more livestock on grain stubble and pasture that was previously consumed by draft animals (Bertrand, 1951; Hatch, 1975; Perelman, 1977).

10. However, he was quick also to note the advantages of mechanization: "The present generation of Americans would be slow to eat bread made of flour from wheat threshed by the treading of horses and cattle" (Quaintance, 1904:28).

11. Furthermore, the cost of replacing eroded soil nutrients is expensive from both a pecuniary and energy perspective (Pimentel et al., 1975).

12. Similar statistics were found for the Canadian Journal of Agricultural Economics.

13. In the words of Shea (1966:36), "The only surprising aspect of these studies is the fact that there are not many more like them." However, this is not so surprising when one realizes the efforts made to undermine and suppress Goldschmidt's work (Goldschmidt, 1978:Part III).

14. So much so that individuals who criticize the changes effected by mechanization are often misunderstood and stereotyped as idealists and romantics glorifying stoop labor, since they have never picked tomatoes by hand, driven a horse-drawn plow, and so forth. Their critical analysis of technological change in rural areas [sometimes strongly polemical; see, for example, the classic study by Hightower (1972)] is dismissed as biased study when juxtaposed with the supposedly "value-neutral" research of other agricultural scientists.

15. There are, of course, exceptions (see for example, Friedland and Kappel, 1979).

16. This is done in several of the European countries (such as Switzerland and France)--a comparative analysis of these countries' farm and food policies would be insightful.

17. Federally funded research (focused on increasing labor efficiency through agricultural mechanization) at the land-grant colleges has been the subject of much controversy by public citizenry groups. Recently, a suit was filed by California Rural Legal Assistance on behalf of nineteen farm workers and a small-farmer organization to contest sixty-nine tax-financed projects at the University of California (Meyerhoff, 1980).

Part 2
Historical Precedents
and Insights

3
The Influence of Farm Machinery on Production and Labor

H. W. Quaintance

Quaintance's monograph, The Influence of Farm Machinery on Production and Labor, was among the first pieces in this century to deal with farm machinery and the social consequences of its widespread use. In his preface, Quaintance wrote, "I have been careful to avoid trying to prove a theory, preferring rather to let the data tell their own story." The story is told with rigorous tabular detail and includes discussions of relative versus absolute displacement, and changes in the class structure of agriculture as a result of mechanized cereal and hay crops.

DISPLACEMENT OF LABOR

The question of the displacement of labor is one of peculiar interest to those who work for hire, because upon it seems to depend the further question of whether the use of machinery decreases the opportunities for earning a livelihood. That the introduction of machinery does frequently deprive workmen of employment in particular lines of work is undeniably true. The introduction of a harvesting machine throws cradlers and binders out of employment just as certainly as the introduction of water drives air out of a jug. It is idle to say that machinery does not

Edited and excerpted from The Influence of Farm Machinery on Production and Labor. Publication of the American Economic Association, Third Series, 5 (4), November 1904. Reprinted by permission.

displace individual workmen and equally idle to contend that such displacement does not entail hardship and suffering, for the more thoroughly and completely one devotes himself to any particular line of work, the less fitted does he become for taking up, and gaining a livelihood in, some other occupation. The extent of change which the introduction of machinery produces in the occupation of individuals is much obscured by the fact that the machine workman is usually given the same name as was borne by his predecessor; as, for example, men who operate a steam threshing machine are called threshers, though they may never have seen a flail and are almost as little fitted for operating a flail and winnowing apparatus as the old time threshers would be to operate the new machine. The old occupation is gone. What we now have is a new occupation passing under the old name. And a new class of workmen (machinists) are in charge.

It is only when we speak of labor as a quantity or of laborers in mass that we can presume to say there has been no displacement of labor by machinery; and yet there may be, in this sense also, a displacement of labor. The displacement may be absolute, as where the labor force in any line of work is decreased, or it may be only relative, as where the rate of increase in the number of laborers employed falls below the rate of increase of laborers employed in industries generally.

THE ABSOLUTE DISPLACEMENT

For the agricultural industry considered as a whole, New England furnishes an instance of the absolute displacement of labor. In 1880, the population, ten years of age and over, engaged in agriculture, numbered 304,679; but in 1900, the number was only 287,829. This decrease was not due to a decadence of agriculture in those states, for the value of the New England agricultural products was more than 50 percent greater in 1900 than in 1880.[1] It must have been due to the introduction of machinery as indicated by the reported valuation of agricultural implements and machines, which increased from $1.68 per acre of improved land in 1880, to $4.49 per acre in 1900.[2]

With respect to the work of cultivating and caring for those nine crops in the production of which machinery appears to be most extensively used (see table 3.1), we may determine what absolute displacement, if any, has taken place by finding in

TABLE 3.1
Days-Work of Man-Labor Required for Producing Various Crops

	Crop of	By Methods of	Days-Work	Difference in Days-Work	Displacement Percent
Barley	1839	1829–30	882,007	---	---
Corn	1855	1855	74,151,217	---	---
Cotton	1841	1841	13,717,188	---	---
Hay	1849	1850	29,176,470	---	---
Oats	1839	1830	20,381,312	---	---
Potato	1866	1866	5,307,260	---	---
Rice	1871	1870–71	124,383	---	---
Rye	1849	1847–48	3,574,396	---	---
Wheat	1839	1829–30	25,905,766	---	---
Total			173,219,999		
Barley	1896	1895–96	630,354	251,653	28.5
Corn	1894	1894	45,873,027	28,278,190	38.1
Cotton	1895	1895	28,178,904	---	---
Hay	1895	1895	18,556,791	10,619,679	36.4
Oats	1893	1893	11,334,266	9,047,046	44.4
Potato	1895	1895	5,134,100	76,536	3.3
Rice	1896	1895–96	108,889	15,494	12.5
Rye	1895	1894–95	2,739,147	835,249	23.4
Wheat	1896	1895–96	7,099,560	18,806,206	72.6
Total			119,655,038	67,930,053	42.5

Crop reports for the desired years could not be found in every case. When the difference between the year reported upon by the investigations of the Department of Labor and the nearest year for which a crop report could be had was greater than one year, a later crop report was preferred as yielding a displacement of labor too low rather than too high.

each case what amount of labor was necessarily employed in the time of production by hand methods and comparing that amount with the amount of labor necessarily employed in the time of production by machine methods. Data of crop production for the exact years covered by the report of the Department of Labor concerning production by hand method cannot be secured for all of the crops, but the best available data are shown in table 3.1.

Table 3.1 shows that in the work of producing each of the crops considered, excepting only the cotton crop, there has been an absolute displacement of man labor. Disregarding the cotton crop, the absolute displacement in the work of producing the other eight crops is 42.5 percent. If cotton be included in the summary and allowance be made for the additional labor employed in the production of that crop, the absolute displacement becomes 30.9 percent.

THE RELATIVE DISPLACEMENT

The relative increase or decrease of the population engaged in agriculture as compared with the increase or decrease of the population engaged in each of the other occupation classes, for the continental portion of the United States, and for the several geographical divisions, during the period from 1880 to 1900, is shown in table 3.2.

In the United States as a whole, and in each division, excepting only the Western division, the rate of increase in the agricultural population has been much lower than in any other one of the occupation

TABLE 3.2
Relative Change in U.S. Population by Occupation Class, 1880, 1890, and 1900

Males & Females Ten Years of Age & Over	Base	1880	1890	1900
UNITED STATES				
Total population	36,761,607= 100		129.0	157.6
In gainful occupations	17,392,099= 100		130.7	167.2
In agriculture	7,713,875= 100		111.0	135.9
In professional srvcs.	603,202= 100		156.6	208.7
In dom. & per. srvcs.	3,423,815= 100		123.3	163.0
In trade & transp.	1,866,481= 100		178.2	255.4
In mfg. & mech. arts	3,784,726= 100		150.0	187.2

——————————— Continued ———————————

TABLE 3.2 (continued)

Males & Females Ten Years of Age & Over	Base	1880	1890	1900
NORTH ATLANTIC DIVISION				
Total population	11,270,090=100		123.2	148.1
In gainful occupations	5,309,722=100		131.3	161.6
In agriculture	1,048,442=100		104.9	102.5
In professional srvcs.	207,551=100		144.3	198.2
In dom. & per. srvcs.	1,211,958=100		121.1	153.2
In trade & transp.	828,802=100		158.9	225.4
In mfg. & mech. arts	2,012,969=100		138.1	167.4
SOUTH ATLANTIC DIVISION				
Total population	5,286,645=100		121.4	144.1
In gainful occupations	2,677,762=100		116.4	149.4
In agriculture	1,622,081=100		102.9	125.3
In professional srvcs.	62,309=100		148.2	191.6
In dom. & per. srvcs.	517,429=100		112.3	154.4
In trade & transp.	177,436=100		174.0	238.0
In mfg. & mech. arts	298,507=100		156.4	210.3
NORTH CENTRAL DIVISION				
Total population	12,760,841=100		132.5	158.9
In gainful occupations	5,625,123=100		136.4	170.3
In agriculture	2,735,525=100		113.9	128.3
In professional srvcs.	230,622=100		161.0	207.4
In dom. & per. srvcs.	1,025,089=100		129.6	171.7
In trade & transp.	595,791=100		193.2	280.5
In mfg. & mech. arts	1,038,096=100		164.3	208.4
SOUTH CENTRAL DIVISION				
Total population	6,076,243=100		128.4	166.6
In gainful occupations	3,022,173=100		120.3	172.4
In agriculture	2,120,525=100		109.5	155.7
In professional srvcs.	73,455=100		155.6	207.4
In dom. & per. srvcs.	464,909=100		112.7	170.7
In trade & transp.	161,449=100		195.3	294.8
In mfg. & mech. arts	201,835=100		178.5	241.3
WESTERN DIVISION				
Total population	1,367,788=100		175.5	236.5
In gainful occupations	757,319=100		176.5	224.9
In agriculture	187,302=100		191.5	248.3
In professional srvcs.	29,265=100		228.6	333.1
In dom. & per. srvcs.	204,430=100		156.1	181.6
In trade & transp.	103,003=100		227.3	320.3
In mfg. & mech. arts	233,319=100		153.3	188.4

Ed. note: Absolute numbers for all three census years appeared in the original.

classes. Not only this, but, subject to the same exception, it has been lower than either the rate of
increase in the total population or in the number of
those engaged in gainful occupations. We must conclude, therefore, that for the period from 1880 to
1900, as compared with the growth in the number of
those engaged in other industries, there has been a
decrease in the number of those engaged in agriculture.[3]

The rate of increase of males and females in the
various occupation classes has been very different.
The relative rates of increase in the agricultural
industry, as reported for the several sections of the
country, are shown in table 3.3.

Table 3.3 shows that women, much more rapidly
than men, are turning to agricultural pursuits. The
introduction of machine power, by decreasing the requirements of physical strength, has placed men and
women upon a more equal footing and women promise now
to invade the agricultural industry as they have
heretofore invaded that of manufactures.

TABLE 3.3
Population Engaged in Agriculture

	Base	1880	1890	1900
United States,				
males	7,119,365=	100	110.78	132.09
females	594,510=	100	114.19	164.39
No. Atlantic Div.,				
males	1,043,497=	100	103.38	99.64
females	4,945=	100	418.07	701.37
So. Atlantic Div.,				
males	1,358,072=	100	104.68	125.00
females	264,009=	100	93.67	126.86
No. Central Div.,				
males	2,720,123=	100	111.64	125.31
females	15,402=	100	520.47	649.38
So. Central Div.,				
males	1,811,486=	100	110.28	155.03
females	309,039=	100	104.80	159.30
Western Div.,				
males	186,187=	100	188.98	241.57
females	1,115=	100	613.36	1379.55

Ed. note: Comparable figures for other occupational
classes besides agriculture appeared in the original.

We may ascertain the extent of the movement to
or from any occupation class during any period by
comparing the distribution of the people among the
various occupation classes at the beginning of such
period with their distribution at its close.

Table 3.4 shows, for the United States and for
the several geographical divisions, what percent of
the total number of those engaged in gainful occupations in 1870 and in 1900 were in the several occupation classes.

Finding the difference between these several
pairs of percents, and representing increases by positive numbers and decreases by negative numbers, we
get the percent of those engaged in gainful occupations who have shifted to or from the several occupation classes, during the period from 1870 to 1900, as
shown in table 3.5.

. . .

The matter of change in the character of farm
work has made it very difficult for any one, from ordinary observation alone, to judge rightly of the effect of machine power on labor. Even so eminent an
authority on agricultural conditions as Professor
Davenport, of the University of Illinois, has been
misled into thinking that the labor power supplanted
by machinery is offset by the demand for labor in new
lines of farm work. In his testimony before the Industrial Commission he stated:

> The introduction of machinery has vastly extend-
> ed agricultural operations. It has extended the
> acreage under cultivation, and has increased the
> amount of labor bestowed upon the land per
> acre. I do not think it has decreased the num-
> ber of men or the total employment of man power
> on the lands of the country. (Report of the
> Industrial Commission, 1901:256)[4]

It is barely possible that Professor Davenport
and the members of the Industrial Commission who examined him, had reference to the absolute and not to
the relative number of workers. If such was the case
then all that can be said is that Professor Davenport
and the commissioners were rather solemnly delibera-
ting upon a subject concerning which the successive
census reports left no room for doubt.

But, one may ask, What becomes of the workers
who are thus thrown out of employment? and, Are there
not some compensating advantages? The first of these

TABLE 3.4
Percent of U.S. Employed Population in Each Occupation Class for 1870 and 1900

		Agri- cul- ture	Prof. Srvc.	Dom. & Pers. Srvc.	Trade & Transp.	Mfg. & Mech. Arts
United States	1900	35.7	4.3	19.2	16.4	24.4
	1870	47.6	3.0	18.2	9.8	21.4
North Atlantic Div.	1900	12.5	4.8	21.6	21.8	39.3
	1870	24.9	3.4	21.4	14.2	36.1
South Atlantic Div.	1900	50.8	3.0	20.0	10.5	15.7
	1870	63.8	2.0	17.5	5.9	10.8
North Central Div.	1900	36.6	5.0	18.4	17.4	22.6
	1870	52.5	3.4	16.7	9.3	18.1
South Central Div.	1900	63.4	2.9	15.2	9.1	9.4
	1870	71.5	2.2	14.0	5.3	7.0
Western Div.	1900	27.3	5.7	21.8	19.4	25.8
	1870	27.2	3.1	25.4	12.4	31.9

Ed. note: Comparable figures for 1880 and 1890 appeared in the original.

questions is easily answered for in the extreme case
of an individual who suffers absolute displacement
the only alternative from idleness is to accept a
lower rate of wages for work in his accustomed employment or to enter as an inexperienced workman, in
some other employment at, most likely, a still lower
rate of wages. His compensating advantage is an uncertain one and one hard to estimate. Besides, it
does not ordinarily accrue until the time of his
greatest need is passed.[5] It arises from the decreased market price of the commodity which he formerly helped to produce. If it is a commodity which

TABLE 3.5
**Relative Percent of Increase and Decrease of U.S.
Employed Population in Each Occupation Class
between 1870 and 1900**

	Agri-cul-ture	Prof. Srvc.	Dom.& Pers. Srvc.	Trade & Transp.	Mfg.& Mech. Arts
United States	-11.9[a]	1.3	1.0	6.6	3.0
No. Atlantic Div.	-12.4	1.4	0.2	7.6	3.2
So. Atlantic Div.	-13.0	1.0	2.5	4.6	4.9
No. Central Div.	-15.9	1.6	1.7	8.1	4.5
So. Central Div.	- 8.1	0.7	1.2	3.8	2.4
Western Div,	0.1	2.6	-3.6	7.0	-6.1

[a]This -11.9 percent does not mean that there was a
decrease, absolutely, in the number of those engaged
in agriculture, but only relatively, and in this
sense; that, whereas the number of those engaged in
agriculture increased during the period from 1870 to
1900, the increase was so much less than in the other
occupation classes that this particular class failed,
by a number equal to 11.9 percent of the total number
engaged in gainful occupations in 1900, to maintain
its former proportion. A similar remark applies to
each one of the other cases where a negative number
appears. The decrease in the class of those engaged
in manufactures and mechanic arts in the Western division is due to the fact that, under the classification used, miners and quarrymen are included in that
occupation class. In 1870, these workers constituted
a high proportion of the total number engaged in
gainful occupations in that division.

enters into his own consumption then the lower price
which he pays for it will, in a measure, offset the
lower wage which he receives in his new occupation.
If it is not a commodity which enters into his own
consumption then his compensating advantage must come
through the stimulus which the decreased price of
this particular commodity gives to other industries
in which it is employed as "raw material" or, more
properly, as a factor of production. Cheaper "raw
material" yields, of course, a decreased cost of production, higher profits, and a stronger demand for
labor.[6]

As to those workmen who suffer only relative
displacement there is, ordinarily, no need for any
compensating advantages. The greatest hardship which
the use of machinery lays upon them is that of avoiding those occupations in which the demand for workmen
is becoming weak. It will be noticed too, that for
every relative decrease in the number of persons engaged in one industry, there is a corresponding increase in some other industry (see table 3.5). As a
matter of fact the persons engaged in gainful occupations constitute a greater proportion of the total
population now than formerly.[7]

THE AGRICULTURAL WORK OF FORMER TIMES
IN THE TOWNS OF TODAY

The element of unreality in the transfer from
agriculture to other occupations consists in this,
that many of those who, at the present time, are employed in the towns and considered as engaged in occupations other than agriculture, are, in fact, doing
work which, in earlier years, was done on the farms;
and the persons who then did the work, if classified
at all, were classified as agriculturists.

There is no need to cite authority for saying
that 150 years ago, not in this country alone but in
all countries, much of that which we now call manufactures was considered a part of agriculture. Agricultural implement manufacture, as a distinct industry, was then practically unknown. Each farmer,
assisted, perhaps, by the village blacksmith, made
his own implements. "Every homestead of any preten-
sion has to be, at the same time, a manufactory of
almost all the things required for daily use" (Smith,
1900:110). "Every housewife spun her own flax and
made her own linen" (McMaster, 1883, Vol. 1:10).
Even within the past fifty years, the business of
ginning cotton has been largely removed from the farm

(Twelfth Census, Agriculture I, 1902:xxx); and, in the report of the Twelfth Census, cotton ginners are classed as manufacturers (Twelfth Census, Population II, 1901:507). The business of cotton ginning, like that of grinding corn and wheat, has become special-ized and has been removed from the farm. Its classi-fication as a line of manufactures followed, of necessity. The Twelfth Census classifies butter and cheese makers as manufacturers (Twelfth Census, Popu-lation II, 1901:506), but in 1870, only the cheese makers were so classified (Ninth Census, Population, 1870:680). Butter was made, in 1870, on the farms and as part of farm work. The development of the ag-ricultural implement industry is another instance. The manufacture of the implements and machines, from being a feature of farm work (Rogers, 1866, Vol. 1:26), has become a distinct branch of manufactures, employing, according to the returns of the Twelfth Census, during the census year reported upon, an "average number"[8] of 46,582 persons besides 10,046 "salaried officials, clerks, etc."[9]

Thus, one after another, functions which former-ly were considered as belonging to agriculture have been differentiated from it and removed from the farm, until the farming business of today appears as a remnant of its former self. He is much mistaken, however, who would, from this fact, conclude that the farmer is sinking to the level of a wage earner. One ought rather to say that it is a sign of the farmer rising to the position of a merchant or manufac-turer. It is specializing his work; it is taking away only that which can be more advantageously done in the towns, and leaving to him just that which he can do most advantageously and, therefore, most pro-fitably. It is lifting him to that place in the industrial organism in which his share in the produc-tion of economic goods counts most effectively.[10] The underlying and controlling fact is this: that the more highly organized society becomes, the farther it advances along the way from barbarism to a perfect civilization, the more does each individual member of society become dependent upon the offices of every other member.

The transfer of occupations from the country to the town is still going on and will go on until divi-sion of labor and labor saving devices shall have ceased to serve their purpose. It is in the nature of things that this should be so, since it can be done more economically; and it is equally in the na-ture of things that people should compete for the better conditions thus offered. It is in vain to try to keep the boy upon the farm where the work is slipping from his grasp. He must follow his work. The zeal which some townspeople manifest in their efforts to persuade the farmers' boys to remain upon the farm betrays a fear that the advent of vigorous blood may diminish the profit which now arises by reason of the somewhat restricted number of competitors.

It must, however, be noted that the introduction of farm machinery is developing work on the farm very much akin to that done in the town, as for example, the cutting and grinding of feed for stock. It minimizes the disagreeable features of farm work,[11] and is giving opportunity for the exercise of a higher order of intellect in farm work.[12] Many advantages, formerly attainable only in towns, are now accessible to the farming classes so that, at the present time, many of the more capable farmers' boys are finding farm life to be the more advantageous avenue to the wealth and social position which they seek.

. . .

SOME CONSEQUENCES RESULTING FROM THE USE OF FARM MACHINERY IN THE REGION MOST DEVOTED TO ITS USE

It has been shown that the cereal and hay crops are those in the production of which machine power plays the greatest part. It now becomes needful to know the relative importance of the cereal and hay crops in the different divisions of the country. Table 3.6 shows for the United States and for several geographical divisions, the total number of acres in all crops; the total number of acres in cereals and hay; and the percent which the total acreage in the cereals and hay bears to the total crop acreage, as reported by the census of 1900.

For the purpose of further narrowing the field of investigation, it may be assumed also, as a matter of common knowledge, that, although machinery is much used in the production of hay, the work of hay production constitutes relatively but a small portion of the total work requisite for the production of both cereals and hay. It is, therefore, the cereal producing regions to which we must look for the most marked effects of the use of farm machinery.

TABLE 3.6
Cereal and Hay Acreage and Their Percentage of
Total Crop Acreage, 1900

	Total Crop Acreage[a]	Total Acreage in Cereals and Hay[b]	%
United States	289,734,591	246,674,289	85.1
No. Atlantic Div.	24,683,365	21,876,493	88.6
So. Atlantic Div.	29,194,661	19,125,863	65.5
No. Central Div.	163,000,561	155,000,940	95.1
So. Central Div.	56,233,143	35,405,091	62.9
Western Div.	16,622,861	15,265,902	91.8

[a]Twelfth Census, Agriculture II, 1902:62.

[b]See appendix A for acreage in all farm crops in 1880, 1890, and 1900.

Table 3.7, taken from the report of the Twelfth Census (Twelfth Census, Agriculture II, 1902:62), indicates the distribution of the cereal crops and the relative importance of the cereal crops, from the standpoint both of acreage devoted to their production and of the value of the product as compared with the acreage and value of all crops.

The North Central division ranked first in the production of cereals, not only in 1899, but also in 1889 and in 1879 (Twelfth Census, Agriculture II, 1902:63). It ranked first also in the production of hay (Twelfth Census, Agriculture II, 1902:215). It is the region of increasing average size of farms and of increasing crop acreage per person engaged in farm work. The North Central states will, therefore, furnish the best field for a study of the effects of farm machinery.

Among the states of the North Central division there were seven which, for the year 1899, reported that over 70 percent of their total crop acreage was in cereals and also that the value of their cereal crops for that year constituted more than 70 percent of the value of their total crop production.[13] The seven states and the percent of their reported cereal acreage and cereal crop values to their total crop acreage and crop values, respectively, are shown in table 3.8.

38

The hay and forage acreage of these seven
states, in 1899, was 35.6 percent of the total hay
and forage acreage of the United States (Twelfth Census, Agriculture II, 1902:215), and their acreage in
cereals and hay and forage was 96.6 percent of their
own total crop acreage.[14] These seven states constitute, therefore, a region in which the cultivated
area is almost wholly devoted to the production of

TABLE 3.7
Distribution of Cereal Crops and Their Relative
Importance by Acreage and Value of Product, 1899

	% of Acreage of All Crops in Cereals	% of Value of All Crops in Cereals	Average Value per Acre of	
			All Crops	Cereals
United States	63.8	51.0	$10.04	$ 8.02
No. Atlantic Div.	36.3	26.6	15.19	11.14
So. Atlantic Div.	58.1	33.6	11.32	6.55
No. Central Div.	73.2	71.1	8.42	8.18
So. Central Div.	56.1	36.3	10.99	7.12
Western Div.	49.4	37.0	11.59	8.69

TABLE 3.8
Acreage and Value of Cereal Crops Compared to
Acreage and Value of Total Crops, 1899

State	Cereal Acreage as % of Total Crop Acreage	Cereal Value as % of Total Crop Value
Illinois	80.4	77.6
Iowa	76.3	76.9
Kansas	72.5	74.2
Nebraska	79.7	82.3
Minnesota	74.0	75.9
North Dakota	71.7	74.4
South Dakota	70.2	78.3

those crops in the cultivation and handling of which farm machinery is most used. Their acreage in the different farm crops, as reported to the Census Office, for the period of 1880 to 1900 was as shown in table 3.9.

The average acreage in farm crops, per farm of ten acres and over[15] was, in 1880, 64.4 acres; in 1890, 86.2 acres; in 1900, 102.5 acres. The average acreage in all farm crops, per person cultivating such crops,[16] was, in 1880, 40.6 acres; in 1890, 53.9 acres; in 1900, 62.4 acres.

Table 3.10 presents these data in a form. showing the relative rates of increase.

The tendency in machine using states, toward a greater crop acreage per farm and per person, is strong and unmistakable.[17]

The persons who cultivated these crops are classified in table 3.11.

Presented from the basis of a common denominator, these data show rates of increase as follows:

	Base	1880	1890[18]	1900
Agricultural laborers	352,565=	100	102.1	173.6
Farmers, planters, and overseers	828,800=	100	131.7	127.4

TABLE 3.9
Acreage of Farm Crops, 1880, 1890, and 1900

	1900	1890	1880
Cereals[a]	82,116,414	58,522,442	39,923,160
Hay & Forage[b]	22,010,381	19,770,323	7,998,365
Tobacco[c]	2,587	4,500	6,906
Hops[d]	911	46	103
Cotton[e]	153	731	---
Totals	104,130,446	78,298,042	47,928,534

[a]Twelfth Census, Agriculture II, 1902:62.
[b]Ibid., p. 215.
[c]Ibid., p. 527.
[d]Ibid., p. 540; Eleventh Census, Agriculture II, 1890:91ff.
[e]Twelfth Census, Agriculture II, 1902:424.

Disregarding the returns of the Eleventh Census, let us consider what these percents indicate. Starting in 1880 with a given ratio between the number of farm employees and employers, we find that in twenty years the employed, or dependent class, has increased 73.6 percent while the employing, or independent class, has increased only 27.4 percent.

In other words, during the twenty-year period from 1880 to 1900, the dependent increased 46.2

TABLE 3.10
Relative Rates of Increase in Acreage per Farm and per Person for 1880, 1890, and 1900

	Base 1880	1890	1900
Average Acreage in All Farm Crops per Farm	64.4= 100	133.9	159.2
Average Acreage in All Farm Crops per Person Cultivating Same	40.6= 100	132.8	153.7

TABLE 3.11
Numbers of Cultivators by Type in 1880, 1890, and 1900

	1900	1890	1880
Agricultural Laborers[a]	612,418	359,894	352,565
Farmers, Planters & Overseers	1,056,237	1,091,867	828,800
Totals	1,668,655	1,451,761	1,181,365

Ed. note: A breakdown of agricultural workers by this classification and by sex in seven states appeared in the original.

[a]This includes 4,264 garden and nursery laborers in the returns for 1900 and probably one-half as many of the same in the returns for 1890 and for 1880; but they were not separately reported by the Tenth and Eleventh Censuses, and, hence, cannot be discarded.

percent more rapidly than did the independent class.
With these figures in mind, one needs but a moment's
reflection to satisfy himself that, at the rates of
increase indicated, the dependent class of farm operators must soon outnumber the independent class.[19]
There is no need here for argument that a large
dependent class is dangerous to society.[20]

The reason for this condition of affairs has
been already indicated. The profitable use of a machine requires that it shall have a field of operation suited to its capacity,[21] just as a man, in
order that he may work to best advantage, requires
more and heavier labor than that suited to a boy.
Hence the movement toward larger farms and greater
average crop acreage per farm so noticeable in the
machine using states. Moreover, the larger farms
call for a corresponding increase in the amount of
capital at the command of the farmer, especially
when, as in this country, there is a tendency toward
more intensive cultivation. This is equally true
whether the farmer be an owner or a tenant. The increasing amount of capital requisite for farm proprietorship makes it more and more difficult for a
member of the dependent class (i.e., an agricultural
laborer), to become a proprietor.[22] His option to
work for himself or to work for wages is more and
more qualified, and, hence, the greater proportionate
increase in the membership of the dependent class.
That there has been a constant increase in the amount
of capital requisite for farm proprietorship will be
evident from an inspection of the following data,
showing for this group of seven states, as reported
to the Census Office:

1. The average value, per farm, of all farm
property, including land with improvements, implements and machinery, and livestock was in 1880,
$3,515; in 1890, $4,859; in 1900, $6,531 (Twelfth
Census, Agriculture I, 1902:688 and 694).

2. The average value, per farm, of lands with
improvements, including buildings was in 1880,
$2,835; in 1890, $3,930; in 1900, $5,358 (Twelfth
Census, Agriculture I, 1902:688 and 696).

3. The average value, per farm, of implements
and machinery on farms: In 1880, $136; was in 1890,
$151; in 1900, $208 (Twelfth Census, Agriculture I,
1902:688 and 698).

The rate at which these several factors have increased is shown in table 3.12.

TABLE 3.12
Relative Rate of Increase in Capital Needed
for Farm Inputs for 1880, 1890, and 1900

	Base	1880	1890	1900
Aver. Value of All Farm Property	$ 3,515=	100	138.2	185.8
Aver. Value of Farms (Land & Improvements)	2,835=	100	138.6	189.0
Aver. Value of Implements & Machines	136=	100	111.0	152.9
Farmers, Planters, & Overseers	828,800=	100	----	127.4
Agricultural Laborers	352,565=	100	----	173.6

WAGES UNDER HAND AND UNDER MACHINE METHODS

. . .

The position of the unskilled workman,[23] meaning
now the workman who is untrained in the use of machinery, is a peculiar one. In a lecture on ballad
poetry, delivered at the University of Wisconsin in
the Spring of 1903, Professor Moulton, of the University of Chicago, called attention to the fact that
before the time of written literature the best literary productions were equally accessible to the free
and to the unfree. The slave, as well as his master, might know and enjoy the choicest of literary
productions. But, with the invention of writing and,
especially, of printing, the best literature came to
be put into book form. Books were expensive and the
knowledge requisite for using them could be acquired
only by a long and difficult course of training.
From the very nature of the case, the best literature
thus became inaccessible both to the slaves and to
the poorer classes of freemen. They could gain no
positive advantage from the new invention; and they
lost relatively, by reason of the intellectual gulf
which opened between them and those others whose more
fortunate stations both gave access to the written or
printed volumes and afforded opportunity for learning
how to use them.

This same process is now working itself out in the matter of labor and machinery. To the skilled workman, machinery opens the way to profit and advancement. But to the unskilled workman, it is as a sealed, or unintelligible, book. He does not understand it; and the hopelessness of competing with one who does understand it, only intensifies his consciousness of inferiority and increases the burden of his struggle for existence.[24] Having, ordinarily, neither machinery nor the capacity for using it, he is practically shut out from all chance of participating in its benefits. His wages, of necessity, are limited by the standard of his efficiency. It is inevitable, therefore, that the unskilled laborer should, relatively, at any rate, sink ever lower and lower in the scale of industrial society.

That we have been experiencing a transition period, not only with respect to the agricultural industry[25] but, also, with respect to all other industries, seems almost self-evident. I do not believe that the transition period is passed, nor do I believe that it ever will be safely and finally passed, until the state, in the interest of the general welfare, and in its capacity of agent for the whole social body, shall have provided for and required, as now so all but universally provided for and required, in the more purely intellectual field, that every child shall be taught, at least, the rudiments of industrial art.

44

APPENDIX A
Acreage in All Farm Crops, as Reported in 1880, 1890, and 1900

	1900	1890	1880
UNITED STATES			
All Farm Crops	272,493,449	214,623,412	164,830,442
Cereals	184,983,220	140,378,857	118,805,952
Hay	61,691,069	52,948,797	30,631,054
Cotton	24,275,101	20,175,270	14,480,019
Cane	386,986	374,975	227,776
Tobacco	1,101,460	695,301	638,841
Hops	55,613	50,212	46,800
NORTH ATLANTIC DIVISION			
All Farm Crops	21,957,338	22,155,561	22,024,776
Cereals	8,957,452	8,869,351	9,913,840
Hay	12,919,041	13,205,321	12,026,364
Cotton	---	---	---
Cane	---	---	---
Tobacco	53,281	44,080	44,852
Hops	27,564	36,809	39,720
SOUTH ATLANTIC DIVISION			
All Farm Crops	26,481,330	23,730,022	22,135,566
Cereals	16,964,662	14,790,108	15,575,701
Hay	2,161,201	1,925,753	1,128,420
Cotton	6,842,489	6,746,292	5,165,175
Cane	47,223	32,888	24,778
Tobacco	465,754	234,981	241,480
Hops	1	---	12
NORTH CENTRAL DIVISION			
All Farm Crops	155,167,564	122,950,427	85,760,874
Cereals	119,324,898	90,584,015	70,154,743
Hay	35,676,042	32,220,468	15,490,866
Cotton	45,749	57,991	32,116
Cane	---	---	---
Tobacco	120,516	86,789	78,038
Hops	359	1,164	5,111
SOUTH CENTRAL DIVISION			
All Farm Crops	53,593,467	36,178,553	29,744,199
Cereals	31,521,429	20,222,568	19,350,718
Hay	3,883,662	1,913,532	633,433
Cotton	17,386,807	13,370,987	9,282,728
Cane	339,708	342,087	202,998
Tobacco	461,855	329,379	274,322
Hops	6	---	---

———————————— Continued ————————————

APPENDIX A (continued)

	1900	1890	1880
WESTERN DIVISION			
All Farm Crops	15,293,750	9,608,849	5,165,027
Cereals	8,214,779	5,912,815	3,810,950
Hay	7,051,123	3,683,723	1,351,971
Cotton	56	---	---
Cane	55	---	---
Tobacco	54	72	149
Hops	27,683	12,239	1,957

Note: By "all farm crops" is meant the following crops: barley, buckwheat, cane, corn, cotton, hay, oats, rice, rye, tobacco, and wheat. These are all of the crops for which comparable data can be had and they constitute nearly the whole of the crop acreage. The only crops of any consequence, from the standpoint of acreage, and not included are: broom-corn, flax, hemp, potatoes, vegetables, and orchard fruits.

The data of hops acreage in 1879 and 1889 are taken from the Report of the Eleventh Census, Agriculture II, 1890:91ff. All other data are taken from the Report of the Twelfth Census, Agriculture II, 1902:63ff.

NOTES

1. The value of New England agricultural product, as reported in 1880, was $103,343,566; in 1900 it was $169,523,435. Twelfth Census, Agriculture I, 1902:703.

2. Twelfth Census, Agriculture I, 1902:698.

3. Bringing together the data concerning the population engaged in agriculture, as presented in tables 3.1 and 3.2, so as to show the relative rate of increase in that class in the different sections of the country, we have the following:

Population Engaged in Agriculture--
(Males and Females)

	Base	1880	1890	1900
United States	7,713,875=	100	111.04	135.88
North Atlantic Division	1,048,442=	100	104.86	102.47
South Atlantic Division	1,622,081=	100	102.89	125.30
North Central Division	2,735,525=	100	113.94	128.26
South Central Division	2,120,525=	100	109.48	155.66
Western Division	187,302=	100	191.51	248.34

4. See also the testimony of Mr. Ketchum on page 132 of the report.

5. "It is small consolation to a working man to be assured that in a year's time he will have plenty of work, if in the meantime he must remain bread- less. Loss of work even for a few weeks may exhaust his credit and the affection and means of his friends, and there may remain nothing for him but starvation, unless poor-laws or private charity come to the rescue" (Nicholson, 1892:30).

6. "Labor-saving methods seem to be a calamity, because the effect is to interfere with present pur- suits and deprive some of their accustomed means of livelihood; to render useless, skill acquired after a lifelong training. The benefits all seem to accrue to the person who first uses an invention, while the ones displaced are apparently shut out of the indus- trial system. It is not noticed how they are gradu- ally absorbed into other channels of employment that open up as the cost of production is decreased. If such were not the case, the whole industrial mecha- nism would soon come to a standstill, considering the progress of inventions supplemented by the army of aliens that arrive yearly and the increasing propor- tion of women breadwinners" (White, 1903:83).

7. Males and females ten years of age and over in the United States:

Year	Total Number	Engaged in Gainful Occupations	Percent
1900	57,949,824	29,074,117	50.2
1890	47,413,559	22,735,661	48.0
1880	36,761,607	17,392,099	47.3
1870	28,228,945	12,505,923	44.3

Ranged on the common basis of 100, for the pur- pose of comparison, the two columns of absolute num- bers in the above table show as follows:

Males and females ten years of age and over in the United States:

Year	Total Number	Engaged in Gainful Occupations
1900	205.2	232.5
1890	168.0	181.8
1880	130.2	139.1
1870	100.0	100.0

These figures show an unmistakable increase in the proportion of those engaged in clearly defined occupations. There are, however, two points which should be borne in mind in any comparative study of the census returns of occupations.

First: the more elementary the industrial organization, the less differentiated are the industrial
functions, and hence the proportion of those who can
report themselves as having definite occupations is
much less than in a highly developed industrial organization in which the workmen are much given to
following special lines of work (Tenth Census, Population I, 1880:710).

Second: the number of different occupations reported upon has been repeatedly changed: the number
of different occupations reported upon by the several
censuses has been as follows (Twelfth Census, Occupations, 1904:xxxii):

Twelfth Census	303
Eleventh Census	218
Tenth Census	265
Ninth Census	338
Eighth Census	584
Seventh Census	323

Any one will readily recognize that the more
minute the classification of occupations, the higher
must be the proportion of those in gainful occupations as compared with the whole population.

8. "The average number of wage-earners (men,
women, and children) employed during the entire year
was ascertained by using twelve, the number of calen-
dar months, as a divisor into the total of the average numbers reported for each month" (Twelfth Census,
Bulletin No. 69, 1901:2.

9. Twelfth Census, Manufactures IV, page 345.
"More than two hundred thousand employees are provided with regular work the year round by the factories
that make the implements and machinery, and nearly as
many more are engaged in selling, transporting and
shipping the products to their final destination"
(Walsh, 1900:147).

10. "Better methods of husbandry, the use of
superior implements, specialization of agricultural
production and vastly improved transportation facilities, whereby large areas of new lands have been
brought under cultivation, have been indispensable to
this increase in productive efficiency, in consequence of which a relatively smaller part of the
world's population is required to produce the food
supply" (Emerick, 1896:436).

11. "The introduction of machinery in many branches of industry--and more especially in agricul-
ture--while increasing, perhaps, the monotony of
employment, has also greatly lightened the severity
of toil, and in not a few instances has done away
with certain forms of labor which were unquestionably

brutalizing and degrading, or physically injurious."
(Wells, 1898:372). "There is no more laborious kind
of farm work than the spreading of manure; so much so
that in farming on a large scale it is difficult to
procure labor for the purpose. This can now be dis-
pensed with. A machine called the manure spreader
does all this work. . . . It does everything in the
manuring line except to use foul language" (Scientific American Supplement, 1900:20528).

12. "The farmer has, by his own progressiveness,
gained a better standing in business and in social
life than he formerly held. The conditions on New
England farms are now such as to attract men of
brains and intelligence" (Phelps, 1902:383).

13. Oklahoma is the only other state, or terri-
tory, in the union which reported so high a percent
of acreage and value in cereals for the year 1899.
But no separate report was returned for Oklahoma in
1880 and it is, therefore, necessarily omitted from
this study.

14. The total crop acreage of these seven states
in 1899 was 108,394,908 acres (Twelfth Census, Agriculture II, 1902:62).

15. Tracts of less than ten acres are excluded
as being vegetable, or truck farms, rather than farms
for the raising of the crops here considered. For
number of farms, see Twelfth Census, Agriculture I,
1902:688 and 690.

16. Agricultural laborers, farmers, planters,
and overseers.

17. "With the coming of the great harvesters,
the planters, cultivators, and scores of other farm
mechanisms, there was an opportunity to double and
quadruple the crops, and the farms gradually
increased from ten and twenty acres to one and two
hundred" (Walsh, 1900:139).

18. The returns of the Eleventh Census are known
to have been very defective in this, that "farmer's
sons and daughters were often reported as farmers
rather than as farm laborers, thus very much compli-
cating the occupation returns in this class." (Letter of Carroll D. Wright, under date of December 29,
1899.) That some such error must have crept into the
returns is evident on a consideration of the rate of
increase of the two classes (i.e., "agricultural laborers" and "farmers, planters, and overseers"), when
taken together. The combined rate of increase appears as follows:

	Base	1880	1890	1900
Agricultural laborers, farmers, planters, and overseers		1,181,365= 100	122.9	141.2

These figures show that the total population engaged in farming increased at a uniform rate and
there seems no good reason for supposing that there
was in fact any such extraordinary movement from the
class of employees to the class of employers and then
back again within the period of twenty years from
1880 to 1900, as indicated by the returns.

19. "Of these evils that which is most serious
and general is the divorce which machinery is bringing about between labor and capital. So far has this
already gone that people have come to think of the
two as things naturally distinct from each other, and
to regard it as a normal state of affairs that the
persons who perform the manual toil of a country
shall be absolutely dependent for employment on a
comparatively small class known specifically as capitalists, in whose hands are concentrated the implements with which alone modern industry can be
successfully carried on. That such dependence is unfavorable to the highest type of manhood will hardly
be questioned; and the enormous extent to which machinery has increased and is still increasing the
percentage of persons subject to such dependence is
surely a most serious matter. The manhood of a nation is its most precious possession, for the loss or
deterioration of which no increase of material wealth
can adequately compensate" (Peters, 1885:2).

20. In 1890 the proportion of male agricultural
laborers reported as unemployed during some portion
of the census year was 17.2 percent; in 1900 it was
36.1 percent. Females in 1890, 18.6 percent; in
1900, 44.3 percent (Twelfth Census, Occupations,
1904:ccxxviii-ccxxxi).

21. "In order to make the steam power machines
of value, the farms must be large and extensive. On
small farms, they would prove too costly either in
the operation or initial expense. For this reason it
has been said that steam power could never supplant
horse power on the farms, for our democratic notions
demand that farming lands shall never be consolidated
in the hands of a few, and farming on a gigantic
scale can never represent more than a very limited
part of the industry in this country. Yet the tendency in the West is to operate enormous farms, combining several rather than cutting up into smaller
ones" (Walsh, 1900:567).

22. "No English agricultural labourer, in his
most sanguine dreams, has the vista of occupying,
still less of possessing, land. He cannot rise in
his calling. He cannot cherish any ambition, and he
is in consequence dull and brutish, reckless and
supine" (Rogers, 1866, Vol. 1:693).

w ve β
machine

23. There is, I think, a great deal of confusion and consequent misunderstanding arising from a loose use of the term "unskilled workman." We speak of paying higher wages to a skilled workman than to an unskilled workman; but, the essential element is not skill but efficiency. Skill means rather proficiency, or dexterity, in the doing of a particular thing. It has reference to the person. But when we speak of a skilled machine workman, we have reference, not so much to the quality of the worker as to the quality of the work done, that is, to the product of his skill. The degree of skill which the machine workman possesses may, in fact, be much below that of the hand worker whom he displaces; but he is a more efficient workman and, therefore, commands the higher wage.

24. "Under conditions where the laborer can offer no resistance and the so-called iron law of wages operates to keep him down to the life line, machinery only adds uncertainty to his other woes. He is, as it were, cut out of civilization. Whenever he presses upward and secures a larger share of an ever enlarging product, machinery becomes an uplifting force" (White, 1903:86).

25. "The introduction of improved agricultural implements and machinery during the latter half of the nineteenth century was a development of such importance as to amount to an industrial revolution in agriculture" (Report of the Industrial Commission, 1901, Vol. 10:xiv).

4

Technology on the Farm

United States Department of Agriculture

*The USDA report Technology on the Farm sur-
veyed major technological developments in
agriculture. Although written more than
forty years ago, the analysis provides an
accurate description of farm problems
today--in particular, those of commodity
surpluses and depressed prices. (Indeed,
many of the authors in Part 2 of this
volume articulate the same concern.) The
authors of the report attempted to estimate
the probable trend and extent of technological developments and to appraise their
probable economic and social effects. Implications of technological changes and the
problems they raise for agriculture and the
nation were discussed. Steps were suggested which might be taken to give more aid
and greater security to those groups most
adversely affected. The authors warned
that "these measures are not in themselves
adequate to meet the situation--their full
effectiveness must await much-needed fundamental adjustments in the whole industrial
economy."*

TECHNOLOGY AND THE FARM PROBLEM

Changes of the kind and magnitude indicated ...
obviously cannot take place without serious consequences to agriculture and the nation. Probably the

----

Excerpted from chapters 14 and 15 of Technology
on the Farm, a special report by an interbureau committee and the Bureau of Agricultural Economics,
U.S. Department of Agriculture, August 1940.

51

52

basic problem will be that of providing employment
and security to the displaced and underprivileged
people who are most adversely affected by these
developments.

Expected shifts in tenure and income raise difficult questions, for they entail loss of position
and income and a progressive piling up at the lower
end of the social scale, and that effect is most
likely in areas of lowest agricultural productivity
where the existing population is already in excess.

This intensification of population pressure is
bound to accelerate population movement. There will
be an increased tendency to migrate between rural
areas and between rural and urban areas. Furthermore, machines alone are expected to displace 350,000
to 500,000 additional farm workers.

The important (but not new) problem of maintaining farm prices and income will be intensified by the
expected technical developments.

Significant increases of corn, soybeans, small
grains, hay and forage, cotton, and other crops and
livestock through improvements in varieties and
strains, in conservation and cultural practices and
in insect and disease control, and through changes in
feed supplies and prices, cannot come without serious
repercussions upon costs, prices, and income of all
farmers, but especially commercial producers.

These changes, furthermore, will not take place
uniformly throughout the country. Fluctuations in
costs as a result of mechanization will be most pronounced in areas where machine methods can best be
used. Similarly, changes in costs and prices will
take place first in localities best adapted to the
new strains, varieties, and new methods of processing, but they soon will spread and produce varying
effects in other parts of the country. They will
have some significant effects upon regional specialization and will intensify the problem of interre-
gional competition. It is clear, therefore, that the
extent and magnitude of these changes will be such as
to render extremely difficult the task of maintaining
farm prices and income at reasonable levels.

Technological developments also raise important
questions of significance to the several national agricultural programs, which at many points are closely
related to technological changes. Many of the problems these programs are trying to meet, in fact, are
intensified by the developments.

The Agricultural Adjustment Administration, for
example, in addition to its acreage allotment and
conservation practice program, strives through these

efforts and through loans and marketing quotas to keep supplies in line with the effective demand of the market so as to maintain farm prices and income at reasonable levels. To keep the supplies of the principal basic commodities at legally defined, normal levels, the acreage allotments are varied each year, depending upon the situation with respect to carry-over, yields, domestic and export demand, etc. Loans and marketing quotas are provided when supplies and prices reach stated levels, but the latter come into operation only when supplies reach rather extreme heights.

Obviously under this adjustment procedure anything which materially increases yields of a particular crop, even assuming domestic and export demand are constant, will decrease the acreage allotment necessary to maintain the supply at normal levels. It is just at this point that technological changes come into the picture and affect the result.

We have already pointed out the rapid strides that are taking place with respect to the development and adoption of hybrid corn in the Corn Belt. Such changes in yields and production, even assuming a reasonably active domestic and export demand, would be difficult to absorb without depressing prices and income. With the domestic and foreign demand in prospect as a result of the present general unemployment situation and the maladjustments that will be accentuated by the war, the problem will be much more difficult.

Because of these factors and a rapidly increasing carry-over, the Agricultural Adjustment Administration put through a 20 percent downward adjustment in the corn acreage allotment in 1939 and has requested an additional downward adjustment of approximately 10 or 12 percent in 1940. With the changes in prospect that have been noted, it seems clear that further downward shifts in acreage will be necessary if supplies are to be maintained at reasonable levels, unless adverse weather conditions interfere to cut the crop or domestic and foreign demand unexpectedly improve greatly.

Growing out of these downward adjustments in acreage is another problem of increasing significance both to the Agricultural Adjustment Administration and to the Farm Security Administration. Reference is made to the growing practice of "bonus" renting, whereby share tenants are forced to pay cash rent for perquisites, buildings, crib space, meadows, pasture, and the like in addition to the usual share of the crop.

Technological developments accentuate this problem in two ways. The first effect comes about through increasing yields which necessitate further downward adjustments in acreage to maintain a given supply. As the acreage of depleting crops is decreased, the released acreage simply swells the total of the acreage of other crops upon which "bonus" rents may be charged.

Another effect is due to the influence of mechanization upon size of farm and the relation of this to the availability of farms for tenants. A few years ago, a farmer upon retirement would go to a town and rent his farm as a unit to a bona fide tenant, but now he is more than likely to stay on the farm and rent it by fields to his neighbors, who thus increase the size of their operating units. Machines help them operate the additional acreage practically as efficiently as if it were a definite part of their home tracts. They stand to enlarge their operations and incomes thereby, but there is one less farm for some other tenant.

This situation apparently is developing to the point where there are more tenants looking for farms than there are farms available; obviously the tenants bid against each other for a farm, and the landlord, with a definite advantage in bargaining, can demand and receive the "bonus" rents. Any such additional charges lower the tenant's income and standard of living.

Because of such situations, the Farm Security Administration is encountering increasing difficulty in finding farms for its tenant-purchase and rehabilitation-loan clients. The problem of the Agricultural Adjustment Administration also is made more difficult, because these "bonus" rents often take the form of "by-agreements" and raise problems very difficult to identify and correct.

Closely related to this development is the influence of mechanization and acreage adjustments upon the shift from a position as tenant and sharecropper to one as wage hand. These shifts have taken place to a considerable degree in the intensive cotton areas of the South where mechanization has increased markedly. Many people attribute the shift in cropper status primarily to this factor. Others lay it also to a landlord's desire to adjust his labor force to his reduced cotton acreage and to get a larger share of the benefit payments. But regardless of the causes, the fact remains that it is a serious human problem and deserves careful consideration.

The problem may become even more intensified in the next few years ahead. The trend toward increased mechanization is very likely to continue. This shift will further displace man labor. Even if it does not cause complete physical displacement, it is likely to result in further "economic" displacement, which comes about because of the tendency of certain land-lords to keep a large supply of labor on the planta-tion for the seasonal peak load tasks of chopping and picking.

Instead of giving the croppers the usual acreage of share cotton, however, they will give them only "nominal" allotments of cotton and use them the rest of the time as wage hands. The consequences are less income for the croppers from the smaller acreages, less wage work, some idleness, a smaller annual in-come, and inevitably a lower standard of living.

Note must be taken also of another problem due to technological developments of significance to the national programs--particularly to the Agricultural Adjustment Administration. This is the decrease in unit costs (resulting from increased efficiency, etc.) and their bearing upon parity payments and the loan program. The question will have to be faced sooner or later whether under the conditions of sup-ply, demand, and prices in prospect, the level of parity prices as now calculated is one that reason-ably can be attained, or whether it may be necessary to recalculate it on a more recent basis so as to take into account these new developments.

In such a calculation, technological and other changes in nonagricultural industries also would come into the picture. In fact, as we have indicated pre-viously, these changes have equalled, (and in some industries have exceeded) those in agriculture, hence, the net result might continue to indicate a relationship between agricultural and industrial pri-ces not greatly different from the existing one. But even so, we still would face the difficult adminis-trative problem of how to attain such levels.

Similar questions arise with respect to the loan program, whether the present loan levels be main-tained, or if not, at what levels they can be made with a reasonable assurance of repayment. There is also the question of the relation of the loan and re-sulting price level on feed grains to the elasticity and efficiency in feeding.

These changes and their effects cannot be disas-sociated from the existing situation, either in agri-culture or industry. In fact, they really intensify an already bad situation, which has had its roots in part in other causes, but also to which past techno-logical developments have contributed.

It is generally recognized that the situation at present, in both agriculture and industry, is characterized by depressed conditions, reduced national and individual incomes, excessive unemployment and relief. It also must be evident that further technological progress either in agriculture or industry simply will add to, and accentuate, these conditions unless we find some way greatly to expand our domestic and foreign markets and absorb the already large army of unemployed.

If some permanent improvement were foreseen in these prospective economic conditions, we could be much more optimistic about the social and economic effects of technology. But unfortunately there is little basis for such optimism. During the next few years, at least, industrial opportunities are not likely to be of such magnitude as to absorb anything like the present industrially unemployed, to say nothing of absorbing the large excess of manpower on the farm.

In 1937 we succeeded in employing about 35 million persons in nonagricultural pursuits. By the end of 1939, when industrial production finally, but temporarily, exceeded the 1929 peak, total nonagricultural employment reached only about 34 million persons, nearly a million fewer than in 1937 and approximately 2 million fewer than in 1929.

There are, at present, probably 42 million to 44 million nonfarm persons available for work, of whom perhaps 2 million are on government work projects and about 2 million normally would be unemployed in prosperity years. Every year probably 500,000 are added to this available working force. Although the tremendous sums that are being employed for defense undoubtedly will speed up business activity and give employment to considerable numbers of unemployed people the next year or so, the effect is likely to be temporary and not on a scale sufficient to meet the problem we are discussing.

Nor are the prospects much brighter for the years ahead. A prolonged European war might alter this prospect, but only temporarily. A short war, on the other hand, might make it even darker. Even when peace is declared it will require a period of years to overcome the maladjustments resulting from the war. There will be extreme competition among all nations for world markets. Because of the major importance of foreign markets to the prosperity of the bulk of our agricultural producers, it appears that agriculture as a whole will be affected particularly by this situation.

Agriculture will be benefitted, however, to the extent that our domestic industrial economy can be made to function more effectively through expanded production, lower prices, and increased employment. But changes in this direction, as we have seen, probably will be slow, so slow, in fact, that agriculture likely will have to take care of not only as many but probably more people than has been the case during the 1930s.

There were in 1937, according to the unemployment census, more than 1,500,000 males living on farms who either were totally or partially unemployed or only had emergency employment. It does not appear that this unemployment situation has improved or will improve much in the next few years, since nearly 400,000 farm males are reaching maturity each year and only about 110,000 farmers are dying each year, with possibly as many more retiring or leaving for other occupations.

Unless there is an unexpected increase in net migration, therefore, the total population in agriculture in 1950 will be higher even than today, when it is the highest on record. Indications are that it may reach a total of 34 million persons, approximately 2 million more than today.

In the South during the 1930s, for example, 275 white persons reached fifteen years of age for every 100 persons over fifteen who died or reached sixty-five years. In other words, for every 100 vacancies there were 275 applicants. Among the Negro population comparable figures indicate that there were 210 applicants for every 100 vacancies. Consequently, there must be a material migration from southern farms or there will result a substantial increase in an area where farm population pressure is already acute.

When it is realized further that there are 3 million farm families in the United States today receiving gross farm incomes averaging only $615 and more than a million and a half males of working age living on farms who are totally or partially unemployed, it is obvious that the further expected displacement of 350,000 to 500,000 workers during the next ten years, because of mechanization alone, will create an extremely bad situation and will make imperative the adoption of remedial measures to meet it.

. . .

58

SOME SUGGESTED LINES OF ACTION

A Need for New Social Direction

Instead of preventing or slowing up technical progress, we need, rather, to speed up and give new direction to social and institutional changes in order to keep pace with technological change. We need to spread the benefits of technology more widely--to extend the benefits to all of the people and to areas where such developments, up to now, have been negligible. We need to encourage the development of new opportunities and greater security for all farm people, particularly the disadvantaged groups.

In this report, we accept neither the optimism of the group that believes that the problem is minor and that reemployment occurs practically automatically nor the pessimistic view that technological advance must be discouraged or held rigidly in check. An underlying assumption in this report is that inventions and technological progress have been a major factor in raising the standard of living of all the people--that by cheapening the means of production, technology has greatly increased efficiency and has brought to the mass of consumers conveniences and luxuries that otherwise would have been available only to a few. But it also has been recognized that these benefits have not always been distributed equally among all groups--that along with them have come certain maladjustments.

As long as our economy was expanding and domestic and foreign markets were growing steadily, these maladjustments were temporary. Labor displaced by new machines and techniques was soon reabsorbed because of the expanded demand for products of particular industries and the new lines of activity opened up by inventions and new techniques. As the era of free land passed, however, as we have shifted from a debtor to a creditor nation, and as our ability to find or to hold foreign outlets for our excess products has progressively declined, maladjustments due to scientific progress have become accentuated.

Some labor supplanted by technological progress continues to be absorbed by reemployment as in the past, to be sure, but by no means does it take place in the rapid, semiautomatic manner of former years. In fact, there has been a distinct slowing up, with a progressively lengthening interval of idleness between the time of displacement and that of reemployment. It is for this reason that consideration needs to be given to measures of a remedial nature--to seek thereby to reduce the impact and to cushion the effect of these changes upon the disadvantaged groups.

The measures proposed relate primarily to steps that might be taken within agriculture itself. It is not assumed, however, that these are the only steps that need to be taken nor that they will in themselves relieve the existing maladjustments. In fact, even more urgent adjustments are needed in the non-agricultural segment of our economy. If such adjustments were made in the direction of greater freedom of enterprise, expanded output, lower and more flexible prices, there would be much less disparity of exchange between agricultural and industrial production and prices and there would be increased opportunity for the excess workers in agriculture to find gainful employment in industry. Such a fundamental development would lessen the need for specific measures in agriculture itself. Over a period of time it not only is desirable but it should be possible to move in this direction. Such a change should make possible a higher level of living for the entire population. But until such adjustments are made it is imperative in the interest of justice and fair play that steps be taken within agriculture itself to cushion the adverse effects of these technological developments.

Suggested ways to attack the major problems created by technological developments are in three groups:

measures to provide employment and security to displaced and underprivileged prople;

measures to stabilize agricultural economic conditions;

and measures to create a wider appreciation for the values and benefits of rural life.

Some of the suggestions are neither new nor exhaustive. Some are now being tried but need increased emphasis. Perhaps no one suggestion or combination of suggestions will meet the problem fully. But if they are developed on a reasonably adequate scale they should be helpful in minimizing the most adverse effects of technology.

Measures to Provide Employment and Security for Displaced and Underprivileged People

First, we need to develop a program which will provide for the immediate relief and rehabilitation

of those now unemployed and in distress and which
will absorb and cushion the shock for the additional
numbers expected to be displaced. This calls for a
conservation works program.

Second, looking beyond the immediate situation,
we need to develop measures for the permanent rehabilitation of these people. Such measures include:
An extension of the present Farm Security Administration program to reach a greater number of the low-
income group, the development of a more adequate
program for farm labor, maintenance and further development of owner-operated family-sized farms, and
assistance to farmers in the development of new
sources of employment and self-help.

. . .

Other Measures Proposed for Permanent Rehabilitation and Security

But other measures are needed to provide permanent security and rehabilitation for these people.
Presumably, after a few years, assuming the works
program were developed on a reasonably large scale,
the most urgent needs of conservation would have been
met. Other devices are needed, therefore, of a continuing and longer-time nature that will give perma-
nency to the effort. Such programs or procedures
might include:

1. a proposal that the present Farm Security Administration program of supervised loans,
   debt adjustment, and the like, be extended to
   reach a greater number of the low-income
   group. . . .

2. a proposal that a more adequate program for
   farm labor be developed. . . .

3. a proposal looking toward maintenance and encouragement of the further development of
   owner-operated family-sized farms. . . .

4. To give assistance to farmers in the development of new sources of employment and self-
   help. . . .

Measures to Stabilize Farm Economic Conditions

Measures are also needed to stabilize the income
from agricultural commodities in order to insure an
even distribution of the advantages of technology.

To the extent that technology tends to increase supplies, this increase manifestly will tend to bear
heavily on agricultural prices unless additional markets are found. And again, to the extent that technology widens the area of production or the area
supplying a given market, it will tend to intensify
competition and work to the disadvantage of many
farmers unless it can be modified. On the other
hand, to the extent that prices and income can be
maintained by increasing demand, a greater number of
workers can be kept gainfully employed in agriculture. But, if solely in the interest of particular
minority groups, restriction is carried to the point
of maintaining an unreasonable or artificial level of
prices, then the reverse situation will result and
there will be further displacement in agriculture.

Measures needed to stabilize agricultural economic conditions may be divided into (1) measures designed to increase consumption and demand, and (2)
measures designed to stabilize returns to commercial
producers, including such devices as acreage adjustment, commodity loans, crop insurance, marketing quotas, and marketing agreements.

. . .

In our consideration of problems and remedies,
we should not assume that industrial expansion--the
best way to absorb those who have no particular desire to remain in agriculture--has ceased for all
time.

Something like a huge defense program may be a
key to industrial expansion; if so, certain of the
suggested remedies no longer will be needed so badly.

But of several considerations we should be mindful: Industrial expansion through armament expansion
may be temporary and lead only to a recurrence of the
problems we have been encountering; we should seek
permanent stability for American farming; over a long
period, it should be possible for the United States
to adjust its economy in a way that will permit expansion of production in industry and agriculture.
That would make possible a higher level of living for
the entire population. That is our goal.

5
The Social Effects of Recent Trends in the Mechanization of Agriculture

C. Horace Hamilton

*Hamilton's 1939 article focused on mechani-
zation in the Cotton Belt, especially the
difficulties which faced displaced tenants,
share croppers, and the rising transient
labor force. Hamilton discussed the dependence of farmers on outside economic
forces--monopolistic farm-machinery corporations and large oil companies--which had
come to control a large share of agricultural income. He argued that services once
provided by the family-farm institution
have been replaced by governmental programs costing billions of public dollars.
Hamilton speculated on whether we can
develop efficient and stable social
institutions which will control machine
technology and promote the same social
values which were enjoyed under a more
simple agrarian organization.*

MECHANIZATION IN THE COTTON BELT

. . . The social effects of mechanization will
now be presented briefly. The displacement of thousands of farm croppers, tenants, and farm laborers is
the most serious problem. Adequate data are not
available to show the complete picture in all its details, but a number of recent studies and surveys do
reveal that the situation is a most critical one.
Bonnen and Magee (1938) have shown that the use of

Excerpted from Rural Sociology 4 (1), 1939, pp.
3-19. Reprinted by permission.

two-row tractor-powered farm equipment on all farm
land in the High Plains of Texas would reduce the
number of farms to 58 percent of the 1935 census
count; and that the use of four-row tractor equipment
would further reduce the number of farms to 33 percent of the 1935 figure. Langsford and Thibodeaux
(1939) have shown how the mechanization of planta-
tions in the Mississippi Delta area would reduce the
plantation labor force per plantation (having 750
acres of crops) from forty families under the horse-
drawn one-row system, to twenty-four families under a
four-row tractor system. This amounts to a decrease
of 40 percent. In this estimate they are quite conservative, because they are assuming that some of the
twenty-four families would be kept there primarily
for the purpose of hoeing and picking cotton. If the
Delta should come to depend upon transient labor as
the Plains and Blacklands of Texas do, then less than
twenty-four families might be kept on the plantation. Already we know of many instances where transient cotton pickers have been transported in trucks
from Texas to Mississippi.

That actual population displacement in Texas
cotton-growing areas has reached serious proportions
is demonstrated by the 1937 Texas Population Changes
Survey which indicated a decrease of over 20,000
farms in the state between January 1, 1937, and January 1, 1938 (Hamilton, 1937). Since many displaced
families from cotton farms probably migrate to non-
cotton farms, the displacement from cotton farms has
probably been greater than 20,000 families. In connection with the annual population surveys for the
past two years scores of letters have been received
from correspondents giving illustrations of the displacement of farm tenants and laborers by tractors.
The displacement of from three to five families by
one tractor is not uncommon. One case was reported
where nine families were displaced by one tractor.
Assuming that one tractor will displace one family
only, more than 60,000 farm families have probably
been displaced from Texas farms since 1930. Also,
since the number of tractors on Texas farms increased
about 50,000 in a three-year period before April 1,
1938, it may be estimated that more than 10,000 families have been displaced annually from Texas farms
since 1935.

"Where do these displaced farm families go?" is
a question which is frequently asked. Many of them,
as I have already indicated, move to poor farms, un-
suited to cotton production. A larger number migrate

to towns and cities and become common laborers, alternating between agriculture and the town. Many displaced tenants and croppers remain in the open country as partially employed farm or common laborers. At the time of this writing, the Texas Works Progress Administration reports a certified caseload of 80,000 farm families--48,000 of whom were awaiting assignment. A late report is that some of these people are to be shifted to the care of the Farm Security Administration, which is already assisting nearly 30,000 Texas farm families. Welfare and employment service offices in the state for the past two years have been reporting unusually heavy requests for aid from these displaced farm families. The 1937 Census of Unemployment showed approximately 130,000 unemployed and partially unemployed agricultural workers in the state. This is almost identical with the number of agricultural wage workers reported as employed by the 1935 agricultural census.

The displaced family faces the prospect of a lower income. The typical farm tenant in the High Plains or in the Blackland may be expected to earn a net farm income of from $800 to $1,000 annually--even with cotton prices as they are today. As either a common or an agricultural laborer the same tenant cannot expect to earn more than from $250 to $300. A survey just completed in Texas shows the farm laborer family median income to have been only $220 in 1937, when opportunities were excellent for cotton picking (United States Government, 1938).

The surplus of farm tenants available has created considerable competition among tenants for places to rent; and, as a result, rental rates are rising. In areas that once followed the straight third-and-fourth share rent systems, cash rents and privilege rents of various types are being used. Pasture land, which tenants formerly received free of rent, now rents frequently for one dollar per acre. In some areas tenants are being charged cash rent for their dwellings. In many areas from three to six dollars per acre is being charged for land planted in feed crops. On many of these farms the cash rent on the feed land amounts to more than the income from cotton. Many cases are being reported also of an increase in cotton share rent from one fourth to one third.

The mechanization of cotton farms has increased what might be called the patch-cropper system. The patch-cropper, similar to a hoe-cropper in some of the southeastern states, may receive a small cash

wage and in addition the cotton produced on a four-
or five-acre patch. In West Texas the patch may be
as large as thirty-five or forty acres, and the cropper may receive a cash wage as well as some perquisites. No surveys are available to show the extent
and characteristics of the patch-cropper system over
wide areas.

The mechanization of cotton farms in Texas and
in some other states has greatly enlarged and intensified the transient labor problem. New social relations, institutions, and problems are arising out of
this situation. Already there has developed a widespread private and unregulated system of transporting
transient labor--a system which has in it great
possibilities of labor exploitation. The labor
contractor furnishes a large open truck, recruits a
group of laborers, and transports them, presumably
free of charge, across the state as the cotton
picking and the truck and fruit harvesting seasons
progress. The contractor, usually a Mexican with a
truck, is a contact man and business agent for the
laborers. He takes the responsibility for contacting
farmers, weighing and hauling cotton (or truck
crops), and of collecting the laborers' earnings from
the farmer. For these services and for transporting
the laborers, the contractor receives from the
laborer from five to ten cents for each 100 pounds of
cotton picked, and from the farmer about $1.50 per
bale.

The rapid increase in the transient labor population has complicated health, sanitation, and housing problems in towns where labor concentrates. The
farm population of some large cotton counties is virtually doubled during the busy part of the picking
season. There is a movement on foot to provide both
temporary and permanent camps for transient laborers
at strategic centers in the state. Already a number
of small towns in cotton centers have cooperated with
the Texas Employment Service in setting up temporary
camps equipped with shower baths and sanitary toi-
lets. These camps serve as point of contact for laborers and employers. On any Sunday during the
cotton-picking season these camps are greatly con-
gested with trucks, old cars, and people--farmers,
cotton pickers, men, women, and children. During the
mornings there will be seen much informal dickering
between farmers, labor contractors, and heads of families. A farmer will approach a group of pickers,
contact the contractor and perhaps two or three of
the family heads. Information as to the number of

pickers, amount of cotton, camping or housing facilities, and wage rates are quickly exchanged. If the preliminary information is suitable to both pickers and farmers, a quick trip is then made to inspect the field of cotton. Large groups or truckloads of pickers prefer, of course, the larger fields and the thicker cotton. If the field is small, the cotton yield low, or the cotton very difficult to pick, the leaders go back to camp and make another contact--unless perchance they are stopped en route by a farmer looking for pickers. If the cotton is satisfactory, the truck returns to the camp and brings the entire group of pickers out to the farm where they usually stay until the crop is picked over once. Because of the fact that most of the transient pickers move in large groups, small farmers quite frequently have difficulty in locating pickers. Labor is also difficult to get for second pickings.

Just how many years the mechanized cotton farms will be able to get an ample supply of cotton pickers at prevailing wages remains to be seen. No strong effort has been made to organize this important group of workers--which, it is estimated, number between 200,000 and 300,000. Under conditions that are developing, some sort of labor organization may appear. If the organization of cotton pickers should be successful, the cost of picking cotton might rise to the extent that the farmers would lose much of what they have gained by mechanization. If such a condition ever arises, we may expect a widespread demand for mechanical cotton pickers. Several mechanical pickers have already been developed. Although their performance is still much below that of hand pickers, the leading agricultural engineers believe that the development of a successful cotton picker is now a possibility. The mechanization of the preharvest operations in cotton production will very probably speed the development of harvesting machinery. In the event of a major war, an acute shortage of labor might be the final and deciding factor in the adoption of mechanical cotton harvesting machines, just as the world war was a great factor in the mechanization of the wheat harvest. Taking all these things into consideration, it seems to me that mechanical cotton picking could very easily become an actuality within the next ten or fifteen years (Horne and McKibben, 1938; Johnston, 1938; Smith, 1938; Bennett, 1938). When that time comes, the southern part of the country may present the nation with its social and economic problem number two!

CONCLUSION

In this paper we have had the time and space to present only some of the more immediate effects of recent trends of mechanization in agriculture. If there are those in this group who would contend that the conditions which have been described are only temporary, may I call your attention to some of the more permanent social effects of mechanization. Mechanization in agriculture has been going on for a hundred years or more. It is likely to continue for many decades. Even though technological unemployment brought about by the introduction of one machine may disappear in time, we would still be faced with problems of a continuously changing technology and hence continuous problems of human maladjustment.

The invention of machines and, what is more important, their exploitation by monopolistic corporations may be considered as one very effective means by which a nonagricultural economic group cuts out for itself a juicy slice of agricultural income. In this sense, farm machinery manufacturers and the large oil companies are engaged in the process of agricultural production, without having to take nearly so many of the risks as does the farmer. Just how these outside interests are able to capitalize on the situation is indicated in a recent report of the Federal Trade Commission. Among other things this report is quoted as saying:

> The ability of the International Harvester Company to make more net profits in 1937 than it made in 1929 (in fact enough to break all records for net earnings before 1937), though the cash income of the farmer for 1937 was nearly 18 percent less than it was in 1929, can, the Commission believes, have only one explanation. It was the result of a policy by the International Harvester Company to advance prices, which policy could not have succeeded if conditions of free and open competition had prevailed in this industry. (Farm Implement News, 1938)

The situation just referred to illustrates only one way in which the farmers of today have become more dependent on outside economic forces than were the farmers of a hundred and fifty years ago. One authority on this subject summarized the results of technological advance in agriculture as follows:

> In 1787, the year the constitution was framed, the surplus food produced by 19 farmers went to

feed one city person. In recent average years
19 people on farms have produced enough food for
56 non-farm people, plus ten people living
abroad. (McCrory, Hendrickson, and Committee
1937)

If this statement is true, then the farmer of today
is sixty-six times more dependent upon outside markets, economic conditions, and organizations than was
the farmer of a hundred and fifty years ago. Temporarily, mechanization increases the individual farmer's income; but ultimately, if mechanization
actually lowers cash costs, he is forced to cut his
prices, and at the same time pay higher costs for
land and fixed costs for both land, machinery, and
motor fuel. The only possible way for the farmer to
maintain the favorable position which he has gained
by mechanization would be to imitate the industrial-
ists and organize a monopoly with or without the help
of the government. Temporarily, farmers might be
successful by adopting such a program; but since this
is a democracy and since the farmer is outnumbered
more than four to one, what chances does he have of
maintaining such a position?

Another way in which the farmer loses some of
the advantages of mechanization is through continually rising standards and costs of living. He has
apparently increased his productivity in doing a few
things; but he has relinquished to others the doing
of a hundred things which he once did himself with
little or no cash costs. Therefore, we may well ask,
"What does the farmer of today have in terms of ultimate human values, contentment, leisure, mental
health, and security that the farmer of 1787 did not
have?" And as "farmer" in this question we must include farm laborers as well as the farmers who operate hundreds of acres with machinery.

Another angle to this question is the fact that
the mechanized farmer and the machinery manufacturer
have shifted a lot of their costs to the shoulders of
the state. There is little need here to enumerate
the many services which the state now performs for
rural and urban residents. True enough, industry and
mechanized agriculture must ultimately bear some of
these costs through taxation or through depreciation
in government bonds; but the economic and political
system by which such an indirect payment of costs is
made necessary is neither desirable nor efficient.
There are too many groups of one kind or another who
are trying to get, and are succeeding in getting, a
larger and larger slice of the producer's income. We

have reached the point where governmental employees
and beneficiaries of governmental assistance are currently cartooned and lampooned as being enemies and
parasites of society.

The development of new governmental functions
and programs, such as social security, farm security,
agricultural adjustment, the works program, and the
housing program, is the fruit of poorly controlled
mechanization--in both industry and agriculture. Under our old rural culture we had developed the
family-farm institution in such a way that our social
needs, such as education, care of the aged, the dependent, and the unemployed were met without any
elaborate political organization or expense. The
fact that we are now spending billions of dollars to
do things which were once done by the farm family for
itself demonstrates in a dramatic manner just how
valuable the family-farm institution was to society.

Along with the machines which the farmer has
bought, he has been furnished with a set of ideas
about the social advantages of mechanization. He
has, for instance, been thoroughly imbued with the
theory of social and technological progress; the
theory that social and historical evolution is always
onward and upward; the theory that older and simpler
forms of agrarian and social organization passed away
because they were bad; and, finally, the theory that
he need not exert any effort to develop new social
organizations and institutions, because what he has
are adequate, and if they were not adequate new ones
would in some mysterious manner come into existence
as a result of more, bigger, and better machines.

We might clarify the issue here by saying that
just as we cannot attribute social evils to the inan-
imate machine, neither should we attribute to the machine some mysterious capacity to mold and develop
our social life. The actual forces that determine
the patterns of our social institutions are more
likely to be human than mechanical in character.
Whether or not machines are to do the wonderful
things claimed for them depends upon how individuals
and groups of individuals make them, how they sell
them, how they manage them, and, finally, how they
distribute their products. In the final analysis we
must evaluate the social effects of mechanization,
not by what these social effects might be under certain ideal conditions yet to be realized, but rather
upon what the social effects are here and now or have
been in recent years.

Still another permanent social effect of farm
mechanization and other technological changes is the

fact that a larger and larger percentage of agricultural products going into the market is being produced by a smaller and smaller percentage of the farm
population.   In 1930 the Census reports show that
about 90 percent of farm products going into the market come from 50 percent of the farms of the nation.
Since today there are more people on farms than in
1930 and since the mechanization of farms has displaced thousands of people from commercial farms, the
probability is that much less than 50 percent of our
farms are producing 90 percent of the farm products
going into the market.   If this were not true, then
600,000 farmers during the past few years have blun-
dered in buying tractors.   As individuals they did
not make mistakes.   Many of them had either to mechanize or to quit.   However, as a group they have,
with the help of their city brothers, contributed to
a very critical social problem.

We might conclude this paper by pointing out
that the social effects of mechanization in agriculture should not be considered as entirely isolated
from other technological and economic trends.   Mechanization of agriculture is rather a part, a very important part, of the current and ever-changing order
of things.   Its significance cannot be appreciated
without an understanding of the entire social and economic order; nor can much be done about it, without
doing something about the rest of the world at the
same time.   As one writer put it, we are in a position where it seems we cannot continue mechanization
without great social cost nor can we stop it without
great social cost (McCrory, Hendrickson, and Committee, 1937).

The question of the hour, it has been said, is
whether or not we can develop some efficient and stable social institutions which will control the machine and give us the same social and human values
which are enjoyed under a more simple agrarian organization.   If you should ask me at this time whether
I think that such institutions could be developed, I
should be forced to reply: "Yes, but it is quite im-
probable."   The social system toward which we are now
evolving seems to be little more than a set of make-
shift compromises in a descending spirit of social
disintegration.   However, if it is necessary that I
end this paper on an optimistic note, it may be said
that a downward spiral is more pleasant than a downward plunge.   So, if it is down that we must go, let
us make the spirals as long and as wide as possible.
Who knows but that we may hit an upward current somewhere and see yet again the mountain heights of freedom and democracy!

6
The Impact of Mechanization of Agriculture on the Farm Population of the South

B. O. Williams

Williams hypothesized that the effects of mechanization would be "of a profound character" and would reshape "the character of the farm population of the South." He predicted many social consequences of agricultural mechanization--disruption of the family-farm institution and changes in the density, age, sex structure, and income of farm populations. He concluded that besides mechanical inventors, we need social inventors who can help surplus labor make adjustments.

Being mindful of the onslaught of technology in industry and of the tremendous dislocations and maladjustments which it has precipitated, let us apply the tools of the analytical techniques of modern research methodology to the probable effects of the mechanization of agriculture on the farm population of the South. These effects may be considered, not only as they work themselves out in the composition and characteristics of the population, but also as they may affect the whole demographic pattern of the farm population. As a means of setting up the analysis, a fundamental hypothesis will be formulated, then a series of propositions bearing upon the hypothesis will be presented, and finally an interpretation will be made of the whole procedure and certain tentative conclusions established. This

Excerpted from Rural Sociology 4 (3), 1939, pp. 300-11. Reprinted by permission.

74

procedure only claims to be based upon a rather careful examination of the literature in the field and
upon a critical application of the ideas so gained to
the analysis.

THE FUNDAMENTAL HYPOTHESIS

**The mechanization of agriculture in the South
will continue to increase, but the increase will be
gradual and slow and will extend over a comparatively
long period of time. The effects of this mechanization will be ultimately of a profound character and
will result in reshaping the character of the farm
population of the South as a whole.**
...Since the transition to mechanization in the
agriculture of the South will be gradual, the effects
will also be gradual, but nonetheless deep-seated, in
the social and economic life of the region. There
are numerous forces operating in connection with the
mechanization of Southern agriculture. These will be
stated in a few propositions, with appropriate
comments.

**Proposition I: The mechanization of Southern
agriculture will develop a technical pattern quite
different from that which characterizes the factory
system of urban industry.**
There are several reasons why the social, economic, and technical patterns that will emerge with
mechanization of agriculture in the South will be
different from those characterizing these patterns in
urban industry. Some of these are as follows:
1. Piecework and piecework rates cannot so con-
veniently be applied to agriculture as to other industries. The separate items and tasks in agriculture are difficult to appraise qualitatively. The
weather and other factors are so tied up with labor
that it is difficult to separate them.
2. It is difficult even to apply standardized
principles of farm management to the individual
farm. The decisions have to be based on the operation of nature's forces and influences and must be
changed in response to nature's pranks and operations.

. . .

**Proposition II: Mechanization of agriculture in
the South has already gone forward much further than
is generally recognized.**

. . .

I think it may be assumed that the rate of mechanization is now increasing and will continue to increase at an accelerating rate in the future. Inventions will beget other inventions until we may in the near future witness the second Industrial Revolution, which will take place in the open fields of agriculture rather than within the borders of cities.

Many observers compare the process of agricultural industrialization to the industrial revolution and believe that it will result in the displacement of the domestic system in farming by large capitalistic operating units. Such changes would inevitably involve a profound transformation in the characteristics and status of the agricultural personnel and an equally significant modification of rural social structure. (Gray, 1937:553)

The prevailing system up to the present with its customs, habits, and traditions has defied change. Inertia and resistance have held back imminent transition. Once these are broken down, the rate of change will speed up.

Proposition III: The mechanization of agriculture in the South will result in a disruption of the family-farm institution.
Assuming that mechanization will increase, it may be assumed also that a shifting in the responsibility of the family as an economic unit will take place. It is probable that the owner-manager type of organization will come to prevail, changing the system of social organization from the family-farm type to the manager-labor type. The labor thus will function, not as a family unit, but as independent units, operating according to the increase or decrease in the demand for labor. The farm will not revolve about the family as a unit, but around the operating unit as a whole.

Thus it is possible that forces and influences that have hitherto developed individuality and independence among the family-farm units will in the future result in the stimulation of dependence and impersonal relationships. The society of the South will thus lose a potent force that has furnished a stable and conservative influence in the past. The strong familism of the South has been one of its most definite integrating influences. But, if mechanization should come to agriculture as it has to industry, and the corporate form of organization should prevail, this positive force of familism might be lost. The increased efficiency in production might not compensate for this loss.

The breaking down of the close relationship between the worker and the individual employer, and consequently of the close personal ties, would likewise be a great loss to the integration of rural life in the South.

Undoubtedly the fairly complete mechanization of agriculture in the South would result in a change from the annual basis of renting and sharecropping to the monthly or daily wage basis. The wage system would be substituted for the tenancy system. This would be only a part of the disruption of the family-farm institution.

There would also come an increased specialization by type of operations and specialties in production. The self-sufficient type of farming would be reduced with the resultant increase of crop specialties.

Proposition IV: The mechanization of agriculture will naturally be associated with large-scale farming, which may be considered to have certain economic and social characteristics.

Some of the more or less obvious advantages of large-scale farming are as follows: (1) Buying and selling may be carried on in larger quantities. (2) Superior managerial ability may be employed. (3) The more efficient use of labor and equipment, especially the largest types of machines, would produce certain economies in production. (4) Overhead expenses, on a per unit cost basis, might be considerably reduced (Holmes, 1932:110-11).

As contrasted with the economic advantages just listed, there are certain other effects of increased mechanization that should be examined. These pertain to the psychological and sociological side of farm life. Some of these are: (1) Through the institution of a new basis of selection in the farm population, there is the possibility of its being remade to some extent. Unquestionably the mechanically inclined would be selected for the farming occupation to a greater extent than previously. Those who like to work with machines would be inclined to stay on the farm and those who do not would be inclined to leave. (2) Mechanized agriculture will demand more positive interest in the business. Costly machinery will demand more capital, which investment may make it more difficult for farmers to leave agriculture and enter other pursuits. (3) The relative social rating of farm and nonfarm people may be changed. There will undoubtedly be a larger infiltration of urban ideologies and folkways into agriculture. The day may, in fact, come when the term "gentleman farmer" will reappear. (4) It is probable that the number of chores to be done about the farmstead will be reduced. This may result in more leisure time, which might result in a shortening of hours in agriculture. This might make possible the operation of multiple shifts of labor on the mechanized farm (Holmes, 1932:93-94).

Proposition V: The mechanization of agriculture in the South will have certain specific effects on the farm population. Some of these may be mentioned as follows:

On density: There is a possibility of a change from open-country homesteads to the village-centered type of community, with a consequential concentration of population in these villages. This would affect markedly the types of service available to farm people. It should be kept in mind that the electrification of farming areas might serve as a hindrance to the concentration in villages, owing to the fact that certain modern services would be available to the people in their scattered domiciles.

On sex: The composition of the farm population might be changed by mechanization so as to affect the sex distribution. Intensive mechanization would open up more specialized jobs suitable to females, especially in the semi-processing phases of commercial agriculture, such as packing, grading, standardizing, etc. As it now stands, more females leave the farms of the South than males, but with jobs suitable to females in agriculture the balance between the sexes might be restored.

On age: Mechanization would unquestionably affect the age composition of the Southern farm population. Whereas at present the farm population contains a higher proportion of the young and the aged, under mechanized farming there would be a greater demand for the middle-age groups, say from twenty to fifty, and this balance would be restored.

On mobility: It is probable that the mechanization of agriculture would speed up the interchange between farming and nonfarming occupations, thus increasing the rate of interoccupational mobility. To the extent that industrial patterns came to be applied to farming there would be less difference between agricultural and nonagricultural occupations.

78

The skills and techniques would have more in common,
as there would not be so much difference between
working with a tractor and many of the mechanical
pursuits of industry. There would also result more
seasonal and part-time jobs in agriculture which
would require a greater fluidity of the farm population. This freer exchange between agriculture and
nonagricultural pursuits would result in a revamping
of the individual and social attitudes of the farming
people, mostly by the spread of urban attitudes among
the farm people.

On race relations: In the South the Negro has
not been admitted freely to diverse occupational pursuits. The mechanization of agriculture would intensify the competition for mechanical and other jobs
that heretofore have not been so accessible to the
Negro as to the white man. If mechanization should
increase the differentiation in skills and techniques, which seems plausible, the more skillful
would be competing for the more technical positions,
and a whole set of new competitive features would be
ushered in. This competitive regime would be extended down the scale from the more skillful to the
less skillful positions. The handling of the tractor
might become, for instance, the key job in farming,
the competition for which would be keen. Greater
wage differentials would consequently result from the
increased specialization. Such changes would increase the general competitive forces and tensions
between the races.

**Proposition VI: The mechanization of Southern
agriculture would result in either (1) a lowering of
material living standards of large numbers of the
farm population; or (2) the migration of large numbers of surplus and displaced laborers to other
areas.**
As to the first phase of this proposition, it
seems obvious that, if mechanization does come on a
broad scale, large numbers of farm workers in the
South would be displaced. The cheap price of farm
labor in the South has retarded mechanization in the
past. It is not economical to substitute machines
for labor until labor becomes dear, and this fact
will without doubt be an active factor in retarding
rapid mechanization of farms in the South for some
time to come. The high rate of natural increase of
the Southern farm population continues to furnish a
large supply of labor for the farms of the region.
If mechanization should result in displacing this
labor, the workers would either be without financial

assistance or else would have to turn to the state and federal governments for relief. This would be equivalent to the maintenance of low material living standards in the area.

As to the second phase of the above proposition, there seems to be little chance that large numbers of Southern laborers can look to other areas for jobs. In most of the sections into which the surplus of Southern labor has gone in the past, there is local unemployment which means that there is little demand for labor from outside these localities.

In the earlier stages of this country's growth it seems that the invention of machines did not to any appreciable extent result in the displacement of labor. But at the present time, with the maturation of the nation's growth, with the fairly high degree of exploitation of natural resources, it seems to the writer that a saturation point has been reached. With the further application of machines, especially to agriculture, there will inevitably result a certain amount of permanent displacement of farm labor. As long as the population was increasing rapidly, as long as free lands were available in the West, and as long as labor remained unorganized, mechanization seemed to absorb, rather than to displace labor. What often happened under these circumstances was that the price of wages was driven downward by the invention of machines. Now, with labor organized, with the national population reaching a stationary level, with the "making of machines to make machines," and with curtailment of production as an assumed policy in agriculture and industry, it seems that further mechanization will result, without question, in the net displacement of agricultural labor. The problem of what to do with its surplus of labor is one of the great challenges that the South will have to face with the further development of mechanical appliances in agriculture.

INTERPRETATION AND CONCLUSIONS

In the foregoing analysis it has been assumed by hypothesis that the mechanization of agriculture in the South will continue to increase but that the increase will be slow and gradual and will extend over a comparatively long period of time. A set of propositions was introduced with comments on each. The attempt has been to show that the South is faced by the probable expansion of mechanization in its agriculture, that the effects would cut across the whole fabric of Southern culture and would result in numerous changes in the characteristics of the farm population.

It was pointed out that there is much resistance and inertia to be overcome in any process of social change, whether induced by mechanical appliances or by the forces of growth and expansion along any front. The South has held rather firmly to the policy of remaining agricultural, except in certain areas where cotton mills have developed to a marked extent. The probable extension of mechanical and technological processes to agriculture in the South will have many and varied ramifications, and it is worth while to the civilization of the South and to the people who live in the region to take stock of the most probable effects of mechanization on the farm population and on the culture of the area. Any analysis of probable effects as they may occur at some future date must of necessity be cast in a theoretical frame of reference. The venture is a speculative one, but there are certain analogies in the field of urban industry that may be useful in projecting possible trends in agriculture. These have been applied in the present paper, but the essential chain of arguments has been based upon deductive reasoning in terms of the problematical approach.

It may be said that one's guess is as good as another's. This would be true, assuming that the guesses were rooted in substantially similar studies and were based on comparable knowledge of the subject matter involved and of a similar insight into the general knowledge of the area. The scientific study of sociology is relatively new, but when applied to the analysis of a concrete problem, the objective treatment of the facts should shed some light upon the projected screen, which is the uncertain future lying just ahead.

With the prevailing rates of natural increase of the farm population of the South, it would appear that, barring migration out of or into the area, the farm population would increase by about 100 percent in thirty or forty years. At the same time, the outlook for the nation as a whole at that time would indicate a practically stationary population. If mechanization should result in the net displacement of labor, as it has been claimed in this paper, then the South will be confronted by the problem of caring for this labor surplus. The states of the South are not financially able to assume this burden, and the federal government will obviously have to share heavily in the expense involved. There does not seem to be any clear prospect of areas outside the South absorbing this surplus because of prevailing unemployment in those areas. An international crisis

might change the nature of the problem, or a wave of
prosperity within the nation might furnish a demand
for the surplus labor. Without some such intervention of unforeseen developments, the prospective picture may be assumed to be somewhat as stated above.

Even if it is admitted that the mechanization of
Southern agriculture would not result in the net displacement of labor, and that the expansion would
merely result in shifting the demand for labor, or
that in the long run the labor would be reabsorbed in
other lines, there would still be the great problem
of caring for temporarily displaced labor growing out
of mechanization. For an individual laborer there is
little consolation in the thought that, even though
he be displaced, some job somewhere else will absorb
some other laborer in his place. The maladjustments
resulting from shifting fall definitely upon the
shoulders of some individuals or groups of individuals. From the long-time standpoint, and from the
view of society as a whole, this might work out all
right theoretically. But the prospect of the imminent wave of unemployment that will result from the
mechanization of Southern agriculture is sufficiently
menacing to cause the leaders of the South and the
nation to consider the implications and develop whatever social devices can be worked out to neutralize
and ameliorate the effects of the extension of mechanical devices to agriculture.

The agriculture of the entire nation must be
kept on a productive basis in the interest of primary
security and of national defense. But at the same
time social efficiency must keep apace with mechanical and technical efficiency. The South needs social inventors as well as mechanical inventors. But
the social inventors must be aware of the concrete
realities and practical aspects of society, as they
must also understand the tenets and doctrines of a
conservative and safe political structure. It is
better that the citizens realize that sudden and dramatic change is fraught with danger and that a sound
and enduring civilization is based upon continuous
adaptation to a continuously changing world. The society which refuses to work out adjustments to a
changing order will become the victim of its own inertia. The society that chases after cure-alls and
get-rich-quick schemes is likewise doomed. The South
faces some real problems; this is obvious. But it
also has resources, human and physical, that furnish
great opportunities for its people. Perhaps a little
more industry mixed in with the mechanization of
agriculture would aid the South in working out some
of its most complicated problems.

7
Social Aspects of Farm Mechanization in Oklahoma

Robert T. McMillan

*The purpose of McMillan's study was to as-
certain what social and economic changes
were associated with the increase of farm
mechanization in Oklahoma between 1920 and
1945. McMillan believed that the findings
furnished a basis for evaluating both the
favorable and unfavorable aspects of farm
mechanization. He concluded that mechanization "should prove highly beneficial to
farm families, but improvement of this nature cannot be achieved without serious
dislocations of populations in their lifeways."*

For more than a quarter of a century the tractor
has been cited in popular literature as one of the
most important factors associated with changes in
farm population, supply and demand for labor, migration, land tenure and use, size of farms, crop and
livestock organization, wealth, income, and level of
living. The study tested this general supposition
through the use of available objective evidence.

. . .

METHOD OF STUDY

The data for this study were taken chiefly from
the federal censuses of 1920 to 1945, inclusive. The
method of study was to compare specified items given

Excerpted from Oklahoma Agricultural Experiment
Station Bulletin No. B-339, Stillwater, November
1949. Reprinted by permission.

in the latest census with those shown in earlier censuses, by counties arranged according to the amount of farm mechanization.

One problem of the study was to select a valid and reliable index of farm mechanization. Several measures were tested in the preliminary stage of work. The index finally selected was the number of tractors per 100 farms with three acres and over in 1945 for each county.[1] The correlation coefficient between this index and the average value of farm machinery and implements per farm was .97. This high degree of relationship is due to the fact that the tractor forms a large part of the value of all farm machinery. The number of automobiles per 100 farms when correlated with the number of tractors per 100 farms gave a coefficient of .89. These coefficients, with other data shown later, indicate that the number of tractors per 100 farms is a valid and reliable measure of farm mechanization.

The procedure of determining "farm mechanization groups" was to array counties according to size of tractor indexes and to divide these arbitrarily into five groups, with counties having the highest number of tractors per 100 farms being placed in Group I and those with the smallest in Group V. . . .

The number of tractors on farms in Oklahoma increased from 6,210 in 1920 to 70,395 in 1945 (table 7.1 and figure 7.1). In 1920, there were 3 tractors per 100 farms. By 1945, this index had increased to 44. The tractor index rose more rapidly than the number of tractors since 1930, which reflects an acceleration of mechanization.

TABLE 7.1
Changes in Number of Tractors on Farms,
Oklahoma, 1920-1945

Census Year[a]	Number of Tractors on Farms in Okla.	% Increase over Preceding Date	Number of Tractors per 100 Farms[b]	% Increase over Preceding Date
1945	70,395	55.2	44.1	74.3
1940	45,369	74.7	25.3	97.7
1930	25,962	137.1	12.8	128.6
1925	10.950	76.3	5.6	75.0
1920	6,210	---	3.2	---

[a]Data for 1935 not available.
[b]Study included farms of three acres or more.

FIGURE 7.1
Number of Tractors on Farms, Oklahoma, 1920-1945

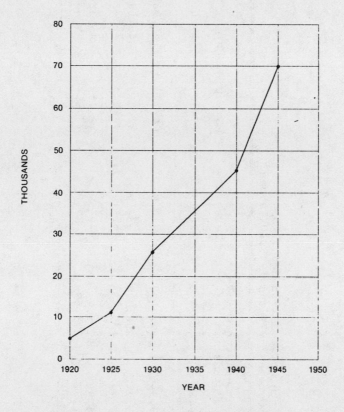

YEAR

FARM POPULATION AND LABOR FORCE

Decreases in numbers of population and farms are associated with farm mechanization. Other factors, however, operate to reduce population and farms in areas little affected by mechanization.

From 1925 to 1945, the population on farms in Oklahoma declined from 925,690 to 639,948, a loss of 31 percent (table 7.2). The decreases were greatest in counties with the largest number of tractors per 100 farms--Groups I and II (figure 7.2).[2] In contrast, the loss of farm population in counties with the smallest degree of mechanization, Group V, was

TABLE 7.2
Changes in Farm Population between 1925 and 1945 and in Number of Farms between 1920 and 1945, Oklahoma

Farm Mechanization Group	Number of Farm Population 1945	Number of Farm Population 1925	Percent Change 1925-1945	Number of Farms 1945	Number of Farms 1920	Percent Change 1920-1945
All groups	639,948	925,690	-30.9	164,790	191,988	-14.2
Group I	135,942	208,928	-34.9	38,069	46,683	-18.5
Group II	85,937	130,113	-34.7	22,823	26,291	-13.1
Group III	92,220	125,842	-26.7	23,575	23,998	- 7.8
Group IV	174,022	235,211	-26.0	43,159	45,584	- 5.3
Group V	151,827	225,596	-32.7	37,164	49,432	-24.8

nearly as large as in Groups I and II, due to heavy
emigration resulting from factors other than mechanization. The decreases of farm population in counties
of Groups III and IV, areas not affected markedly by
farm mechanization, were smaller proportionally than
for the state as a whole.

It is possible to estimate with some precision
losses of population associated with increasing numbers of tractors. In Group I counties, between 1925
and 1945, there was an average loss of three rural-
farm persons for each increase of one farm tractor.
In Group II counties, there was an average loss of
four rural-farm persons for each tractor added.[3]
Elsewhere in the state, the estimated losses of persons per tractor were not reliable, because other
factors were more important than mechanization in
effecting reductions of population.

. . .

FIGURE 7.2
Percentage Loss of Farm Population, Oklahoma,
1925-1945

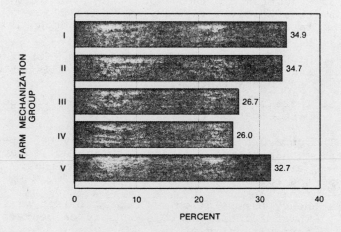

SOCIAL IMPLICATIONS OF FARM MECHANIZATION

The findings of this study furnish a basis for evaluating both favorable and unfavorable aspects of farm mechanization. It is not always possible to measure specifically the cause and effect relationships of a great cultural force like the tractor and other mechanical inventions. Indirect causes and effects sometimes may be more important than the direct causes and results of machines. Often the appearance of a particular machine itself may be an effect, or an adjustment to, a sequence of deeply underlying complex causes. Whatever the cause, trends point to more rather than less farm mechanization in Oklahoma and elsewhere. It is, therefore, appropriate to indicate the possible correlated tendencies.

The following changes, which may be expected as mechanization of farms increases, should result in improvement of Oklahoma agriculture:

1. Consolidation of many uneconomic farm operating units.

2. Increased average wealth and income of families remaining in agriculture, especially farm operators' families.

3. Reduction in the amount of hand labor and time involved in many work activities of the farm and home, and consequent economies in production.

4. Higher material level of living for farmer and farm laborer families than existed with less mechanization.

5. Increase in the amount of leisure and social participation for farm families.

The unfavorable tendencies which may be expected as farm mechanization increases, though not so apparent now, are nevertheless potentially serious. They include the following:

1. Heavy depopulation of farms, and of villages which fulfill the role of service centers for agricultural families.

2. Increase of technological and frictional unemployment.

3. Increase of large-scale commercial farms with potential capacity to produce more food and fiber than can be consumed under probable peacetime effective demand.[4]

4. Concentration of farm ownership among relatively few large landholders.

5. Increased dependence of farmers' welfare upon fluctuations of the business cycle and upon government, with subsequent loss of traditional self-sufficiency and autonomy.

Farm mechanization facilitates, and is facilitated by, the reduction of uneconomic size units. Since early settlement Oklahoma has had many thousands of farms too small to provide occupant families with decent housing, health, and otherwise wholesome living. The consolidation of small farms into more adequate units, therefore, is desirable.

The substitution of motor or electric power for much of the horse and hand power reduces the amount of labor necessary for, and speeds up, farming operations. Consequently, members of farm families should have more time for recreational, educational, religious, and various social activities than formerly. With an improvement in the general level of living, families who remain on the farm should experience more satisfaction with country life.

While not listed either as a favorable or unfavorable aspect of farm mechanization, the trend toward smaller farm families will result in a greater income per person.

As farm families decline in number and size, fewer schools and churches will be needed in the open country. Farm mechanization should accelerate the townward movement of those institutions. The decline and disappearance of neighborhoods can be expected as rural social organizations become located increasingly in nearby trade centers.

Coincident with the enlargement of farms is the tendency toward concentration of ownership among a few large landholders and the restriction of opportunities for farm youth who wish to become farmers. Increased capital requirements in agriculture will tend to discourage young men from entering agriculture. The sons of farm owners will gain a decided advantage over sons of tenants and farm laborers in the acquisition of ownership and control of land.

Large farms develop tremendous productive capacity which proves to be a boon in times of need for food and fiber but is a serious economic and political problem in times of depression. (Seventeen percent of all farms in Oklahoma—those with products valued at $4,000 or more—accounted for 63 percent of the value of all farm products sold in 1945.) Farmers who produce primarily for market become vulnerable to extreme production and price fluctuations. Because farming is a business characterized by relatively high fixed costs and usually increasing variable costs, large-scale commercialized agriculture probably will rely increasingly upon government assistance in production control and price support programs. This will mean, curiously enough, that full scale agricultural production can be maintained only at a cost of lower levels of living for the general population.

The impacts of farm mechanization probably have been greatest upon the landless classes in agriculture--tenants and laborers. World War II solved the problems of technological unemployment resulting from farm mechanization at least temporarily, through the creation of economic opportunities in villages and cities of Oklahoma, Texas, the Pacific Coast states, and other states to which Oklahomans migrated. High rates of employment in nonfarm industries must continue if large numbers of war-boom migrants are to avoid having to seek refuge and lower living costs in farming areas of Oklahoma and other states.

During the past twenty-five years tractors on farms increased at an average rate of 2,600 per year. Farms with tractors now are concentrated in western Oklahoma where fairly level topography, comparatively large acreages and capital per unit, and a specialized cropping system favor mechanization.

The diffusion of the tractor and other machines into central and eastern Oklahoma has been slower and probably will continue to be slower, in terms of actual numbers, than in the western part of the state due to these factors:

1. Uneven to hilly topography
2. Greater density of population on farms
3. Prevalence of small farms and small capital per unit, and
4. General and self-sufficing agriculture, which is not easily adapted to use of tractors.[5]

Considering these and other factors it is not unreasonable to expect that Oklahoma will have between 100,000 and 115,000 farm tractors by 1965. This prediction indicates that from 60 to 75 percent of the farms in the state eventually will have tractors as compared with 37 percent in 1945. Wide variations in the incidence of tractors appear likely, with probably not more than 30 percent of the farms in counties of Group V having them two decades hence.

Machine technology has resulted in great social and economic changes in agriculture. Its effects on farm people and their activities have been tremendous. In the long run, the increased use of tractors and other labor-saving machines should prove highly beneficial to farm families, but improvements of this nature cannot be achieved without serious dislocations of populations and disruptions of their lifeways.

NOTES

1. The chief weaknesses of the measures considered unsatisfactory for this study can be stated briefly. Both the number of tractors per 1,000 acres of land used for crops and the value of farm machinery per 100 acres of cropland reflect variations in crop acres per farm, intensity of cropping, and major crops. For example, in the panhandle counties of the state, characterized by relatively large farms and high proportions of cropland in wheat and grain sorghums, the number of tractors and the value of farm machinery per 1,000 acres of cropland are comparatively low, even though there is a tractor on nearly every farm. The number of trucks per 100 farms is not a satisfactory measure of the amount of farm mechanization since trucks are used most widely in those areas of the state where wheat and beef cattle are the principal farm enterprises. Accessibility to electric power lines influences the proportion of farms with electricity. The objection to the number of automobiles per 100 farms as a measure of mechanization is that nearness to cities or to oil and mining industries seems to affect this index unduly.

2. The correlation coefficients between increases in numbers of tractors per 100 farms and net changes of farm population between 1925 and 1945 for the five mechanization groups were as follows:

All groups	.29	Group III	.51
Group I	.54	Group IV	.03
Group II	.35	Group V	.05

3. Regression coefficients were calculated for each group of counties. Actually, the loss of population per tractor probably was much larger than indicated by regression coefficients, because only net population changes were used. The excess of births over deaths in Oklahoma amounts to about 10 per 1,000 population each year, and no adjustment for this factor was made in the calculations.

4. See charts on wheat and cotton in <u>1949 Agricultural Outlook Charts</u>, U.S. Department of Agriculture, Bureau of Agricultural Economics, U.S. Government Printing Office, Washington, D.C., October 1948:61-62 and 67.

5. The development of small inexpensive tractors or the cooperative ownership of tractors might counteract the retarding effects of items 3 and 4.

8
Agricultural Mechanization and Social Change in Rural Louisiana

Alvin L. Bertrand

*This article is one of several in which
the socioeconomic consequences of mechanization are analyzed, as well as the underlying causes for a rapid shift to mechanization. Through analysis of census data
and field surveys of county extension
agents and farm operators, Bertrand examined the rate of agricultural mechanization between 1930 and 1945. He believed
that social change occurring in rural
areas represented both a warning and an
opportunity for rural sociologists to be
aware of these changes and to monitor
them.*

INTRODUCTION

Agriculture in the South is in an era of
change. It is undergoing what might well be termed a
"technological" revolution. This fact has been acknowledged by almost every writer or speaker on the
southern region within the last ten years. Observers, however, seemingly have been so absorbed in the
chronicling of this trend that they have, with few
exceptions, overlooked causation and social and economic implications.[1] Present developments make it
evident that the above considerations merit the
immediate attention of the social scientists of the
region. This fact is emphasized by Ogburn and
Nimkoff. They state:

Excerpted from Louisiana Agricultural Experiment
Station Bulletin No. 458, Baton Rouge, June 1951.
Reprinted by permission.

94

> Mechanization is one of the most striking and
> pervasive phenomena of our times. Unfortunate
> ly, its study has been neglected by the social
> sciences, which have not sufficiently recognized
> that while technology itself belongs to the
> field of the natural sciences, its far-reaching
> effects on social life make it a vital subject
> for study by the social sciences. (Ogburn and
> Nimkoff, 1950:52)

Already it is obvious that changing techniques in agriculture have drastically altered the economic nature of farming itself and have been responsible for
profound changes in rural social institutions. Over
and beyond this, problems have appeared which stem
from the dislocation of populations. The above facts
set the stage for the following research report.
    More specifically, the present study is an at-
tempt to answer questions in connection with the relatively sudden advent and spread of agricultural
mechanization in Louisiana. How quickly the change
has come about may be seen in Table 8.1, which shows
the increase in the number of tractors in the state
in the last fifteen years. Since this is one of the
first works of its kind to appear, the procedure is
exploratory to a high degree. It is felt, however,
that sufficient information is presented to answer
many of the questions which have been raised. At the
same time, the findings should be useful in predicting trends--an important task--as mechanization in
the state is far from its peak and will presumably
continue to advance at a fairly rapid pace.

TABLE 8.1
**Changes in the Numbers of Tractors in Louisiana,
1930-1945**

Census Year	Number of Tractors	Percent Increase over Previous Census Year
1930	5,016	....
1940	9,476	88.1
1945	17,630	86.2

Source: Sixteenth Census of the United States, 1940,
and United States Census of Agriculture, 1945.

OBJECTIVES

The major objectives of this study may be listed
as follows: The first was to discover how far mechanization had progressed in the various areas of the
state. Information of this sort is not only important to the State Agricultural Extension Service and
Agricultural Experiment Station but to persons in
private and public life concerned with Louisiana agriculture. Also, a knowledge of the extent and degree of mechanization in each area of the state will
shed light on the factors associated with the acceptance and diffusion of technological improvements in
rural areas of the southern region.

The second purpose was to acquire information
relative to underlying causes for the rapid shift to
mechanization by southern farmers. In this connection, knowledge was sought at two levels, i.e., regional as well as local. The aim was an understanding, not only of the overall developments related to
the advent of machines in southern fields, but [also
of] the actual reasons of farm operators for mechanizing. Information on reactions to mechanization
was considered relevant in this connection. Agricul-
turalists and others who possess this information
will, of course, be in an advantageous position to
understand what has happened and in appraising possible future changes on the farm scene.

A third objective, and perhaps the major one of
the study, was to find out, insofar as possible, the
number and nature of socioeconomic changes in agricultural areas of Louisiana which are attributable to
the adoption of mechanical power on farms. It is
known, as has been mentioned, that the abruptness and
speed of southern agriculture's shift to machines has
already created some problems and others may be anticipated. Such information, then, is of significant
value to many people.

Finally, it was felt that there might exist certain social changes in rural areas of Louisiana not
clearly attributable to mechanization or, for that
matter, to any other single factor, yet representing
phenomena of great importance. Consequently one objective of the study was to point out changes of a
social nature occurring in the rural areas of the
state. It was believed that this objective could be
carried out incidental to the presentation of the
role of mechanization in social change. Such knowledge, of course, is of use in appraising the sum
total of change and can be invaluable to agricultural
planners.

METHODOLOGY

Since this study is one of the first of its kind, there was little precedence to follow.[2] The first task undertaken was the assembling and tabulating of basic relevant data from the Federal Census. After review of these materials, it was felt that many questions were not explained and could only be answered by a field study. To determine what direction such a study should take, a list of questions pertaining to the advent and effects of mechanization and social change was sent to every county agent in the state. The response to these questions was gratifying, and ample information for the development of a field schedule was obtained.

Census data and county agent reports indicated wide differences in degree of mechanization from one part of the state to another. Therefore, it was deemed desirable to make a sounding in as many different localities as possible. The problem was to select a valid and reliable index of farm mechanization so that sample enumerations would represent the state or stage of mechanization in a given group of parishes within the state. This problem was complicated by the fact that a realistic definition of mechanization must include the shift from hand or horse power to combustion engine or electric power in any part of the operation of the farms instead of just in the fields.

In the preliminary work to decide upon an appropriate index, many measures of mechanization appearing in the 1945 Census of Agriculture were tested. After careful analysis, it was decided that, in view of the above definition of mechanization, no one index would suffice. Rather a combination of two, the number of tractors per 1,000 acres of cropland and the dollar valuation of implements and machinery per acre of cropland, was selected as most satisfactory. Acres of cropland instead of land in farms was used as the bases of the indices because of the many acres of land not utilized on some farms.

The procedure for determining Farm Mechanization Groups was to array parishes according to the two indices named above and arbitrarily divide the sixty-four parishes of the state into four groups. The parishes having the highest indices were placed in Group I, those with the second highest in Group II, those with the third highest in Group III, and those with the smallest in Group IV. In the few parishes where the indices indicated different categories, an intermediate position was selected. For example, if the number of tractors per 1,000 acres of cropland indicated Group I and the dollar valuation of implements and machinery per cultivated acre indicated Group III, the parish was placed in Group II. . . .Table 8.2 shows the difference in numbers of tractors and value of implements and machinery for each group.

TABLE 8.2
Number of Tractors and Value of Implements and Machinery Related to Land in Cultivation, by Mechanization Groups, Louisiana, 1945

Farm Mechanization Group	Tractors per 1,000 Cultivated Acres	Implements and Machinery per Cultivated Acre
State	3.4	$11.87
Group I	5.9	20.15
Group II	4.6	13.39
Group III	3.0	10.95
Group IV	1.4	7.26

Source: United States Census of Agriculture, 1945.

. . .

To satisfy the requirement for obtaining a representative sample in each group of parishes representing a particular state of mechanization, the following procedure was used. Four circular survey areas with a thirty-mile radius were selected, each with its midpoint located as near as possible to the center of the largest cluster of parishes falling in a particular Mechanization Group. With the exception of a few persons not available for interview, every farm operator and nonoperator with a ten-year history of continuous residence within the sample areas, regardless of race, was interviewed by a carefully trained enumerator. In this connection, it should be noted that operator and nonoperator schedules were of a necessity not identical. Many of the same questions were asked each group of interviewees, however. The survey schedules called for a considerable variety of information, although an attempt was made to keep the time required for interviews reasonably short. Altogether 485 schedules were taken. Of these, 275 were from farm operators and 210 from nonoperators. The distribution of operator schedules was as follows: 55 in Group I parishes, 54 in Group II parishes, 82 in Group III parishes, and 84 in Group IV parishes. Sixty-three nonoperator schedules were taken from Group I parishes, 72 from Group II parishes, 35 from Group III parishes, and 40 from Group IV parishes.

The information obtained from the Census and the survey was sorted and tabulated in the conventional manner. Comparisons by Mechanization Groups are emphasized because these are considered the most significant for the purposes of the study. In this connection, differentials such as race, religion, etc., while not maintained in the data, are used in making interpretations. Where comparable data from the Census and the survey are available, both are used in the analysis for the sake of a clearer and more up-to-date picture. The analysis is simple and straightforward. For comparative purposes, the Census data for 1930 and 1945 are used whenever available, as this period is the most important in the change to mechanization.

. . .

SUMMARY OF RESULTS

1. All farm areas of the State of Louisiana have been characterized by substantial gains in agricultural mechanization during the last twenty years. The most highly mechanized region of the state centers in what is commonly known as the Sugar parishes of south Louisiana. The next highest mechanized parishes are somewhat scattered. Included in this group are the inner tier of the upper Mississippi Delta parishes, the lower tier of the so-called Florida parishes in southeast Louisiana, and several southwest Louisiana rice-growing parishes. The third highest group of parishes, according to degree of mechanization, includes the remaining rice-growing parishes of southwest Louisiana, several adjacent mixed-farming parishes, three upper Red River Delta parishes, and four outer Mississippi Delta parishes. Parishes with the least concentration of mechanization, except for three upper Florida parishes and one south central parish, are all found in the north and central Hill and Cut-over areas.

2.   Although the depression, AAA program, and
World War II are given credit for setting in motion
processes which precipitated agricultural mechanization in the southern region, individual farmers over
the state name economy, labor shortage, and efficiency, in that order, as the most important reasons
why they have mechanized. A lack of necessary finances has deterred farmers who have not mechanized but
who intend to do so, while age, lack of finances, and
lack of land have discouraged operators who are not
mechanized and who do not plan to mechanize.   Nonoperators have mixed emotions about mechanization.
However, those on mechanized farms are favorably inclined toward machines.
       3.   In Louisiana, the mechanization of farms has
been directly associated with a steady advance in the
number of tractors, trucks, implements, and machinery; a decrease in draft animals; an increase in
livestock other than workstock; an increase in
owner-operated farms; a decrease in numbers of sharecroppers and laborers; absentee ownership; a decrease
in the number of farms; an increase in the size of
farms; an increase in total value of farm products
produced; and a higher level of living.
       4.   Social changes taking place in rural areas
of Louisiana, which are more or less associated with
agricultural mechanization, include decreases in
rural population; improvements in the equipment,
faculty, and attendance of rural schools; a loosening
of the ties on individual members of the rural family; a loss of many of the rural family's functions
to other social institutions; a decline in the influence of the rural church; a decrease in mutual aid
practices; an increase in leisure time; an increase
in social participation; and improved town-country
relations.
       5.   In the final analysis, it may be pointed out
that there is an increasing commercialization of
farming and an increasing urbanization of rural populations in Louisiana. Both of these trends are in
large measure due to the mechanization of agricultural systems.

· · ·

CONCLUSIONS

The salient findings of the above report may be
stated in succinct form as follows. Agricultural
mechanization stimulated by the economic motive is

proceeding at a rapid rate in Louisiana. It has been
responsible to a greater or lesser degree for many
changes on the farm and in farm people. Together
with other technological advances and changes in ideologies and philosophies it has worked and is working
to reduce the differences between the two heretofore
quite distinct residential segments of the popula-
tion--the rural and the urban. The fact that much
social change is taking place in farm areas emphasizes that rural society is dynamic and not static in
nature--that characteristics which describe it today
may not hold tomorrow. There is both a warning and
an opportunity for Rural Sociologists in the above
knowledge. They must ever be on the alert to detect
and call attention to changes in rural life. At the
same time their work will never be done or become
uninteresting.

NOTES

1. This does not mean to imply that there has
been no study of the social effects of the mechanization of southern agriculture. On the contrary, several scholars have done commendable jobs of taking
inventories of the immediate social effects and of
hypothesizing on possible changes of the future. For
some examples, see: Hamilton (1939:3-19); Raper
(1946:21-30); Williams (1939:300-313); Vance (1945
and 1946); and McMillan (1949).
2. The most helpful study to the writer was
McMillan (1949).

Part 3
Recent Concerns
with New Technologies
in Agriculture

9
Mechanized Agriculture and Social Welfare: The Case of the Tomato Harvester

Andrew Schmitz
David Seckler

In this study, both social costs and social benefits of mechanization were analyzed. The authors showed that gross social returns to aggregate research and development expenditures were approximately 1,000 percent. Even if displaced labor were compensated for wage loss, net social returns would still be favorable. However, since compensation was not actually paid, it cannot be concluded that society as a whole has benefited from the tomato harvester. The authors concluded with several suggestions for compensation strategies that would allow the social costs and benefits of technology to be more equitably distributed throughout society.

At the beginning of the industrial revolution in the 19th century gangs of workmen known as the Luddites roamed England, systematically destroying machinery. To their compatriots in the Netherlands we owe the word "sabotage," after "sabot," the heavy wooden shoe that Dutch workmen threw into the grinding gears of the new technology.

The other side of the coin is well illustrated by the lament of John M. Horner, one of the inventors of the wheat combine.[1] Writing to his friend, Colonel Warren, editor of the California Farmer, in July 1869 (Higgins, 1958:22), Horner said,

we were brought more particularly to reflect upon our position by the burning of one of

------

From American Journal of Agricultural Economics 54 (4), 1970, pp. 569-77. Reprinted by permission.

our machines. . . . We ask ourselves: Have we
injured anyone so that personal vengeance is
pursuing us, and this burning was done to grat-
ify a revengeful feeling? No. We have had no
misunderstanding with anyone, in fact, not an
enemy in the world, a conscience void of offence
to all men. We entered that neighborhood to
perform honest labors, and harvested (1,600)
acres in a good workmanlike manner to the entire
satisfaction of our employers--so much so that
most of them wanted us to consent to harvest
their next crops.

Colonel Warren promptly responded with an editorial in his paper (Higgins, 1958:23):

Such acts as the one named upon a man like Mr.
Horner because he had invented a labor-saving
machine should arouse the spirit of the lion
among all good men and they should unite and
hunt up the offenders and make them feel the
heaviest penalties of the law for damages and
then be driven from every civilized community.

The rhetoric of this ancient conflict has
changed, but not its substance. "Technological displacement"--as it is now euphemistically called--
remains the source of some of our greatest social
problems. This is particularly true in agriculture.
We point with justifiable pride to the fact that now
only a small percentage of the total population produces our food needs. But we tend to forget the
painful process of adjustment that accompanied the
transition from a rural to an urban society. We have
forgotten that for many people the transition was in-
voluntary; that many people have been forced off the
farm only into an economic and social limbo in rural
towns and urban ghettos.
The overall purpose of this paper is to provide
a means whereby the broad social costs of technological innovation can be mapped into the framework of
economic analysis. It focuses specifically on a recent technological change affecting agriculture--the
mechanical tomato harvester.

DEVELOPMENT OF THE TOMATO HARVESTER

The history of the development of the tomato
harvester is a subject of interest in itself. It is
an outstanding instance of the parallel development

of innovations dovetailing into a viable system. As Rasmussen (1968:532-533) states,

> The invention of the mechanical tomato harvester contrasted decidedly with the development of the cotton picker. The tomato harvester resulted from the "system approach." A team made up of an engineering group and a horticultural group, with advice and assistance from agronomists and irrigation specialists, developed suitable plants and an efficient harvester at the same time. The necessary changes in planting, cultivation, and irrigating were developed concurrently. . . .
>
> The systems approach was also followed in the development phase of the harvester. Manufacturers, scientists, and extension personnel worked closely with farmers, first in growing the new tomato varieties, then in getting the tomatoes harvested. Processors subsidized the first crops by lowering their purchasing standards on the new tomatoes and by adjusting their production techniques to accommodate the changed inputs. In the opinion of E. Blackwelder of the Blackwelder Manufacturing Company, which produced one of the first harvesters, it would have been virtually impossible to develop the harvester without an industry-wide integration of efforts. Thus, the harvester represents a social as well as a scientific and engineering success. Through coordinated efforts on many fronts, the industry was able to achieve results not economically available to any individual member.
>
> The first 25 harvesters were used in California in 1961. By 1964, 75 were in use; a year later, 250. The number increased to 1,000 in 1967 (Lynch, 1968), when approximately 80 percent of the California acreage was harvested by machines. However, in other tomato-producing states the harvester was adopted after this period.

PURPOSE AND FRAMEWORK OF ANALYSIS

Like the cotton harvester, the mechanical tomato harvester has created important production economies but has also undermined the livelihood of numerous agricultural laborers. In this paper we attempt to appraise both the heightened production efficiency and its effect on the welfare of workers. The pioneering work of Schultz (1953) and Griliches (1958)

106

is carried one step further--into an appraisal of important social costs as well as social benefits.

Both gross and net social rates of return to the tomato harvester are computed; the difference is the wage loss of the displaced workers. To compute the gross social rate of return, we employ as a basis the framework used by Griliches (1958) and Peterson (1967) who estimated, respectively, the benefit to society from the introduction of hybrid corn and from poultry research.

Using the concepts of consumer's and producer's surplus, Griliches analyzed two polar cases. In figure 9.1 supply is completely elastic and the original supply curve is S'; after the development of hybrid corn, the new supply curve is S. Since supply is completely elastic, producer surplus does not exist and the net gain, E+F, represents the addition to consumer surplus. In figure 9.2 supply is perfectly inelastic; with the introduction of hybrid corn, supply shifts from S' to S. The gain in consumer surplus is A+B; the gain in producer surplus is -A+D; and the net gain to society is A+B+(-A+D)= B+D, from which is calculated the gross social rate of return.

Peterson, on the other hand, used the inbetween case of a positive sloping supply curve. Thus, as demonstrated in figure 9.3, the net benefit to society is G+F+H+I, that is, the area between the two supply curves and the demand curve, as in figure 9.2. This is so since the net gain in consumer and producer surplus is E+G+F+(-E+H+I). As previously, the gross social rate of return is calculated from the area remaining after accounting for the changes in surpluses.

FIGURE 9.1

FIGURE 9.2

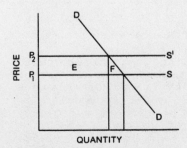

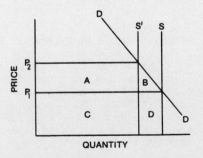

Consumer's and Producer's
Surplus, Supply elastic

Consumer's and Producer's
Surplus, Supply Inelastic

Various attempts at estimating the elasticities
of demand and supply of processing tomatoes have met
with little success.[2] Therefore, in computing the
gross social returns from the harvester, we take the
total production after the new equilibrium is
achieved and multiply this by the ensuing cost savings per ton of tomatoes harvested. Thus, we are essentially measuring area EGFK in figure 9.3, where Q_1
is the equilibrium level of tomato production prior
to the implementation of the harvester and Q_2 is the
equilibrium level of production when the harvester is
in use. Therefore, we would overestimate consumer
surplus, and hence the gross social gain to society,
by K if the demand for tomatoes were DD and supply
were perfectly elastic. However, if the supply curve
for tomatoes is not perfectly elastic, our calculations underestimate the gross social rates of return
if the true demand and supply functions for tomatoes
are approximately those represented by DD and S_0'
(compare EGFK and GFHI).[3]

To compute the net social rate of return from
the development of the harvester, we explicitly took
into account its effect on farm workers. With reference to figure 9.4, prior to mechanization the demand
for tomato workers is D_0 and supply is S_0, but subsequent to the harvester the demand becomes D_1. As one
extreme, we computed $W_0(Q_2-Q_1)$--the unemployment
caused by the harvester--assuming no alternative employment possibilities and assuming that the remaining employed workers receive wages at least as high
as those obtained prior to the implementation of the
harvester. In addition, we calculated the net social
rate of return assuming different levels of employment for farm workers in nonagricultural industries.

FIGURE 9.3

FIGURE 9.4

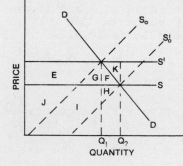

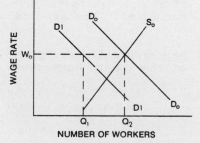

Gross Social Rate of Return   Net Social Rate of Return

GROSS SOCIAL RATE OF RETURN

Gross Social Returns

We use "gross social returns" (GSR) to mean the value of the reduced costs of harvesting tomatoes by the mechanical harvester.[4] These returns differ from "net social returns" by the value of the costs incurred by workers displaced by the harvester.

Only for California have definitive studies been made of the comparative costs of hand and mechanical tomato harvesting methods (Parsons, 1966; Zobel and Parsons, 1965), and these data are used here for other tomato-producing states as well. According to the California studies, mechanical harvesting reduces costs by $5.41 to $7.47 per ton,[5] including amortization and interest charges at 6 percent on the machine costs. The data apply only to tomatoes for processing since tomatoes for nonprocessing are still handpicked.

In order to estimate GSR from the harvester for the United States as a whole, it is necessary to estimate its rate of adoption. These estimates, presented in table 9.1, are based on a total U.S. acreage of tomatoes for processing of 322,010, the average for 1966-1969.[6] We estimate that California will harvest 95 percent of its acreage by machine in 1973 and that the maximum rate of adoption by other states will be 60 percent. Webb and Bruce (1968:1-5) have estimated the total U.S. average rate of adoption to be 80 percent.[7]

Given these data and an estimated average yield of 22 tons of tomatoes per acre, we can now compute the GSR to the harvester for the United States. All estimates have been carried to the year 1973 when, by assumption, tomato acreage attains a constant amount. Thus, the annual GSR for each year, 1965-1973, are calculated at 6 percent interest to 1973 and then converted to an annual perpetual sum.[8] This, together with the annual GSR in 1973 and thereafter, constitutes the annual value of GSR to the harvester. The results are shown in table 9.2.

Research and Development Costs of the Tomato Harvester

Several universities and private firms contributed to research and development (R and D) of the tomato harvester. Reasonably good information is available on the costs incurred by two of the major

TABLE 9.1
Rate of Adoption of the Tomato Harvester,
United States, 1965–1973[a]

Year	Percent of Tomatoes Harvested by Machines		Total U.S. Acreage of Tomatoes Harvested by Machines
	California	Other States	
1965	25	0	48,302
1966	60	0	112,704
1967	80	0	144,905
1968	85	10	161,005
1969	90	20	193,206
1970	95	30	209,307
1971	95	40	225,405
1972	95	50	241,508
1973	95	60	257,608

[a]The rate of adoption was negligible before 1965 and is assumed to be zero for estimation purposes.

Sources: Adoption rates prior to 1968 were taken from Lynch (1968); succeeding adoption rates are the authors' projections (see footnote 7 of text). Estimated tomato acreage harvested by machine for 1965-1968 was derived by applying the above percentage rates of adoption to the acreage figures reported by the U.S. Department of Agriculture (1961-1968). The equilibrium acreage in processing tomatoes was estimated to be 332,010, of which 257,608 are mechanically harvested.

TABLE 9.2
Gross Social Returns to the Tomato Harvester

Returns	Estimated Cost Reduction at	
	$5.41 per Ton	$7.47 per Ton
	Dollars	
1. Cumulated GSR, 1965-1973	199,124,897	274,792,805
2. Annual value of cumulated GSR,1973	11,947,494	16,487,568
3. Annual GSR,1973	30,660,524	42,335,299
4. Total, 2 and 3	42,608,018	58,822,867

110

parties to this invention--the University of California at Davis and Blackwelder Manufacturing Company of
Rio Vista, California. The University of Michigan,
the University of Florida, and the University of
Maryland also have engaged in research and development; and some other firms, including H. D. Hume
Company, Food Manufacturing Corporation, Massey-
Ferguson, and Button Manufacturing Company, have incurred significant R and D costs in the development
of tomato harvesters. Estimates of costs incurred by
these universities and firms represent only an educated guess based on interviews with knowledgeable
persons. Total R and D estimates compounded to 1967
are given in table 9.3.[9]

TABLE 9.3
Research and Development Expenditures
on the Tomato Harvester

	Expenditures[a]
Universities (to 1967)	
University of California, Davis	
Non-Extension activities	$ 588,000
Extension and related activities	100,000
Other universities (including Extension)	600,000
Total universities	$1,288,000
Private firms (to 1967)	
Blackwelder Manufacturing Company	$ 491,000
Other firms	1,473,000
Total firms	$1,964,000
Total 1967 value	$3,252,000
Total R and D costs: 1973 value (cumulated at 6 percent)	$4,585,320

[a]Figures rounded to the nearest thousand.

Rate of Return

Given the above data on benefits accruing from the tomato harvester and the R and D costs to make the harvester a reality, it is possible to calculate the gross social rate of return (GSRR) to R and D costs as follows:

$$GSRR = \frac{\text{total annual value}}{\text{research and development costs}} (100).$$

Thus, assuming the low-cost saving of $5.41 per ton,

$$GSRR = \frac{\$42,608,018 \text{ (Table 9.2)}}{\$4,585,320 \text{ (Table 9.3)}} (100) = 929 \text{ percent.}$$

Similarly, for the cost saving of $7.47 per ton, the GSRR is 1,282 percent ($58,822,867 ÷ $4,585,320). Hence, the gross social rate of return may vary from 929 to 1,282 percent.

To this point we have followed traditional analysis to calculate the rates of return from an innovation in which the distributional effects are assumed to be zero. In the next section, this assumption is relaxed and the costs incurred by workers due to adoption of the tomato harvester are explicitly taken into account; but first we discuss welfare criteria relevant to this expanded view.[10]

WELFARE CRITERIA

The concept of Pareto optimality implies that one cannot recommend a change from a state "A" to a state "B" unless everyone is better off in B than in A—that is, no one is worse off in B and at least one person is better off than in A.

A major problem arising is that Pareto optimality favors the status quo. But almost every conceivable change leaves someone worse off. Consequently, making recommendations on grounds other than "whatever is, is right" involves the inextricable difficulties of interpersonal comparisons of utility. If, for example, one is willing to recommend a change that will leave someone worse off than before, he is implying that he can cardinally evaluate the increase

in welfare of the beneficiaries, subtract the decrease in welfare of the losers, and find a net
increment in welfare. This is indeed a heroic pre-
sumption.

As a kind of halfway house between these ex-
tremes, the following "compensation" test has been
proposed by Kaldor and Hicks. It is a necessary condition to recommending a change that the gainers
shall be able to compensate the losers and still be
better off. If the benefits of the change are not
sufficient to pay its ordinary costs and compensation, it cannot be considered socially desirable. It
should be noted, however, that it is not sufficient
that compensation could be paid--it must actually be
paid if a change from the status quo is to be recommended. Otherwise, the problem of interpersonal comparisons of utility still remains.

The implications of this general analysis to the
specific problem of the tomato harvester are clear.
In order to determine the value of the harvester, we
have to determine whether the gainers (producers,
consumers, etc.) could compensate the losers (workers) and still be better off than before.[11]

NET SOCIAL RATE OF RETURN

The tomato harvester displaced roughly 91 man-
hours per acre of tomatoes harvested (Parsons,
1966:1-9).[12] Using the acreage and adoption rates of
table 9.1, 478,637 man-hours were displaced in 1965;
in 1973 and every year thereafter, 19,477,227 (see
Appendix for calculations).[13] The average wage of
harvest labor in California was approximately $1.65
per hour in 1967 (Parsons, 1966). With these
figures, we computed the net social rate of return
(NSRR) under varying assumptions of alternative employment opportunities and, hence, the amount of compensation (C) needed to offset the impact of technological change. The formula used is:

$$NSRR = \frac{GSR - C}{R \text{ and } D} (100).$$

The results are given in table 9.4. For the low-cost
savings estimate of $5.47 per ton, NSRR varies be-
tween 929 and -8 percent as the amount of compensation changes from 0 to 100 percent of the estimated
displaced wage bill. For 100 percent compensation,
it is assumed that displaced tomato workers have no

alternative employment opportunities. For the cost savings of $7.51 per ton, NSRR varies between 1,288 and 345 percent.

We have not attempted to estimate the actual amount of unemployment created by the harvester since this would require knowing all displaced workers' future employments.[14] The estimated wage loss from 1965 through 1972 has been compounded forward to 1973 and then converted to an annual flow. Thus, assuming a wage of $1.65 per hour, the cost to the workers is overestimated because, while the conversion to an annual flow makes it possible to calculate the NSRR, this assumes an infinite life for the displaced labor. This assumption is untenable unless one believes that there is a lasting effect on the workers' families in denied educational opportunities and the like resulting from unemployment caused by technological change.

ACTUAL PAYMENT OF COMPENSATION

We have shown that the rates of return to R and D expenditures on the tomato harvester were highly attractive when measured in the conventional way. More important, the rates of return remain attractive

TABLE 9.4
Net Rates of Social Return to
Research and Development on the Tomato Harvester

% of Displaced Wage Bill Paid in Compensation	Annual 1973 Amount of Compensation	Net Rate of Social Return to R and D Estimated Cost Savings at $5.47 per Ton	$7.51 per Ton
	Dollars	Percent	
0	0	929	1,288
25	10,746,610	694	1,048
50	21,493,262	460	814
75	32,239,892	226	579
100	42,987,523	-8	345

after deducting reasonable amounts of compensation
for costs incurred by displaced workers. However,
since compensation has not actually been paid, it
cannot be concluded that society as a whole has
benefited from the tomato harvester.

Our analysis has focused on unorganized workers
confronted with technological displacement. Compensation was not paid because they lacked the organization to compel it. Contrast this situation with one
in which workers were powerfully organized--the International Longshoremen's and Warehousemen's Union.
Under the leadership of Harry Bridges, this union was
able to mitigate the impact of technology on worker
displacement through "featherbedding" provisions in
its contracts, which it provided for many years. In
the late 1950s, however, it became apparent that the
momentum of technological development, particularly
in the containerization of freight, would eventually
overpower employment-preserving rules. Bridges recognized this in 1957 (Hartman, 1966:145):

> I would say that we have resisted the impact of
> labor-saving machinery, mechanization, automa-
> tion, whatever you want to call it, possibly
> with greater success than any other organiza-
> tion. It has been a combination of ways and
> means of doing things, and it has involved
> strikes, slow-downs, and what-not. However, we
> have reached the point possibly, and some of the
> demands that you are putting in (take this reso-
> lution, for example) and some other proposals
> for changes reflect the feeling that you have
> reached the point, where the battle against the
> machine for us has become a losing one. And we
> can continue to fight a losing battle, and we
> will lose in more ways than one, and finally af-
> ter we have thrown away a lot of energy and a
> lot of bargaining power we will put on a show-
> down, last-stand fight, and we will lose that
> one, too.

Under Bridges' leadership, the union entered ne-
gotiations to trade its featherbedding prerogatives
for job and income security and won a settlement of
$5 million per year for 1961 through 1965; this, to-
gether with previous payments, totaled $29 million
(Hartman, 1966:176). In the union's view, $18 mil-
lion of this, or approximately $3 million per year,
was compensation for technological change or, as they
put it, "the men's share of the machine" (Hartman,
1966:180).

The essence of the contract for the union was the principle of "sharing the machine." As Hartman (1966:344) says,

> In the longshore experience, the older workers won a great deal; the retirement bonus was the equivalent of more than a year's pay. The younger workers were offered less but their prospects for promotion were enhanced by accelerated withdrawal of the older men. Further, they believed that the principle of 'sharing in the machine' had been established and would provide benefits to them in the years to come.

The longshoremen achieved a share in the machine of approximately $3 million per year on an estimated annual industry net savings (in 1965) of no more than and probably considerably less than $59.4 million (Hartman, 1966:332). Thus, the settlement was certainly no less than 5 percent and probably no more than 10 percent of industry's benefits. While the two cases are perhaps noncomparable, it is interesting to observe that, had the tomato workers received a similar share in the machine, their compensation would have been between $2 and $4 million per year. On this basis, the conservatively estimated net social return to the harvester would still have exceeded 700 percent.

CONCLUDING OBSERVATIONS

Our study of the development of the mechanical tomato harvester provides a microscopic look at a general social dilemma. The talents of science and industry combine to create enormously productive innovations, but the very success of these sectors of society creates consequences which bear unfavorably, as Fuller ("Political pressures and income distribution . . .," pp. 255-63) has pointed out, on less organized and therefore more vulnerable sectors.

In order to illustrate this fact, we briefly examined the contrasting impacts of technological change on tomato workers and longshoremen. But labor unions are not the only means of protecting vulnerable sectors of society. Indeed, as Schultz (1961) has stressed, it is the social scientist's task to devise a variety of institutional structures appropriate to the problems with which society is afflicted.

Thus, for compensation purposes, an alternative to unionization may be a form of state intervention in which a tax is imposed on units of output. The proceeds from this tax would then be used to finance retraining, relocative, and retirement programs. This solution is theoretically sound, but if extended through all sectors of the economy that are subject to technological displacement, it would be an organizational monstrosity. Before embarking on programs of this type, it would be wise to seek more general solutions to this general class of problems.[15] Specifically, we might explore whether there are any possibilities that general social programs could significantly reduce the need for compensation itself. We believe there are.

The process of adjustment is particularly painful for displaced tomato workers because they are highly immobile, mainly because of limited occupational versatility. If a fraction of the great economies generated by such technological innovations as the harvester could be allocated out of general taxes and applied to destroying the "vicious cycles of poverty" that afflict society, immobilities--and thus the social costs accompanying such innovations as the tomato harvester--would be substantially reduced. Interventions of this sort would allow social costs and benefits to fall more or less randomly on the population as a whole and thus, in a sense, cancel each other. If this were to occur, "everyone" would be better off with technological change. That is, to us, the moral of the tomato harvester.

APPENDIX
TOTAL MAN-HOUR DISPLACEMENT
BY THE TOMATO HARVESTER

The base acreage used prior to 1965 (that is, prior to the year when the harvester was used substantially) is 297,289, the average from 1958 to 1964. The base acreage used subsequently is 322,010, the average from 1966 to 1969. California is assumed to harvest approximately 55 percent of the processing tomatoes grown in the United States. Using the computations of Parsons (1966), 163 man-hours were employed per acre prior to the harvester; with the harvester, this was cut to 72 man-hours.

Thus, prior to the harvester, 48,458,127 man-hours were employed (297,289 X 163). After the harvester was adopted, in 1965 for example, the number of man-hours employed dropped to 47,979,490, computed as follows: 322,010 [(163 X .85) + (72 X .15)]. This represents a displacement of 478,637 man-hours (48,458,127 - 47,979,490).

It is estimated that in 1973 only 28,980,900 man-hours will be employed, computed as follows: 322,010 [(163 X .20) + (72 X .80)]. Total displacement will then be 19,477,227 man-hours (48,458,127 - 28,980,900).

NOTES

[The authors] appreciate the data made available for this study (Giannini Foundation Paper No. 310) by various departments at the University of California, Davis, and the University of Michigan. Ernie Blackwelder, Clarence Kelly, Philip Parsons, Gordon Rowe, Loy Sammet, and Ron Schuler also provided valuable information. We thank Roy Born for computational assistance and Bill Martin and Loren Ihnen for critical comments.

1. We are indebted to Paul Barkley for this reference.

2. For consumer tomato demand, Babb et al. (1969) estimated the price elasticity to be -.76, but this was statistically insignificant. They attributed their difficulty in estimation to data problems. For supply response of planted tomato acreage, they estimated the short- and long-run price elasticity to be 2.18 and 4.49 in Indiana; 1.05 and 2.65 in Ohio.

3. Other configurations for supply could lead to an overestimate of the gross social rates of return.

4. Some benefits of the harvester have been omitted from our estimates. We neglect benefits accruing to foreign countries (Germany, the U.S.S.R., and Israel, for example) that have imported these machines. Manufacturers' profits from the sale of the machines were not independently estimated, but enter our analysis as a cost of the machines. Royalties received by the University of California, which holds a patent on the most commonly used machines, were not included in our estimate of benefits; these amounted to $224,782 by 1969.

5. These cost savings are not given explicitly in the studies; they were computed from Zobel's and Parsons's work (Parsons 1966; Zobel and Parsons, 1965, 1969). Detailed calculations are available on request from the authors, as are the detailed calculations underlying the remainder of this paper.

6. Since this study was completed before 1969 acreage figures were available, total 1969 acreage was estimated to be 80 percent of the 1968 figure.

7. Accurate estimates on the current rate of adoption do not exist. It appears, however, that for California at least 90 percent of the acreage is now mechanically harvested and could easily reach 95 percent by 1973. On the other hand, several people have expressed the opinion that our 60 percent adoption figure by 1973 for other states is too high. It may well be, however, that more processing tomatoes may be grown in California than the 55 percent of the acreage figure used. Therefore, we feel that the total acreage of 257,608 mechanically harvested of a possible estimated 322,010 acres is a conservative estimate.

8. We cannot predict the ultimate impact of the harvester on wages, prices, and output; so, unless otherwise stated, we have assumed these to remain the same as in 1965-1969.

9. Estimates include only direct R and D costs of developing the harvester. Costs to farmers and processors of transition to the new technique are not included, nor are the effects of the harvester on processing costs. R. Schuler of California Canners and Growers Association indicated that it is extremely difficult to determine whether the net effect on processing costs is positive or negative. Finally, we have not entered the discussion as to whether the new tomato grown for mechanical harvesting is of inferior quality than that grown prior to mechanization. If the new variety is inferior, which is debatable, then the costs incurred because of inferior quality are not accounted for.

10. We cannot go into all the complexities of welfare theory here. The interested reader is referred to Little (1950) and Mishan (1960).

11. The main losers from this particular technological change are farm workers. Undoubtedly there are other people who also lose, but these are not discussed in this paper. Furthermore, it becomes clear that cost-benefit studies must consider both allocative and distributional problems [see, for example, Prest and Turvey (1965), Musgrave (1969), and Knetch et al. (1969)]. Compensation is a necessary but not a sufficient condition for appraising an improvement. See Little (1950: ch. 6) for a discussion of the Scitovsky reversal problem.

12. The amount of the labor saved by the mechanical harvester is given in Parsons (1966:8). The man-hours saved per acre vary from 29 for excellent

workers to 178 for poor workers. The figure used, 91 man-hours, while substantially above that for poor workers, is only slightly below the man-hours displaced for good workers. However, it should be pointed out that Parsons's calculations are based on the specific type of harvester available in 1966 when approximately twenty good workers were needed per machine. A new tomato harvester will soon be made available which will require substantially less labor to operate; the use of an electronic sorting device can reduce the requirement to less than eight workers per machine. In view of these recent developments, our estimates of labor displacement resulting from the harvester are probably conservative.

13. When calculating the displacement by the tomato harvester, the analysis would become extremely complex if one attempted to distinguish between domestic workers and temporarily admitted aliens. In our analysis, we have assumed that had the tomato harvester not been invented the total workers employed would be the same as in the early 1960s.

14. As Robinson (1958:2) points out, "Nearly four million workers were employed in 1957 in industries which did not exist or hardly existed in 1900. If we had been looking for jobs for those workers in 1900, we should never have foreseen the present number of workers in the motor industry and motor transport, in the making of gramophones, wireless or television sets, in electricity, or aviation. At any moment it is hard to foresee how those workers will ultimately be absorbed, for whose services in their former occupations there is likely to be less demand."

15. See, for example, H. G. Johnson (1962:180-95).

10
Assessment of the Economic and Social Impacts of Agricultural Technology: A Case Study

Ahmed M. Hussen

*In this article, Hussen reviews models and
methodologies used for technology assessment, all of which tend to overemphasize
economic factors and underemphasize
secondary and tertiary impacts of technology. He argues that many of the models do
not take into account all the distributional effects (social and economic) arising from agricultural technology. Hussen
uses a framework for analysis similar to
Schmitz and Seckler's to estimate gross and
net social returns resulting from use of
the mechanical strawberry harvester in
Oregon. He includes a discussion of the
factors not explicitly accounted for in the
model and their potential repercussions on
the estimated social returns.*

The primary objectives of this study are: (a) to
briefly discuss the complex theoretical and empirical
issues facing economists in assessing the economic
and social impacts of technological change in agriculture; (b) in light of these issues, to evaluate
the net social benefits arising from the proposed
mechanization of strawberry harvest in Oregon. This
case study demonstrates the strengths and weaknesses
of the most contemporary economic models and methodologies used to evaluate the economic and social

Edited and excerpted from the Western Journal of
Agricultural Economics, December 1979, pp. 17-31.
Reprinted by permission.

impacts of new and existing agricultural technologies.

. . .

MODELS AND METHODOLOGIES USED
FOR TECHNOLOGY ASSESSMENT

According to West (1976), technological assessment entails "the formal systematic examination of
existing, newly emerging, or prospective technology
with the objective of estimating first and second order costs and consequences (beneficial and adverse)
over time in terms of the economic, social, demographic, environmental, legal, political, and institutional dimension of the impacts of the technology."
Hence, technological assessment involves a careful
and objective consideration of both the social and
economic impacts of technology. In assessing agricultural technology, however, economic factors have
been given unjustifiably heavy weight in the past,
while the social (distributional) effects of technology [have] received little consideration. In this
regard, Hightower (1972) criticized the land-grant
colleges and universities for ignoring the effects of
introducing new technology (mechanization) on the
small family farms and the rural poor.

The overemphasis on economic factors and the un-
deremphasis of the secondary and tertiary impacts of
technology are partly attributed to such facts as:

(a) Until the last two decades, the distributional impact of introducing new technology
appeared less severe because of the growing
industrial sectors' ability to absorb labor
leaving the small farms. However, even
though past events have changed, economists
have been assessing the effects of technology in conventional ways.

(b) Economic impacts generally are easier to
quantify and analyze using the tools and experiences most economic researchers acquire
during their training.

A number of researchers have addressed the issues of the economic and social impacts of new and
existing technology in the agricultural sector (Griliches, 1958; Schmitz and Seckler, 1970; Hertford and
Schmitz, 1977; Martin and Johnson, 1978). Since a

comprehensive review of these works is not the primary goal here, only a brief illustration of the scope, models, and methodologies is presented. Broadly speaking, researchers have used two approaches in analyzing the impacts of agricultural technology—statics and comparative statics.

Static Approach

This approach considers whether the new technology is economically beneficial (usually in terms of profits) to the producers of immediate concern and in some cases to a narrowly defined group of consumers (Parsons, 1966; Holtman et al., 1977; Hussen, 1978). It assesses the cost effectiveness of a proposed or existing technology strictly from the viewpoint of the immediate beneficiaries. Factor and product prices are assumed constant and no distributional effects of the technology are considered. This limited scope does not allow for any definitive conclusions about whether a given technology is socially desirable or not.

Comparative Statics

This approach is broader than the static approach. The objective is to estimate the social return (gross, net, or both) arising from a given agricultural technology. The concepts of consumers' and producers' surplus are used to achieve this goal (Griliches, 1958; Peterson, 1967; Schmitz and Seckler, 1970).[1] In most of these types of analysis, the secondary and tertiary distributional effects of technological change are simply overlooked (Griliches, 1958; Peterson, 1967). Recently, however, researchers using similar approaches have attempted to account for the secondary and tertiary impacts of technological change (Schmitz and Seckler, 1970; Hertford and Schmitz, 1977; Martin and Johnson, 1978).

Even though some of the shortcomings of the static approach are lessened, the comparative static approach still falls short of comprehensive and well-integrated analysis which fully satisfies everyone concerned with the subject. Among the major drawbacks of the comparative static approach are conceptual and theoretical problems arising from the use of the consumers' and producers' surplus as a measure of the social benefits. For example, are compensated demand curves used in measuring the consumers' surplus? Is a derived or final demand curve used? How small is the income elasticity of demand? Also, for producers' surplus, how elastic are the supply curves of the variable inputs? Other drawbacks are the lack of practically applicable criteria for compensating the losers who are negatively impacted by technological change, and the fact that the results from partial equilibrium analysis may not coincide with the results of a more general equilibrium analysis. This fact is especially true when a product with many substitutes is evaluated.

In the next sections of this paper, an attempt is made to evaluate the benefits and the costs arising from the proposed mechanization of strawberry harvesting in Oregon. Concerted effort is made to demonstrate the complexities and the magnitudes of the practical problems associated with the assessment of the social and economic impacts of technology.

ESTIMATED SOCIAL BENEFITS AND COSTS FOR MECHANIZATION OF STRAWBERRY HARVEST

Problem Setting

The strawberry is one of the most popular and widely used small fruits in the United States. Although nearly all states grow strawberries of some kind, for the last two decades over 85 percent of the commercially marketed, processed strawberries [have been] grown in California, Oregon, and Washington (figure 10.1). Climate and soil are the major contributing factors for the domination of the Pacific Coast states in strawberry production.

Besides being second in strawberry production, Oregon is a pioneer, having grown strawberries commercially since the early 1900s. In its peak, Oregon produced over 45 percent of the total U.S. processed strawberries (figure 10.1).[2] However, since 1971, Oregon's share of strawberry production has been declining steadily. In fact, since 1973 strawberry production in Oregon [has] constituted less than 20 percent of the nation's total processed strawberry production, which is the lowest since 1951. Increased harvesting costs, without an offsetting increase in the farm prices of strawberries, are the main causes for the continuing decline of strawberry production in Oregon.

Oregon's strawberry growers depend largely on children between the ages of ten and sixteen for harvesting their crop. However, in recent years, the enactment of child labor laws has caused a shortage

FIGURE 10.1
Relative Market Shares of Processed Strawberries,
by Major Producing States

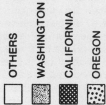

OTHERS
WASHINGTON
CALIFORNIA
OREGON

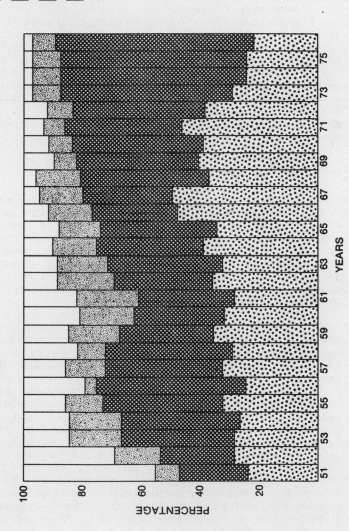

of strawberry pickers, resulting in a substantial
increase in harvest costs which account for 30 to 40
percent of the price growers receive in Oregon (Martin, 1976). Cost prospects for the future are even
gloomier because of the continuing pressure from the
various legislative bodies to extend the nation's
minimum wage to farm workers. In order to alleviate
the problems associated with increased harvest costs
and by so doing regain its competitive edge, since
1967 Oregon has been actively seeking to mechanize
its strawberry harvest.

Mechanization of strawberry harvest requires,
among other things, (a) change in the present strawberry varieties, and (b) development of a technically
sound and efficient harvester. In the last ten
years, considerable progress has occurred in developing a mechanical harvester and new strawberry varieties suitable for machine harvesting. If the past
achievement is indicative of the future, it will not
be too long before Oregon strawberry harvesting is
mechanized (Booster et al., 1970).

FRAMEWORK OF ANALYSIS

Successful implementation of mechanical strawberry harvesting should create significant production
economies.[3] However, it also may have a considerable
negative effect on the livelihood of numerous agricultural laborers. To compute the gross and net social returns arising from the use of a strawberry
harvester in Oregon, the framework used by Griliches
(1958), Peterson (1967), and Schmitz and Seckler
(1970) is employed.

To illustrate the main points of the analysis,
in figure 10.2 let S_1' and S_1, respectively, represent
the supply curve with and without mechanization. The
supply curve of the processed strawberry is assumed
to shift from S_1 to S_1', because successful implementation of mechanical strawberry harvest in Oregon is
expected to reduce the cost of harvesting (see note
3). As a result of mechanization of strawberry harvest in Oregon, the equilibrium output and price of
processed strawberries will change from Q_1 to Q_2 and
P_1 to P_2. The area $R + S + T$ represents the increment to the consumers' surplus as a result of mechanization of the strawberry harvest, and the increment
to the producers' surplus is measured by the area $-R
+ V + W$. Thus, the benefit to society in terms of
consumers' and producers' surplus is the area $(R + S
+ T) + (-R + V + W) = S + T + V + W$; that is,

FIGURE 10.2
Estimation of Gross Social Returns When the
Long-Run Supply Curve Is Positively Sloped

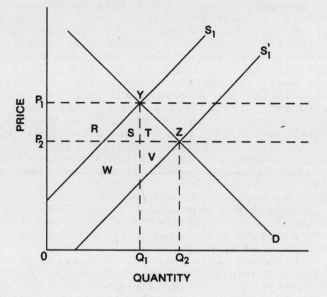

the area between the two supply curves and below the
demand curve, as shown in figure 10.2.

In addition, using the formula derived by Peterson (1967), the area S + T + V + W in figure 10.2 can
be approximated by

(1) Gross Social Return (GSR) =

$$KQ_2P_2 + \frac{1}{2} K^2 P_2 Q_2/\eta - \frac{1}{2} Q_1 K^2 P_2 \; \frac{P_2}{P_1} \; \frac{\epsilon\eta}{\eta-\epsilon} \; \frac{\eta-1}{\eta}^2$$

When ε = O, the above equation is reduced to:

(2) $GSR = KQ_2P_2 \left(1 + \frac{1}{2} K \frac{1}{\eta}\right)$

where the Greek letters ε and η represent supply and
demand elasticities, respectively. K represents the
relative shift in the supply function, i.e.,
$K = (Q_2 - Q_1)/Q_2$.

If there were no harmful effect to any member of
society, the movement from the old equilibrium Y to
the new equilibrium Z in figure 10.2 would be considered an improvement in social welfare (Pareto Opti-
mal). However, in cases where a technological change
is expected to negatively affect some segment of society, in this case the strawberry pickers, the movement from Y to Z cannot be judged unequivocally as an
improvement in social welfare. To measure the social
benefits in this case, the Kaldor-Hicks (K-H) criterion is used. The Kaldor-Hicks criterion states that
if the gainers (the consumers and producers of strawberries) can compensate the losers (strawberry pickers) out of their gain and still be better off in Z
than they were in Y, then the movement from equilibrium Y to Z can be viewed as an improvement in social
welfare. However, using the K-H criterion does not
imply that actual compensation need be given to the
losers. In other words, the movement from Y to Z
would be considered an improvement in social welfare
if a potential positive social return occurred after
accounting for all distributional effects.

To estimate the dollar value of the loss to the
displaced strawberry pickers, the following scheme is
used. In figure 10.3, prior to mechanization the demand for and supply of farm laborers were D_0 and S_0,
respectively, and the equilibrium wage rate was W_0.
With the introduction of the mechanical harvester,
the demand is assumed to shift to D_1. Hence, the new
equilibrium wage rate and employment level will be W_1
and N_1, respectively. For analytical convenience,
let us assume farm laborers to be producers of a service so that we can estimate the change in producers'
surplus resulting from the shift in demand. This results in original surplus of area W_0 L O reduced to
an area of W_1 M O by the shift in demand. The loss
to the displaced workers (or the surplus from labor
service) is then obtained by subtracting area W_1 M O
from area W_0 L O which is equal to the area W_0 L M
W_1. The area W_0 L M W_1 can be estimated as:

$$(3) \quad (W_0 - W_1)N_1 + (N_0 - N_1)W_0 - \int_{N_1}^{N_0} f(Z)d\,Z$$

FIGURE 10.3
Estimation of the Values of the Displaced Workers

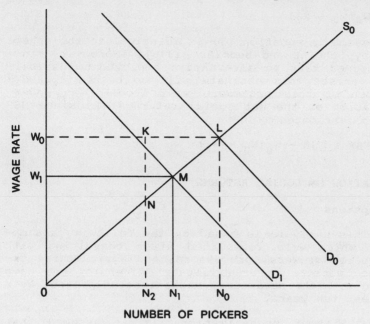

which can be reduced to:

$$N_0 W_0 - N_1 W_1 - \int_{N_1}^{N_0} f(z) \, dz$$

where:

$f(z) \Rightarrow$ factor supply function.

On the other hand, if wage is fixed at W_0 (say, minimum wage), the value of the loss in surplus as a result of the shift in demand is the area K L M N which is obtained by subtracting the area W_0 K N O from W_0 L O. The area K L M N can be estimated as:

$$(4) \quad K \, L \, M \, N = W_0(N_0 - N_2) - \int_{N_2}^{N_0} f(z) \, dz$$

130

and the estimate in equation (4) can be approximated by

(5) $W_0(N_0 - N_2)$

The result in equation (5) is identical to the scheme used by Schmitz and Seckler (1970). Moreover, since it assumes that no alternative employment possibilities exist, this estimate will be biased upward.[4] The use of this procedure will lead to an underestimation of the net social return (NSR) since NSR will be estimated as

(6) $NSR \equiv GSR - W_0(N_0 - N_2)$

ESTIMATION OF SOCIAL RETURNS

Assumptions

This analysis is based on the following assumptions which were formulated after consulting with strawberry growers, processors, and agricultural extension workers at Oregon State University who have worked with the strawberry mechanization project over the last ten years.

1. Without mechanization, it is assumed that strawberry production in Oregon will stabilize at 5,200 acres (present level). If the harvest trend of recent years continues, this assumption will probably overestimate the level of future harvests and, as will be evident later, lead to an overestimation of the value of the labor loss (in terms of wages) resulting from mechanization.

2. Commercial use of mechanical strawberry harvesters is expected to start by 1981, and by 1985, 50 to 70 percent of Oregon strawberry acreage is expected to be harvested mechanically. In addition, for lack of reliable information, a constant rate of adoption of the harvesting machinery is assumed. Under this assumption, the annual diffusion rate will be 10 percent or 14 percent depending on whether 50 or 70 percent of the strawberry fields in Oregon are mechanically harvested by 1985.

3. Under the assumption of a 50 percent adoption rate, annual harvest of Oregon [strawberry acreage] is expected to reach 9,000

acres, which is approximately the level of acreage harvested before the enactment of the child labor law of 1973. With a 70 percent adoption rate, 10,400 acres (or twice the present level) would be harvested. Provided that mechanization reduces harvesting cost substantially (Hussen, 1978), 9,000 to 10,400 acres of strawberry harvest by 1985 is a conservative estimate.

4. The acreage is assumed to increase at a constant amount over the five-year period (1981-1985); hence, annual increases are 760 acres $\left(\dfrac{9000 - 5200}{5}\right)$ with the adoption rate of 50 percent and 1,040 acres $\left(\dfrac{10400 - 5200}{5}\right)$ with the adoption rate of 70 percent.

5. The strawberry varieties to be harvested by machine are expected to have a "marketable yield" of four tons per acre. Again, in light of the experimental results from the Oregon State University strawberry breeding program, this yield estimate is fairly conservative (Lawrence, 1975).

6. Aggregate U.S. processed strawberry production excluding Oregon remains at an annual level of 137 million pounds which is its recent four-year average. This assumption is made to isolate the increment to the consumers' and producers' surplus resulting from the increase in Oregon strawberry production.[5]

Using these assumptions and the theoretical framework developed earlier, the annual gross social returns resulting from mechanization are estimated. Tables 10.1 and 10.2 present the annual gross social return assuming that the diffusion rates by 1985 are 70 and 50 percent, respectively. Except for this difference, the same approaches are used to estimate gross social returns in both tables.

Columns 1 and 2 of table 10.1 present the expected total annual strawberry acreage in Oregon and the portion of the total acreage which is expected to be harvested mechanically. Column 3 shows the aggregate U. S. processed strawberry production excluding Oregon. The entries in column 4 are the total processed strawberry production in Oregon. The first

TABLE 10.1
Estimated Values of Annual Gross Social Returns Net of Extra Processing Costs Arising from the Proposed Mechanization of Strawberry Harvesting in Oregon, Assuming 70 Percent Mechanization by 1985

	Expected Annual Strawberry Harvest in Oregon (Acres)	Expected Annual Machine Harvest (Acres)	Aggregate Processed Straw.Prod. Excluding Oregon (mill.lbs.)	Aggregate Processed Straw.Prod. in Oregon (mill.lbs.)	Estimated Value of K	Predicted Farm Price (¢/lb)	Estimates of Price Flexibility $(1/\eta)$	Gross Social Return (GSR) (mill.$)	Extra Processing Costs (EPC) $480/acre (mill.$)	Estimate of GSRNEPC (mill.$)
	(1)	(2)	(3)	(4)	(5)	(6)	(7)	(8)	(9)	(10)
1976-80	5,200	—	137.0	41.0	—	23.0	—	—	—	—
1981	6,240	874.0	137.0	50.0	0.0481	22.3	0.279	2.019	0.420	1.599
1982	7,280	2,038.0	137.0	58.0	0.0871	21.6	0.3006	3.717	0.978	2.739
1983	8,320	3,494.0	137.0	67.0	0.1274	20.75	0.3274	5.505	1.677	3.828
1984	9,360	5,242.0	137.0	75.0	0.1604	20.1	0.351	7.027	2.516	4.511
1985	10,400	7,280.0	137.0	83.0	0.1909	19.8	0.37	8.609	3.494	5.115

The Gross Social Returns in the above table are estimated assuming that 70 percent of Oregon's strawberries will be harvested mechanically by 1985 and that mechanization is expected to diffuse at a constant annual rate of 14 percent between 1981 and 1985.

TABLE 10.2

Estimated Values of Annual Gross Social Returns Net of Extra Processing Costs Arising from the Proposed Mechanization of Strawberry Harvesting in Oregon, Assuming 50 Percent Mechanization by 1985

	Expected Annual Strawberry Harvest in Oregon (Acres)	Expected Annual Machine Harvest (Acres)	Aggregate Processed Straw.Prod. Excluding Oregon (mill.lbs.)	Aggregate Processed Straw.Prod. in Oregon (mill.lbs.)	Estimated Value of K	Predicted Farm Price (¢/lb)	Estimates of Price Flexibility $(1/\eta)$	Gross Social Return (GSR) (mill.$)	Extra Processing Costs (EPC) $480/acre (mill.$)	Estimate of GSRNEPC (mill.$)
	(1)	(2)	(3)	(4)	(5)	(6)	(7)	(8)	(9)	(10)
1976-80	5,200	—	—	41.0	—	23.0	—	—	—	—
1981	5,960	596	137	47.7	0.0363	22.4	.274	1.502	0.286	1.216
1982	6,720	1,344	137	53.8	0.0669	21.8	.291	2.810	0.645	2.165
1983	7,480	2,244	137	59.8	0.0957	21.4	.306	4.089	1.077	3.012
1984	8,240	3,296	137	65.9	0.1228	20.8	.325	5.389	1.582	3.807
1985	9,000	4,500	137	72.0	0.1483	20.3	.342	6.451	2.160	4.291

The Gross Social Returns in the above table are estimated assuming that 50 percent of Oregon's strawberries will be harvested mechanically by 1985 and that mechanization is expected to diffuse at a constant annual rate of 10 percent between 1981 and 1985.

entry in this column (41 mill. pounds) is the present
level of Oregon processed strawberry production.
Other entries in this column are found by multiplying
the corresponding entries in column 1 by the assumed
yield of four tons per acre. Column 5 presents the
estimated value of parameter K which is the relative
shift in the supply function resulting solely from
the increased strawberry harvest in Oregon. For example, parameter K for 1981 is estimated as the ratio
of the difference in Oregon strawberry production before and after mechanization (9 million pounds or 50
- 41) and the expected total U. S. strawberry production including Oregon (187 million pounds or 137 +
50). Entries in columns 6 and 7 are the predicted
aggregate farm prices for processed strawberries and
the estimate of the price flexibility, respectively.
The predicted prices and the estimate of the price
flexibilities are derived from the demand equation in
endnote 6. Finally, the annual gross social returns
from the mechanization of Oregon's strawberry harvest
are estimated using equation (2), where the elasticity of supply is assumed to be zero,[7]

$$GSR_j = K_j Q_j P_j \left(1.0 + \frac{1}{2} K_j \frac{1}{n_j}\right)$$

where K_j = the value of the parameter K for year j;
Q_j = the estimate of the aggregate United States processed strawberry production in year j (the sum of
the entries in columns 3 and 4); P_j = the predicted
price of processed strawberries in year j; and n_j =
the point elasticity of demand associated with Q_j and
P_j. The results of these estimates are shown in column 8 of tables 10.1 and 10.2.

Gross Social Returns Net of
Extra Processing Costs (GSRNEPC)

Since the berries will be uncapped when they are
harvested by machine, additional work is required to
cap the berries in the processing sectors. Therefore, the value of extra processing cost must be subtracted from the estimate of GSR. Based upon experimental work in Michigan (Holtman et al., 1977), the
value of the extra processing cost was estimated to
be between 5 and 6 cents per pound or $400 and $460
per acre assuming a yield of 4 tons per acre. Hence,
the upper bound of the value of the extra processing
cost for any given year will be $460 times the

expected total acres harvested by machine (column 2). These estimates of extra processing costs are shown in column 9 of tables 10.1 and 10.2.

The entries in the last column of tables 10.1 and 10.2 are the value of the gross social returns net of extra processing costs (GSRNEPC).

Discounted Value of the Total GSRNEPC

Let C_1, C_2, ..., C_5 represent the values of the flow of GSRNEPC for the years 1981 to 1985, respectively. Then, the cumulated GSRNEPC for the years 1981 to 1985 discounted to the year 1980 is estimated by:

$$(7) \quad \sum_{t=1}^{6} \frac{C_t}{(1+r)^t} = C$$

Furthermore, if we assume the strawberry acreage in Oregon to stabilize at the level existing by 1985, then the cumulated GSRNEPC for the year 1986 and thereafter discounted to the year 1980 is estimated to be:

$$(8) \quad \sum_{t=1}^{\infty} \frac{C_6(1+r)^{-6}}{(1+r)^t} = \frac{C_6(1+r)^{-6}}{r} = C^*$$

Therefore, the discounted value of the total cumulated GSRNEPC over an infinite planning horizon is estimated to be:

$$(9) \quad C + C^* = C^{**}$$

Using the above formulations and the information in column 10 of tables 10.1 and 10.2, the discounted value of the total cumulated GSRNEPC is estimated to be:

136

	Case 1: 70% Adoption Rate by 1985	Case 2: 50% Adoption Rate by 1985
1. Discounted value of the cumulated GSRNEPC 1981-85, C	$12,154,000	$ 9,861,000
2. Discounted value of the cumulated GSRNEPC 1986 and thereafter, C*	$33,877,778	$28,422,222
3. Total discounted value of GSRNEPC, C**	$46,031,778	$38,283,222

Net Social Returns (NSR)

Net social return is defined as the difference between gross social returns net of extra processing costs and the cost of displaced workers. Hence, an estimate of the cost of the displaced strawberry pickers is needed to derive net social returns. Based on a field study by Oregon State University Extension Service, the cost of handpicking strawberries with a yield of 4 tons per acre was estimated to be $902 per acre. In this analysis, allowing for general price increases, the cost of hand harvesting is expected to be $1,000 per acre. Using this estimate, the values of the estimated cost to the displaced pickers are computed (tables 10.3 and 10.4). Tables 10.3 and 10.4 show the cost of the displaced pickers corresponding to the gross social benefits estimated in tables 10.1 and 10.2, respectively. The entries recorded in column 1 of tables 10.3 and 10.4 are obtained in the following manner: First, the total strawberry acreage that would be available for hand harvesting is obtained by subtracting the entries of column 2 from the corresponding entries of column 1 in tables 10.1 and 10.2. Then, 5,200 acres is subtracted from the above result since strawberry pickers would have harvested a total of 5,200 acres, assuming no mechanization. Finally, the net difference between acreage available for hand harvest with mechanization, and harvested acreage without mechanization (5,200 acres) is the loss or gain of acreage for hand harvesting as a result of mechanization (column 1 of tables 10.3 and 10.4). To estimate the cost of the displaced pickers, entries in column 1 of tables 10.3 and 10.4 are multiplied by $1,000, which is the per-acre benefit forgone to the strawberry

TABLE 10.3
Values of the Annual Estimated Loss to the Displaced Strawberry Pickers (70 Percent Adoption Rate)

	Loss or Gain of Harvestable Acreage to the Pickers	Value of the Loss or the Gain $1000/acre (mill.$)
1976-80	---	---
1981	+166.0	+0.166
1982	+42.0	+0.042
1983	-374.0	-0.374
1984	-1,082.0	-1.082
1985	-2,080.0	-2.080

TABLE 10.4
Values of the Annual Estimated Loss to the Displaced Strawberry Pickers (50 Percent Adoption Rate)

	Loss or Gain of Harvestable Acreage to the Pickers	Value of the Loss or the Gain $1000/acre (mill.$)
1976-80	---	---
1981	+164.0	+0.164
1982	+176.0	+0.176
1983	+36.0	+0.036
1984	-256.0	-0.256
1985	-700.0	-0.700

pickers. These results are indicated in column 2 of tables 10.3 and 10.4. From these results, using similar procedures as outlined in equations (7), (8), and (9), the total cost of the displaced strawberry pickers is estimated to be:

138

	Case 1: 70% Adoption Rate by 1985	Case 2: 50% Adoption Rate by 1985
1. Discounted value of the cumulated cost of displaced pickers 1981-85	$ 2,036,200	$ 284,400
2. Discounted value of the cumulated cost of displaced pickers 1985 and thereafter	$13,780,000	$4,637,778
3. Total discounted value of the displaced pickers	$15,816,200	$4,922,178

Thus, the net social returns for cases 1 and 2 are $30,215,578 or ($46,031,778 - 15,816,200) and $33,610,044 or ($38,283,222 - 4,922,178), respectively. It is important to note that accounting for the effects of displaced workers makes net social returns higher for the lower adoption rate. This result differs from the ranking based on GSRNEPC.

Social Returns Net of Research and Development Costs

Thus far, the various social returns are estimated and for making decisions with regard to the desirability of strawberry mechanization in Oregon, the estimated social returns have to be compared with the estimate of the total research and development costs associated with the overall strawberry mechanization project in Oregon. The total research and development expenditures estimate compounded to the year 1980 is expected to be $1,448,361 before mechanized strawberry harvesting is fully adopted for commercial use (Hussen, 1978:97).[8] Therefore, when this estimate of total research and development costs is compared with the above estimates of the gross and net social returns, it suggests that an endeavor to mechanize strawberry harvesting is, indeed, a profitable venture with respect to the society as a whole. For the 70 percent adoption rate, the estimate of net social returns exceeds the research and development costs by $28,767,217 valued as of 1980. Similarly, for the 50 percent adoption rate, the estimate of net social returns exceeds the research and development costs by $32,161,683.

However, while measures of gross or net social rates of return after accounting for the research and development costs can provide decision makers with criteria to assess projects, other factors that influence the desirability of mechanization should be considered.

Factors Affecting Social Rates of Return

1. Using the K-H criterion to estimate the loss of the displaced workers does not imply that actual compensation need be given to the losers. If, in fact, the strawberry pickers were compensated, then, depending on the source of the revenue for compensation, there could be an added social cost which is not accounted [for] in the model above. Moreover, if compensation is effected, what is the criterion used for compensating the losers?

2. This analysis assumes that (a) strawberry varieties suitable for machine harvesting, as well as an efficient mechanical harvester, will become available; (b) the necessary adjustments, both in the farming and processing sectors, will be undertaken to accommodate the technological change in strawberry harvesting; and (c) the demand for strawberries will not change due to the introduction of new varieties or the technological change in strawberry harvesting. How realistic are these assumptions? For example, are the new varieties likely to be readily accepted by the consumers? If not, how would that affect demand?

3. Mechanization may favor large-scale farmers (Hussen, 1978). If so, what is the distributional effect on small-scale farmers? In general, how significant is the adjustment cost? For lack of reliable information, this cost is not explicitly considered in the model.

4. This study uses the farm demand for processed strawberries to estimate the consumers' surplus resulting from mechanizing the strawberry harvest. This farm demand is a derived demand. Is the consumers' surplus estimated using this demand equivalent to an estimate based on final demand? The answer depends on the difference between the price elasticities of the derived demand and the final demand (Hertford and Schmitz, 1977). The final demand is not estimated because there is no one final demand

140

for processed strawberries; processed strawberries as a final product appear in different forms. Also, there is a difference in net social benefits calculated from a partial equilibrium analysis as opposed to those calculated from a general equilibrium analysis. For example, if there are close substitutes for strawberries, then social benefits are overestimated.

5. Oregon is expected to harvest no more than 10,400 acres, which is slightly above the acreage harvested before the enactment of child labor laws in 1973. However, if mechanization occurs, the acreage allotted for strawberries could exceed the estimate used here. If so, the gross social return is underestimated.

6. In Oregon most strawberries are harvested in June, when the processing and canning industry has substantial unutilized capacity. Increased production of strawberries resulting from mechanization would enable the processing and canning industry to operate at fuller capacity in the early part of the season. Since most processing and canning firms are located in rural areas, this increased use of capacity would also contribute to an increase in employment in the rural community.

7. Finally, mechanization of the strawberry harvest likely would end the use of child labor which is thought to be socially undesirable. This would have a positive social benefit that is not accounted for here.

SUMMARY AND CONCLUSION

Before the mid-sixties, economists gave little consideration to the distributional effects of technological changes. Hence, agricultural research tended to recommend or encourage technological changes which were favorable to large-scale farmers at the expense of small-scale farmers and farm laborers (Hightower, 1972). In recent years, in response to the growing number of agricultural critics, economists attempted to specifically account for some of the distributional effects of agricultural technology (Schmitz and Seckler, 1970; Martin and Johnson, 1978). Although recent attempts to account for the distributional impacts of technological change have significantly strengthened the credibility of economic models, these models still do not take into account all the distributional effects (social, economic, or technical) arising from agricultural technology.

However, the fact that the models are not complete enough to account for all distributional effects should not discourage a continuing effort to assess the economic and social impacts of agricultural technology when the need arises. It is important, however, to be aware of the inherent weaknesses of the models employed. With this in mind, this paper has been an attempt to evaluate the economic and social desirability of mechanical strawberry harvest in Oregon. Using a partial equilibrium analysis approach, the gross and the annual net social returns were estimated. In addition, other factors which were not explicitly accounted for in the model were also discussed because of their potential repercussions on the estimated social returns.

NOTES

1. For comprehensive treatment of the concept of economic surplus and its use in economic analysis, see Currie et al. (1971).
2. Almost all of Oregon strawberry production is marketed in the processing sector.
3. In most instances the use of a mechanical strawberry harvester in Oregon is found to yield a significant positive return to the growers (Hussen, 1978).
4. This estimation formula will overestimate the displacement cost of the strawberry pickers. Not all the strawberry pickers who are displaced will be unemployed. Some of the strawberry pickers will find new jobs and will earn income to compensate for their loss, and the above formula does not account for the economic effects of workers moving to their next best job.
5. Note that mechanization is expected to affect only Oregon's strawberry production, mainly for the following reasons: (a) success in mechanization depends on the development of strawberry varieties suitable for mechanical harvesting, in which Oregon has a substantial lead over other strawberry-growing states; (b) California, which is the leading strawberry-growing state, is not expected to mechanize without substantial time lag because the high yield that California growers enjoy presently can be sustained only if multiple harvesting is possible (the mechanical strawberry harvesters developed so far operate as once-over harvesters); and (c) the strawberry varieties developed in Oregon may not be easily adapted to other areas without losing some of their desirable characteristics.

$$6. \; PP^S = 7.675 - .0333X_1 + 0.844X_2$$

$$(3.37)* \; (0.00735) \; (0.18624)**$$

$$+ \; 1.984X_3 - 4.419X_4$$

$$(.91744)* \; (0.7855)**$$

$$tR^2 = .82 \qquad DW = 2.1125 \qquad N = 26$$

where PP^S = average farm price for processed strawberries (¢/lb.); X_1 = total processed strawberries
marketed (mill. pounds); X_2 = average farm price of
fresh strawberries (¢/lb.); X_3 = average farm price
of peaches (¢/bushel); X_4 = average hourly earnings
for labor employed in food and kindred products
($/hour); and n and DW are demand elasticity (evalu-
ated at the mean value) and the Durbin-Watson statistics, respectively. In terms of expected signs of
all coefficients and general "reasonableness" of results, the above specification of the demand relationship was thought preferable to the other various
alternatives considered (see Hussen, 1978).

7. Equation (2) assumes that the supply elasticity for processed strawberries is zero, which is restrictive unless it is reasonably justified. In the
beginning, I attempted to fit a supply equation for
processed strawberries so as to derive the supply
elasticity. However, I was unable to estimate a statistically meaningful supply equation for processed
berries. Hence, due to lack of information about the
precise magnitude of the supply elasticity for processed strawberries, I estimated GSR by assuming that
the supply elasticity of processed strawberries is
perfectly elastic. To estimate GSR when the supply
elasticity is infinity, equation (1) was used. For
this problem the ratio of the value of GSR when the
supply was perfectly elastic ranged from 1.012 to
1.019. Therefore, the difference between these two
extreme assumptions implies less than a 2 percent
difference in the final estimate of the GSR. Since
this difference is so small, estimation of the supply
elasticity for processed berries would not contribute
much to the accuracy in estimating GSR.

8. The cost estimates include, among others, the
outlays incurred in developing and sustaining the research program by the farmers, the agricultural extension programs, and other organizations that are
directly or indirectly involved in the program. For
details on the expenditure for research and development of the harvester and new strawberry varieties,
see Hussen (1978).

11
From Lug Boxes to Electronics: A Study of California Tomato Growers and Sorting Crews, 1977

O. E. Thompson
Ann F. Scheuring

The years 1975 to 1977 saw a rapid growth in the use of electronic sorting devices and, consequently, the decline of the seasonal labor force of tomato sorters in California. Through extensive interviews conducted with growers and farm workers in Yolo and San Joaquin counties, Thompson and Scheuring estimate the rate of adoption of the electronic sorter and resultant labor displacement; they discuss work alternatives for sorters, assess growers' attitudes, and develop comprehensive work histories for selected workers. Thompson and Scheuring conclude by asserting society's need for both economic pragmatists and social critics.

A PERSPECTIVE ON TECHNOLOGICAL CHANGE IN AGRICULTURE

. . .

Undeniably, farm productivity has increased vastly in the past three decades. The causes have been a variety of technological developments in plant and animal breeding and in cultural practices, as well as the mechanization of cultivation and harvesting. Yet, from a human standpoint, a price has been

Edited and excerpted from Monograph No. 3 of the California Agricultural Policy Seminar. Department of Applied Behavioral Sciences, University of California, Davis, December 1978.

paid for that efficiency and productivity; it has been hard to determine just how high the price has been.

The alterations in agriculture parallel changes that have already occurred in other industrial sectors. For some reason, however, the issues are especially poignant when viewed in the context of farming. Technological change in agriculture has brought about a greatly enhanced standard of living for the average consumer, yet that achievement has been accompanied by the displacement of farmers and workers, the concentration of property and resources, some undesirable environmental consequences, and a shift in the economic structure from the small entrepreneur to large businesses and corporations. Agriculture is not different from other industries in those respects, but many people somehow feel it should be.

Why, for example, has agricultural mechanization in the tomato fields lately become such a controversial topic? The number of workers affected is relatively small when compared with worker displacement in other industries.[1] The jobs involved are only seasonal. Nor are farmers generally faulted for wanting to reduce drudgery and severe working conditions. It is unlikely that anyone seriously wants to revert to stoop labor in the fields. Yet the issue has caught the public imagination, and advocates on both sides debate the value and the cost of agricultural mechanization.

Doubtless there are many contributing factors, but three stand out when serious discussions are held:

1. **The immediate political issue.** In doing legislative battle for their constituents, farm worker advocacy groups find it necessary to appeal to the public. Political decisions on the framing of legislation or the disbursal of funds for special-interest groups are always made in the context of the climate of public opinion. The allocation of resources for various types of public-assistance programs is made both rationally and emotionally, on the basis of what decision makers consider appropriate for the times.

A leader of the United Farm Workers, quoted in the Los Angeles Times, pleads powerfully for his constituency by making machines villains:

...in the workers' view it is a cruel irony that the rapid spread of machines--bringing hardship and suffering to countless thousands of displaced men and women--is spearheaded by one of

the great institutions of public education....
Before mechanization some 100,000 workers found
jobs in the cotton fields. More were employed
in cotton than in any other single crop. By the
late 1950s, thousands of families who relied on
cotton harvesting for their livelihood were left
without jobs or a future...never able to find
new jobs. Their children, an entire generation,
were raised in these hamlets of unemployment
unable to find work and subsisting on welfare.
(Los Angeles Times, 1978)

The focus on mechanization by farm-worker organizations and by other groups is partly a political
manipulation of symbols intended to benefit what is
undeniably a needy constituency. Farm-worker advocacy groups have only relatively recently exerted any
political power; by raising the mechanization issue
as a symbol they are doing what other special-interest groups have been doing for years.

  2.   The longer-term policy issue. Apart from
the immediate concerns of advocacy groups, the mechanization debate is concerned with significant considerations of public policy. What role should public institutions play in implementing technological
change? Should publicly funded research and development efforts be required to assess their potential
social and economic impacts? If certain kinds of
research efforts appear to be inequitable in their
benefits, should they be discontinued or modified?
To what extent should society allocate funds to aid
workers disadvantaged by technological development?
What is the proper role of government in assisting
citizens caught in broad social changes? The political issue almost immediately becomes a policy issue
for decision makers who have to set priorities and
shift resources to solve society's many problems.

  3.   The essential-values issue. More deeply, a
basic conflict in values seems to pervade our entire
society. There are those who embrace the industrial
model and believe that efficiency and enhanced production, as the ultimate goal of technology, are a
means to better human life for all. They see technology as a way of reducing human suffering and
increasing human potential. Others, however, believe
that technology, uncontrolled, inevitably leads to
increasing disparities between social strata, and
they believe that the dispersion of work, ownership,
and power are of primary importance to a healthy
society.[2] More than that, the ramifications of technology seem to many critics to result in a less human
life, i.e., a physical and social environment in

which human beings are increasingly cut off from the natural world of which they are biologically a part. In particular, modern technology, based so heavily on the consumption of fossil fuels, seems to lead to a world "out of joint" ecologically as well.

Those views are not necessarily polarized, although some would have them so. They have co-existed, often uneasily, but with a certain kind of dynamic tension, in American life since the early days of the Republic.[3] The agricultural mechanization issue, which is the concern of this case study of tomato harvest workers, is one that calls up significant questions centered on this values conflict. It can only be healthy to recognize that questions of value need periodic reexamination in the light of changing circumstance.

THE CALIFORNIA CANNING-TOMATO INDUSTRY AND CONCERN FOR THE CONSEQUENCES OF MECHANIZATION

. . .

Initiation of a Case Study

Apart from the academic publications that appeared on the subject [of mechanization], public concern was exhibited in a variety of ways. In 1976 and 1977, numerous articles on mechanization appeared in the press. Student advocacy groups wrote papers, put together displays and slide shows on the negative effects of mechanization research, and encouraged opposition to "agribusiness." The United Farm Workers and other advocacy groups kept the issue alive by picketing various University of California meetings and by criticizing agricultural research before state legislative budget hearings in 1977. The Regents of the University also held hearings on mechanization research in February 1978.

In the State Capitol, requests for information resulted in a report by the Assembly Office of Research suggesting that as many as 8,000 harvest jobs had already been eliminated in 1977 by the electronic sorter in California tomato fields. Another report was circulated in the Department of Benefit Payments on the potential impact of the electronic sorter on welfare caseloads. Yet public agency personnel, extension agents, and others involved in the collection and use of information about workers agreed that there was a lack of current information on which to base discussions of the issue of farm labor displacement.

This increasing concern over the social consequences of technological change prompted the administrators of the Agricultural Experiment Station to
encourage research on the impact of mechanization on
people in agriculture. Publicity on the growing
adoption of the electronic sorter in the tomato harvest served to direct the attention of the researchers toward that subject as a case study. Although
the harvest of canning tomatoes was mechanized in the
1960s, it had always been necessary to have a crew of
sixteen to twenty on the machines to sort the green
fruit from red. With commercial release of the automatic electronic color-sorting device in 1975, the
crew could now be cut by more than half. The device
is built into the new generation of tomato harvesters
or can be mounted as a unit on older machines. It
represents another clear stage in the mechanization
process, which may ultimately culminate in the development of a one-man machine somewhat similar to a
grain combine, according to some engineers and
producers.[4]
In the fall of 1977, survey research was undertaken, under the auspices of the Agricultural Experiment Station, to assess the rate of adoption of the
electronic sorting device on the mechanical tomato
harvester and its impact on seasonal farm workers.

Project Methods

Fifty-seven processing-tomato growers were interviewed in Yolo and San Joaquin counties, which
rank first and third, respectively, in the production
of processing tomatoes in California. A random sample was taken from Cooperative Extension lists of
tomato growers in those two counties. Some growers,
when contacted, opted not to participate, but cooperation was generally good. Extension agents and representatives of the California Tomato Growers' Association reviewed the data and found it reliable.
The objectives of the grower interviews were:

1. to collect some factual data on the numbers
   of workers employed as tomato sorters; the
   rate of adoption of the electronic sorter;
   the trends in employment of farm workers
   during the last three years; the employment
   outlook for sorters in the immediate future;

2. to collect some information on the overall
   farming operations of tomato growers and
   their use of farm labor in tasks other than
   tomato sorting; to determine their general
   experience with the electronic sorter; and

3. to assess to a limited degree growers' attitudes on the social issue of labor displacement.

At the same time, 200 interviews were conducted
with persons employed as tomato sorters in the harvest of 1977. Ninety percent of the interviews took
place in Yolo County and 10 percent in San Joaquin
County. Over 40 percent of the interviews were conducted with workers in tomato fields, with the cooperation of their employers. Another 30 percent were
conducted with workers living in farm labor camps,
and the remaining 30 percent were with individuals
who had been suggested by various growers, and with
persons living in public housing and farm-labor
neighborhoods in Yolo County. It is recognized that
this is not a true random sample but, as many others
have discovered in farm labor surveys, it can be extremely difficult to sample farm laborers in a scientific, consistent way. From Department of Employment
Development estimates on the basis of "man-weeks,"
there were about 3,320 seasonal workers employed in
tomatoes at the peak of harvesting in Yolo County in
September 1977. This group of 200 interviews thus
represents roughly 6 percent of the total. . . .
The objectives of the farm-worker surveys were:

1. to assess the composition of the work force
on the [mechanical] harvesters by identifying
the people who work as sorters;

2. to develop comprehensive work histories for
two years for individuals working as sorters
in order to assess the economic importance of
this work to them;

3. to assess the levels of general education and
job skills characteristic of sorters so that
some estimate might be made of the increase
in service demands likely to occur with decreasing employment in the tomato harvest.

One interviewer collected all the information
about growers; a team of bilingual interviewers collected the farm-worker data. The information was
coded for computer analysis, which consisted primarily of frequency distributions and cross-tabulations
of demographic data.

GROWER INTERVIEWS IN YOLO
AND SAN JOAQUIN COUNTIES

Nearly 90 percent of the growers sampled identified themselves as owner-operators. Of those, half
were in family corporations, 28 percent were sole
proprietors, and 15 percent were in partnerships.
About 60 percent of the growers lived on their
farms. Only 15 percent grew all their tomatoes on
their own land. Over half the growers grew most or
all of their tomatoes on leased land.

Nearly all growers were born in the United
States. Their average age was 45, although the range
was from 22 to 65. About 45 percent had ended their
formal education with high school; about one-fourth
had "some college," and an equal number had a four-
year college degree. Of the college graduates, one-
third had done some graduate work. The college-edu-
cated growers had studied agriculture (65 percent),
business (18 percent), engineering (15 percent), and
other fields as diverse as law, art, and comparative
literature (2 percent).

The tomato growers had from two to forty years
of experience in farming, averaging twenty-one
years. The average grower had raised tomatoes for
more than twenty years, and only 10 percent had grown
tomatoes fewer than five years. Over 90 percent
expected to be growing tomatoes three years from now,
or hoped to be, since tomatoes are a high-cash crop.
Commitment to tomatoes as an annual crop appears to
be stable, no doubt because of the heavy investment
in specialized machinery.

The tomato acreage ranged from 22 to 13,000
acres, while half of the growers had 400 acres or
less.5 Average acreage was higher in 1977 after a
decline in 1976, although still somewhat lower than
1975, reflecting variable market and weather conditions.

The tomato acreage of the thirty Yolo County
growers was 26,655 (including 13,000 for one grower
alone), and of the twenty-seven San Joaquin County
growers was 9,004.

Average yield per acre in 1977 was over twenty-
six tons, ranging from sixteen to forty tons. One in
eight averaged over thirty tons. Weather conditions
reduced the 1976 average per acre to about nineteen
tons, while the 1975 yield was about the same as in
1977. Yields appeared not to differ particularly between large and small growers.

. . .

Experience with the Electronic Harvester

The reason given most frequently for investing in the electronic device was that growers expected to save money on labor costs. The second most frequent reason was that they hoped to avoid some of the headaches and anxieties associated with labor management. Only a few growers mentioned potential labor contracts as a motivating force for adoption of the new device, although that consideration clearly entered into some of their perceptions of possible difficulty in dealing with workers. Several also mentioned that it was natural to invest in the most modern equipment when replacing old machines.

Although commercial growers are often viewed as hard-headed businessmen, nearly a fifth of these growers had done no cost analysis before buying the electronic sorter. One grower with a history of labor difficulties responded, "Oh, I thought it might save money, but it was really an emotional decision." Most growers, however, had done some kind of cost analysis; about one-third had a fairly specific set of figures. Two-thirds of the respondents thought that the decrease in the need for sorters would pay off the additional cost of the electronic machine within four years. Maintenance costs on the electronic sorter were reported to be between $3,000 and $4,000 a year, about the wages of three seasonal workers.

Most growers using electronic sorters had had good experience with them. Ninety percent said harvesting was faster, although several pointed out that it was probably the new generation of machine rather than the electronic device that made the difference. Half the growers thought there was less waste of tomatoes with the electronic unit, whereas 30 percent thought that waste was about the same as with human sorters. Nearly half thought that working conditions on harvesters were better with electronic sorters than with manual sorting; others thought there was not much difference.

For most respondents, the chief advantage of the electronic sorter was that it reduced labor management worries and made farming a little easier. Some growers commented, however, that the manual-sort harvester offered more flexibility in operation since the electronic devices required ideal field conditions for best performance. They added that manual sorting still resulted in better quality of marketed fruit (if the crews were dependable).

Outlook for More Electronic Sorters

One-fourth of the growers planned to add electronic sorters in 1978, either their first or additional. A large majority expected total adoption of the electronic sorter by tomato growers within the next five years. San Joaquin growers were less enthusiastic about the new machines than Yolo growers, because of the different growing conditions. The number of electronic sorters owned by the fifty-seven growers in the sample grew from eight in 1975 to sixty-one in 1977, with an anticipated ownership of eighty-seven by 1978 (table 11.1). Adoption was faster in Yolo County.

Only a small minority thought that complete adoption of the device would have an adverse effect on their own operations, perhaps by making it more difficult to compete on small acreages.

Opinions on Work Alternatives for Displaced Workers

The manual-sort harvester was reported to average fifteen or sixteen workers and the electronic harvester six to eight. That is a displacement rate of between 50 and 65 percent.

The majority of growers felt no particular responsibility for workers displaced by the new technology, often commenting that the problem was not new in agriculture and was shared with industry in general. They felt that this responsibility belonged to the wider society or to the individuals themselves. Common comments by growers were that workers should actively seek other jobs or get into training programs, and that work was available for most individuals if they would look for it. In responding to this question, most of the farmers reflected a belief in individualism and self-reliance, traditionally rural values.

TABLE 11.1
Adoption of Electronic Sorters Starting in 1975
(57 Growers)

| County | Number of Harvesters | | | |
	1975	1976	1977	1978[a]
Yolo	5	33	44	58
San Joaquin	3	12	17	29

[a]Planned at time of study

When questioned about job possibilities for displaced tomato sorters, they responded by mentioning
other crops and other farm jobs, and work in the
urban sector. Nearly a fifth, however, thought that
tomato sorters were not really interested in other
kinds of work, because many of them were housewives
who did not want steady jobs.

Few growers thought that language was a big barrier for farm workers. Several spoke negatively of
bilingual educational programs, particularly those
[growers] whose parents had come from other countries
and had had to learn English (Japanese, Italian, and
Basque growers among them). Many interviewees mentioned that farm workers lacked basic education and
job skills. A quarter of the growers commented
negatively on unemployment-insurance programs as reducing worker willingness to seek work actively.
Other growers mentioned a variety of farm-worker
problems in finding work, ranging from alcohol to
family structure. Many growers spoke favorably of
their employees and felt that they would have no
trouble in getting other employment if they wished
it. Some growers had had long associations with some
worker families, and spoke positively of their
efforts to upgrade themselves educationally and
financially.

INTERVIEWS WITH TOMATO SORTERS
IN YOLO AND SAN JOAQUIN COUNTIES

. . .

California farm workers--sorters, in this case--
are distinguishable from other laborers by reason of
their ethnicity and generally low education and
standard of living. The historical material cited
suggests that the last fifteen years or so have seen
a decided shift toward identification of farm workers
as of Mexican origin. Reports from the early '60s
indicated a wider spread of ethnic groups among
California field workers than seems to exist now.

Most workers function in family groups and are
engaged in agricultural occupations as a family.
Because of this tradition, the age range of workers
is wide. Although younger workers may find it relatively easy to train for other kinds of occupations,
older ones may find it difficult to adjust to decreasing employment in agriculture.

There is diversity among farm workers; there is
no composite picture of the typical tomato sorter.

In these two counties at least, however, many tomato sorters are local women who produce part of the family income, though not all. Because their family incomes tend to be low, their contribution is important.

Tomato sorting is a means of earning a limited amount of income, usually about a thousand dollars. Some workers are very dependent on that money; for most, however, it is only one in a series of multiple jobs, or a percentage of the family income, earned in a variety of ways.

An important distinction exists between local and migrant workers. Migrancy is associated with lower education, lower family income, and higher dependence on public assistance. Local residents have a somewhat higher education and family income as well as, presumably, more opportunity to seek stable work and training. Migrants appear to be losing ground in this particular labor market. Some growers have remarked that their field workers have become less migrant over the past few years, and the growers prefer that. Some also predict a decline in the number of migrants coming into the area in the future.

Most seasonal workers get some form of supplementary income during the year to add to their low family earnings. Most of this additional income is in the form of unemployment compensation, which they have earned. About one in four workers accepts public assistance in the form of food stamps, welfare, or medical benefits. Since seasonal workers are needed in agriculture, transfer payments of these kinds are a way of subsidizing them for the periods when they must inevitably be out of work. Growers sometimes complain about such subsidies without realizing that these programs, allowing workers to subsist during slack periods, help keep the seasonal work force available when it is needed.

These seasonal workers have little experience outside agriculture; over half have done no other kind of work; their educational levels are much lower than in the general population. For these reasons, many of them are locked into low-paying farm work.

Only one worker in three expresses a preference for seasonal work. An overwhelming majority express dissatisfaction with agricultural work. Two-thirds of these interviewees said they would prefer nonfarm work even if they could make a higher income from farm work than they presently do. The reasons given varied, but the two mentioned most commonly were difficult working conditions and lack of job security. Nearly 90 percent expressed a preference for nonfarm work for family members, perhaps a reflection of higher aspirations for children than for oneself.

Growers' and workers' reports agree in many factual respects, although their perspectives diverge on some attitudinal questions. Growers, for example, sometimes suggested that workers were not motivated to seek permanent work, preferring in some cases to live hand-to-mouth, and [that they were] unwilling to commit themselves to steady jobs. Workers, on the other hand, often reported [wanting] steady work off the farm but [said they were] unable to find it, perhaps because of lack of skills and education.

IMPACT OF THE ELECTRONIC SORTER ON EMPLOYMENT IN THE TOMATO HARVEST

1. How likely are workers to be displaced by the electronic sorter in the tomato harvest?

The electronic sorter is being very rapidly adopted among tomato growers, and will probably be used by all growers within the next five years. The displacement rate for harvest workers is estimated conservatively at about 60 percent. This means that, by 1982, the number of seasonal jobs on farms in the tomato harvest may be less than half the number of jobs in 1975, the first year that the electronic sorter was used commercially.

2. How many people are likely to be affected by displacement?

Several different researchers, using different methods, have come up with estimates of the loss of tomato harvest jobs statewide, ranging from 6,600 to as high as 16,000 (Kumar et al., 1977; Linfield, 1977; Hernandez and Costa, 1977). Since those estimates are based on slightly different methods of calculation, the figures vary. What is important is not the actual number of jobs affected (which is probably impossible to arrive at with any real accuracy), [but] the indicated range. Our own figures suggest that, over a period of years, all other things being equal, between 12,000 and 14,000 fewer tomato-sorting jobs might be available for workers than in the years immediately preceding adoption of the electronic sorter.[6]

3. Who are the workers most likely to be affected? How much impact will the loss of sorting jobs have on them?

The data show several different groups of sorters. The majority of tomato harvest workers are now female local residents, often housewives who supplement family income rather than earn it all. However, a number of migrant families and green-card Mexican workers are also still involved. In local areas, who is affected will depend on the source of the labor supply. A loss of sorting jobs will affect individuals differently, depending on their alternatives for employment. Since the income typically derived from sorting tomatoes is about $1,000, a loss of that income will affect individuals according to their own situations. The lower their family incomes, the more important the loss. Some workers will have to depend more on public assistance; others will find work to replace tomato sorting. Some workers might have dropped out anyway, since the rate of attrition appears to be fairly high.

4. What are the alternatives for workers who can no longer find work sorting tomatoes?

Briefly, we can suggest the following alternatives:

(a) Workers no longer finding field sorting jobs can look for similar jobs on farms, in canneries, in packing sheds, or elsewhere, using personal information networks and private or public employment agencies. That has been the customary response of labor to unemployment in any sector. Present unemployment rates are high, and some of these unskilled workers will doubtless be unable to find other work easily.

(b) Workers can attempt to make themselves more "marketable" by developing their skills through education and training. It appears that most agricultural workers would prefer other kinds of work yet are locked into farm work by their own lack of skills.

(c) Workers can apply for various forms of public assistance for the needy.

(d) Specific public provision may be made for a more orderly transition of farm workers out of agricultural work, through short-term emergency aid, if necessary; referrals for other types of employment through public agencies, with special attention to the problems of farm laborers; training programs

for other types of employment; and job creation in the public and private sectors,
specifically for the unskilled and semi-
skilled.

Theoretically, all of those options are already
available, although some observers say that they do
not adequately serve the present specific needs of
farm workers. In many cases, laborers do not know
their options, or existing services may be poorly
distributed. If the superstructure for these services is already in place [Comprehensive Employment
and Training Act (CETA) programs, regional occupational programs, Economic Development programs, and
others], a leading question is why they are not more
effective in easing the transition of farm workers
into the mainstream.

POLICY IMPLICATIONS OF MECHANIZATION IN AGRICULTURE

The Myth of the Machine: Historic and Economic Rationales for Mechanization

Americans have always been inventive. The task
of making habitable a continent of wilderness encouraged them almost from their beginnings to devise a
multitude of mechanical gadgets to make their labors
easier. The land was immense; the population was
sparse; and mechanical inventions often speeded the
work of shovels and axes. Throughout most of America's westward expansion, the steam engine--driver of
locomotives and steamboats--stood for "progress." As
the continent absorbed an ever-increasing population
in its industrializing cities and on its developing
frontier, the dream was that accumulating national
wealth would raise the level of life for all. And it
has.

Times change, however, and the locomotive is not
the symbol it once was. Still, for a great many
Americans, the machine as a labor-saving device continues to stand for progress. Farmers, in particular, are close enough to memories of back-breaking
toil in fields and orchards to make them sympathetic
to any device that seems to promise a reduction of
physical strain, or a means of reducing risk.

Agricultural mechanization is, in fact, a reaction to risk. The development of agricultural technology in general has been an evolutionary process of
trying to minimize the high risks already present in
the natural cycles of reproduction--death, pests,

disease, and disastrous weather. Farmers have mechanized out of reaction to new kinds of economic and
managerial risk as well. In recent years, for example, production costs have escalated more rapidly
than the income derived from agriculture. Farmers,
caught in the classic cost-price squeeze, look for
ways to cut costs, and labor seems a likely place for
reducing cash outlay, particularly if mechanization
promises greater speed. Uncertainty of the labor
supply has also been a perennial problem for farmers. The traditional unstructured migrant-labor
force has recognized disadvantages. Even when farmers have stable relations with seasonal workers,
there is still the possibility that sufficient labor
may not be available exactly when needed. The mechanization of peak seasonal tasks such as harvesting
permits some farmers to operate with regular year-
round employees, even perhaps not much more than family labor.[7]

No one can deny that another cause contributing
to farmers' labor headaches and anxieties has been
the polarity between organized farm labor and management that has been fermenting for years. Some
growers have resented being forced to interact with
unions; some have seen mechanization as a way of
avoiding the threat of unionization and increasing or
regaining control over their operations by reducing
their labor force to a minimum. Even the paperwork
caused by new legislation, such as minimum-wage increases, housing codes, and unemployment compensation, has contributed to farmers' desires to hire
fewer short-term employees.

Changing Times: Perspectives and
Values in Different Worlds

Viewed as a reaction to perceived risk, agricultural mechanization is a rational response to changing circumstance. Many factors bearing on the farm
economy have made mechanization of laborious tasks
seem eminently logical. The object- and task-
oriented applied research done in public and private
institutions supports and encourages that view, and,
at least on the surface, technological developments
(including but not limited to mechanization) in agriculture have resulted in spectacular achievements in
efficiency and productivity. Other effects of technological change have, however, been increasingly
noted, and critics...have been harbingers of what may
be a changing perspective on current agricultural
technology. Mechanization, though perhaps historically inevitable, has been an important cause of farm

change in the United States, and thereby of social
change in general. Some perceptive and intelligent
observers are not willing to have the process continue without closer examination of the consequences.[8]

. . .

Without examining any of the assumptions that
lie behind [the popular arguments for and against
agricultural mechanization], it may be pointed out
that many of those arguments are based essentially on
value judgments. The persuasiveness of the arguments
for any individual may depend on what frame of reference he or she brings to the discussion.

In spite of conflicting arguments, there are
some broad areas of agreement on this issue. The
present farm labor system is regarded as a "thorn in
the side" by many growers and workers. Many workers
want out, and many growers wish for far less dependence on them. The migrant system that has been inherited has been the cause of many social ills. The
unstructured labor system lends itself to uncertainty
on both sides.[9] In spite of the rhetoric employed by
advocacy groups, it is also generally agreed that no-
body really wants to stop mechanization. "Our union
does not oppose progress," says Cesar Chavez. "We do
not even oppose mechanization" (Los Angeles Times,
1978). No one wants stoop labor made permanent; what
is really needed--and both sides agree--is short-term
assistance for disadvantaged workers, and long-range
research on alternatives for a group of workers that
has only very limited options as of now.

The issue is, however, broader than what is described as "displacement" of workers by machines.
The subject is really the whole complex of technological change and its impact on the whole structure of
agriculture and of society at large. Both sides
agree about that, too; we need to know more about
what we are doing.

Research and Policy Implementations

The social effects of technological change in
agriculture have drawn concentrated attention only
relatively recently. Work is needed not only to determine the long-range impacts of various kinds of
change but to determine what kinds of strategies
would be best for minimizing ill effects. Land-grant
institutions, in cooperation with public agencies,
could provide the facilities and expertise for such
public-service research. Concerning agricultural

mechanization, at least several questions might appropriately be examined: What constraints operate to keep farm workers from successfully moving into the mainstream of society? What are the successes and failures of the current training and employment system? How significant are Mexican workers, legal and illegal, in the American agricultural scene today? What have other nations done to stabilize employment and farm communities while modernizing agriculture? What is the relationship between mechanization and farm size and viability? What is the effect of farm change on rural community structures? Research on those and other questions might help provide information for rational decision making on public policy. For, in the end, the social effects of technological change must be dealt with at the public level, either by conscious judgment or (by default) by public sentiment responding to new crises.

Some of the public-policy issues engendering debate are these:

-- whether to compensate workers displaced by technological change; if so, who, how, how much, and for how long
-- whether to encourage or phase out special public services to aid the migrant farm worker
-- how to deal justly with minority groups in the larger society; whether to encourage or discourage diversity through bilingual facilities, special education, community development, and other programs for the disadvantaged
-- how to deal with unemployment in the whole economy
-- whether to allow public monies to be spent for research and development with possible negative social consequences.

Many recommendations on policy have already been made by national task forces. The optimism of the sixties about social programs, however, has shifted to pessimism as to the efficacy of public solutions. The current taxpayer revolt is only one symptom of this malaise. Social change remains much harder to engineer than technological change.

Mechanization as Metaphor

The mechanization issue is not a new one. Economists and social historians have been examining the consequences of agricultural mechanization since the

thirties both in the United States and abroad.
Nevertheless, the issue has surfaced in California as
a political hot spot in 1977-78. And it has captured
the imagination of many observers because it can be
viewed so simply: man versus machine, muscle versus
metal, peasant versus patron (for there are many
ethnic and class overtones), "nature" versus all the
chemical and mechanical artificialities that cut man
off from direct experience with the earth. Yet an
issue is not diminished in importance simply because
the naive can so quickly reduce it to an emotional
argument through the manipulation of symbols.

The mechanization issue may be viewed as a meta-
phor for at least two very central human concerns:
man's relationship with the earth itself; and the
distribution of economic and social power among human
beings. Far from being only an economic issue, the
controversy has philosophical overtones dealing with
human values. The currents in present-day criticism
of mechanization may be compounded by nostalgia for
bygone days, when life is supposed to have been
simpler, slower, more satisfying (was it ever,
really?); by some private resentment against "rich
farmers"; by uncertainty in a fast-moving society,
which leads to a grasping for simple answers; and by
a need for a visible adversary--the machine--in a
world that seems somehow intangibly threatening. But
there is also in the controversy an honest grappling
with some fundamental questions, a frustrated ideal-
ism, and a reexamination of American life as it lives
out today the principles that the architects of the
American dream committed to paper in their founding
documents.

We need our economic pragmatists--they feed us
well. But we also need our social critics--they keep
the dream alive.

NOTES

1. "...in June of 1977, there were 244,000
fewer employees building transportation equipment
than there were in 1953....In the primary metals industry [which includes the production of iron and
steel] the number of production workers declined by
214,000...100,000 jobs lost at American Telephone and
Telegraph since 1974....The longshore work force, in
the port of New York, dropping from 40,000 to less
than 12,000 between the mid-fifties and 1977...coal
production up 7 percent while 227,000 coal miners,
some 55 percent of the work force, lost their

jobs...800,000 jobs eliminated on the railroads since
the end of World War II...over the span of a generation, the cumulative effect of job losses because of
new technological changes has been incredible and
devastating." From a keynote speech by Frank Runnels
at the First National All Unions Conference to
Shorten the Work Week, April 11, 1978.

2.   Martin sees these conflicting values in
broadly similar terms, though he states them differently. "If the concept of culpability were exorcised
from farm mechanization discussions, the issue could
be seen as one in which society is pursuing incompatible social goals. Society strives for both full employment and increased agricultural production.
These goals inevitably collide." (Martin and Hall,
1978)

3.   A thoughtful examination of the conflict between Jeffersonian agrarianism and the march of in-
dustrialism is found in Leo Marx's The Machine in the
Garden: Technology and the Pastoral Ideal in America (1964).   The book examines the stresses and
strains of developing America as reflected in American literature. To the symbols of the locomotive,
the steamboat, and the dynamo as used by American
writers, we might add the tomato harvester.

4.   It has been a popular misconception that the
electronic sorting device was developed at the University of California. Although research on color
sorting of lemons was done there some years ago, the
addition of the electronic sorter to the tomato harvesting machine has been done by commercial engineering companies. The principle upon which color sorting of tomatoes is based is different from that used
in the lemon-sorting research.

5.   The statewide average would certainly be
less, according to the California Tomato Growers
Association.

6. First, a caveat: in playing numbers games,
it can happen that no two sets of calculations come
up alike, depending on the base data, the assumptions
governing the calculations, and the point the player
may wish to prove. We performed our simple calculations thus: using a base figure of 28,000 employed
in the California tomato harvest (average from EDD
figures of 1972 through 1976), we subtracted 7,000
(25 percent) for the harvest jobs that will not be
affected by the electronic sorter--drivers of tractors and trucks, machine operators, etc.--then calculated a 60 percent displacement rate based on 21,000
which we assume to be the probable number of sorting
crew workers. Arriving at a figure of 12,600, we

suggest that this may be a general guide to the mag- nitude of job decline for sorters between 1975 and 1982. This is a somewhat higher estimate than that suggested in the Chancellor/Garrett report (Kumar et al., 1977), which was based on the measurement of man-hours of labor utilization rather than jobs per se. The latter report, moreover, was less specif- ically concerned with canning tomatoes than with overall trends across all crops.

7. This can be demonstrated with reference to Yolo County seasonal labor requirements as collected by the Employment Development Department from 1974 through 1978. Seasonal peaks of employment (August through October) have been somewhat flattened (down 15 to 20 percent), while overall monthly employment has increased. It appears that although fewer workers are needed for seasonal highs, more workers are being employed year-round or for longer periods. This corresponds with some growers' statements that they are trying to spread out work over the year for regular employees while reducing their dependency on a peak force.

It should be noted, however, that employment statistics are not the same as unemployment statis- tics. Very little is really known about the number of people who would like to find farm work but can- not. It may well be possible that the available "pool" of workers is actually increasing even faster than employment figures are declining. (There are three plausible reasons for this hypothesis: 1) There is an undetermined influx of workers, both legal and illegal, from Mexico. 2) There may be an increasing number of workers coming into the state from other states because of more attractive wages, working conditions, and the whole "package" of California living. 3) The farm worker population has been characterized by a relatively high birth rate.)

8. For a well-balanced discussion of the causes and results of mechanization, see Donaldson and McInerney (1973).

9. On the other hand, an unstructured system offers opportunities for growers to pick up cheap labor quickly; and offers relatively easy-entry jobs for immigrants, the unskilled, and young workers. Occasional work is also what some people want; and there will always be a need for some seasonal farm work as long as agriculture reflects the exigencies of biology and time.

12
University Involvement in Social Impact Analysis of Changing Agricultural Technologies: Tobacco Harvest Mechanization in the Southeast

Leon B. Perkinson
Dale M. Hoover

Flue-cured tobacco has traditionally been one of the most labor-intensive crops in the United States. Tobacco production and marketing systems, combined with a farm structure that was stabilized by the Agricultural Adjustment Act of 1938, have ensured that the size distribution of farms has remained much as it was in the mid-thirties. In the 1970s, researchers at North Carolina State University began to analyze the labor displacement effects of tobacco mechanization. Funded in part by the U. S. Departments of Agriculture and Labor, several publications have appeared which are unique in that they attempt to predict the negative effects of mechanization--and possibly ameliorate them--before displacement occurs. Here, Perkinson and Hoover discuss some results of the research, including problems and prospects for similar ex ante labor impact studies.

HISTORY OF CONCERN

In a progressive economy, the amount of labor used per unit of output is expected to fall and real earnings are expected to rise. Unless output increases more rapidly than labor productivity, employment in a given area of production declines. People

Leon B. Perkinson is an economist with the U.S. Department of Agriculture. Dale M. Hoover is Department Head and Professor in the Department of Economics and Business, North Carolina State University.

lose jobs if the decline in labor demand exceeds the rate of attrition.

U.S. agriculture has been going through such labor adjustments for more than fifty years due to the increase in productivity of farm labor. Every region and farm enterprise has experienced a considerable decline in the demand for farm labor. Agricultural labor used in the United States declined by more than 75 percent between 1939 and 1977 (Durost and Black, 1977). Between 1967 and 1977 alone, a 30 percent decline occurred in aggregate agricultural labor utilization, and rapid rates of adjustment have continued into the 1980s.

The general public has not been greatly interested in the labor displacement resulting from farm mechanization. There was some interest among academicians in the potential effects of cotton-harvest mechanization before it was well along (Taylor, 1938), as discussed in two articles included in this book (Hamilton, 1939; Williams, 1939). But there was little formal analysis of how much households would be affected by mechanization, or of the numbers of people who would migrate because of it. Estimates of the impact of cotton mechanization on rural-urban migration have increased over the past several decades. The debate over how much "push" (reduced farm labor demand) versus how much "pull" (reduced farm labor due to nonfarm labor-market forces) was at work in cotton mechanization remains unresolved (LeRay and Crowe, 1959; Padfield and Martin, 1965; Pederson, 1954). Even so, the widely held notion of the effect of cotton mechanization on workers was the primary basis for the interest in the potential impact of tobacco-harvest mechanization in the late 1960s and early 1970s.

Concern about reduced demand for farm labor has focused primarily on mechanization although most forms of technological change raise output per unit of labor. Harvest mechanization seems to create the most concern, perhaps due to the rapidity of adoption once a technology is perfected. Decreasing the seasonal peak labor demand may cause fundamental changes in farm tenancy and rural residence, especially in the South. This could lead to migration from rural to urban areas and, in turn, urban problems.

In addition to causing social problems, a reduction in the demand for farm labor can lead to a reduction in the wage rate and incomes of farm workers. Insofar as the farm wage falls and farm workers have low incomes, mechanization may also be

associated with a worsening of the real income position of low-income farm-worker households.

Tobacco mechanization, like mechanization of
many other crops, has been a long process. Labor input per acre began to decline well before World War
II as some of the tillage operations were mechanized
(table 12.1). The process continued as semimecha-
nized transplanting and curing processes were developed. As a result of increased yield per acre,
successive reductions in the national quota and
loose-leaf marketing, labor utilization in flue-cured
tobacco production in 1970 was only 39 percent of the
level it had been in 1947 (table 12.1). At the onset
of adoption of bulk curing and mechanical defolia-
tion, there was less labor left in tobacco production
than had existed in the previous twenty-five years.
Even so, potential problems that would face flue-
cured tobacco laborers were numerous. The possible
problems were cited by a United States Department of
Agriculture study (USDA, 1969) and by Calvin L. Beale
(1972). Both studies noted that rapid mechanization
could lead to large reductions in employment and
possibly sizable amounts of rural-urban migration.

TABLE 12.1
Flue-Cured Tobacco Output, Labor Requirements
per Acre, and Employment in North Carolina

	1930	1947	1956	1965	1970
Man-years of work (thousands)	133	167	123	92	58
Total output (1947 = 100)	61	100	102	94	87
Labor input per acre (1947 = 100)	130	100	71	58	39

Labor input requirements were taken from Pierce and
Pugh (1956), Farm Management Extension (1965), and
Allgood et al. (1971). Output data were taken from
published sources and used to estimate man-years of
work from input requirements. Flue-cured tobacco
accounted for 60 percent of all U.S. tobacco labor.

In early 1972 the United States Department of Labor (USDL) was interested in studying the impact of the new technologies available to flue-cured tobacco producers. Consequently, USDL, together with USDA and North Carolina State University (Department of Economics and Business), organized a workshop which was held in Raleigh in February 1972. Researchers from USDA, USDL, and North Carolina State University (NCSU) participated. In general they agreed that more research on the probable impact of mechanization was needed. Representatives of the Department of Economics and Business (NCSU), USDA, and USDL agreed to coordinate research concerning the labor-market effects of mechanization. A substantial grant was provided by USDL to NCSU to support a field survey of households in the flue-cured tobacco production region, emphasizing labor-supply and employment changes. The results of the survey are reported in the next section. The problems and prospects for similar ex ante labor impact studies are discussed in the final section.

TOBACCO-HARVEST MECHANIZATION: HOUSEHOLD RESPONSE TO CHANGING LABOR CONDITIONS[1]

The Study Area and Sample

Flue-cured tobacco is produced in about two hundred counties in six Southeastern states stretching from Virginia to Florida. Since about two-thirds of the total output is produced in North Carolina, labor adjustments from adopting the mechanical harvester are apt to be more concentrated in North Carolina than elsewhere. Within North Carolina, the area selected for study was where: (1) tobacco production was concentrated, (2) the crop was amenable to mechanization (level land, large fields, etc.), and (3) nonfarm alternative uses of labor were relatively scarce.

The area with these desired characteristics contained eight counties extending from the Virginia border through the central coastal plain to the north-south midpoint of the state. Nineteen percent of tobacco production in the state and 12.4 percent in the nation was produced in the eight-county study area in 1972. Tobacco allotment acreage was slightly less than 10 percent of cropland acreage in the study area: roughly twice the mean ratio for all flue-cured counties in the state. Peak seasonal agricultural

employment in the area was about 2.5 times as important in percentage terms as for the state as a
whole. Even then, only a little over one-fourth of
the work force was employed in agriculture. There
were only two important urban centers within the
study area with populations exceeding 20,000 in
1970. The total population of the area was just over
a quarter of a million in 1970.

The objectives of the study were to measure all
hours worked and all income of workers, especially
harvest workers; to determine the socioeconomic characteristics of workers' households; to simulate the
distribution of change in employment and income among
workers and households in response to projected harvest mechanization; to estimate the potential income
lost from mechanization; and to identify the potential demand for retraining and other social services
during the period of rapid adjustment.

A 3 percent sample of all households in the area
was drawn to determine the importance and distribution of tobacco-harvest work relative to other work.
Usable questionnaires were obtained for 1,515 households.[2] Excluding households with small amounts of
work or no work prohibited generalizing about all
residents of the study area, as those not effectively
in the labor market were excluded.[3]

Work Force and Household Characteristics

About one worker in four had work in the tobacco
harvest in 1972. Almost 60 percent of these were
hired workers; the remainder, workers on their own
farm. Despite the relatively large number of workers
involved in tobacco harvest, the work hours in tobacco represented about 6 percent of total work time of
the area's population. More than 50 percent of the
hired workers were less than eighteen years old.
More than 75 percent of those working on their family
farm were eighteen or over.

The average hired tobacco-harvest worker earned
less than $350 and the average own-farm worker had
imputed wages of less than $650. These harvest earn-
ings represented approximately one-half of all earnings for hired workers and more than one-fourth of
the earnings of own-farm workers. Few earned substantially more: about 3 percent of hired workers and
18 percent of own-farm workers earned more than
$1,000. In contrast, about 40 percent of hired work-
ers and 29 percent of own-farm workers earned less
than $250.

Most harvest workers did not generally participate in other labor markets. Tobacco-harvest earnings represented over 75 percent of the total
earnings for more than three-fourths of hired workers. Tobacco-harvest earnings were not particularly
high but were an important part of total earnings for
the individual.

The changing demand for labor affecting individual workers also spreads to the individual's household. Household reactions to lost employment depend
upon the importance of such losses on household earnings and whether such losses represent an offspring's
spending money.

Of all households in the work force, about 18
percent had hired harvest workers and 9 percent had
own-farm harvest workers. Of those households with
hired workers, harvest earnings averaged less than
$600 per household and represented less than 10 per-
cent of household earnings. Of the own-farm households, imputed harvest earnings averaged over $1,500
and represented less than 25 percent of household
earnings. Household income included all earnings as
well as interest payments, rent, royalties, unemployment, disability and retirement compensation, the
value of bonus food stamps, and welfare payments.

Projecting Labor Loss

Survey data were used to project harvest labor
utilization under a variety of hypothetical tobacco
cost and output situations (Grise et al., 1975; Hoff
et al., 1977). The usual assumptions of net farm
income maximization were used in developing projections of labor utilization for an aggregate estimate
of labor demand. Given 1972 price, quota,[4] and farm
structures, mechanization was projected to reduce
harvest labor demand by 35 percent by 1980. Even if
quota increased 50 percent, harvest labor demand was
projected to decrease by 23 percent. If quota decreased 50 percent, harvest labor demand was projected to decrease 71 percent from 1972 conditions.

The new harvest technologies were expected to
reduce the demand for labor in many traditional
tasks. In addition, farmers adopting new techniques
might increase their production to take advantage of
economies of size by leasing quota from owners facing
higher costs of production. Such consolidation would
release labor from those leaving tobacco production
for other farm and nonfarm activities. On the other
hand, there could be an increase in demand for labor
to perform those tasks associated with the new machines.

Estimates of the division of work loss were based on changes in harvest tasks and labor requirements and on changing tenure arrangements of workers (hired vs. own-farm workers), as given by Hoff et al. (1977) and Grise et al. (1975). The distribution of work time was then applied to the estimated work time expected to remain after mechanization.

Projecting work loss among hired workers required two steps. First, the percentages of work done by males and females for each task were applied to estimate the work loss for each sex group. Then the displacement of workers within each sex group was specified. The 1972 age-sex distribution of workers for each task and the changing physical requirements of the new technologies were used to formulate a hierarchy of worker release. Workers were ranked on the basis of work requirements (tasks) changing from manual dexterity to physical strength. We assumed that the most productive hired workers of a given sex retain employment without reference to the tasks previously held. In general, females were expected to lose more hours than males, and young and elderly workers were expected to lose more than middle-aged workers.

The demand for own-farm workers could decrease either as quota was consolidated among farms or as tasks of family workers were eliminated by mechanization. Two steps specified the change in expected employment. First, the change in farm numbers, and the differential labor requirements by farm size classes, were obtained from Hoff et al. (1977) and Grise et al. (1975). The decrease in labor requirements from the 1980 projected farm size distribution was considered the "consolidation effect." Any additional decrease in employment was attributed to mechanization. The shift from own-farm tobacco harvest was then constructed—first from those farms most likely to leave tobacco production, and then from the age and sex of own-farm workers most likely to lose employment as tasks are mechanized.

Mechanization by 1980 with the 1972 level of production was projected to result in a 46 percent decrease in total harvest work hours.[5] About 42 percent of hired work time and 44 percent of own-farm work time would be released. The work done by hired males was projected to decrease 31 percent and the work of hired females by 60 percent. This represented about 10,000 harvest jobs: 3,000 from males and 7,000 from females.

About 15 percent of own-farm workers' lost harvest time came from farm consolidation; mechanization accounted for the remaining 29 percent of hours. As

the consolidation effect removed entire producing
units from tobacco production prior to the removal of
individual workers, the own-farm adjustments were
confined to the household effects.

Of the 11,087 households containing at least one
hired harvest worker in 1972, 29 percent were projected to lose harvest workers from mechanization.
Black female-headed households and white households
with at least one hired harvest worker would decrease
by 32 percent; black male-headed households would decrease by 24 percent (table 12.2). Of those households losing hired-worker tobacco-harvest earnings,
more than one-half of each race-sex category of heads
lost less than $250. About 38 percent of households
with black female heads were expected to lose 10
percent or more of their income, compared to about 18
percent of the black male-headed households.

The projected labor reduction resulting from
mechanization was more severe for own-farm households, especially black households. In addition, the
loss in earnings and income was greater. Compared
with hired-worker households, a smaller percentage of
own-farm households lost less than $250 and a larger
percentage lost $500 or more (see table 12.2). The
projected losses were larger for black households
than for white households. There was no attempt to
project expansions in substitute activities.

Estimated lost earnings indicated the direct impact from tobacco mechanization. The potential for
replacing lost earnings through different jobs or income transfer programs was not known. Therefore, the
potential for income replacement, job training programs, income transfer programs, or potential migration was evaluated.

Household Responses to Change

Projecting losses of employment and earnings was
useful only as a first step in analyzing the impact
of mechanization because many workers adjust to lost
work opportunities. Some adjustments involve the
household as a unit; others are more strongly related
to individuals. Therefore, several household and individual labor-adjustment responses were modeled.
Each adjustment was treated independently of the others for simplicity. However, households would consider alternatives simultaneously for decision-making
purposes, choosing the combination of activities appearing to maximize the household's utility. Adjustments likely to occur if the 1972 level of tobacco
production was produced in 1980 were analyzed and are
summarized below.

TABLE 12.2
Projected Losses of Earnings among Tobacco-Harvest Workers' Households after Mechanization

| | Percent of Households | | | | |
| | Black | | White | | |
	Female	Male	Female	Male	Total
Hired-worker households					
Decreases in:					
Households with earnings	32.4	24.2	32.0	32.0	29.0
Harvest earnings	45.6	42.0	30.0	51.6	44.8
Total earnings	12.0	5.3	2.4	2.0	4.0
Total income	7.3	4.7	1.9	1.7	3.4
Households with losses					
Losing earnings of:					
Less than $250	52.8	56.4	77.4	67.1	60.0
$500 or more	20.2	20.8	0.0	7.4	15.3
Households with income losses of:					
Less than 10 percent	61.6	81.7	87.4	95.8	81.3
25 percent or more	12.3	5.0	12.7	0.0	5.1
Own-farm households					
Decreases in:					
Households with earnings	36.5			29.8	32.3
Harvest earnings	29.2			37.2	41.5
Total earnings	13.1			8.2	9.7
Total income	10.5			5.2	6.6
Households with losses					
Losing earnings of:					
Less than $250	26.7			50.5	41.6
$500 or more	48.9			36.7	41.2
Households with income losses of:					
Less than 10 percent	52.3			80.1	69.7
25 percent or more	15.0			8.3	10.8

Nonfarm employment. Work replacement from other activities in the area was examined. Those of prime working age with educational qualifications and experience in nonfarm employment would be the most likely to seek and obtain other jobs. Those least likely to seek and find replacement employment were the youngest workers still in school and unavailable for regular employment and the oldest workers. Workers under eighteen were excluded from this analysis and the nonfarm employment experience of those over sixty-five was ignored.

Based on our assumptions of work release, almost 4,000 hired harvest workers, all females, and over 5,800 own-farm workers were projected to lose part or all of their harvest employment by 1980. Less than one-fourth of these hired workers and less than one-fifth of the own-farm workers had nonfarm work experience in 1972. Of those with nonfarm work experience, about one-fourth of the hired workers and over one-half of the own-farm workers were less than forty-five years old.

Predicting the number who would seek nonfarm work is complicated since some own-farm workers may seek new farm employment in expanded nontobacco farm enterprises. Nonfarm work accounted for almost half of the income on the smallest farms analyzed by Grise et al. (1975), the farms most likely to leave tobacco production. Also, the Bureau of the Census found in a similar area that only 25 percent of part-time workers between sixteen and sixty-four were interested in a full-time nonfarm job (U.S. Bureau of the Census, 1972). Therefore, while there might be a desire to replace lost part-time work with other part-time employment, probably less than 2,000 of the 9,800 displaced harvest workers either desire or have nonfarm work experience.

Retraining. While the pressure for additional training would be felt by all unskilled workers in the region, the most direct effects would probably be on laborers released from harvest work who were not in school. Workers less than eighteen years old were excluded from the analysis because most would not have completed their formal schooling. The group considered for potential retraining was therefore identical to those considered for work replacement.

Only one out of four hired harvest workers had completed twelve or more years of schooling and most of these were less than twenty-five years old. More than 50 percent--almost exclusively older workers-- had eight years or less of formal education. If the potential benefits from retraining were greater for those with less than high-school completion, almost 75 percent of the displaced workers could benefit from retraining. The benefits shrink with age, however, because the increased earnings power from retraining would be applied to a shorter time in the job market.

Almost one-third of the displaced own-farm harvest workers had completed twelve years of school; 42 percent had completed no more than eight years of schooling. However, only 9 percent of the workers, equally divided between races and sexes, were under thirty-five and with less than twelve years of schooling. An additional 13 percent were between thirty-five and forty-five with less than twelve years of schooling. Between 10 and 20 percent of all workers directly affected by mechanization were likely to seek retraining directly in response to mechanization.

CETA influence. The impact of the Comprehensive Employment and Training Act (CETA) on the total agricultural work force was also estimated. There were 11,515 tobacco-harvest households and another 2,850 households with someone seasonally employed in farming but not in the tobacco harvest. Using the CETA program eligibility requirements for seasonal farm workers, 13 percent were eligible for assistance, double the national rate. Of the eligible households, 4 percent were headed by a black female and 41 percent were headed by a black male. The average age of the household head was forty-eight, somewhat older than the average of all households with farm workers. The educational level of the household head was also low, averaging no more than eight years. The age distribution diminished the potential for technical and on-the-job training except for some younger households. Family service, especially day-care services for participating families headed by a female, would be more likely utilized in conjunction with other CETA services.

Migration. One possible response to employment losses is to move in search of a new job. The move may take two forms: youth who mature and expect to relocate in the future may migrate sooner than planned, or entire households may relocate if earnings losses are big enough. Household migration was considered because it is socially important and is probably more easily predicted. As the psychic benefits and costs of migration were not directly

observable, the best guide to the incentive to migrate was the household's loss of earnings arising
from harvest mechanization. If household earnings in
the study area were approximately equal to earnings
available if the household had lived in some other
area, then the potential lost annual earnings from
harvest mechanization represented the gain from moving to a new area. The potential for out-migration
increases as the ratio of lost earnings to income increases.

Specifying a dollar loss stimulating migration
is arbitrary, but other studies indicated that a minimum loss of $500 per year would be likely to stimu-
late migration. About 1,700 households with hired
harvest workers and 2,200 own-farm households would
lose at least $500. These represented about 15 per-
cent of all hired-worker households and 40 percent of
own-farm households. Only 10 percent of these heads
were less than thirty-five years old. The average
educational level of those thirty-five or over was
less than eight years while the average for those
under thirty-five was ten to eleven years. Of those
losing at least $500, about one-fourth lost at least
20 percent of their household income.

The average household most likely to migrate
from loss of harvest work would be impeded by the educational level of the head, except for the younger
ones. Eligibility for income transfer programs might
also impede migration, given the potential lag to re-
qualify after moving if employment is not found.
Most hired harvest-worker households likely to migrate (i.e., those that lost 20 percent of income or
$500) were already receiving some form of transfer
payments. Few own-farm households received transfer
payments. Using these guidelines, we found that
about 3,900 families might lose enough earnings to
stimulate migration. If the migration was spread
evenly over the eight-year time span of the analysis,
488 households would leave each year. Spread over
eight counties, the out-migration averaged slightly
more than sixty households per county per year.
Households with heads sixty-five or over or those for
whom $500 represented less than 10 percent of gross
income would not be likely to migrate, reducing potential migrants to forty-three per county per year.
Even for those most prone to migrate, many impedi-
ments to migration existed. Taking into account age,
sex, and education of the head, existence of transfer
payments, and the existence of some local employment
opportunities, the probability that most would migrate because of lost harvest earnings seemed quite

small.   Consequently,   the   estimated   out-migration
would be about twenty-five households per county per
year.   Migration as a result of mechanization should
be negligible.

   Income replacement. Two types of transfer programs were examined for their potential impact for
replacing lost harvest income: the Food Stamp Program
(FSP) and Aid to Families with Dependent Children
(AFDC). · Although the programs had different rules
for determining eligibility, neither program included
earnings of dependent children in household income so
long as the dependent was a full-time student. Hence,
losing dependents' earnings would not increase program benefits in the event of mechanization and worker displacement.   Since more than 50 percent of the
hired work force was under eighteen and since most of
the income losses were projected for the young, much
of the lost earnings would not be recoverable through
increased welfare benefits.
   FSP benefits as of 1976 were used to estimate
household eligibility and benefit levels and the
anticipated "benefits" and eligibility for 1980, assuming mechanization and no change in tobacco production levels.   Use of a standard FSP for both 1972 and
1980   conditions   permitted   the   identification   of
eligibility and benefit changes arising from mechanization. Of all households containing harvest workers
in 1972, almost 36 percent were eligible for food
stamps, with potential benefits averaging $1,275 per
eligible household.   With mechanization, the number
of eligible households was projected to increase 7
percent. Projected losses in earnings for adults and
workers under eighteen in households eligible for FSP
were approximately $1.4 million each.   Only adult
losses were potentially replaceable from increased
food stamp benefits.   The adult losses would increase
potential benefits by almost 5 percent from the 1972
level or $400,000, offsetting 29 percent of adult
losses.   Hired-worker households were eligible for
the bulk of estimated 1972 benefits but increased
eligibility would come more from own-farm households.
   Aid to Families with Dependent Children (AFDC)
was available to households with dependent children
where one or both parents were absent and household
income was below specified levels.   As with the FSP,
the same rules were used for the 1972 level and the
projected 1980 level of eligibility.   About one-half
of the female-headed households containing harvest
workers were estimated as eligible for AFDC benefits
in 1972.   Estimated program benefits averaged $1,535

per household. Almost all eligible households were headed by a black female. The reduction in employment due to mechanization was projected to eliminate about 12 percent of adults' harvest earnings, $195,000, and 41 percent of dependents' earnings, $321,000. These losses would make an additional 3 percent of the households eligible for AFDC benefits. More than one-half of the adult losses would be recoverable from added AFDC benefits although total estimated AFDC benefits would increase only 5 percent from the 1972 level.

Increases in AFDC and FSP would benefit the lowest-income households. The total increased benefits from the two programs was $508,000. These two programs may overlap but we made no attempt to analyze both benefit programs simultaneously. Less than one-half of the estimated eligible households reported receiving program benefits in 1972. If lost harvest earnings encouraged those previously eligible, but not participating, to participate, program payments could increase substantially. A change in participation rates could increase benefits much more than a change in eligibility caused by mechanization.

Summary of Findings and Projections

With no change in acreage, mechanization between 1972 and 1980 could have led to a loss of 44 percent of own-farm family harvest labor and 47 percent of hired harvest labor. Over 10,000 fewer seasonal harvest jobs would have been available. Even so, the income losses would have represented less than 4 percent of their households' total income. The losses would not be distributed equally: 20 percent of the black households and 7 percent of the white households were projected to lose more than $500 per year. Nearly half of the projected displaced workers were too young to be expected to seek or to be able to obtain other nonfarm work. Perhaps 5 to 10 percent would be expected to benefit from retraining activities. Relatively few households would be induced to migrate, given the low level of income loss experienced by most households. Income replacement through food stamps and AFDC benefits would be low--less than 10 percent of the losses incurred by all workers in the area studied--unless the participation rate of eligible households increased because of mechanization.

The effects of a reduction in quota were also estimated in the study. However, quota actually increased. Also, the projected rate of mechanization for the study area was not realized. These forces worked together to reduce the impact of mechanization to less than that projected in our study.

OVERVIEW OF RESEARCH ON
AGRICULTURAL LABOR MARKETS

Our analysis of the flue-cured tobacco labor situation and estimation of the possible impact of mechanization were undertaken to provide "an early warning" of dire consequences that were feared possible. Choosing "worst-case" assumptions, we concluded that in general massive migration was highly unlikely and that the income effects would be widely distributed and relatively small per household when compared to other sources of income. The study produced data on the diverse characteristics of households involved in the seasonal agricultural labor markets of eastern North Carolina. The heterogeneity of household economic situations which we were able to document may be important information for developing research for other agricultural labor markets, both in the United States and abroad. Certainly, future mechanization and other technological changes will have a much more dramatic effect in developing countries than in the United States or, probably, in other industrialized countries.

The results of our study raise questions about the generally held opinion that mechanization of other crops affected hired farm-labor markets in a simple, straightforward manner. If hired farm labor employed for seasonal peak demands such as harvesting cotton was as widely distributed among households as in the case of flue-cured tobacco harvest, perhaps mechanization was less important than generally assumed for the observed migrations of thirty to forty years ago. Consider some potential forces. First, cotton acreage was decreased by changed allotments in the late 1930s and mid-1950s, and by other land-diversion programs in the late 1950s and the 1960s. These programs idled as much as 20 percent of total cropland in some years. Demand for labor would be expected to decrease about proportionately with acreage diversion. Second, cotton moved westward during and after World War II when the allotment program was not in force, reducing the demand for labor sharply in the Southeast and Delta states. This westward movement was due in part to publicly subsidized irrigation in the West along with harvest mechanization, which was not initially useful in humid areas. Consequently, one can conclude that factors other than mechanization affected the demand for hired workers and sharecroppers in the Cotton Belt of the Old South.

An argument favoring the hypothesis that cotton mechanization was the crucial factor setting off large-scale migration was the absence of farm-nonfarm labor-market integration in the 1930s. In the 1970s most hired farm workers and most farm households reported nonfarm earnings. Consequently a decline in farm earnings might not be expected to trigger migration in the 1970s as in earlier decades when labor markets were less integrated. The net effect of cotton mechanization needs to be reexamined in light of current theory and research methods to see if earlier appraisals are sustained or rejected.

Identifying research topics in agricultural labor supply and demand problems is a public policy issue. Almost all of the analyses to date have been sponsored by state and federal agencies. Public policy analysis can be defined as the use of costs and returns concepts (from economics) as applied to the allocation processes of public agencies to derive descriptions of how decisions are made, who is benefited, who pays, etc.

The demanders of agricultural labor have had more impact in the research decision process than the suppliers. Generally farm producers have more of a focused interest in the price and availability of labor than the laborers themselves. Workers often work in several industries. The wage bill of a single producer is larger than the wage receipts of a single worker. This difference in economic impact may explain why farm operators band together more than farm laborers to affect agricultural research decisions.

The study of labor supply and household labor decisions is complex and generally more difficult to model than are factor demand decisions. There are more motivations and considerations at work in a household made up of two or more individuals, each with several options including home production, human capital production, and market/wage employment to consider both singularly and jointly.

Also, concepts vary as to the benefit of the results of labor-supply studies. The fact that public intervention might occur to retard mechanization or restrain migration makes an estimate of workers' responses to changing employment conditions of more value than in an era when public intervention was not expected.

Those assuming that knowledge of supply responses are unimportant tend to believe that labor markets function smoothly and efficiently. In this situation, well-informed workers, appropriately trained
to work in a variety of industries, would be able to
respond to shifts in demand without great personal
loss or social externality. Studies of tomato mechanization (Schmitz and Seckler, 1970) and flue-cured
tobacco harvest (Martin and Johnson, 1978) estimate
some social costs but not at a level that warrants
prohibiting the adoption of the harvesters in either
case. The opposite position is the belief that labor
markets do not function efficiently and that individuals should be protected by extending to them a
property right in their chosen employment.

Clearly the public-choice framework throws some
light on the current and past status of research into
labor-market supply questions. It is true that laborers will not become much more highly organized and
influential in the research allocation process than
they have been in the past, with the possible exception of one or two states with the largest concentrations of hired workers per farm. If labor-market
integration (two or more wage and income sources per
household) grows, the pressure for more studies of
supply will lessen. If migration is perceived to im-
pose sizable externalities on the receiving area or
the "home" area, labor studies may receive more emphasis. Of course, a higher level of public education could lead to lower social or community impact
of migrants and with it a lesser interest in labor
supply/migration studies. The development of the
household labor-supply model has contributed to
greater emphasis on supply analysis and will generate
additional work both in the United States and abroad
in the years ahead.

NOTES

1. This section is based upon and summarized
from Hoover and Perkinson (1977a and 1977b) unless
otherwise cited.

2. Many household background characteristics
were available in Hoover and Perkinson (1977b) that
are not included in this summary because of space
limitations.

3. Thus, population estimates in this paper refer to households whose sum of all labor-market time
exceeded 160 hours during 1972; households not meeting this criterion were ineligible for the survey.

4. A quota is a production quantity, denominated in pounds, which is set by the U.S. Department of Agriculture to regulate yearly total tobacco production.

5. This decrease in harvest hours differs from the 35 percent noted on page 168 because wages were assumed to increase and farm consolidation was allowed: neither condition existed for the 35 percent reduction.

13
Can Tobacco Farmers Adjust to Mechanization? A Look at Allotment Holders in Two North Carolina Counties

Gigi M. Berardi

Berardi studied allotment holders who were no longer producing tobacco in Greene and Wayne counties, North Carolina, partly to determine how former growers had replaced tobacco income. Berardi found that income adjustments were made primarily through lease and transfer of tobacco quota, and to a lesser extent through participation in income-distribution programs. Berardi concluded that premature attrition as a subtle form of labor displacement, the replacement of earnings for the elderly, and the expectations of younger allotment holders need to be studied more thoroughly. Researchers and policymakers often assume that those who are displaced from agriculture either participate in federal, state, or private income-transfer programs or find off-farm employment. Berardi showed that this is not necessarily true, particularly for the rural South.

In recent years, people from all segments of the political spectrum have called for the preservation of the family farm. Yet the numbers of farms and farmers have been plummeting at an alarming rate in virtually every commodity sector, now even in tobacco. Flue-cured tobacco has always been one of

Chapter 5 in The Tobacco Industry in Transition: Policies for the Eighties, William Finger, ed. Lexington, MA: D. C. Heath and Co., Lexington Books, 1981. Reprinted by permission.

the most labor-intensive crops in the United States
and has remained so much longer than almost all other
crops.[1]   A unique production and marketing system,
combined with a farm structure that was stabilized by
the Agricultural Adjustment Act of 1938, preserved
the tobacco belt as a kind of laboratory, perhaps the
best remaining example of the Jeffersonian ideal of
an independent yeomanry.[2] But the vast sweep of agricultural mechanization and the escalating pressures
common to all farmers, from fertilizer and fuel prices to labor costs and international competition,
have begun to transform tobacco farming.

In the last twenty years, two "push" factors--
technological innovations and changes in the federal
support program--have prompted a dramatic shift in
the patterns of tobacco production. And to a lesser
degree, the "pull" force of increased industrialization has also caused people to quit farming tobacco.
Consequently, a dramatic displacement in the tobacco
labor force has begun, a transition that affects
every type of tobacco farmer: allotment holders,
growers who own land without quotas and have to lease
allotments from others, growers who lease land and
quota, sharecroppers who farm someone's allotment for
a portion of the profits, permanent hired labor, and
seasonal workers.

Changes in production technology have had a dramatic impact on the tobacco work force. Chemical
controls have virtually eliminated the summer labor
bottleneck when sucker leaves must be removed from
the plant. A single machine operator can handle up
to twenty acres a day, "topping" the plants and
spraying them with a sucker-inhibiting chemical in
one pass down the row. Transplanting, although still
labor intensive, now requires far fewer hours because
of the mechanical transplanters. But the most publi-
cized and perhaps the largest impact on tobacco labor
resulted from the introduction of the mechanical harvester and bulk curing barns.

As early as the 1950s, members of the Agricultural Research Service faculty at North Carolina
State University (NCSU) had begun to design work on
the functional principles needed for a machine that
could remove and handle tobacco leaves. The state's
land-grant university, NCSU, supported this early
work through its ongoing federal and state funding
received for agricultural research.[3] In the early
1960s, two commercial manufacturing companies attempted to produce a mechanical harvester; they were
unsuccessful, primarily because field-harvesting
methods had not yet been developed to take advantage

of the harvester. (See the discussion of changes in the federal price-support program later in the chapter.)

In the mid-1960s, R. J. Reynolds Tobacco Company, anticipating the need for a harvester in the future, made grants to NCSU to help sustain the research that had begun a decade earlier. Reynolds itself also began design research, utilizing the functional principles developed at NCSU. By 1969, Reynolds--with the close cooperation and assistance of NCSU researchers--had designed, constructed, and field-tested a prototype harvester. In 1970, Reynolds and the Harrington Manufacturing Company announced an agreement for commercial production. Within a few years, mechanical harvesters began appearing in the field.

Although the average tobacco allotment in North Carolina was about three acres at that time, the new harvesters had a break-even capacity of forty to fifty acres. The machine's designers felt that it was impractical to develop a harvester with only a three- to four-acre capacity and that tobacco farming units would move toward larger operational sizes as the harvester became widely available (Suggs, 1972).

In 1975, the United States Department of Agriculture (USDA) released the first major study of the harvester's impact.[4] The USDA analyzed data from an area that produced about three-fourths of the flue-cured tobacco in the country, and found that in 1972, 1 percent of the acreage had been harvested mechanically and 8 percent of the crop had been cured in bulk barns. With the technology available in 1972, a farmer could harvest an acre with only 58 hours of labor, a dramatic change from more traditional methods that took up to 257 hours of labor per acre harvested. The USDA then predicted that by 1978, tobacco farmers would harvest 23 to 36 percent mechanically, cure 65 to 80 percent in bulk barns, and reduce the labor needed during the harvest by some 50 percent.[5]

Since the USDA study in 1972, a number of researchers have collected data that support these predictions. Some have found an even more rapid pace of mechanization than the USDA anticipated, especially in the North Carolina belts. In 1980 Tobacco Information, for example, Rupert Watkins of the North Carolina Agricultural Extension Service reported that 46 percent of North Carolina's crop was harvested mechanically (Watkins, 1979).

These technological innovations took hold in such a short time primarily because of three major

changes in the federal tobacco program. First, in
1961 Congress passed Public Law 87-10 which author-
ized intracounty (that is, within a single county)
lease-and-transfer of flue-cured allotments on a limited basis. Subsequent amendments expanded the leasing provision (for example, a 1967 action eliminated
the five-acre limit on the amount that could be
transferred to a single farm). Intracounty leasing
facilitated a consolidation of quotas into larger tobacco management units at central locations. A farmer no longer had to go from one part of a county to
another, from farm to farm, to acquire more tobacco
quotas. Second, in 1965, federal legislation changed
the flue-cured allotment system from an acreage to a
poundage basis. A poundage quota eliminated a critical barrier to mechanization: the tobacco harvester's
high leaf loss in the field. (Mechanical harvesting
can result in up to 15 percent leaf loss.) On a
poundage basis, unlike the acreage method, the leaf
left in the field was not a loss. Third, in 1968,
the "tying" requirement for flue-cured tobacco was
eliminated. Marketing flue-cured leaf in loose-leaf
"sheets" rather than in tied "hands" required far
fewer labor hours and made possible large investments
in bulk-curing barns, where loose-leaf sheets (but
not tied hands) could be easily stacked.

The rapid spread of mechanized tobacco produc-
Although changes in technology and the federal
tobacco program were "pushing" people out of tobacco,
nonfarm occupations, to some extent, were "pulling"
them with the lure of a steady wage. From 1965 to
1977, North Carolina's employment in nonagricultural
sectors increased from 1.4 to 2.1 million. But research published in the last four years indicates
that people moving into the state accounted for much
of this increase, not persons leaving tobacco farms
(Perkinson, 1979; Hoover and Perkinson, 1977b; Long
and Hansen, 1977). Some tobacco laborers were losing
their old jobs in the fields but failing to find work
in the state's newly built factories.

The rapid spread of mechanized tobacco production, facilitated by adjustments to the federal support program, is resulting in increased labor
efficiency and decreased per acre production costs
for some growers. But those who have not been able
to invest in the technology have had to either produce tobacco at relatively higher costs (at a time
when costs common to all agricultural sectors were
skyrocketing and agricultural labor came under
minimum-wage law) or quit tobacco farming completely. Leaving tobacco farming in the largest numbers
are sharecroppers, full-time laborers, and seasonal

workers. They are not needed, and they can no longer be afforded except in far fewer numbers on the larger, more mechanized farm units.

All types of tobacco farmers have already experienced, or will soon face, some adjustments in employment, income, and possibly location. But persons who own no factor of production other than their own labor face the most severe adjustment problems, which are often exacerbated by age, race, education levels, and lack of vocational training. In 1977, researchers at NCSU reported on the effects of mechanization on harvest workers in eight of the state's coastal counties, an area that produced one-eighth of the nation's flue-cured tobacco. They found that less than 10 percent of the total lost earnings of harvest workers would be replaced by two income-transfer programs: food stamps and Aid to Families with Dependent Children (AFDC).[6] [The research is reported in chapter 12 of this volume.]

ALLOTMENT HOLDERS: ADJUSTING TO DISPLACEMENT

Although some income-transfer programs such as food stamps or AFDC have a stigma, others do not. The federal tobacco program, through its lease-and-transfer provisions combined with its other features, effectively functions today as a redistributor of income for allotment holders. Because of such income transfers, one can assume that allotment holders in general adjust to displacement more easily than people who have no land equity. Indeed, a study of displacement among allotment holders (such as the one I have completed) examines minimum-hardship patterns. But it also suggests the degree and form of adjustment that other types of tobacco "farmers" experience.

In the summer of 1980, I coordinated a study of tobacco allotment holders in Greene and Wayne counties, North Carolina. This research had two primary objectives: (1) to document the socioeconomic characteristics of allotment holders who are no longer producing their quota; and (2) to determine if former tobacco growers who had allotments made the transition out of agriculture successfully, and to record how they replaced tobacco income.

In this two-county area, located in the coastal plain of North Carolina, 12 percent of the cropland in 1977 was tobacco allotment acreage, 10 percent higher than the state average. In 1979, these two counties produced 6 percent of North Carolina's tobacco; Wayne ranked eighth and Greene thirteenth

among the state's counties in total production. Because of this concentration of tobacco production,
labor adjustment problems were expected in this
area. Cost constraints prevented extending the study
into other tobacco-producing counties and sampling
other groups such as seasonal and permanent workers.

The North Carolina State Agricultural Stabilization and Conservation Service (ASCS) provided the
names of the 43,298 tobacco allotment holders in
these counties. A systematic sample of 431 allotment
holders was drawn.[7] Sixty-one percent of the sample
(261 out of 431) were ineligible: they either were
still producing their own quota or owned quota in
counties other than Greene and Wayne. Of the remaining 170 allotment holders, 32 percent (54 out of 170)
refused to be interviewed. The response rate was
thus 68 percent (116 interviews completed out of 170
eligible respondents). The respondents completed a
three-page questionnaire that was developed with the
assistance of North Carolina State University staff
and pretested to identify unclear or ambiguous questions. A random sampling of the allotment holders
who refused to complete the questionnaire determined
that no significant differences existed between the
eligible nonrespondents and the respondents for the
variables tested.

The allotment holders tended to be lifelong residents of their respective county, over sixty years
old, and high-school educated. Sixty-nine percent of
the respondents were sixty years of age or older; the
average age was sixty-three. Two-thirds of the respondents were male, one-third female (most of these
women were widowed). The average years lived in the
present county of residence was fifty-three, and 98
percent of the respondents planned to continue living
in the same county. Two-thirds had completed high
school, thus increasing their qualifications for off-
farm employment relative to other residents in the
area without this level of education. Nevertheless,
the older age of the population puts a constraint on
their participation in the nonfarm labor force. The
nonfarming allotment holders who responded to this
survey thus have not migrated, nor have they joined
the nonfarm labor force at the rates that their educational backgrounds might indicate.

After quitting tobacco farming, these allotment
holders either retired (52.8 percent), worked in off-
farm employment (30.0 percent), remained a housewife
(11.3 percent), or farmed crops other than tobacco
(5.9 percent). Most of the off-farm employment was
in industry.

It is important to note that although 52.8 percent listed themselves as retired, less than one-third gave "retirement" as the reason they no longer farmed their allotment (table 13.1). Of those who did state "retirement," one out of four were less than sixty-five years old (primarily fifty-five to sixty-four) and had some off-farm employment. Retirement age, then, is only one of several factors involved in the decision to stop growing tobacco, despite the age of this population. High production costs, including investment in new technology, were discussed at length by respondents, especially by the elderly persons.

Only 13.7 percent of the respondents had never grown tobacco, and they are grouped in table 13.1 as those who "discontinued" because they inherited a quota. Three-fourths of this 13.7 percent were over fifty-five years of age, and 80 percent earned more than $20,000 a year. But one must remember that 13.7 percent is barely more than one person out of every eight who is not growing his or her allotment. A common assumption among some critics of the tobacco program is that it benefits primarily those who have never farmed their allotment, insuring from birth a source of income that requires no work. The results in table 13.1 indicate that this is not the case.

Generally, the allotment-holder population has replaced its tobacco earnings by combining income from four sources: lease and transfer of quota, special services (particularly social security), crop

TABLE 13.1
Reasons Given by Allotment Holders in Greene and Wayne Counties for Discontinuing Tobacco Production

Reasons	Percent of Allotment Holders
Retired	30.5
Health	16.8
Inherited quota	13.7
Labor problems	12.6
Off-farm employment	10.5
Other[a]	15.9
Total	100.0

[a]High cost of machinery, "larger profit to be made from lease and transfer of quota."

and livestock production, and off-farm employment
(table 13.2). These income sources are only mutually
exclusive in some cases. For example, those dependent on special services most likely would not have
off-farm employment. On the other hand, both groups
might get some income from crop and livestock production.

Almost all the respondents (95.3 percent) received income from the lease and transfer of their
quota, reflecting the extent to which the tobacco
allotment system now functions as an income-transfer
program for allotment holders. In 1979, the average
number of pounds leased and transferred out for production was 10,412 (the range was 178 to 64,000).
The average payment received was $.44 per pound and
thus the rental earnings (based on average price and
weight) were $4,581 (the range was $78.32 to $28,160)
per year per allotment holder. These earnings constituted a large portion of the yearly household income for allotment holders in Greene and Wayne
counties (the average yearly household income ranged
from $10,000 to $14,999).

Approximately half (46.7 percent) of the households made less than $10,000 in 1979. Of these
households, 29 percent had only one household member,
whereas 71 percent had two or more members. Most of
these incomes (calculated on a per-household-member
basis) would be considerably lower than the 1979
North Carolina state per capita income average of
$7,359. The income data for age and occupational
classes reflect more hardships among the elderly than
among the younger respondents, and lower incomes for
housewives and the retired than for those in off-farm
jobs and other farm sectors (tables 13.3 and 13.4).

TABLE 13.2
**Replacement of Tobacco Earnings by Allotment Holders
in Greene and Wayne Counties**

Income Sources	Percent of Allotment Holders
Lease and transfer of quota	95.3
Special services	56.6
Off-farm employment	31.1
Crop and livestock production	29.2

One quarter (26.6 percent) of the allotment
holders stopped producing their own quota before
1970. Thus, the decision to lease and transfer quota
was made by most allotment holders during the period
in the 1970s when mechanization was increasing. Furthermore, the decision is fairly permanent; 98.2 percent had leased and transferred out quota every year
since they began transferring their quota. Even so,
almost 40 percent said that if they wanted to produce
their own quota, they would have the equipment and
curing barns to grow tobacco again. Only 10.9 percent (these are younger individuals with off-farm

TABLE 13.3
**Distribution of Allotment Holders in Greene and
Wayne Counties by 1979 Household Income and Age**

| Age | % of Allotment Holders with Household Income | | | |
	Less than $10,000	$10,000-19,999	Greater than $20,000	Total
65+	59.6	29.7	10.7	100.0
64-55	46.0	32.4	21.6	100.0
54-46	30.0	30.0	40.0	100.0
43-34	9.1	18.1	72.8	100.0

TABLE 13.4
**Distribution of Allotment Holders in Greene and Wayne
Counties by 1979 Household Income and Occupation**

| Occupation | Percent of Allotment Holders with Household Income | | | |
	Less than $10,000	$10,000-19,999	Greater than $20,000	Total
Retired	62.8	23.5	13.7	100.0
Off-farm employment	27.2	36.4	36.4	100.0
Housewife	88.9	11.1	0.0	100.0
Farm operator[a]	16.7	33.3	50.0	100.0

[a]Most of these farm operators had off-farm income.

employment) stated that they may want to grow tobacco again.[8]

As table 13.2 shows, 56.6 percent of these persons are supplementing their incomes from special services. But very few of the allotment holders participated in programs other than social security and disability (table 13.5). Income-transfer programs such as food stamps and AFDC were not used at all, although households did qualify.

Those replacing some of their tobacco income by producing other crops (29.2 percent of the population; see table 13.2) were growing primarily corn and soybeans for cash sale and vegetables for home use (table 13.6). Only 21 percent produced vegetables for personal consumption, and only 6 percent or less produced livestock for themselves. Since one-half the households earned less than $10,000 yearly (71 percent of these households had two or more members), and since none of them were participating in the food-stamp program, the nutritional adequacy of the diets of these households might have been in jeopardy.

Off-farm employment was a source of income for 31.1 percent of the sample population no longer growing tobacco (table 13.2). About 40 percent of this group's household income was over $20,000 and only 27.3 percent earned less than $10,000, a sharp contrast to allotment holders who depended more on special services--68.4 percent of whom earned less than $10,000 (table 13.7).

TABLE 13.5
Distribution of Allotment Holders in Greene and Wayne Counties Receiving Income from Special Services

Special Services	Percent of Allotment Holders
Social security	55.7
Disability	6.6
Workman's compensation	0.0
Food stamps	0.0
Other (pension, and so on)	6.6

TABLE 13.6
Distribution of Allotment Holders in Greene
and Wayne Counties Receiving Income from
Crop and Livestock Production

Crop/Livestock	Cash Sale	Home Use
Peanuts	0.0	1.7
Corn	29.2	5.2
Soybeans	20.7	0.9
Vegetables	6.0	20.7
Forest products	5.2	1.7
Poultry	5.2	1.7
Hogs	2.6	3.4
Dairy	0.0	1.7
Other	0.0	2.6

TABLE 13.7
Distribution of Allotment Holders in Greene and
Wayne Counties, by 1979 Household Income and
Method of Replacement of Tobacco Earnings

Replacement of Tobacco Earnings: Income Source[a]	Percent of Allotment Holders with Household Income			
	Less than $10,000	$10,000-19,999	Greater than $20,000	Total
Prod.of crops & livestock	41.4	34.5	24.1	100.0
Off-farm employment	27.3	33.3	39.4	100.0
Special services	68.4	26.0	5.6	100.0

[a]These income sources are not necessarily mutually exclusive.

CONCLUSION

The changing structure of tobacco production in Wayne and Greene counties suggests ways to view the impact of labor displacement throughout the flue-cured tobacco belt. First, a subtle but widespread form of labor displacement must be recognized: premature attrition, that is, persons retiring from tobacco farming before they normally would want to retire. This necessitates some special attention for the elderly. Second, replacement of earnings for the elderly and for all other displaced tobacco farmers demands careful attention, particularly the role of off-farm employment, special services, and lease-and-transfer income. Third, the expectations of younger allotment holders need to be viewed in relationship to the changing tobacco structure in an era of mechanization. Finally, the impact of labor displacement on those "farmers" without equity in land must be more thoroughly studied and understood.

Although most of the respondents in this study could be characterized as elderly, only one-fourth listed "retirement" as the reason for quitting tobacco farming. Sixty percent of those over sixty-five years of age and 46 percent of those from age fifty-five to sixty-four earned less than $10,000 a year. Tobacco policymakers should note especially that much of this income came from lease and transfer of quota. A change in the tobacco program that affects this source of income would have a severe impact. If the tobacco program is changed so that it no longer functions as an income-transfer program for allotment holders, some other type of income transfer will have to replace it or an additional hardship will be placed on this group of people.

Individuals who can successfully obtain off-farm employment have a substantially higher income than those who must depend on social security or income-transfer payments. Special-service payments are lower than industrial wages (even in North Carolina, which has one of the lowest average industrial wages in the country). Moreover, people are hesitant to utilize income-transfer programs commonly labeled "welfare."

Almost one-third of the population did replace tobacco earnings with off-farm employment. One would expect that individuals who are no longer employed in agriculture in North Carolina could successfully obtain off-farm employment, given the growth rate of industry in the state. During the decade following

1966, only Texas and California gained more manufacturing jobs than North Carolina. Yet who is benefiting from this shift in manufacturing location? As stated earlier and corroborated by these research findings, North Carolina's displaced tobacco farmers may not be able to compete for industrial jobs as well as people moving into the state in pursuit of employment. This is primarily a result of educational and age constraints (particularly true for the population of tobacco allotment holders in Greene and Wayne counties), and the lack of retraining programs for older adults.

The primary objective of this study was to determine the socioeconomic characteristics of allotment holders who are no longer producing their quota. However, information was also obtained from allotment holders who are still producing their quota. These people have a strong commitment to tobacco production, and most are planning to grow tobacco until retirement.[9] But as this study demonstrates, "retirement" can mean quitting tobacco farming long before age sixty-five. As leasing costs increase to one-third and more of the value of tobacco production, the profit margins of tobacco growers (and in particular, small-scale producers who might have higher production costs) are narrowing.[10] This could lead to a greater decline in the number of tobacco growers and an increase in average acreage of tobacco farming units.

In sum, tobacco allotment holders who are no longer producing their own quota have made employment and income adjustments primarily through participating in special services (mainly social security) and leasing and transferring their tobacco quota; fewer than one-third have off-farm employment or other farm income. But it is difficult to draw conclusions as to whether nonfarming allotment holders have successfully made the transition out of agriculture either completely or partially. One-half of the households had yearly incomes of less than $10,000, but no data were obtained to compare income figures before and after allotment holders began to lease and transfer out their quota.

The population of allotment holders sampled in this study had some distinct advantages over other members of the tobacco work force, in terms of replacing tobacco earnings. Allotment holders derived a considerable portion of their income from lease and transfer of their quota, a source not available to those tobacco growers who own no allotment. Furthermore, this particular population did not have the educational constraints (the average number of school years completed was much higher than the state's average) one might expect of the tobacco work force in general.

More research needs to be conducted in the flue-cured tobacco belt on target populations for which adjustment may be particularly difficult, given lower education levels, vocational training, and political power base (for example, for migrant workers).[11] In the same way that concerns have been raised about the adjustment of farm operators to mechanized and modernized tobacco-production technologies (for example, the Ford Foundation and others have suggested programs for training farm operators in mechanical skills and management), so too should concerns be raised about the majority of the tobacco labor force who will no longer be deriving income through employment in tobacco production. Although some adjustment programs, such as special education grants, have been suggested by other researchers, ex ante facto research focusing on this group must be expanded.

Researchers and policymakers often assume that those who are displaced from agriculture either participate in federal, state, or private income-transfer programs or find off-farm employment. However, the little research that has been conducted on the adjustment process indicates that changes in employment and location may indeed be difficult, and for some, impossible (Hamilton, 1939; Raper, 1946).

NOTES

I wish to thank Professor Dale M. Hoover (Department of Business and Economics) and Professor Michael Schulman (Department of Sociology and Anthropology) at North Carolina State University for their assistance in the design and implementation of this study. Mr. Eugene Naylor (North Carolina State Agricultural Stabilization and Conservation Service office) assisted in obtaining the sampling frame used in the study. In particular, I wish to acknowledge the assistance of Ms. Lisa Bosley in the research design, data collection, and data analysis phases of this project.

1. According to the USDA, Agricultural Statistics 1977 (Washington, D.C.: USDA, 1978), the 1971-1975 average man-hours per acre required to produce tobacco was 281.0 (compared with 5.1 for corn, 2.9 for wheat, 23.0 for cotton, 42.6 for potatoes, and 161.5 for tomatoes).

2. Throughout the last sixty years, writers have recorded the consequences of labor displacement caused by agriculture mechanization—during the great agricultural depression of 1921-1936, with the arrival of an automated cotton harvest in the 1950s and 1960s, and following the mechanization of the tomato harvest in California in the late 1960s. Many of these researchers were attempting to explain the unique circumstances of a particular farming sector and then to suggest possible adjustment programs to ameliorate the hardships of labor displacement. Unlike most of this type of research, several studies on the mechanization of the flue-cured tobacco industry have attempted to anticipate this displacement so as to offer some understanding of its effects prior to large-scale mechanization (Grise et al., 1975; Hoover and Perkinson, 1977b). This chapter represents another effort at exploring policy options prior to full-scale farm displacement.

3. Federal funding of research that is focused on increasing labor efficiency through agricultural mechanization has been the subject of much controversy by academicians (Friedland and Barton, 1975) as well as public-interest groups. Recently, California Rural Legal Assistance filed a suit on behalf of nineteen farm workers and a small-farmer organization to contest sixty-nine tax-financed projects at the University of California that benefit large farming operations (Meyerhoff, 1980).

4. See Grise et al., 1975. The USDA gathered data from four census-of-agricultural subregions: 29 (Ga.), 17 (Coastal Plain, N. C.), 18 (Piedmont, Va.-N.C.), and 16 (Pee Dee-Lumber River).

5. See Grise et al., 1975. The USDA released a follow-up study (Hoff et al., 1977), based on the same 1972 data, which projected the most profitable farm structure within this mechanization process. In 1979, the USDA began a new study of the same magnitude as its 1972 survey. A report based on the 1979 data will be released in 1981.

6. Research from Legal Services of North Carolina, Pennsylvania State University, State University of New York (Binghamton), and others has shown that monetary and nonmonetary income-transfer programs in North Carolina are vastly underutilized, failing to reach about half of those who qualify.

7. The sample size for the survey was calculated using estimates for the population variance of key variables. We assumed that 50 percent of the list would be ineligible and that there would be a 60 percent response rate.

8. This result is interesting from a policy perspective since there has been some discussion of mod-
ifying the tobacco program so that allotment holders
would be required to produce their own quota periodically.

9. Most of these farmers planned to grow tobacco
until retirement (79.5 percent) or were undecided
(12.8 percent). Only 7.7 percent were considering
leasing and transferring out their quota in the future, and they still planned to farm part-time or
full-time until retirement. Slightly more than two-
thirds (69.2 percent) of the growers had no source of
income other than farming. Of those who did have
other income, the majority of them had jobs in industry. The average size of quota for this group was
24,614 pounds (range: 150 to 330,000), more than
twice the quota of allotment holders no longer growing tobacco.

10. As rental rates and thus production costs
increase, the price of United States flue-cured tobacco also increases. This has resulted in a decrease in the United States flue-cured share of the
domestic and foreign market. To compete more strongly in the world market, the tobacco program might
have to undergo changes that will result in lowered
production costs (and perhaps loss of rental income
for current tobacco allotment holders). This situation has generated much discussion.

11. Results may show that incomes are higher for
former members of the tobacco labor force who have
off-farm employment. However, it is also possible
that off-farm employment will not be an option for
many of these individuals. Migration and participation in income-transfer programs may or may not be
viable options. All these hypotheses need to be
tested with data collected through surveys, especially longitudinal case studies.

14
A Programmatic Approach to the Social Impact Assessment of Agricultural Technology

William H. Friedland

Social impact assessment (SIA) of agricultural technology has been accomplished in several research projects during the last decade at the University of California, Santa Cruz (UCSC). The research has been conducted in part by students participating in an innovative curriculum in the Community Studies Department of UCSC. In this chapter, Friedland, who developed the "second curriculum," discusses the program, its background and objectives, and the dissemination of results of his research projects on various agricultural commodity systems. He also discusses the "social sleepwalker" characteristics which he sees as typical of researchers in the land-grant college system, and makes a convincing case for further SIA studies in agriculture.

INTRODUCTION

This report describes combined research and curriculum development in social impact assessment at the University of California, Santa Cruz (UCSC). The project had two concurrent dimensions: (1) research expanding SIA methodology to agricultural technological change; and (2) integration of this research into an undergraduate teaching program. These SIA

William H. Friedland is Professor in the Departments of Community Studies and Sociology, University of California, Santa Cruz.

studies of mechanization in California agriculture were not undertaken because of explicit concern or involvement with SIA methodology; rather, the projects originated because of concerns about other issues, especially those involving agricultural labor, its displacement through technology, and the way in which decisions were made about the substitution of capital-intensive technology for labor. The use of an SIA approach began once the research got underway.

What is perhaps most striking about publicly funded agricultural research is that it provides a basis for SIA in embryo. One need only consult the forms used by the United States Department of Agriculture (USDA) and the state agricultural experiment stations that researchers use in seeking funding support. Researchers are asked to justify their research in terms of the benefits to the public or how the results will help agriculture. Although such questions are routinely asked and answered, little attention is devoted to responses and, in most cases, research funds are allocated less because of the formal process and more as a result of historic relations linking departments and colleges of agriculture, on the one hand, and funding agencies such as the USDA, on the other. Thus, despite the requirement for what could potentially be social impact assessment, the opportunity is not taken seriously.

It was the discovery of these relationships that underlay the development of my initial interest in SIA. During a sabbatical leave in California during 1967 and 1968, I learned that the mechanical tomato harvester had been introduced only several years before. Several interviews and some reading on processing tomato production gave me an initial familiarity with the topic when the sabbatical year ended. I did not return to it until I moved to California in 1969. I devoted my immediate attention to a new department of community studies at Santa Cruz, an enterprise that was to play a significant role in facilitating my SIA research in agriculture.

Around this time Professor Isao Fujimoto of the Department of Applied Behavioral Sciences at the University of California, Davis, had been generating considerable discussion on the social aspects of the decline in small-scale farming in California. I was drawn into this debate and found myself in accord with Fujimoto on many issues. Most important was our agreement that the agricultural research establishment of the University of California was too closely tied to the large capitalist enterprises that characterize California agriculture; little or no research could be "captured" by smaller farmers. Fujimoto and I tried in vain to convince the head of the agricultural experiment station about this research bias, suggesting that a small percentage of the resources of the experiment station be explicitly committed to research sustaining small-scale agriculture.

An important paper came to my attention around this time. This was the study by Schmitz and Seckler (1970; reprinted as chapter 9 in this volume) on the development of the mechanized tomato-harvesting system. This study, which joined a burgeoning literature on "returns to research," showed that the costs of development of the harvesting system were minute compared to its benefits. Despite the fact that Schmitz and Seckler (1970:575) acknowledged that "the very success of these sectors (science and industry) creates consequences which bear unfavorably. . . on less organized and therefore more vulnerable sectors," I had certain problems with their study. Although they had made a brief attempt to assess man-hour displacements of the new system, they did not deal with the specific numbers of workers affected nor with any additional, unquantifiable social effects. Moreover, despite their warning about the unequal effects of the new harvesting system, their paper was generally seen as demonstrating the effectiveness of new agricultural science and technology.

Having done the earlier research in California, I was aware of some consequences and processes which Schmitz and Seckler had omitted. For example, it was clear that a shift had occurred in production locations within California and that a large number of women were employed on the harvesting machines. Schmitz and Seckler thus left open the opportunity to conduct a study elucidating social effects that they had not uncovered. The fortuitous circumstance of there being a dean in the College of Agriculture at Davis committed to pushing research in new directions provided the impetus for a project to do just this.

At the outset I confronted a methodological dilemma. All of my prior research had involved hands-on activity close to data sources. My research orientation had always been committed to direct experience and empathic understanding of social reality, i.e., verstehen (Abel, 1948). But there were two problems in this new venture. First, I was personally ill-suited to agricultural labor (despite seven years of hard experience as an auto worker, several days of field labor during my earlier California sabbatical had left me groaning and crippled). Second, the activity of building a new department, even one centered on the idea of incorporating field study into the undergraduate curriculum, did not permit extensive absences for field study activity. It was therefore clear that a key part of the research project would have to involve students who could act as primary data collectors. Thus developed the second curriculum within the Community Studies Department.

INTEGRATING ACADEMIC CURRICULUM WITH RESEARCH

The original curriculum in community studies was constructed around the idea that students should design an academic program of study incorporating a field study of not less than six months. This study had to be oriented toward social change and conducted within an existing organizational context. Students were discouraged from operating simply as observers, visitors, or as initiators of new, personal projects. Each student chose his or her field study location after classroom preparation. On completion of the field study, students returned to the classroom to prepare a senior thesis derived from the field experience--one that integrated literature relevant to the individual field circumstance.

The second curriculum followed a model I had previously developed at Cornell in what was called the Cornell Migrant Labor Project (Friedland, 1969). In the Cornell project, a group of students was recruited and trained for field study in migrant labor camps. On their return from the field, they prepared a series of papers as a way of consolidating their experience and relating it to relevant social science literature.

In the second curriculum developed at Santa Cruz, students were recruited to a research project directed by a faculty member. They spent an initial term working with the instructor, learning about the research area, doing assignments and research exercises related to project substance, and learning more about each other. It was understood that, at the end of the introductory period, the individual students could withdraw from the relationship; once agreement was reached to continue, the participants were obligated to see it through to completion in the form of a senior thesis.

As we initiated the tomato research, it became clear that we should not limit the approach solely to specifics of tomato harvest mechanization. Rather, the mechanization research should be considered in the larger social milieu within which agricultural research is conducted. Accordingly, two research strategies were developed. The first involved placing students recruited through the second curriculum with agricultural scientists at Davis. The intent was to understand how these researchers define their problems, work, and relate their problems to larger social contexts. The second strategy involved research on the tomato-mechanization transition, accumulating statistical data from whatever sources existed, interviewing whatever participants were available, etc.

As a result of the first strategy, as well as through auxiliary data-collecting processes, we learned almost immediately that only a few agricultural scientists paid any attention to the broader ramifications of their research. Most scientists gave some consideration to the immediate consequences of their research: all were aware, although to varying degrees, of the existence of constituencies for their research and were concerned with the maintenance of good relationships with such constituents. The very structure of agricultural knowledge production enforces such consciousness. Not only do college of agriculture officials continually remind scientists of constituent expectations, but the presence in each department of an extension person provides an important link to these groups.

It was equally clear, however, that few scientists with whom we met and worked placed their research in a larger social context. "Social," in other words, was limited to the organized constituencies and linkages which fed funds and research problems to the researchers. The larger social context--for example, the ownership and control of trucking and railroads, seeds and fertilizers, processing and retailing, credit and technology essential to agriculture by a relatively small number of corporations, financial institutions, and families-- seemed lost on the researchers. With only very minor exceptions, they operated as if the social context with respect to the farm was neutral. The results of this first field period with students working in the laboratories of agricultural scientists at Davis were summarized in Social Sleepwalkers (Friedland, 1973b), formulated around an argument that agricultural scientists should be encouraged to broaden their social horizons. This short monograph argued for SIA procedures in all publicly funded research conducted on agriculture within the University of California.

Social Sleepwalkers recognized that agricultural scientists had little training or incentive to consider the broader social ramifications of their work. Accordingly, it proposed a procedure for all funding applications in the agricultural experiment station, in which researchers would set out projected social consequences of their proposals. Because few scientists had experience with this approach, Sleepwalkers recommended that appropriate technical consultation be made available to them. These consultants should have experience in SIA methodology and be able to advise the researchers in how to consider first-, second-, and third-order consequences. Realizing the still-primitive state of SIA methodology,[1] Sleepwalkers also suggested the need for a second group of experts dedicated to evaluation. This unit would select, after some time had elapsed, various projects to determine the accuracy of their original assessment. The body of experience acquired through such monitoring would improve SIA methodology and reduce the variability of predictiveness.

After the publication of Social Sleepwalkers, a few scientists took the work seriously, and some of the associate and assistant deans at Davis read it and reacted to it. Its main readership, however, was found among scholars interested in SIA outside agricultural research circles.

In the meantime, research was proceeding on tomato-harvest mechanization. A draft manuscript of a monograph and the first senior thesis by Robert J. Thomas were completed.[2] We shared a draft of Destalking the Wily Tomato (Friedland and Barton, 1975) with a number of experts who had participated in the research on tomato mechanization. Although this was at least four years after the complete transition to mechanized harvest, the draft was received with some hostility. Several factual points were disputed with vigor. The basic contentions of the study remained intact as far as we were concerned following this exposure.

Destalking followed the approach of the inventors of the mechanized harvesting system by treating tomato production systemically, considering it from beginning to end.[3] In the course of conducting the tomato research, we fortuitously stumbled on the idea of the agricultural commodity system, an idea already well developed among agricultural economists but essentially unknown in rural sociological circles. Once we began to treat tomato production as a system, it was feasible to relate this work to other commodity systems in agriculture. Further, we began to draw on the extensive literature on commodity systems that had been generated after the second world war in industrial sociology and the sociology of work. Much of this literature took the form of using the commodity as the unit of analysis.

The substantive findings were set out not only in the monograph Destalking the Wily Tomato, but also in a shorter article, "Tomato Technology," in Society (Friedland and Barton, 1976). What we found confirmed my original unhappiness with the Schmitz and Seckler (1970) article. There were, indeed, a variety of consequences, some of which could be quantified and others that could not, that went beyond the cost-benefit efficiencies that Schmitz and Seckler had emphasized. Among the most dramatic were the startling reduction in the number of workers (from 50,000 in 1964 to 18,000 in 1972) and the transition from male harvesters to women of all ages and to students of both sexes. Equally startling was the efficiency of the system, which "saved tomatoes for California" by concentrating production in the state (to the detriment of tomato production in New Jersey, Ohio, Indiana, and other states). There were dramatic increases in acreages and tonnages and a sharp drop in the number of tomato growers; thus, production more than doubled while the number of growers decreased from approximately 4,000 (before) to 600 (after). Subsequently, a study by the California Agrarian Action Project (1978), a public interest research group at Davis, showed that the economic benefits of the transition had not been passed on to consumers, i.e., the retail price of processed tomatoes had risen more rapidly (111 percent) than that of all other processed fruits and vegetables (76 percent).

FROM POST-FACTUM TO PROJECTIVE METHODOLOGIES

With the publication of Destalking the Wily Tomato, our first attempt at curriculum-related SIA was complete. We now confronted an interesting criticism. This was not so much directed at the substance of Destalking (which appears to have withstood the tests of time) as at the fact that the research was conducted post-factum, i. e., after the phenomenon was completed. Some readers raised the point that "anyone" could find out what had happened after the fact. This criticism was especially painful since Social Sleepwalkers had argued for a projective or predictive methodology, i.e., before the fact. This led to a consideration of research sites that would permit (1) the development of a predictive or projective methodology; (2) comparative analysis of other commodity systems; and (3) the formulation of proposals for institutional change in the agricultural research system.

Again, fortuitous circumstances affected the research design. As we considered a series of studies to examine other agricultural commodities entailing different kinds of systems, a major event was unfolding in California agriculture. For the first time in history, agricultural worker unionism had been successfully estabished. The success of the United Farm Workers (UFW) in organizing grape workers led the lettuce grower-shippers, a powerfully organized segment of California agriculture, to support two major research and development efforts at mechanized lettuce harvesting—one at Davis and the other at the USDA research station in Salinas. The time was ripe for an ante-factum study. Encouraging us at Davis, despite the resignation of the former dean, was a new associate dean employed to create a program in community development. Through his offices, new funding became available for this study. With this support it was feasible to undertake a projective study[4] of mechanized lettuce harvesting and to begin planning for future research on grapes and citrus.

Unlike the study with tomatoes which involved interviewing principals who had developed the system, studying extant data and materials, and participation in harvest activities by students, the lettuce study required an understanding of the ante-factum system. This meant, for example, that interviewing of principals would have to be very different. In the case of tomato mechanization, it was impossible to interview workers who had been harvesters prior to mechanization transition. These workers, with only few exceptions, had all been braceros, i.e., workers imported under contract from Mexico for specific harvests and periods of work. While many ex-braceros could be found working in California agriculture, to locate them for interviews would have been very difficult. Nor would it have been very useful to interview them about conditions under which they had worked almost ten years previously.

In contrast, it was relatively easy to interview currently employed lechugeros (lettuce workers). Unlike our experience in tomato harvesting, however, it was impossible to find field employment for students with the lettuce-harvest crews[5] because the social organization of lettuce production is very different from that of tomato harvesting. In lettuce

production, harvest crews are essentially self-re-
cruited, self-directed, and autonomous. There are
supervisors, of course, and they play roles in the
production process, but these are far more limited
than in tomato harvesting. Moreover, the lettuce industry is very highly organized and concentrated; it
constitutes more of an enclave system than exists in
processing tomatoes. Ever since it was founded in
the 1920s, the industry has required far greater co-
ordination in production and distribution than is
found in a commodity intended for processing.

In preparing a social impact assessment of the
potential transition to mechanized harvesting in lettuce, we confronted three problems. First, we had to
grasp the industry as it existed and how it had
evolved to its present complexity. Second, it was
necessary to formulate an understanding of the conditions precipitating mechanization. Third, we had
to project the social consequences of a transition
that had not yet moved beyond the R&D phase.

The lettuce research continued in fits and
starts because of interruptions in funding and competing academic demands. Not until we obtained funding from the National Science Foundation's (NSF) program in Ethics and Values in Science and Technology
(EVIST) were adequate resources available to complete
the study. As part of the NSF proposal, we created
the Project on SIA and Values (PSIAV) at the University of California, Santa Cruz. This was to be the
project name under which we would continue and conclude the lettuce research, and undertake the grapes
and citrus studies.

While much of the lettuce research had been completed under Davis sponsorship, NSF funding not only
permitted the completion of the research but the establishment of a procedure in which we could expose
the draft manuscript to a series of lettuce "constituencies." These included lettuce grower-shippers,
lettuce-union officials, lettuce workers, lettuce
consumers, and scientists involved with lettuce (and
agricultural) research. One intended meeting with
university officials proved to be a failure when only
one person showed up. But a final joint conference
of all the constituencies involved almost twenty-five
persons. Perhaps the most interesting session was a
bilingual one in which lechugeros were given a summary of the report in Spanish and had an opportunity
to react to it in a full-day's session. Simultaneous
translation was dogged by technical problems in the
equipment and the difficulties of using Spanish-
speaking academics whose knowledge did not include

any of the technical aspects of lettuce production;
the lettuce workers introduced our translators to a
galaxy of new technical terminology.

We used the constituency meetings and the general conference to elucidate various issues including
a number of values questions. One thing became clear
almost at the outset: the higher up one went in the
university bureaucracy, the broader was the vision,
but there was no impetus or incentive to deal with
constituency issues other than those with which the
university was familiar. Thus, neither unions, nor
workers, nor consumers played any significant role in
anyone's thinking. To the extent that such constituencies had been addressed, it had taken the form of
a thrust to develop mechanized harvesting procedures. Subsequently, university research was to be
initiated to develop managerial skills, but this research too has taken an exclusively grower viewpoint,
being concerned exclusively with the management of
labor, with no attention being given to workers'
viewpoints or to their unions.

The constituency meetings and the conference
proved valuable in exposing the draft to groupings
with intense knowledge about discrete aspects of the
industry. Grower-shipper representatives were able
to explain aspects of the production process that we
had not covered adequately. Similarly, the union
representatives presented data specific to their organizational locations. The lechugeros introduced
facts regarding the work process that were un-
matched. The resultant monograph, Manufacturing
Green Gold (Friedland, Barton, and Thomas, 1978), was
issued through the auspices of the Department of Applied Behavioral Sciences at Davis.

This form of departmental publication provided
us with several opportunities. First, as the monograph circulated, it generated discussions that
pressed us to move the research to a comparative
frame of reference more rapidly. Largely as a result
of the reaction to Manufacturing Green Gold, we began, along with a number of others (primarily but not
exclusively in rural sociology departments), to talk
about an emergent sociology or political economy of
agriculture.[6] Second, questions began to be raised
as to why sociology as a discipline had so thoroughly
ignored agriculture. While it was clear that industrial sociologists and sociologists of work could
have studied agricultural problems, it was equally
clear that they had eschewed such research with a
vigor almost equivalent to that of the rural sociologists. We therefore saw the opportunity to reach a

broader audience of sociologists through the Rose
Monograph series of the American Sociological Association.

Exposing the monograph to the editorial committee of the Rose Monographs proved to be rather un-
nerving because of its mixed response. While some
members of the committee were interested in the lettuce material, others failed to see the relevance of
a study of a small (though valuable in terms of dollars), obscure industrial system. The criticism by
members of the committee and their outside readers
proved to be valuable in that it forced us to system-
atize our approach to the sociology of agriculture.
This became the foundation not only for revisions to
the lettuce study but to the developing research in
grapes and citrus. Extensively revised and expanded,
Manufacturing Green Gold (Friedland, Barton, and
Thomas, 1981) was published by Cambridge University
Press in the Rose Monograph series.

While the research phase of the lettuce study
was nearing completion, a two-student contingent
(Anne Fredricks and Tim Kappel) was recruited to a
new second-curriculum project. These students provided a bridge between the lettuce study and the succeeding grapes study. One of the students, Anne
Fredricks, prepared a senior thesis in the form of an
organizational analysis of Bud Antle, Inc., one of
the two or three largest lettuce firms and the one
with the longest history in technological
innovation. This study is reported in chapter 17 of
the present volume.

Yet another opportunity for follow-up research
developed through the University of California's Appropriate Technology Program. Looking for research
projects that were not simply technological but also
had a social dimension, Tim Kappel (the other student
in the second curriculum) and I developed a proposal
for a study on agricultural research priorities.

With sustained contributions from Amy Barton and
Anne Fredricks, Kappel and I produced a short monograph that expanded the earlier argument in Social
Sleepwalkers. The new study, Production or Perish
(Friedland and Kappel, 1979), augmented the argument
about the importance of developing SIA procedures in
publicly funded agricultural research. It went much
further, however. It recognized that, left to itself, there was little that would move the institutional monolith of the land-grant research system to
generate SIA research on changing agricultural technologies. Accordingly, we argued for the legislative
establishment of social goals for which the land-
grant research apparatus should be held accountable.

Such goals could include bringing to a constant level
the consumption of nonrenewable energy in agriculture, halting the decline in the number of farms, increasing the proportion of food produced by various
forms of self-production, obtaining a more equitable
distribution of income within agriculture, and holding constant or dropping the volume of chemicals applied in agriculture. Further, we proposed that the
funding of the university's agricultural research by
the state legislature be tied to attainment of these
goals. Thus, if certain goals were not achieved
within five, ten, or fifteen years, an increasing
percentage of the university's budget would be cut
and the funds put aside for research projects outside
the university that would fulfill the social goals.
Production or Perish (Friedland and Kappel,
1979) set out an SIA procedure and evaluative process, examined some of the problems implicit in such
a process based on experience with environmental impact assessment, and concluded with an analysis of
some of the problems that would have to be confronted
if the proposal were to be implemented. This short
monograph was published by the Project on Social
Impact Assessment and Values and was circulated in
appropriate-technology and agricultural-science circles, particularly in California. On the whole, some
interest was manifested in appropriate-technology
circles, but little response was generated among the
agriculturists. There was an early flurry of interest among some of the legislative aides in Sacramento, but this soon disappeared when criticism of
the agricultural-science system began to decline.

GRAPES AND BEYOND

The next study undertaken involved grapes. This
research marked the beginning of a departure from SIA
methods. Reflecting the programmatic concerns of the
NSF grant, we focused increasingly on the agricultural sciences and agricultural scientists, on the
one hand, and on the commodity system as a unit of
analysis, on the other.
The grapes study permitted the use of some SIA
approaches motivating our earlier studies on agricultural mechanization. The mechanized harvesting of
wine grapes represents a transition that has now been
underway for approximately a decade, and one that
will probably continue for a considerable time. Full
transition to mechanized harvesting of grapes for
wine production is probably not feasible, although it

is likely that the process will continue until a substantial proportion of the wine-grape harvest is conducted through mechanical means. Some varieties of grapes and some geophysical conditions of grape production, however, require hand harvest. Similarly, raisin grapes do not permit mechanized harvesting, although some aspects of the production process are passing through limited forms of mechanization. The harvesting of fresh table grapes by machine is unforeseeable at the present time.

The grapes study has emphasized for us the importance of the separateness and the interrelationship of agricultural commodity systems. Though all three major uses (wine, raisin, table) are derived from a single biological entity, and though many varieties of grapes (in particular, Thompson Seedless) are intermixed in actual usage, three distinct systems of production exist. None, however, can be considered in isolation. A shortfall of wine-variety grapes increases demand for Thompson Seedless which might otherwise go to the fresh market or to raisins; similarly, a surplus of fresh table grapes drops prices so that growers turn to raisining or the wineries to maximize income. Each commodity form entails sharply different activities, labor requirements, and risks.

In conducting the research on grapes, the SIA approach has proven to be of limited value. Each of the three uses is different in terms of the "maturity" of the system. Thus, raisin and table-grape production tend to be relatively stable and unchanging, although the former commodity is showing some tendencies toward technological change. Wine production shows the sharpest tendencies toward change because of the enormous increase in U.S. consumption and production. SIA methods have their greatest utility when things are changing, not when a system is stable or "mature."

This point has been strongly reinforced during the research on the final commodity group we have been researching, citrus.[7] Much of the change in this set of systems[8] is occurring in only one commodity form, frozen concentrated orange juice, and much of the significant change in this system is occurring outside the United States, in Brazil. SIA methods have been of relatively limited use under these circumstances.

210

CONCLUSION

SIA methodology for research in agricultural technological change has proven to be useful in several research projects. As a method, we have found SIA to have utility for both post-factum and projective purposes. Two important conclusions that can be drawn from our experiences are that SIA methods are most useful in circumstances of change and are of restricted utility in "stable" or "mature" situations; and that in applying SIA methodology, one is driven to consider the totality of a system and its interrelations with other systems.

In this latter respect, I have found that SIA methodology has emphasized a gestaltist approach for me, which stands in sharp contrast to the strong tendencies in positivistic science to consider singular phenomena in isolation from other phenomena. In addition, I would consider an SIA approach to simply constitute "good" social science, i.e., the kind of social science that ought to be done as a matter of professional respectability. SIA is not always useful and there are some circumstances in which one may not want to think in terms of how some social impacts will develop. In agriculture, on the whole, however, where technological change is fairly consistent, it is surprising that SIA has been as little used as it has. Considering that agriculture has been a major locus for adoption-diffusion research, rural sociologists might have used SIA methodology with greater frequency. Perhaps, by virtue of the fact that SIA calls attention to the need for policy development (since technological change produces change in social organization), rural sociologists have felt somewhat uncomfortable with the approach.

Finally, it should be noted that, while the research activities involving undergraduate instruction explicitly sought to develop a breadth of research approaches, several cohorts of students were introduced to SIA and can be expected to be oriented to this methodology in the future.

NOTES

Support for the research reported is acknowledged to several agencies of the University of California including the Faculty Committee on Research at Santa Cruz, the Agricultural Experiment Station at Davis, and the Appropriate Technology Program of the University of California; and the Program on Ethics

211

and Values in Science and Technology of the National
Science Foundation, Grant No. OSS78-24814. The opinions, findings, and conclusions are those of the author and do not necessarily reflect the views of any
of the sponsoring agencies. The editorial support of
Janet Burton is also appreciated.

1. Although environmental impact assessment had
already begun to blossom, the social impact variety
was still, at best, in seedling stage. The first major publication on this subject (Finsterbusch and
Wolf, 1977) was not to appear for another four years.

2. A second senior thesis was completed after
several years of delay by Vicki Bolam. This involved
a multimedia treatment of the tomato research. Of
the four undergraduates who began the second-curriculum project on the tomatoes research, two decided
that the subject was too specialized and did not complete the project. Bob Thomas, the first student to
complete his senior thesis through the second curriculum, subsequently became deeply involved in the lettuce research and coauthor of the lettuce monograph.

3. As a practical research matter, this proved
to be beyond our resources. We did not have sufficient funding to pursue the consequences of the mechanization transition into the packing sheds where the
tomatoes were processed. Conceptually we recognized
the need to follow the tomatoes through to the consumer, but were never able to complete this phase of
the research.

4. Conceptual terminology gave us considerable
problems. We had originally been talking about an
ante-factum study as "predictive" but were increasingly uncomfortable with the term which seemed, in
the literature, to imply a level of accuracy that we
were not attempting to accomplish. Ultimately we
dropped the term "predictive" and used "projective"
as a way of indicating general parameters of our projections rather than any intended specific predictions.

5. At the beginning of the lettuce study, I did
not actually have a second-curriculum project operating and therefore had no undergraduate participants
to begin with. As the study progressed, a small co-
hort of two students was recruited. They participated in the final stages of the lettuce study and in
the grapes research that followed.

6. This also led me to focus some personal research on rural sociology as a body of knowledge, and
to raise questions as to why rural sociologists knew
more about agriculture and land tenure outside the
United States than inside it; I subsequently prepared

several papers dealing with these issues (Friedland, 1979, 1982).

7. A final group of four students, Suzanne Ludlum, Ayn Schmit, Catherine Sonquist, and Vincent Valvano, were involved in the second-curriculum project on citrus.

8. Even a single commodity such as oranges forms two distinct commodity systems, with a sharp differentiation between production for the fresh market (centered mainly in California) and for juices, especially frozen concentrated orange juice, which is located primarily in Florida. Lemons constitute a distinctive system, as does grapefruit, both for fresh market and for processing as juice.

15
Sustained Land Productivity: Equity Consequences of Alternative Agricultural Technologies

Charles C. Geisler, J. Tadlock Cowan, Michael R. Hattery, Harvey M. Jacobs

The analysis reported here, conducted for the Office of Technology Assessment (OTA) of the U.S. Congress, investigated a series of social-equity problems associated with changing agricultural technologies. Three agricultural technologies were examined for their contribution to sustained land productivity and their implications for social equity: (1) center-pivot irrigation, (2) no-till agriculture, and (3) organic farming. The authors suggest that the U.S. agricultural system manifests certain social inequities. By its almost exclusive reliance on economic efficiency and conventional productivity criteria, current agricultural technology is biased against social equity for small farmers and rural communities. Simultaneously, the system masks growing threats to soil and water resources which--being central to community sustenance--are viewed here as social indicators.

INTRODUCTION

The contribution of technology to changing social well-being is complex, dynamic, and poorly delineated. Isolating the social impacts of agricultural technology is challenging and requires a

Edited and excerpted from the Cornell Rural Sociology Bulletin Series, No. 19, Cornell University, Ithaca, NY, February 1981.

214

willingness to rethink long-term "human-land" relationships. Implicitly, this requires a reformulation
of much that has been previously analyzed as well as,
by extension, much that has been left unanalyzed in
the American agricultural system. It is the purpose
of this paper to describe the social-equity impacts
that result, or are likely to result, from changes in
agricultural technology. More specifically, this paper focuses on the social effect of agricultural
technologies that affect the sustainable productivity
of U.S. croplands and rangelands.

In this report the distinctive emphasis on sustainable productivity is important because there are
other definitions of productivity. Conventional productivity in agriculture has meant the continued
ability to increase yields while decreasing the
amount of labor used in the production process. According to these criteria, the U.S. system has been
extremely successful. As of the late 1970s, 3 percent of the U.S. population grew most of the food
which fed the rest of this country, and provided more
than 86 percent of the world's surplus food. Since
the end of World War II, total farm output has increased by more than 50 percent, while output per
unit of labor has increased more than 250 percent.
Today a single U.S. farm worker feeds close to fifty
people, in contrast to 1950 when the same farm worker
fed only fifteen people.

However, these figures do not say whether these
production outputs can be sustained or increased in
the future to meet growing food demands in the United
States and abroad. For the purpose of this report,
sustainable productivity in agriculture is defined as
the retention of the natural capital stock of the agricultural production process, i.e., soil depth and
health, water reserves and quality, and energy stocks
and options. The assumption used here is that if
these natural elements are retained in the system,
productivity can be sustained. But if one or more of
these elements become unavailable, sustained productivity will be extremely difficult, if not impossible.

. . .

The response among Americans to foreboding projections of this nature will surely be tempered by
the successful historical experience in the United
States with technological innovation. The National
Academy of Sciences (1975) has warned, however, that
the bounty afforded by technological improvements may

soon run its course. The findings of the current
study suggest that massive injections of capital-
intensive technology into the U.S. food and fiber
production system may in fact be masking the rise of
unsustainable production, even at present levels of
output, while also incurring a complex array of inequitable consequences for rural people and communities.

In addition to the term productivity, two other
terms used in this report must be defined at the outset. The term technology is used broadly to mean
"applied knowledge in the social and political context in which it is employed" (Bereano, 1974:6).
That is, technology is not an island unto itself.
Technological changes do not occur without changes in
the social and political system into which a technology is introduced. Applied to agriculture, technology does not simply mean a mechanical device, such as
a tractor or picking machine, but rather an entire
complex or system of production. Technological
changes in agricultural systems have implications for
the inputs and outputs of agricultural production.
The former include labor, land, and capital requirements. The latter involve the quantity and quality
of food and retention (sustainability) of the productive elements of the production process.

The term social equity is used to denote two
separate but interrelated issues--equality of access
to decision processes, and justice in the substantive
outcome of policy action. In actual application,
this term comprises equity to those in the future, or
intergenerational equity, and equity to those in the
present, or temporal equity (Jacobs, 1980). Here intergenerational equity will mean the maintenance of
the natural capital stock of the agricultural production process. Intergenerational equity is therefore equivalent to agricultural sustainability. Temporal equity will mean the fairness of policy to
present persons and groups. For the purpose of this
report, temporal equity specifically encompasses issues of tenure (the concentration or decentralization
of control over land resources), environmental
health, local economic multipliers, and the viability
of local community institutions. This definition is
consistent with the requirement placed on the authors
by OTA of assessing social equity among those people
and communities living in the immediate area in which
the technology is introduced. More macro issues of
social equity, such as food costs to consumers at the
supermarket and impacts on foreign trade, are not
treated here in systematic fashion.

This report treats three examples of agricultural technology with known impacts on land productivity and social equity. One of the cases is a now-common technology, center-pivot irrigation. Two of the cases are on emerging technologies--no-till agriculture and organic farming. Each case contains a statement of background and history, identification of equity effects, a discussion of relevant public policies, and a summary statement of the key equity issues raised by the technology. These technologies were chosen because they represent a range of technology types, with a range of sustainability and social-equity impacts. Together they also cover a range of geographical areas.[1]

. . .

CASE STUDY: CENTER-PIVOT IRRIGATION

Background

Center-pivot irrigation (CPI) is a highly capital- and energy-intensive agricultural technology, currently in use in thirty-eight of the fifty states (Servin, 1979). The diffusion of CPI in recent years has substantially added to crop yields in the United States and, in so doing, has "literally moved the Corn Belt from eastern Nebraska to the Rocky Mountains" (Splinter, 1979a:42). The existing research and literature on the relationship between CPI and social equity is minimal. Some initial analysis has been conducted for the Sandhills region of Nebraska (Holt County in particular) and for the Columbia Basin of Washington and Oregon. The assessment of social equity will be limited, in general, to the case materials for these two areas.

History

CPI was one in a series of significant irrigation innovations evolving since World War II. These innovations were based upon the advent of rotating sprinkler nozzles and the availability of comparatively cheap aluminum pipe. An important feature of CPI, within the context of the historical development of irrigation technology, is that it dramatically reduces labor inputs and costs. This tremendous reduction in the labor intensity of CPI technology distinguishes it from the pattern of increased employment associated with other irrigation technologies (Stone, 1977).

In addition to automation, two other important
features underlie CPI's adoption. First, such systems apply water frequently and lightly, thus minimizing soil erosion and enabling increased production
on coarse-textured or sandy soils that hold little
water and often have minimal capacity for soil nutrients. Nutrients and other crop applications can be
added to the sprayed irrigation water, and the light,
frequent spraying maintains appropriate soil moisture. Second, the mobile CPI arm can adjust to
grades of up to 30 percent. Thus, land that is usually too costly or fragile to grade (change the slope
of) and therefore unfeasible to irrigate by other
methods can now be productive. Studies in Nebraska
(Center for Rural Affairs, 1976; Stone, 1977) and in
the Columbia Basin of Oregon and Washington (Muckleston and Highsmith, 1978) point to the rapid adoption
of CPI with the goal of converting low-grade, often
rolling, grazing land into productive irrigated
units.

Intergenerational Equity

In Nebraska, what was seen as an abundant under-
ground water resource for CPI as recently as a decade
ago is now subject to concerted water-management
planning. CPI has contributed to severe water-table
drops and "aquifer mining," depleting a nonrenewable
stock of water. Such aquifer mining is occurring in
Nebraska, Kansas, Texas, Colorado, New Mexico, and
other states. According to Splinter (1979a:42),
"there is not much hope for recharge in many of these
areas, and once the water table is depleted, it will
force farmers back to dry land production." Inadequate supplies of water have already resulted in crop
failures for land under CPI (Council on Environmental
Quality, 1978). Energy use of CPI in Nebraska indicates that CPI uses ten times the fuel needed to
till, plant, cultivate, and harvest a crop such as
corn (Splinter, 1977) as conventional agriculture.
The use of CPI also has important implications
for maintenance of soil quantity and quality. As noted above, a threat to area water flows can undermine
the continued operation of CPI and the attendant increased yields. Therefore, the effects of CPI on
soil erosion and soil quality are important when and
if lands are returned to dryland or other non-CPI
forms of production. The Center for Rural Affairs
(1976) notes that CPI technology has not been in use
long enough for a long-range analysis of its effects

on soil. However, its report points up several important trends observed in an examination of CPI in Holt County, Nebraska.

The increase in CPI-irrigated areas in Nebraska could produce a drop in the percent of acres under irrigation which are arable. This is a noteworthy development from the standpoint of landscape changes (and therefore sustainability). The eight-foot-high rotating irrigation arm requires the removal of many normal features of the landscape, including treelines that aid in soil conservation. Replacement of treelines would require substantial investments when reversion to dryland farming becomes necessary. In the interim, during the growth of the tree line, substantial soil erosion could occur.

Another important feature is the rise of investor-owned CPI operations. Center for Rural Affairs' research indicates that the investors' share of the nonarable land being irrigated increased from 27 percent in 1974 to 52 percent in 1975, and might have gone as high as 67 percent in the following years (based upon applications for permits, etc.). The soil type in Holt County undergoing most rapid development by the investor-owners was considered by the United States Soil Conservation Service to be "suitable only for grass, trees or wildlife. . ." (USDA, 1963:16). As the rapid recent growth in CPI is increasingly investor-owned, this trend may indicate an increasing tendency toward less sensitivity to important soil and environmental characteristics. Over time this could adversely affect the sustained yield capabilities of lower-quality soils. A recent report by the Economics, Statistics, and Cooperatives Service of the U.S. Department of Agriculture (USDA) which dealt with investment in soil conservation, drainage, and irrigation in the United States found that soil and water conservation improvements are declining in the United States while expenditures on irrigation improvements are increasing (USDA, 1979).

Temporal Equity

The resource intensity and the increased pattern of absentee/corporate investment are the two major sources of interest in evaluating CPI's temporal-equity effects.

Size Neutrality

The effects of absentee investment mechanisms and ownership have led to increased size of landholdings and changes in tenure patterns. Some 96

percent of owner-operators in Holt County own four or
fewer pivots (Center for Rural Affairs, 1976). Only
56 percent of the investor-owners, on the other hand,
were in this category, and one investor owned 127
pivots.

Tenure

Perhaps the most important social consequence of
CPI is the change in ownership and ultimate control
of land and production that has occurred because of
the high-cost financial packaging and low labor intensity surrounding or characterizing the technology. The financial barriers for the normal operator
to adopt CPI are formidable. The initial capital investment can normally run well over $61,000 for a
single pivot unit, and estimates of annual fixed and
variable costs (1976 figures) total $46,500 per 160-
acre section of corn (Sheffield, 1977:20-21). Thus,
while in the early days of CPI, farm operators were
the principal adopters of the technology, the situation has rapidly evolved to the point where most new
investment in CPI is done by off-farm and absentee
investors, who also buy land and make use of the investment to shelter income. The increase in absentee
control of land and production has increased the role
of hired farm labor and tenant farming where CPI is
used (Center for Rural Affairs, 1976).

Economic and Labor Multipliers

The direct economic benefits of CPI are substantial. In Nebraska, CPI has increased yields of corn
by 100 bushels per acre in comparison with dryland
production. Using capital investment multipliers,
the total economic impact of CPI investment on the
Nebraska economy in 1976 was estimated to be $223.7
million (Sheffield, 1977). On-farm labor demand differs significantly from the high capital multipliers,
however. The labor required to operate land under
CPI is one-half or less the labor required to manage
equivalent acreage with surface or gravity irrigation.

Community Structure and Impact

In the Columbia Basin region of Washington and
Oregon, water for CPI is drawn directly from the
Snake and Columbia rivers. Here, the energy impacts
are somewhat different than in areas where ground-
water sources are used (Muckleston and Highsmith,

1978). By drawing down the flow of river water, adoption of CPI has decreased the electrical generating capabilities of downstream hydroelectric plants. This lost hydro power increases demand for higher-cost thermoelectric generation, which in turn increases electricity costs to area consumers.

Moreover, because CPI uses such high volumes of electricity, it qualifies for lower rates. Whittelsey et al. (1976) estimated that the net annual cost of this rate disparity for every acre of land irrigated (in a specific region of the Columbia Basin known as Horse Heaven Hills) would be about $60 for other area energy consumers.

In its historical context, the effects of CPI on farm size and population are not typical of old-style irrigation technologies. Intensification of production through traditional irrigation in Great Plains communities has allowed farm size to remain smaller and farm population to remain larger than in nonirrigated areas (Stone, 1977). The increase in the number of CPI adopters has been concurrent with relatively rapid growth in the size of individual irrigated farms in Holt County, Nebraska. Stone (1977) therefore observes:

> Had there never been a center pivot machine, other sprinkler types would no doubt have eventually occupied much of the same landscape, but hardly as an attraction for an investor or an absentee owner. Investor-operators would have been tempted to farm with the smaller-scale, labor-requiring sprinkler. Growth of the irrigation economy would likely have been slower, and would probably have remained in the hands of the small farmer.

These results would indicate that, in comparison with other irrigation technologies, CPI could have more adverse impacts on local community viability (Goldschmidt, 1978). In particular, the CPI bias against a small-farm structure could erode local economic multipliers and the viability of community institutions.

Public Policy

To our knowledge, there is no specific national public policy concerning CPI. It is noteworthy, however, that in several states—particularly Washington, Nebraska, and Oregon—public policy initiatives have been put forth to monitor or regulate some aspect of CPI's extensive resource use. In the state of Washington, a family farm act has been passed that limits permanent water rights to family-owned units not exceeding 2,000 irrigated acres per person in the farming family (Muckleston and Highsmith, 1978).

Summary

CPI has led to dramatic increases in per-acre production yields. These increased yields are dependent on high levels of water, energy, and capital usage. Because of certain constraints on long-term water and energy availability, it is presumptuous to consider the increased yield made possible by CPI as "sustainable." In certain contexts, such as the Columbia Basin of Washington, CPI has had clear adverse impacts on the surrounding region and communities. In terms of the structure of agricultural production, CPI is increasingly dominated by corporate owners external to the community, which in turn contributes to real change in the social relationship between people and land as well as in the size and distribution of farm parcels. CPI appears to have thrived on an absence of local or regional policy that would regulate or monitor the large-scale appropriation of water, land, soils, and energy resources.

CASE STUDY: NO-TILL AGRICULTURE

Background and History

No-tillage agriculture is one of the oldest methods of crop production. No-tillage represents a family of related terms—zero-till, direct seeding, direct planting, no-plow, and spray-plant-harvest. Under a no-till system, a crop is planted either entirely without tillage or with the least tillage necessary to allow placement and coverage of the seeds with soil sufficient to allow them to germinate and emerge (Phillips et al., 1980). No soil preparation is done other than that of opening a trench of adequate width and depth to obtain seed coverage (Phillips and Young, 1973). No Till Farmer magazine defines no-tillage as cultivation where only the seed zone and up to 25 percent of the land surface area is worked (USDA, 1975a).

No-till agriculture contrasts sharply with conventional tillage practices. For centuries farmers have developed myriad practices of plowing, smoothing, and pulverizing the soil, principally through

use of the moldboard plow followed by several disc-
ings. Such "complete tillage," thought necessary to
control weeds, manage field trash, aerate the soil,
and aid normal root development, was supported by
generations of practice (Phillips and Young, 1973).
Fifty to sixty years ago farmers thought four to five
cultivations after row planting were essential; making, in all, some ten trips across a tilled field by
harvest time (Triplett and Van Doren, 1977).

In 1943, E. H. Faulkner's book, Plowman's Folly,
appeared. In the wake of the dust bowl, Faulkner
criticized the plow as the basis of most if not all
problems related to soil quality and crop production. Indeed, he argued that "no one has ever advanced a scientific reason for plowing" (Faulkner,
1943). The book was both widely praised and criticized within the ranks of organized agriculture
(Friends of the Land, 1943; Truog, 1944) and had the
effect of subjecting conventional tillage to more
critical evaluation. The book's most controversial
proposition--that plowing was unnecessary--supported
growing concern that conventional agricultural practices exposed soil to severe erosion from wind and
water.

Increasing awareness that conventional tillage
threatened the finite resource of soil coincided with
the introduction of herbicides in the late 1940s. It
was the introduction of 2, 4-d in the late 1940s that
proved a solution to the broadleaf weed problems in
corn production. By controlling perennial weeds,
herbicides reduced the need for multiple tilling operations and made reduced tilling practices more
widely accepted. This chemical revolution, in conjunction with the constant market pressure to cut
production costs, brought about a reevaluation of
time-honored tillage practices.

Since the mid-1950s, the land area for row and
forage crops in no-till has increased rapidly. In
1974, the USDA estimated that U.S. cropland under no-
tillage was 5.5 million acres and that by the year
2000 nearly 45 percent of U.S. cropland will be no-
till (USDA, 1975a). An estimated 65 percent of the
seven major annual crops (corn, soybeans, sorghum,
wheat, oats, barley, and rye) will be grown under no-
till by 2000 and nearly 78 percent by 2010 (Phillips
et al., 1980). Thus it has been stated that

> no-tillage systems of husbandry could con-
> ceivably facilitate an increase in food produc-
> tion comparable to that made possible by the
> shift from animal power to machine power in

agriculture that occurred in the United States during the last half-century. (Shear, 1968)

The potential for multicropping may well be the most important factor in no-till agriculture acceptance. Formerly considered a practice available only to farmers in the Southeast, multicropping is now moving to the northern Corn Belt of the United States (Phillips and Young, 1973; USDA, 1975a). Under no-till, harvesting of one crop can be followed by immediate planting of the next crop. Corn-small grain for silage, corn-barley for grain, and corn-barley-sorghum are some combinations of multicropping possible under no-till. Getting two or more crops, although not confined to no-till, is enhanced by the reduced time required to plant following harvest (USDA, 1975a). This enhanced opportunity to multicrop could also compensate for any loss in yield under no-till agriculture with certain soil types (USDA, 1975a).[2]

Conventional methods of tillage require considerable expenditures of energy. Currently, about one-third of the energy used for food production is consumed in the crop-production phase, that is, plowing, discing, planting, and cultivating (Phillips et al., 1980). Under conventional moldboard plowing and discing, an average of almost 200 gallons of diesel fuel per 100 acres is not unusual. In contrast, no-till estimates average less than 50 gallons of fuel per 100 acres (Triplett and Van Doren, 1977). Despite these estimates, energy savings are dependent on a variety of factors, including type of crop; fertilizer; herbicide use; and the match between tractor, equipment, and field size. Although no-till does save fuel, it may require greater expenditures for fertilizer, seeds, and chemicals. Because farmers are primarily concerned with total production costs, the fuel-savings feature of no-till may not be perceived as a major net advantage.

A review of the research literature concerned with reduced tillage speaks almost exclusively of such issues as erosion control, crop yields, energy consumption, and herbicide/insecticide use. With few exceptions, the social aspects of no-tillage agriculture have scarcely been investigated. Considering the relatively advanced state of current no-till adoption, as well as estimates for expanding the amount of land under no-till by the year 2000, the lack of social-impact investigations of no-till on the sustained productivity of U.S. farmland is a significant gap in the nation's knowledge of this expanding technology.

Intergenerational Equity

Soil erosion and soil compaction increase as tillage increases and as plant cover decreases. There is strong research evidence that no-tillage agriculture reduces erosion to practically zero where surface mulch of two to four tons per acre is used (Harold, 1972). Other researchers have found that no-till reduces soil erosion by as much as fifty-fold over conventional tillage (Phillips et al., 1980). On slopes of up to 15 percent, no-till methods have reduced erosion to nearly zero. This would appear favorable to erosion reduction and sustained-yield agriculture, but no-till could conceivably facilitate the cultivation of slopes or rangeland for which long-term cultivation is ill advised.

Reducing soil erosion from wind and water is vital to sustained land productivity, and also has implications for reducing pollution of water supplies. Farmers have been increasing the use of herbicides and insecticides for the past several decades. An estimated increase of 300 million pounds by the year 2000 will be required to be consistent with USDA projections for no-till increase (USDA, 1975a). Because this increase in pesticides will occur largely on the seven major annual crops, severe environmental problems could result. However, the adverse effects of pesticide pollution of water supplies is partially a function of the amount of runoff from treated acres. With the decline in water runoff and subsequent erosion, the transport of pollutants is reduced. Most of the persistent pesticides are strongly attached to soil particles so that a reduction in erosion will likely translate to a reduction in pesticide pollution of water supplies (Hahn, 1971).

There is a question of soil exhaustion raised by multicropping under no-till, although research evidence is limited. It is reasonable to question whether, with enhanced capability for multicropping, needed fallowing periods will be neglected in favor of increased fertilizing. For example, soybeans are a typical second crop in the United States, and have demanding nutritive requirements of the soil. In 1969 nearly two million total acres were double-cropped with almost all soybean production under a no-till system (USDA, 1975a). In other words, a technology with broad potential for intergenerational inequity could, depending on national priorities, merely expedite monocultural agriculture and other soil-jeopardizing practices.

Temporal Equity

Research to date implies that no-till methods are size-neutral, i.e., they do not benefit large farmers more than they benefit small farmers. There is, though, room for speculation about the validity of such an assumption.

Whether a switch to no-till is financially attractive to a farmer is influenced by initial investment costs. For example, a new no-till planter costs slightly more than a conventional one. The decision to buy is partially related to credit available to small farmers and to whether the opportunity costs for labor are low. Part-time and small farmers' labor opportunity costs are generally lower and their access to credit more restricted than is true for large farmers (Perelman, 1977). It is questionable whether labor savings offered by no-till are sufficiently attractive to the small farmer to encourage a move into no-till. All other things being equal, larger farmers may find the labor savings attractive enough to offset the costs of switching to no-till (Choi and Coughenour, 1978).

A change to no-till agriculture has other equity considerations significant to local farmers and farming communities. Although empirical support is tenuous, no-till adoption does raise questions about farm tenure changes, no-till's contribution to crop specialization trends, and increases in farm size. In a recent single-county case study of Kentucky farmers who had adopted no-till methods, early adopters of no-till had enlarged their farming operations over time--generally by renting additional lands (Choi and Coughenour, 1978). Smaller farmers tended to specialize in tobacco products and to use conventional tillage, while larger operators incorporated no-till and specialized in cash-grain crops. Part-owner operators were more reluctant to give up tobacco raising than were full-owner operators, suggesting that the risks associated with changing to no-till and grain, at the same time forgoing the security of a tobacco income, were greater for part-owners than for full-owner operators (Choi and Coughenour, 1978).

The exact role of no-till in differential land-ownership and land use is ambiguous in the absence of further research. As with any new technology, no-till presents immediate farm-management problems that qualify its contribution to social equity. No-till requires considerably more management expertise than conventional agriculture, including a greater knowledge of soil characteristics and a more detailed knowledge of the proper use of farm chemicals. No-till farmers must be more concerned than conventional farmers with selection of crop varieties, planting depth, seeding rates, and crop-residue management. It is therefore arguable that competency in mastering no-till techniques is directly related to educational level (Choi and Coughenour, 1978). Under these circumstances, it is not surprising that smaller, often less educated operators are at a disadvantage in the use of no-till methods while larger, better educated operators have an advantage.

Public Policy

There has been no enabling legislation specifically facilitating no-till adoption, though public policy exists that makes no-till extremely relevant to intergenerational equity as defined here. The USDA spends several hundred million dollars annually on various soil-conservation programs. The most promising piece of legislation for erosion control in some time is Section 208 of the Clean Water Act of 1972. While there are currently no mandatory controls on pollution, each state, under this legislation, is required to submit a plan to the Environmental Protection Agency for controlling pollution from all sources, including farmland.

As mentioned earlier, much ground- and surface-water pollution originates from nonpoint runoff from pesticide- and fertilizer-laden farmland. If voluntary efforts to reduce nonpoint pollution fail, regulations may eventually be imposed setting fertilizer and pesticide use restrictions. In that event, no-till agriculture could offer one of the best ways of achieving erosion control while maintaining current productivity levels. It is also conceivable that Congress could require sound erosion-control measures as a condition for future farm subsidy programs administered by USDA.

Summary

Evidence is strong that, where adopted on lands that have been in conventional tillage, no-till is a superior technology for reducing erosion and maintaining a high soil moisture level, thus controlling runoff and soil-borne pollutants. There is some question whether the increased pesticide use often accompanying no-till methods has implications for altering soil quality over time. In addition, successive multicropping under no-till agriculture raises questions about the possibility of soil exhaustion and the overburdening of marginal lands. There is also initial evidence that no-till may not be a size-neutral technology, contrary to popular belief. The proportionately greater risk associated with farm-production failure may be less of a problem to the large farmer. Further, in the absence of public policies correcting information differences, the relatively demanding farm-management problems under no-till may favor larger, better educated operators with better access to extension and related services.

CASE STUDY: ORGANIC FARMING

Background and History

Organic farming, like no-till agriculture, is a whole system of agricultural productivity. As a system of production, and a system that stands as an explicit alternative to so-called conventional agriculture (Rodale, 1980a), it can have completely different implications for the inputs of production--machinery size and use, labor needs, soil and water use and retention, and fertilizer type and application--and for the outputs of production--food quantity and quality.[3] In a recent study report on organic agriculture, the United States Department of Agriculture defined organic farming as follows:

Organic farming is a production system which avoids or largely excludes the use of synthetically compounded fertilizers, pesticides, growth regulators, and livestock feed additives. To the maximum extent feasible, organic farming systems rely upon crop rotations, crop residues, animal manures, legumes, green manures, off-farm organic wastes, mechanical cultivation, mineral-bearing rocks, and aspects of biological pest control to maintain soil productivity and tilth, to supply plant nutrients and to control insects, weeds and other pests. (USDA, 1980b:xii)

Modern organic farming originated with the work of Sir Albert Howard in England in the 1930s. Howard advocated greater attention to soil, the environment of growth, rather than to plants, the product of growth. For Howard, soil was capital which, if wasted, ceased to render crop dividends. Howard developed composting practices to replenish the soil and emphasized a holistic approach to food production, distribution, and consumption (Oelhaf, 1978).

Organic "technologies" thus concentrate on soil development, whereas conventional agricultural technologies focus on the end product, plant development. Organic farmers tend to avoid monoculture production practices--the planting of a large amount of a single crop for successive years--as antithetical to successful soil building. In combination with mixed planting and crop-rotation practices, this leads to long-term production security for the farmer. Among organic farmers this offsets any decrease in yearly income which may result from switching to organic farming methods (Oelhaf, 1978).[4,5]

The current interest in organic farming (USDA, 1980b; Rodale, 1980a) arises from the most obvious shortcomings of conventional farming: the decline in soil productivity due to erosion and sterility, the questionable availability of water for irrigation in the future, the increasing costs and uncertain availability of energy and energy-related products, and the cumulative effects of these three factors on environmental quality, human and animal health, and the general demise of the family farm (USDA, 1980b; Crosson, 1979; Louis Harris and Associates, 1980).

Characteristics

Empirical studies on the composition and structure of organic farming are few and very region-specific. In terms of the total number of organic farmers, the USDA has estimated that at most 1 percent of all American farms are organic (USDA, 1980b). While there now is a registration system for organic farmers, it understates the adoption of organic technologies. In southern Minnesota in 1975 there were only 33 registered organic farmers; yet reliable estimates placed the actual number at closer to 300 (Oelhaf, 1978). More recently, Robert Rodale's organization did a survey of the 80,000 readers of New Farm magazine. Results would suggest that over 11,000 of the readers are complete organic farmers (though not all of these are full-time farmers), and that over 24,000 are mixed organic and conventional farmers (Data Probe, 1980).

The size of organic farms is extremely variable. The USDA study found farms ranging in size from 10 to 1,500 acres. A study in the Corn Belt matched organic and conventional farms for the purpose of comparing energy use. These farms averaged

429 acres in size and ranged from 175 to 844 acres
(Klepper et al., 1977). Full-time farmer respondents
to the Rodale survey farmed on the average 200 acres,
part-time farmers less than 30 acres (Data Probe,
1980). Organic farms are present in every region of
the United States, though there seem to be fewer organic farms in the South (USDA, 1980b).

Organic farming is much less energy-intensive
than conventional farming. Klepper et al. (1977)
found in their study of Corn Belt farms that organic
farms used 2.7 to 2.8 times less energy than conventional farms. This difference was highly correlated
with reduced use of inorganic fertilizer, and with
the conservation-farming methods of organic farmers
(Klepper et al., 1977).[6] Studies on the labor intensity of organic farming are mixed, but seem to indicate that organic farms are more labor-intensive than
conventional farms.

Organic farming is less capital-intensive than
conventional farming. This is particularly related
to the decreased use of petroleum-based production
inputs such as fertilizers, and to the decreased
amount of land planted in row crops which can require
petroleum-based field drying (USDA, 1980b). Lower
capital intensity leads to two other important characteristics of organic farmers. They tend to carry a
lower debt load than comparable conventional farmers
and, if the Rodale survey is representative of organic farmers in general, they own outright a higher
proportion of the land they farm (USDA, 1980b).

Finally, while the net crop yield per acre
planted is roughly equivalent for organic and conventional farms, the total farm output of equal-sized
farms is lower among organic farms. The reason for
this is that, as mentioned, organic farms plant less
land to crops because of their mixed crop-rotation
production practices.[7] Consequently, organic farmers' gross income is lower than that of conventional
farmers of similar size in the same region, though
their net income may be equal because of the lower
cost of production inputs (USDA, 1980b).

Intergenerational Equity

Organic farming is a system of sustainable agriculture that retains the natural-resource capital
stock necessary for future food production. Organic
farming practices build soil fertility, retard or
eliminate soil erosion, conserve water, reduce or
eliminate pollution and environmental health risks,
and reduce use of nonrenewable petroleum resources

(Oelhaf, 1978; USDA, 1980b). Organic farmers generally implement those types of farming practices that the USDA has recommended for the last fifty years as a way to bountifully provide food while sustaining food-production resources.

Temporal Equity

While organic farming exists on a wide variety of farm sizes, it is a system of production that can be said to be biased toward smaller production units. It is biased because of lower "barrier-to-entry costs," meaning that less capital is needed to get into organic farming (Oelhaf, 1978; USDA, 1980b). Related to the size neutrality of organic farming are its effects on land tenure. As noted, decreased capital needs for expensive petroleum-based products make it easier to enter and stay in organic farming (Lockeretz, Shearer, and Kohl, 1981). In addition, organic farmers are more stable because of their mixed planting practices, lower indebtedness levels, and higher landownership ratios (Oelhaf, 1978; USDA, 1980b).

Organic farming is much more healthful for the farmer, farm family, farm livestock, and area wildlife. Oelhaf notes that many organic farmers adopt organic methods specifically because of the adverse health impacts of pesticides associated with conventional farming (Oelhaf citing Wernick and Lockeretz, 1977; National Rural Health Council, 1980). "Such farmers express a sense of relief that they can allow their children to wander freely about the farm again" (Oelhaf, 1978:147).

While evidence is inconclusive, a system of organic farming is likely to require more farm labor (USDA, 1980b). Whether this would then translate into an economic and community multiplier is unclear. If it is assumed that a widely adopted organic system of agriculture would in fact be composed of smaller farms than the current system of production promotes, then studies such as those by agricultural economists Heady and Sonka (1974) and anthropologist Walter Goldschmidt (1946) suggest that a system of smaller farms would have significant local multipliers that would facilitate economically stronger and socially more viable local communities and their attendant institutions. Oelhaf suggests that changes that encourage organic farming would ultimately result in benefits for "the smaller, poorer, traditional, [and] poorly financed farmers" (Oelhaf, 1978:149).[8]

Public Policy

There is little federal, state, or local policy directly aimed at organic farming. On the other hand, a USDA study found examples of current policy in programs, designed to support conventional agriculture, which discriminate against organic producers. These examples include the local price-support program administered by the Agricultural Stabilization and Conservation Service. This program requires certain tillage practices and commercial fertilizer applications, and does not count protected grassland among lands eligible for price support. Also, USDA marketing orders are likely to discriminate against the cosmetic quality of organic food (USDA, 1980b).

The availability of credit is another policy area in which organic producers are at a disadvantage. Generally, financial institutions are reluctant to lend money for a farmer to convert to organic, though they willingly assist in a shift to conventional agriculture. Because of this, organic farmers, particularly smaller ones, are likely to pay more for their capital needs (Oelhaf, 1978; USDA, 1980b; Perelman, 1977). "For the most part those who have chosen to farm organically have done so in spite of financial incentives rather than because of them" (Oelhaf, 1978:146).

Summary

On the basis of net yield per acre, the quantitative output of organic farming is equivalent to that of conventional agriculture. If a national organic and gardening system were established, the shortfall in total output of crops and livestock need not be drastic. Ecologically speaking, organic farming effectively retains the capital stock of production: soil, water, and energy. Since organic farming does not require many of the petroleum-based inputs of conventional farming, it is a less capital-intensive farming method. Because of lower debt levels stemming in part from higher landownership ratios, organic farming is cheaper to get into and easier to stay in, though greater labor inputs are entailed. Organic farming can facilitate stable smaller farms, which have the potential for significantly contributing to local economic and social multipliers.

. . .

SUMMARY, CONCLUSIONS, RECOMMENDATIONS

Our purpose has been to examine the social consequences and equity implications of agricultural technology as they pertain to sustained land productivity. The conclusions which follow depend very much upon the definition of productivity used. The prevailing view of agricultural productivity or rangeland productivity draws attention exclusively to efficiency and returns on investment. Social consequences are accorded secondary consideration, as are those of the biological community upon which human communities depend. In the present review, by contrast, productivity is construed as long-term system sustainability wherein both present and future yields are of equal concern.

Soil and water are the "capital stock" of sustainable agriculture. Most present and past agricultural technology applications have embodied an efficiency/productivity bias, and have helped to deplete this societal capital. As a consequence, the renewability of our agricultural system from one generation to the next can no longer be taken for granted. Given the redefinition of productivity as sustainability, however, soil and water protection becomes a social indicator with important implications for future social impact assessment (SIA) of agricultural technologies.

Agriculture is a sociotechnical system of production and technological changes occurring within this context. It is this sociotechnical structure that preserves the efficiency orientation of conventional production and that selects technologies favoring large-scale producers. Acceptance of sustainability-oriented technologies presupposes contextual changes in the structure of agriculture, changes that are likely only with public-sector intervention.

Conclusions

The following conclusions emphasize (1) the key factors behind the equity/productivity/technology relationship, (2) the usefulness of SIA for evaluating the relationship, and (3) relevant survey research on public attitudes.

American agriculture is decreasingly productive in its present form, given a broader definition of productivity that encompasses both present and future social equity. We are abandoning sustained-yield agriculture for short-term productivity gains and for

an improved balance of payments. Concurrently, public opinion shows considerable support for soil conservation (sustainable agriculture), and for small
farm redevelopment (Louis Harris and Associates,
1980).

The spread or increased use of capital-intensive
agricultural technology is likely to have adverse
social-equity impacts at the local level. Such technology tends to favor large farm units and to deplete
or diminish basic human and natural resources. Thus,
while this may increase current benefits, it generally does so at the cost of temporal and intergenerational equity. Labor-intensive agricultural
technologies, like organic farming, are competitive
with their capital-intensive equivalent on a current
productivity basis, while simultaneously improving
social equity for small farmers and rural communities. The alleged trade-off between "productivity
and equity" therefore appears to be a false dichotomy.

The size neutrality (lack of farm-size bias) of
emergent technologies is ambiguous, given the effi-
ciency-productivity bias of capital-intensive technologies. To the extent that emergent technologies
do not undermine small-farm and small-community
viability, they are more apt to foster social equity.

There is genuine need for an unbiased approach
to social impact assessment of agricultural technology. The cost-benefit framework of traditional SIA
is inadequate for conducting social-equity analysis.
A body of social impact/evaluative studies exists
which is not bound by a narrow cost-benefit approach.* This alternative work begins to address
important social-equity issues and provides direction
for future SIA work on agricultural technology. . . .
Currently, there is a critical lack of public policy
for monitoring, anticipating, and making restitution
for the real and potential social consequences of
agricultural technology.

Recommendations

Research should be undertaken to investigate
more fully the theoretical and methodological implications of using social-equity concepts in SIA, especially in agriculture. These concepts take into
consideration both biological and social spheres in

---

*Ed. note: These studies appear in the original
bulletin from which this article is taken.

future as well as present time periods. Further
assessments of agricultural technologies are needed
integrating local, regional, and international social
equity.

SIAs should be prepared, using the social-equity
concept, on programmatic agricultural research in the
United States. A research project conducted at the
University of Nebraska Law School suggests that such
anticipatory evaluations might have helped in understanding the likely impact of center-pivot irrigation
on Nebraska localities (New Land Review, 1980). SIAs
should consider various technological alternatives,
as opposed to assessing the likely impacts of a
single option.

Evaluative research should be conducted on past
public programs which granted compensation, reset-
tlement, or other considerations in the wake of technological innovations in agriculture with social
impacts.

Survey research should be conducted which ex-
plores the relationships between social equity, technology, and land productivity. Existing opinion data
in related areas should be carefully reviewed for
relevance to these concerns, and new research should
be undertaken to illuminate public attitudes and perceptions toward the social consequence of technological innovations that impact land productivity.

The OTA and other federal agencies are encouraged to hold workshops concerning the issues raised
in this report--the shortcomings of existing SIA
theory and methodology; the potential utility of the
social-equity concept in the SIA process; and, more
generally, the social consequences of technological
innovations that impact land productivity. Meetings
which bring together the general public with profes-
sionals, academics, and SIA practitioners would provide a wealth of information, insight, and needed
public feedback on this topic of national interest.

NOTES

1. These studies were integrated into a final
report published by OTA (Office of Technology Assessment, 1982), which lists all commissioned technical
papers in an appendix.

2. Acceptance and adoption of no-till practices
has shown regional variation. In the southern half
of the eastern Corn Belt, no-till has been well received; but, in part because of differences in soil
types, adoption of no-till in the northern half has

been less widespread. Indeed, soil type and especially drainage are important considerations in the
degree to which no-till practices can be employed.
Research has indicated that poorly drained soils are
less suited to no-till than those that do drain well
(Phillips and Young, 1973).

3. In one of the principal scholarly works on
organic farming, economist Robert Oelhaf identified
four distinct subgroups to the organic-agriculture
movement: organic farming, biodynamic agriculture,
French intensive farming, and eco-agriculture. All
are organic in that they emphasize (1) the building
of soil over the direct feeding of plants, (2) the
general rejection of pesticides, and (3) the importance of measuring productivity in terms of food
quantity and quality. The rejection of pesticides by
organic farmers has to do not only with their inorganic nature but, even more importantly, with pesticides' emphasis on plant growth over soil building
(Oelhaf, 1978).

4. In studies of farmers' attitudes toward production, farmers are often found to place high value
on the avoidance of risk. At the same time, farmers
also want to be independent proprietors. However,
the importance of the former value over the latter
often leads them to enter into contractual arrangements with food suppliers--so-called vertical integration of the production process--which can greatly
decrease their independence (Oelhaf, 1978; Davis,
1980).

5. Most full-time organic farmers in the United
States have had substantial previous experience as
chemical/conventional farmers (USDA, 1980b).

6. Conservation farming refers in part to the
use of terracing; contour plowing; a fallow or green-
manure system of crop rotation which decreases the
total amount of land planted to crops; and a mixed-
crop pattern of planting which decreases the amount
of cropland given over to row crops that have high
short-term value but which deplete soil productivity
and tilth.

7. However, a 1979 Gallup poll on home gardening
found that the vegetables produced in home gardens
constitute one-third of the total retail value of all
produce grown in the United States (Gallup Organization, Inc., 1979). Robert Rodale suggests that home
gardens yield two to four times more crop per unit
area than current commercial yields (Rodale, 1980a).

8. This is not to suggest that an organic system
of production is without its problems. At present a

wholesale shift into organic agriculture is impossible in the United States due to lack of sufficient organic wastes and lack of labor. Even if possible, it would be difficult because a shift from conventional to organic farming methods requires a three- to four-year transition period during which time there are decreases in total yields and, hence, on-farm income; also, the current technical support structure for conventional agriculture, which provides substantial public investment in university agriculture extension, research, and teaching programs, does not exist for organic farming (USDA, 1980b).

In addition, it should be noted that an organic system of production may result in increases in food prices. Also, it has been suggested that an organic system in the United States may shift temporal and intergenerational equity burdens onto populations in less developed countries. If the United States shifted to organic production, and if total production yields dropped, less developed countries which now import U.S. crop surpluses may seek to boost in-country production through use of capital-intensive fertilizers, pesticides, and mechanization. While these actions might offset import drops, they are also likely to hasten soil erosion and sterility (Oelhaf, 1978).

16
Agricultural Mechanization: Physical and Societal Effects and Implications for Policy Development

Council for Agricultural Science and Technology: James Copp, Task Force Chairman

In July 1979 the Council for Agricultural Science and Technology (CAST) approved the establishment of a task force which would prepare a report on the impacts of agricultural mechanization. The task force was formed mainly as a response to an antimechanization, antitechnology lawsuit filed against the University of California in January 1979. Task-force members included twenty-three scientists with collective expertise in agricultural economics, agricultural engineering, agronomy, rural sociology, and other agricultural sciences. Excerpts from the report include a discussion of the nature of agricultural mechanization and a summary of social impacts. Implications for policy development are also discussed.

INTRODUCTION

At various times, penetrating questions have been raised about the social consequences of agricultural mechanization. For example, during the Great Depression, agricultural engineers were accused of creating unemployment (Stewart, 1979). More recent ly, the Land Grant Colleges' involvement in agricultural mechanization research and other technology

---

Excerpted from Report No. 96 to the Council for Agricultural Science and Technology, Ames, Iowa, February 1988. See note 1 for listing of task force members.

development was criticized (Hightower, 1973). Statements by the past Secretary of Agriculture[2] are an even more recent expression of reservations about mechanization and its effects upon agriculture, farm people, and the general public.

Such criticism has been disturbing to agricultural engineers, who believe they have been serving humanity by lightening physical labor, increasing agricultural production, and contributing to human welfare in the broad sense. Strong criticism, however, has become a common phenomenon in our times, and its frequency probably will increase rather than diminish. Organized groups are playing an increasingly active role in issues affecting the common welfare, and agriculture is one of those issues. The focus on agriculture may reflect (1) the general public's longstanding, genuine interest in agriculture and rural life; (2) the public's concern about rising food prices; and (3) the fact that the agricultural constituency has become such a small minority that decisions on many public issues affecting agriculture are now heavily influenced by the nonfarm majority.

This report is offered as a "state of the art" summary of current knowledge and perspectives on the consequences of agricultural mechanization. . . .

NATURE OF AGRICULTURAL MECHANIZATION

This section includes a definition of agricultural mechanization and a discussion of the reasons it has occurred. These topics are intended as background for developing the major focus on the physical and societal impacts of mechanization.

Definition

Agricultural mechanization includes devices and systems that apply work energy to agricultural tasks in a controlled manner. Mechanization overcomes limitations imposed by the human body on the amount of agricultural production that can be generated per unit of human energy input. . . .

Reasons for Mechanization

Two broad classes of reasons may be given for agricultural mechanization. The first has to do with invention and research development which creates new mechanical systems. The second has to do with motivations for adopting these innovations.

Farmers have been, and continue to be, a source
of many innovations. The Agricultural Experiment
Stations in the Land Grant University system were
created by the public to do the basic and applied research needed to create technological innovations
(Kellogg and Knapp, 1966). Private industry also is
important, especially in fields in which some of the
benefits of invention can be captured via the patent
process (Just et al., 1979).

Beyond invention, and the availability of innovations in a general sense, two additional points
help explain the flowering of agricultural mechanization. The first, especially relevant for North
American agriculture, is that labor historically has
been scarce relative to land, in contrast to the situation existing in much of Asia. Development of
labor-saving technology has been attractive to
farmers and profitable to developers because of that
historic imbalance in factors of production
(Binswanger and Ruttan, 1978).

Second, the development of mechanical technology
has been attractive because, until recently, fossil
fuel supplies have been ample and relatively inexpensive (Dorner, 1977), and energy has been available
even in remote locations. Transportation systems,
fuel storage and distribution networks, and rural
electrification have made mass markets for mechanical
technology feasible. In short, the potential has
been high for attractive returns on investment in the
development of mechanization technology.

Diffusion of mechanical technology in American
agriculture has been dramatic in recent decades, due
primarily to its saving of labor. Labor saving is
important for operators of both large and small
acreages, and for some tasks labor-saving machinery
is available that can be used economically by both
classes of operators. Thus, while large, powerful
tractors are important labor-savers for farmers with
large acreages, small, low-power tractors that are
much less expensive are important lavor-savers for
farmers with small acreages. As another example, operators of both large and medium acreages have been
able to take advantage of the reduction in labor requirement made possible by the introduction of relatively economical, one-man, large-package, haymaking
systems in the early 1970s (Bowers and Rider, 1974;
Buchele, 1982). Previously, mechanized haymaking was
either a labor-intensive operation or one requiring
expensive equipment that was best suited to large
farms and custom operations.

Labor availability also has been an important
factor in the diffusion of mechanical technology in

American agriculture. Most agricultural labor requirements are seasonal, and this characteristic has
been intensified by the increasing quality standards
that have emphasized the importance of performing
tasks at the most appropriate time relative to
weather conditions. Both this situation and the uncertainty of the labor supply have promoted mechanization (Friedland et al., 1979). The labor supply
has been influenced also by the gradual increase of
urban employment, the strong surges in off-farm employment during wartime mobilization, the hourly wage
differentials strongly favoring nonfarm employment
(Hayes, 1978), and the nonmonetary attractiveness of
nonfarm jobs relative to that of jobs in agriculture. The relationships involved here are complex
and often indirect (Dillingham and Sly, 1966).

Even when farm labor is available, management
problems have tended to favor agricultural mechanization. Agriculture, though increasingly specialized, still involves a diversity of tasks which
require supervision if they are to be performed by
laborers. The traditional stress on self-direction
has not served the farmer well in supervising the
work of others. Nor has assistance in solving management problems been available in a manner comparable to assistance with other production problems.
Finally, unionization of farm workers, often viewed
as a threat, has added to the store of only partially
resolved management problems which have tended to encourage reduction of labor usage through mechanization (Ford, 1973; Friedland and Nelkin, 1972).

Adoption of new agricultural technology, including mechanization, has been an important means by
which farm operators could increase their returns.
Historically, farm incomes have been low relative to
urban incomes (Dorner, 1977; Tweeten and Huffman,
1980). In recent years, the gap has been narrowing
(Carter and Johnston, 1978; United States Department
of Agriculture, 1980a), and in the period from 1975
through 1979 the total per capita disposable personal
income from all sources, including income received by
farm residents from nonfarm sources, was 91 percent
of that of the nonfarm population (United States Department of Agriculture, 1980a). Currently, however,
farm income is down. In 1980 and 1981, per capita
farm income from all sources averaged 85 percent of
that of the nonfarm population (United States Department of Agriculture, 1982). The current year (1982)
is expected to yield net farm income only 62 to 77
percent as great as that in 1981 (Lucier and Smith,
1982).

With mechanization, farmers can reduce the need for labor or increase the size of the farm enterprise while increasing the returns to the remaining labor. The results include increased personal and family income, and decreased incidence of labor-management problems and risks.

Farmers can expand their enterprises with increased profits (Madden and Partenheimer, 1972), and they can expand also on borrowed money or on consumption forgone when justified by the profitability of the prospective enterprise. The incentive to expand beyond a farm of moderate size is usually greater profits rather than increased economic efficiency, as indicated by the finding by Miller et al. (1981) that ". . . as farm size increases, per-unit costs decline at first and then are relatively constant over a wide range of sizes." Of course, the role of mechanization in farm growth varies considerably across types of farm enterprises (Zahara and Johnson, 1979).

Certain other factors that may be classed as financing also contribute to the acceptance of farm mechanization. Attempts to minimize income tax liability may lead to year-end investments in machinery and equipment. Rapid depreciation allowances and deduction of interest payments foster equipment purchases and periodic replacement. Credit practices favor purchase of items which can serve as collateral rather than other farm inputs, such as labor. Credit for mechanization generally has been available (Dorner, 1977).

Finally, a range of less tangible factors also may contribute to acceptance of agricultural mechanization. The attractiveness of mechanization to agricultural producers may hinge to a degree upon the enhancement of available options both on and off the farm. On the farm, the possibility of multicropping or adding additional enterprises can be affected strongly by the use of labor-saving machinery. Time-saving makes off-farm activities and leisure options feasible as well. Mechanization enables operators on small acreages to remain financially solvent by holding a part-time or full-time job elsewhere. Other themes current in American society, such as equating bigness with success, considering machine power as an extension of personal power, and keeping up with one's neighbors, also may contribute to the perceived attractiveness of agricultural mechanization (though the extent of such influences may be hard to assess).

Up to now, the decision to adopt agricultural technology has been considered the exclusive

242

prerogative of the farmer. However, this decision has ramifications for farm workers, the community, and society in general.

. . .

SUMMARY OF THE EFFECTS OF
AGRICULTURAL MECHANIZATION

. . .Agricultural mechanization greatly increases productivity per unit of labor. It also increases the farmer's ability to produce food and fiber by eliminating the maintenance of draft animals. Additionally, mechanization facilitates the application of other agricultural production technologies, such as fertilizers, pesticides, improved crop varieties, and animal care, that increase the yield of crops and food-animal products per acre.

Agricultural mechanization and other technologies affect the quantity, quality, organization, location, and stability of production. As a consequence of technological change, agricultural production in the United States in the past half century has increased several fold, and output per person has increased many fold.

In the short run, a substantial part of the economic benefit from the increases in agricultural productivity associated with mechanization and other new agricultural technology is captured by early adopters of the new technology. Late adopters derive less benefit. In the long run, consumers are the principal beneficiaries of adoption of new agricultural technology. Landowners benefit from the bidding up of the price of agricultural land, a development to which agricultural mechanization appears to have contributed. Suppliers of mechanized equipment and other technological inputs as well as processors and other links in the agribusiness production-marketing chain also share in the economic benefits.

Adoption of agricultural mechanization is stimulated by the potential for increased profits. Saving of labor, facilitation of management, and advantageous financial arrangements are major contributors to the profitability. Other, less tangible factors such as governmental regulations, agribusiness practices, and farmers' subjective preferences also may be involved.

With continuation of mechanization beyond that required to eliminate virtually all draft animals, other changes in agriculture have occurred. These include a decrease in the numbers of small and medium-sized farms; an increase in the numbers of large farms; more part-time farms; increased quantities of nonland resources used in agriculture; increased land values; increased production, sales, debt, and net income per farm; greater differentiation of farm ownership, management, and labor; a decline in the absolute numbers and relative importance of family-operated farms; and entry of large corporations and investor groups into agriculture. These changes were a consequence of a number of factors. Mechanization, however, was a necessary condition for some of the changes, and it played a major role in others.

The decrease in agricultural employment over the years has affected many agricultural communities. Most of the out-migration occurred among young people just entering the labor force. The eventual consequences of this depopulation include closing and consolidation of schools, decline in community morale, closing of small-town businesses, abandonment of country churches, withering of social organizations, inactivity of community and civic organizations, and a decline in relative value of property in affected communities.

Urban society has benefited from agricultural mechanization and other agricultural technology. The transfer of more and more agribusiness activity to the nonfarm sector has created new jobs; the release of workers from agricultural employment has provided workers for both agricultural and nonagricultural industry as well as the professions, and the productivity permitted by agricultural technology has assured what by historical standards has been an abundant food supply at moderate prices for the urban majority. On the other hand, urban society has inherited some of the unemployment associated with the release of agricultural workers who then competed for jobs with urban workers.

. . .

IMPLICATIONS FOR POLICY DEVELOPMENT

The foregoing discussion leads to some general implications for policy development. These are discussed in the following paragraphs.

The Probability that Agricultural Mechanization and Related Technological Development Will Continue

There is very little likelihood that agricultural mechanization will cease. The alternatives to mechanization are unlikely to be adopted. For performing the labor required in farm tasks, human beings and animals are less efficient users of energy than are appropriate mechanical devices (Splinter, 1979b). Continued improvements in the lightening of labor, in agricultural productivity, and in profit potential for early adopters are not likely to be given up even if the cost of energy becomes substantially higher. Agricultural mechanization is not likely to be halted or reversed; that is not the issue. The issue seems to involve the rate of adoption of mechanization and the socioeconomic consequences.

Scale-of-Farming Implications

Economies of scale affect agriculture as well as other business activities. Thus, very few developments in agricultural technology are scale-neutral (i. e., have no effect on the size of operations). Often the implications are indirect and unintended. For instance, early research on disease control among chickens was eventually an aid in the raising of large flocks, although this consequence was not necessarily the objective of the research (see, e.g., Hays et al., 1981). Most technological developments require increased levels of management, and many are implemented with the aid of mechanization; thus, they lead indirectly to advantages for larger units. Other technological developments are less subtle in their scale consequences, requiring utilization of high-capacity machines. The economies associated with large farming units vary from item to item and do not necessarily imply advantages for large units under all conditions, but the balance appears to be in favor of larger rather than smaller units. Modern developments in producing animals in confinement result in a smaller acreage requirement to produce a given quantity of product than did the extensive operations used previously. They do depend upon mechanization and specially designed buildings and feedlots, however, and units with large numbers of animals are favored because the cost of the facilities per animal is less with large numbers of animals than with small numbers.

Complexity of Causal Relationships

The cause-and-effect relationships between agricultural mechanization and social consequences are
complex and often mediated by many factors, including
hourly wage differentials favoring nonfarm employment, nonmonetary attractiveness of nonfarm jobs,
unionization of farm workers, competition among producers, the lengthened work-life of farm workers,
management, the technological approach in general,
and societal values. Agricultural mechanization is
only a tool that responds through management to much
wider economic and political forces. Thus, dislocations attributed to agricultural mechanization might
better be viewed within this larger societal and economic context.

The Need for Information

The data required to answer some questions about
the societal impact of agricultural mechanization do
not exist, and the information available on many
questions is inadequate. Through the years, the major part of the budget of the Agricultural Experiment
Stations has underwritten research related to the
various production aspects of agriculture rather than
research related to the social consequences of changing agricultural production techniques.

Public Involvement

According to Ruttan (1982), public involvement
in agricultural research can be justified on three
bases: (1) In many areas, the incentives for research
in the private sector are inadequate to induce the
optimum rate of investment because a large share of
the social gains from research is captured by other
firms, producers, and consumers rather than the firm
that makes the research investment. (2) A strong
synergistic, mutually reinforcing interaction exists
between research and education in agricultural science and technology. (3) Public-sector research contributes to the maintenance of a competitive
structure in the supply, production, and marketing
sectors of agriculture.

Most of the funds for agricultural research in
the public sector are supplied by state legislatures
and the Congress, which answer primarily to urban
people. Members of the agricultural sector and their
representatives in state legislatures and the Congress are now distinct minorities. In such an

environment, heavy involvement of nonagriculturally oriented persons in decision-making about funds for agricultural research must be expected. Also to be expected is participation of the nonfarm sector in the debate over agricultural mechanization because of the high visibility of mechanization in the complex of factors affecting the gradually changing character of agriculture as well as the role of government in influencing the change.

Full and adequate information on the social costs and benefits of agricultural technology is not presently available for informed decision-making by either the agricultural sector or the nonagricultural sector. Some scientists have suggested that, as a part of the information-development process and to improve the methods of making social impact analyses, new technology should be monitored for social impact as it is put in place (Friedland and Kappel, 1979) and over time as adoption proceeds (Just et al., 1979; Madden and Baker, 1981).

The Basic Social Issues

Basic social issues remain unresolved: (a) What is the magnitude and incidence of the social costs and benefits of agricultural mechanization? (b) How should unemployment associated with advances in agricultural mechanization be handled? (c) Should changes be made in the current system by which the public supports the work of public institutions that provides information which may lead to mechanization? (d) Should changes be made in the current system by which the public guides the adoption and monitors the effects of new mechanization?

Much remains to be learned about the costs and benefits of agricultural mechanization. The problem is complex because of the need to assess economic costs and benefits, which is a difficult undertaking, and noneconomic costs and benefits, which is even more difficult.

Although the massive transfer of population from the farm to nonfarm sector that occurred in the past can no longer take place, future mechanization of labor-intensive crops, such as certain fruits and vegetables, can be expected to produce significant local and regional effects. A major question, therefore, is whether and what sorts of programs are necessary to deal with these employment dislocations.

In the past, decisions regarding adoption and use of agricultural mechanization technology have been made by individual entrepreneurs. The economic

pressures guiding these decisions have arisen partly
in the private sector and partly in the public sector. Pressures from the public sector have originated in part from the public subsidy of research
that has led to advances in agricultural mechanization technology. They have originated also from
other government programs, such as price supports,
acreage limitations, tax incentives, and regulations
affecting machinery design. At present, there can be
no doubt that, in the aggregate, the decisions made
by individual entrepreneurs have social and society-
wide ramifications. In view of this, the question is
whether the system used in the past should be retained, with or without adjustment, or whether some
other, better system can be devised.

NOTES

1. Task Force Members were James H. Copp (Chairman of the Task Force), Department of Rural
Sociology, Texas A&M University; J. F. Bartholic, Agricultural Experiment Station, Michigan State University; Robert F. Becker, Cooperative Extension, Seed
and Vegetable Sciences, New York State Agricultural
Experiment Station at Geneva; Wendell Bowers, Extension Administration and Supervision, Oklahoma State
University; D. K. Cassel, Department of Soil Science,
North Carolina State University; Frederick C.
Fliegel, Department of Agricultural Economics, University of Illinois; William Friedland, Departments
of Community Studies and Sociology, University of
California at Santa Cruz; Roger E. Garrett, Department of Agricultural Engineering, University of Cali-
fornia at Davis; Waymon A. Halbrook, Department of
Agricultural Economics and Rural Sociology, Univer-
sity of Arkansas; G. C. Harris, Department of Animal
Sciences, University of Arkansas; Joseph Havlicek,
Jr., Department of Agricultural and Resource Economics, University of Maryland; David W. Holland, De-
partment of Agricultural Economics, Washington State
University; Dale M. Hoover, Department of Economics
and Business, North Carolina State University; W. H.
Lange, Department of Entomology, University of Cali-
fornia at Davis; Max Lennon, College of Agriculture,
University of Missouri-Columbia; J. Patrick Madden,
Department of Agricultural Economics and Rural Soci-
ology, Pennsylvania State University; Marshall A.
Martin, Department of Agricultural Economics, Purdue
University; Richard D. Rodefeld, 3420 Highway BB,
Madison, Wisconsin; John W. Schmidt, Department of

248

Agronomy, University of Nebraska; William E. Splinter, Department of Agricultural Engineering, University of Nebraska; R. T. Toledo, Department of Food Science, University of Georgia; Jerome B. Weber, Department of Crop Science, North Carolina State University; Kenneth L. Wells, Department of Agronomy, University of Kentucky.

2. On December 13, 1979, Bob Bergland (1980), then United States Secretary of Agriculture, said at a news conference in Fresno, California, "I do not think that federal funding of (research into) labor-saving devices is a proper use of federal money. This is something to be left to private enterprise and to the state universities. . . . But I will not put federal money into any project that results in the saving of farm labor. The economic incentives in the market place should be powerful enough so that that kind of research work can be done by private enterprise." Later, in a prepared statement, he wrote "we will not put federal money into research where--other factors being equal or neutral--the major effect of that research will be the replacing of an adequate and willing work force with machines." At the same time, he noted that he had "no intention of cutting off federal funding of all research into mechanization" and that he had no objection to labor-saving devices that could "mean easing the drudgery of work" and could "lighten a person's workload." He noted also that "when machines are used because the labor force in a particular area can't fill the work requirement--or when they enhance the competitive status of an individual operator without large-scale labor displacement--that's another story."

17
Technological Change and the Growth of Agribusiness: A Case Study of California Lettuce Production

Anne Fredricks

In this chapter, Anne Fredricks traces the development and expansion of one large California agribusiness interest--Bud Antle, Inc. Antle has traditionally led the lettuce industry in technological change, implementing original ideas for methods of production, distribution, and marketing. Fredricks assesses the corporation's process of internal growth and the role of technological change in capital accumulation and concentration. She concludes that the primary motivation for the transition to mechanization derived from the need to reduce uncertainty in the production process and gain greater control over the labor component of production. Bud Antle, Inc., has followed the successful corporate pattern of technological change, domestic expansion, and now--as a subsidiary of Castle & Cooke, Inc.--further expansion into a larger, more diversified, global corporation, from which it will continue its process of growth and control.

"Agribusiness" corporations are increasingly dominating American agriculture. They grow, process, finance, and market food, and they manufacture many of the inputs necessary for food production. Even where growing or harvesting operations remain in the hands of independent or "family-sized" farmers,

---

Anne Fredricks is a city planner with the San Francisco Department of City Planning.

249

corporate interests exercise considerable control over access to capital, raw materials, machinery, and product markets (Pfeffer, 1980).

The impacts of capital concentration and centralization in agriculture have recently been chronicled. Martinson and Campbell (1980) investigated the effects of agribusiness on farmers in the United States; Thomas (1980) analyzed the impacts on farm workers; and Valvano (1981) examined the consequences for farm size and structure. Few studies, however, have focused on internal corporate growth within influential agribusiness firms. In an effort to contribute to the literature on the political economy of agriculture, my research traced the development and expansion of one large California agribusiness interest--Bud Antle, Inc.--one of the most important domestic and international shippers of iceberg lettuce. Here, the Antle company's process of internal growth is assessed, emphasizing the role of technological change and its relationship to and impact on capital accumulation, economic concentration, and agricultural labor.

Choosing Antle for a case study of corporate agribusiness was not arbitrary. Nowhere does the specter of agribusiness production loom more dominant than in California's lush fruit- and vegetable-growing regions, home of Antle headquarters. California accounts for 40 percent of the nation's fresh produce, much of it commanding a profit rate far above that of other agricultural commodities. Of the numerous crops which have contributed to the state's reputation as a leader in fresh food production, iceberg lettuce--Antle's mainstay--has been termed the "financial backbone," the "cash crop" of the vegetable industry (Cargill and Garrett, 1975). In 1977, the iceberg lettuce industry accounted for over $250 million a year of California's agricultural revenue, with shipments of 105 million cartons having a market value of $325 million (Smith, 1977).

Corporate agribusiness has settled comfortably in California's fresh fruit and vegetable areas. A drive through the state's fertile agricultural valleys illustrates the extent to which traditional farm communities are absent from the landscape. Huge tractors and mechanical harvesters roll across fields which measure into the thousands of acres. The presence of large agribusiness interests in fresh fruit and vegetable production has not been extremely longstanding. While corporate agriculture and large-scale, capital-intensive technologies historically flourished in the food processing, marketing, and distribution sectors, their move into fresh fruit and vegetable production has been recent. The speculative and risky nature of producing, transporting, and marketing an extremely perishable crop makes fresh food production inherently more uncertain than the production of crops that undergo processing prior to shipping.

Iceberg lettuce epitomizes the riskiness of the fresh fruit and vegetable industry. Because lettuce is strictly a fresh market crop with a short "shelf life," its selling price can fluctuate wildly from day to day based upon varying conditions of supply and demand, changes in the weather, or the reliability of transportation or harvest. The lettuce market is so sensitive to changes that a delay of even one day in shipping can set off a rise in price. Conversely, a high-quality crop may be disced under in the field if supply suddenly increases and prices fall too low.

Because of daily demand and extreme perishability, lettuce producers and marketers require steady year-round production schedules, complex transport and marketing systems, and a reliable and highly skilled labor force. Although different varieties of lettuce may be grown throughout the country at various times of the year, consistent commercial production of the hearty iceberg variety is limited to the warm-weather climates of California and Arizona. These areas have conditions particularly suited for growing lettuce, so growers can schedule more easily and regulate more closely the growth of their valuable crop. Ninety-two percent of U.S. lettuce is produced in California and Arizona, and shipped eastward for national marketing (Friedland, Barton, and Thomas, 1981).

As producers of a delicate, perishable, and highly speculative crop, lettuce-industry leaders have demanded a series of highly sophisticated technological innovations for lettuce production, marketing, and shipping. Huge capital expenditures are now necessary for entry and success in the industry. While it is possible to reap the sometimes large windfall profits of a good year, the risk inherent in lettuce growing and marketing has eliminated many growers who cannot absorb the production costs involved during a bad year. Between the years 1959 and 1970, the number of lettuce growers in a five-state area including California declined from 1,800 to 1,000 farmers--a drop of 44 percent in eleven years (Garoyan, 1974). Accompanying the reduction in the number of growers has been both an increase in farm size of the remaining growers and a rise of large grower-shipper firms. Lettuce shippers such as the Antle company have integrated backwards into other aspects of the industry to assume successive phases of the production process. A handful of large grower-shipper firms now dominate the lettuce industry. In 1978, the twelve largest firms handled 51 percent of the California crop, approximately 40 percent of the combined California-Arizona crop, and 37.2 percent of all U.S. lettuce (Friedland, Barton, and Thomas, 1981).

Foremost among lettuce-industry leaders is Bud Antle, Inc., a Salinas-based firm which was, until its purchase in 1978 by Castle & Cooke, Inc., of DOLE pineapple and banana fame, the world's largest independently owned lettuce grower and shipper. Founded in 1943 as a small packing and shipping operation, and begun with a $1,500 investment, Antle expanded into a worldwide corporation with diversified operations throughout California, Arizona, Europe, and Africa. Its activities include the production and sale of several different vegetables in addition to lettuce, as well as some related nonfarming investments in machinery manufacture, marketing and distribution subsidiaries, and real estate. At the time of its sale to Castle & Cooke, Inc., Antle grossed over $80 million per year in sales from its shipments of fresh market vegetables (Castle & Cooke, 1977).

Technological change allowed for the lettuce industry's relatively recent domestic and international expansion. Antle's success is due in large part to the company's technological experimentation. While Antle became known as a "maverick" and a "troublemaker" among its competitors, its leadership in technological change stimulated its spectacular corporate growth. From its earliest innovations to its most recent developments, Antle has led the industry in the implementation of original ideas for lettuce production, distribution, and marketing. Unique among its competitors, the company has employed its own engineering facilities and agricultural engineers; machinery and implements are often designed directly to Antle specifications. Many of the company's inventions have set production standards industry-wide. Successful technologies have provided Antle with increased control over production, over labor, and over the erratic lettuce marketplace. Reduction of uncertainty, particularly labor uncertainty, in this highly competitive industry has given Antle an edge on predictability and profit, and has enabled the company to expand and invest further in its own growth and development.

To illustrate more fully the relationship between new technologies and the growth of Bud Antle, Inc., we will examine the impact of several of the firm's specific innovations.

THE INTRODUCTION OF VACUUM COOLING

In the infancy of modern lettuce production in the 1920s and 1930s, stationary packing sheds played a major role in the lettuce marketing process. The crop was harvested and immediately sent to the sheds to be trimmed, packed, cooled with ice, and shipped via rail cars refrigerated by ice packed over and around the crates. Since huge tonnages of ice were essential to packing and shipping operations, the lettuce industry depended upon major capital investments in permanent packing sheds which housed ice storing, handling, and crushing machinery (Segur, 1974).

By the 1930s, a new system of packing technology began to appear. Lettuce was harvested, packed in crates, and covered over with ice in the field, for shipment directly to local markets. The process had marginal impact, however, because field-packed lettuce, though ice-cooled, would not keep as long and could not be shipped as far as shed-packed. Packing sheds remained prominent throughout the 1930s and 1940s.

It was during this period that Antle entered the lettuce industry. Founded by Lester V. "Bud" Antle, the company started packing and shipping fresh vegetables from Watsonville, California, twenty miles north of Salinas. By 1949, Antle held in partnership, or owned outright, 2,000 acres of land and had expanded to Salinas and the Imperial Valley from Watsonville (Salinas Californian, 1972). The process of increasing acreages and entering new production areas continued throughout the 1950s.

The introduction of vacuum cooling, a process which chills the lettuce in airtight chambers down to thirty-three degrees in thirty minutes, represented one of the first major technical breakthroughs of the lettuce industry. In 1949, Lester "Bud" Antle met the inventor of the vacuum-cooling process, endorsed the invention, and had the first vacuum-cooling plant built on Antle property in Watsonville. The original railroad cars of vacuum-cooled lettuce left Antle's fields in the spring of 1950 (Padfield and Martin,

1965). Vacuum cooling was a crucial step in the history of Antle's phenomenal growth, and it paved the way for a complete transition from traditional shed packing of lettuce to field packing.

A major impetus behind the innovation of vacuum cooling was the lettuce industry's agricultural labor situation. In the era of packing sheds, packing-shed employees working in permanent operations obtained some measure of job stability. They organized under the auspices of the United Packinghouse Workers of America (UPWA) and received top union wages (Padfield and Martin, 1965). In contrast, field-workers were unorganized. As field-packed lettuce was considered inferior to shed-packed, field-workers were relegated to a subordinate role in the industry. California's packing sheds were reserved for white workers; Mexican and Filipino workers remained in the fields (McWilliams, 1971).

The fact that packing-shed labor organized and bargained for higher wages than field-workers gave growers a significant economic interest in packing lettuce in the fields, and in substituting field labor for packing-shed labor. Prior to the introduction of vacuum cooling, the process of chilling field-packed lettuce was not sufficiently advanced to enable growers to convert to field packing on a large enough scale. With vacuum cooling's inauguration in 1950, growers began to shift their packing operations into the fields, and packing-shed workers lost their economic importance and organized strength.

Though the majority of lettuce growers were at first resistant to vacuum cooling, perhaps due to the required capital expense, "Bud" Antle was convinced it was the wave of the future. He was right: almost 80 percent of the industry switched to vacuum cooling in just three years. In retrospect, "Bud" Antle remarked in 1972: "If they had kept fighting it, we would have wound up with all the business" (Hull, 1972).

In terms of reducing labor and shipping costs, vacuum cooling technology was unprecedented. Growers replaced wooden crates with cardboard cartons, and moved all of their packing procedures into the fields. They were able to hire exclusively the lower-paid field-workers, which expedited the decline of the packing-shed workers' union (Glass, 1966).

The power of farm-labor organizing was an important aspect of the growers' interest in the cooling technology. In 1950, C. B. Moore, secretary of the Western Growers and Shippers Association, warned that technical change in the lettuce industry was inevitable, due to wage increases granted California's packing-shed workers. The introduction of vacuum cooling successfully fought unionization by eliminating up to 75 percent of the packing-shed laborers (Glass, 1966). While not in itself labor-saving, vacuum cooling was extremely cost-efficient. Growers and shippers escaped union domination and controlled field-workers' wages: though "labor requirements were 7 percent to 42 percent higher than for shed packing, labor costs were cut phenomenally" (Glass, 1966).

Packing-shed workers were displaced from their jobs and given little opportunity to transfer into fieldwork positions. Not only did the new vacuum-cooling technology serve to displace them, but at precisely the same time--1951--the United States and Mexican governments agreed upon the passage of Public Law 78, known as the "bracero program." The law secured the importation and documentation of Mexican citizens to work in American fields. The use of "foreign supplemental workers" allowed the maintenance of an inexpensive and overabundant supply of labor and, in conjunction with the advent of vacuum cooling, caused the rapid demise of the UPWA in vegetable packing. For Bud Antle, Inc., technical innovation and the disappearance of the powerful packing-shed workers' union combined to increase Antle's control over production and to enhance its potential for growth. The increased profit derived from lowered labor costs, and the improved predictability earned through increasing the labor supply and therefore maintaining labor control, assured Antle's position of dominance.

TECHNOLOGY FOR FIELD WRAPPING

With the success of vacuum-cooling technology and the complete shift to field packing of lettuce, interest arose in a new field technology--field wrapping of lettuce in a "breathable" plastic film. In the winter of 1960-1961, Antle began the pioneering tests on film-wrapped lettuce, utilizing a newly developed "Trycite" plastic, in conjunction with a modified Antle carrot harvester. Field wrapping, like vacuum cooling, caused a significant change in the lettuce-production process. Just as vacuum cooling eliminated the need for packing-shed workers and enabled growers to set their own terms for control of the yet unorganized field-workers, the introduction of the lettuce-wrapping machine continued the process

of grower control by again reducing the labor force.
The very first wrap machines, put into use by Antle
in 1961, cut the work force in half. With the new
technology, a crew of twenty-six workers could harvest 320 cartons an hour where previously forty-six
workers cut and packed only 275 cartons an hour
(Newsweek, 1961).
    From the start of the field-wrapping experi-
ments, Antle took the lead. The company was the
first to utilize the wrap-pack procedures, and to
this day remains the largest shipper of field-wrapped
lettuce. Nearly 50 percent of Antle lettuce is
wrapped in the field, in polypropylene plastic, on
machines designed and manufactured by the company.
The advantage in marketing field-wrapped lettuce lies
in its higher profit rate and in the advantages
gained from the labor process involved. The wrapping
procedure relies upon the use of a machine which
moves through the field while some workers cut and
others immediately wrap the lettuce in the field.
The machine-paced harvest results in increased control over the work force.[1] In addition, Antle sales
representatives add between seventy-five cents and
ninety cents per carton onto the price of their film-
wrapped product over and above the officially quoted
lettuce price for the day. Because wrapped lettuce
has its protective outer leaves removed, it takes up
less room in the carton and allows for more heads--
hence, more revenue--per box.
    The promotional value of field-wrapped lettuce
is also important. By wrapping lettuce in its own
logo, Antle strives to create brand-name identification for its produce and to improve its market position. The advertising of brand-name goods, allocated
huge budgets in the processed-food industry, has now
entered the realm of the fresh market commodities.
By packaging even perishable crops such as lettuce
and celery, Antle attempts to secure both customer
loyalty and a premium price for its products. Field-
wrapped lettuce has played a large role in Antle's
profitability and market position.

ANTLE'S FARM LABOR CONTRACT:
SOCIAL INNOVATION FOR CONTROL

    In 1961, Antle introduced an innovation which,
if not technologically significant, would prove the
most socially significant of its actions in terms of
agricultural labor relations in the lettuce industry. The company became the first lettuce firm to

sign a union contract, with the International Brotherhood of Teamsters, to represent some of Antle's field-workers. Antle's move marked "the first breach in growers' solidarity against a union in the fields" (Salinas Californian, 1961a). For years, along with all the other lettuce growers, Antle had strongly resisted any farm-labor unionization efforts. The company's signing of the Teamster contract came as a shock to other lettuce growers, who were organized together as the Salinas Grower-Shipper Vegetable Association. After years of antiunion sentiment, the association maintained that they had "no foreknowledge that Bud Antle, Inc. was going to sign with the Teamsters" (Salinas Californian, 1961a).

For its break with grower solidarity, Antle was expelled from the California Council of Growers. Antle resigned from the Grower-Shipper Vegetable Association, citing its members for "an apparent and complete area of misunderstanding as well as an obvious lack of respect for the Antle company" (Salinas Californian, 1961b).

In terms of management tactics, however, Antle was far ahead of other firms in the lettuce industry. The Antle-Teamster agreement was very favorable to Antle, as the company was assured the right to determine the number of workers required for any job and was given the prerogative of hiring and firing workers. The union agreed that there would be no strikes, slowdowns, job actions, or any other interruptions of work during the contract period. The Teamsters promised to give immediate notice to the company when it could not furnish enough workers, and guaranteed Antle assistance in obtaining foreign supplemental workers through the federally sponsored United States-Mexico bracero program.

Significantly, at the time the union agreement was signed by Antle, the company employed approximately 500 Mexican nationals through the bracero program, and these workers were exempted from contract coverage. In addition to the bracero workers, the new labor agreement also excluded Antle's cooler workers, who were covered by the United Packinghouse Workers of America, and the general farm workers engaged in hoeing, thinning, irrigation, and tractor driving. In fact, the new Teamster contract covered only about 150 employees, as opposed to 50 covered previously by UPWA (Lester, 1961).

For the Teamsters, the Antle contract also proved advantageous. By covering even a small number of field-workers, the Teamsters obtained vertical integration in their representation of agricultural employees. They added field-workers to those they already covered--truck drivers, certain cooling-plant workers, and workers in the canneries and on the freight cars (Glass, 1966). Vertical integration gave the union a greater degree of security. If field-workers under Teamster contract were prohibited from striking, they would not adversely affect the Teamster cannery workers or truck drivers, dependent for their jobs upon harvested field crops. Conversely, if a strike were called by the union, the Teamsters had the power to remove workers from all aspects of production, giving the Teamsters greater bargaining leverage.

The Teamster contract clearly brought Antle a measure of labor security, which had been its most troublesome of production uncertainties. In 1961, the Agricultural Workers Organizing Committee (AWOC) and the UPWA, both of the AFL-CIO, led a large lettuce strike in California's Imperial Valley. As the largest lettuce grower, Antle was hurt badly by the action. It caused the company to lose all of the Mexican nationals employed during the winter season. "Bud" Antle complained that his labor troubles had started several years before the Imperial Valley action, and that he had "fought alone for five or six years against striking packinghouse workers." After experiencing all this labor turmoil, Antle management was anxiously "looking for a way to assure labor peace" (Lester, 1961).

The fact that Antle signed a union contract with the Teamsters, however, did not exempt the company from further labor disputes. If anything, the Teamster contract infuriated the agricultural workers who had staged labor strikes throughout the 1950s, and who were represented by the Agricultural Workers Organizing Committee, not the Teamsters. Throughout the 1960s the Antle-Teamster contract was cause for conflict.[2] The United Farm Workers Organizing Committee (UFWOC), the successor to AWOC, continued the farm-labor fight against Antle in the 1970s.

TECHNOLOGY FOR LABOR REPLACEMENT: LETTUCE-HARVEST MECHANIZATION

With the persistence of agricultural labor strife in the lettuce industry throughout the 1960s and 1970s, industry leaders and state and federal scientists and engineers began pursuing research and development of lettuce-harvest mechanization. Interest in designing a mechanical lettuce harvester was

expressed as early as 1961 (Western Growers and Shippers Association, 1961).   The bracero program was
under political attack, and growers became increasingly worried about their abundant supply of cheap
labor.   They gave serious attention to possibilities
of technological change.   Researchers at the University of Arizona termed the development of a mechanical lettuce harvester "top priority" (Western
Growers and Shippers Association, 1961).   At the
University of California, Davis (UC-Davis), research
on lettuce-harvest mechanization began "even before
the Bracero Program ended" (Friedland, Barton, and
Thomas, 1981).

Work on the development of a mechanical lettuce
harvester continued throughout the 1960s.   By 1975,
two separate prototype harvesters had been built, one
at UC-Davis and one at the U.S. Department of Agriculture Experiment Station in Salinas.   In addition,
the Iceberg Lettuce Research Advisory Board, funded
by a self-imposed tax on growers under the laws of
the California Marketing Order Act, agreed upon a
contract with FMC Corporation for developing, testing, and building a prototype machine.   The terms of
the contract stipulated that growers would pay FMC
$150,000, and that FMC would finance the rest of the
estimated $440,000 cost of the lettuce harvester's
research and development.   All hardware, prototypes,
and technical information would remain the property
of FMC.   The contract did provide a clause, however,
which would have made possible a return of some of
the funds contributed by the growers.   If the harvester was successfully developed and marketed outside of California, "the parties (would) consider an
arrangement to repay the lettuce advisory board for
its portion of the development costs."

The FMC contract with the growers was vetoed by
the director of the California Department of Food and
Agriculture on the grounds that it constituted a "gi-
ft of public funds."   Had the marketing order been
approved, all lettuce growers in the state would have
been required to pay a tax, based on the amount of
lettuce they produced, to support the development of
harvest mechanization.   Not all growers would have
benefited from their contribution, however, as the
cost of a mechanical harvester would be prohibitive
to many small growers.   Estimates placed the cost of
the machine at $40,000 in 1975, escalating to over
$75,000 by 1977 (Manning, 1977).   Only the largest
lettuce growers could have adopted the new capital-
intensive technology.   As the developers of the machine at UC-Davis themselves pointed out,

the change to a mechanical harvest system will require an investment of capital in machines and equipment, better management, possible changes in production schedules with a probable increase in lettuce acreage to make efficient use of the machine and equipment. (Zahara, Johnson, and Garrett, 1974)

The effects of mechanical lettuce harvesting on the displacement of farm workers would be similar to the historical effects of innovations such as vacuum cooling and field wrapping. The number of available jobs would decline, a surplus of unemployed farm workers would result, and wage rates and farm-labor bargaining power would be depressed still further. Control over wages and working conditions would rest securely in the hands of the growers.

Implementation of the mechanical lettuce harvester is not imminent. Technical problems, as well as the availability of a stable supply of reliable, efficient, and inexpensive workers, has made less than urgent the adoption of lettuce-harvest technology. Further development on the machine ceased in January 1978, when both the U.S. Department of Agriculture (USDA) and UC-Davis engineers announced the end of their lettuce-harvester research (Santa Cruz Sentinel, 1975).

As in many other technical innovations affecting the lettuce industry, Bud Antle, Inc., took a visible role in the development of harvest mechanization. While other growers relied upon the USDA or UC-Davis to design and build a machine, Antle, in conjunction with its internal research and development on other technical changes, experimented independently with harvest mechanization. Antle "obtained nonexclusive license to produce a machine developed by the University of California at Davis" (Santa Cruz Sentinel, 1975). Company engineers then modified the Davis harvester to enable it to cut four rows of lettuce at one time, instead of two (Friedland, Barton, and Thomas, 1981). After publicly funded research on lettuce-harvest mechanization had ended, Antle continued to assess the machine's feasibility.

RECENT TECHNOLOGICAL INNOVATIONS

Harvest mechanization is not the only recent technical innovation that Antle has explored. One of the company's latest inventions is the introduction of very capital-intensive "lettuce-processing" equipment, designed to cut fresh lettuce in the fields into shredded salad for sale to institutional and individual consumers. With its new processing technology, Antle has broadened its market for the sale of lettuce and increased its lettuce-harvesting efficiency. Because the lettuce is shredded prior to sale, workers do not have to pick lettuce conforming to strict Antle appearance standards. Though the company emphasizes that the lettuce used in its shredding operations is the same "top-quality" product, "the harvest crews connected with the precut operations do not have to worry about head shape or size, thus utilizing a portion of the crop that formerly stayed in the field" (Franta, 1975). Antle has also expanded the international market for its products, shipping bags of shredded lettuce by air to McDonald's restaurants in Germany and Hong Kong. The company recently introduced the supermarket sale of bagged, shredded cabbage, finally fulfilling "Bud" Antle's 1961 prophecy that his firm would "make coleslaw in the fields, pack half- and quarter-cabbages, and bundle carrots and everything else. We can do anything" (Newsweek, 1961).

In 1976, Antle began experiments on the greenhouse production of transplantable lettuce seedlings, a technique designed to increase company productivity. By using the transplant method, Antle can plant three crops of lettuce in one season instead of the normal two. One crop of seedlings can be maturing in the greenhouses while the previous crop is still out in the field. An Antle subsidiary was created, Transplants, Inc., to specialize in growing the young seedlings. As of 1976, Antle operated fifty-two greenhouses and supplied 25 percent of the firm's internal California lettuce-seedling requirements (Razee, 1976). The high cost of land and the scarcity of growing space in the Salinas area, where most of the transplants are grown, were cited as the main reasons behind the establishment of the greenhouse program (Winslow, 1976a).

The entire transplant process is highly mechanized. A complex setup is utilized to automatically fill and inject with seeds 120 "inverted pyramid cells" filled with a special peat and vermiculite mixture in which the lettuce seedlings mature. The plants are grown in the greenhouses in polystyrene trays which each hold 120 plants (Winslow, 1976b). The trays are suspended off the ground to allow for air circulation, and irrigation is supplied by a system of spray booms which move down the greenhouse center.

262

The advantages of transplants can be tied directly into other forms of production mechanization. The seedlings can be mechanically planted, spaced, and positioned in rows with a machine designed especially by Antle engineers. Few workers are needed for mechanized planting, and only a small crew is required to move through the field afterwards to check that the seedlings are properly placed. The seedling transplant method eliminates much of the labor and expense involved in irrigation, hoeing, thinning, and weeding, all "very costly hand operations." Until now these operations have been the most labor-intensive. According to the California Farmer (Razee, 1976), labor problems were again the primary motivation for the interest in preharvest mechanization.

> Labor problems brought on by the demise of the short-handled hoe, and union activity, have renewed interest in precision planting and transplanting. The Antle operation is now semi-automated, but their goal is full automation. Good labor is hard to find, and the fluid union situation makes this the only real option open to growers. (Razee, 1976)

Should Antle ever choose to mechanize the harvest of lettuce, a somewhat futuristic possibility, the use of "speedling" transplants will be ideally suited. Transplants allow for an increase in the uniformity of the entire crop, in spacing, maturity date, and yield per acre. According to one Antle executive, there are expectations that "with some refinement of seed and more experience in growing transplants, it will be possible to obtain the uniformity necessary for a one-time harvest in the field. Then the mechanical harvester will come into its own" (Winslow, 1976b).

CONCLUSION

The history of Bud Antle, Inc., makes clear that a primary motivation for the transition to mechanization stemmed from the need to reduce uncertainty in the production process and gain greater control over labor. Important technical changes in the lettuce industry correspond to the unique requirements of the crop as well as to the specific demands of agricultural production.

With the seasonal requirements of fresh fruit and vegetables, a temporary labor force and seasonally available laborers are crucial to the success of

the industry. Due to the perishability of certain
commodities, labor supply and control is imperative,
and the threat of harvest-worker unrest poses a potentially devastating problem for agricultural employers. Because agriculture, specifically lettuce
production, is highly speculative and historically
fraught with labor strife, technology has played a
major role in the attempt to reduce production uncertainty. Firms without the capital resources to invest in new technologies have often been forced out
of agricultural production.

For the Antle company, labor-supply uncertainty
was somewhat eased by the introduction of mechanization for field wrapping and packing. There was a major reduction in the number of workers required for
the lettuce harvest and, with the machine, there was
a concomitant rise in labor control. The innovation
of seedling transplants again reduced Antle's labor
requirements and provided predictability in other
production areas such as crop maturity and yield.
The acquisition of Bud Antle, Inc., by Castle & Cooke
provides testimony to the success of the Antle enterprise. The merger represents part of a larger phenomenon occurring in United States agriculture.

> The independent farms that are being merged into
> the large corporate structures are not failures,
> not inefficient competitors on the verge of
> folding. Quite the contrary, they are being
> bought by the giants precisely because they are
> competitive, innovative, and exhibit favorable
> growth potential. Frequently, the companies
> that are bought are the leading producers of
> their respective products. (Hightower, 1973)

With the purchase of the Antle company, Castle &
Cooke has used its massive capital resources to invest in the leading lettuce grower and shipper. Taking minimal risk by relying on an experienced and
established organization to conduct the business of
its subsidiary, Castle & Cooke can afford to expand
Antle's profitable operations even further.

Undeniably, Bud Antle, Inc., followed the corporate pattern of technological change, domestic success, international expansion, and finally absorption
into a larger, more diversified, global corporation.
It has successfully grown, only to be subsumed by a
larger corporation as a measure of its success.
Antle, as a subsidiary of Castle & Cooke, will now
have an even firmer base from which to continue its
process of growth.

264

NOTES

1. For further discussion regarding managerial control over the work force in the mechanized lettuce harvest, see Thomas (1980).

2. In 1963, two years after signing its first Teamster agreement, Bud Antle, Inc., received a $1-million loan from the Teamsters' Central States Southeast and Southwest Areas Pension Fund. The loan became the center of controversy when the United Farm Workers (UFW) filed a $20-million suit against the Antle company, charging an "irreconcilable conflict of interest because of the financial interest which the Teamster fund holds in Bud Antle, Inc.'s operation." Throughout the 1960s the Antle firm was sued by the UFW for misrepresentation of workers, violation of California health and safety laws, and collusion with the Teamsters in conflict of interests.

18
Agribusiness in the United Kingdom: Social and Political Implications

Howard Newby
Peter Utting

Although relationships between agribusiness and technological advances in production have been explored for some time in the United States, such relationships are only now being investigated in other developed countries. This chapter presents a penetrating treatment of the structure and implications of agribusiness in Great Britain. Newby and Utting assert that since World War II, agribusiness companies have become a major agent in promoting social and economic change in rural Britain. This has occurred through the companies' system of advisory and consultative services which aid certain farmers in adopting new technologies of production while assuring quality control over the finished product. Newby and Utting predict that many more technological innovations will be adopted in agriculture which will increase the control of the agribusiness companies, promising far-reaching changes in rural society.

Since World War II, rural Britain has been transformed by a process which is often referred to, with pardonable hyperbole, as the second agricultural revolution. Essentially this has involved the increasing application of scientific and technological principles to the pursuit of profit in the production

---

Revised version of a paper presented at the British Sociological Association Annual Conference, University College, Aberystwyth, Wales, April 1981.

of food. It should be emphasized that, in itself, the commercialization of agriculture is nothing new. Farming has been organized around the principle of profit at least since the eighteenth century, and therefore long ago became disciplined to the exigencies of the market. All that has occurred in recent decades has been a transformation in the technology[1] of most branches of food production, accompanied by state intervention in agriculture which has granted farmers the conditions of production under which they could embark upon a program of increasing productivity and cost-efficiency. The most visible consequences of these changes have involved the mechanization of agriculture and the "drift from the land" of a large proportion of its former labor force. Elsewhere, advances in genetics have produced unprecedented increases in output from both plant and animal breeding, while the application of nutritional science has also resulted in immense benefits from the scientific application of animal feed and fertilizers. Husbandry has also been improved by the introduction of complex forms of vaccine and pesticides.

In these ways agricultural production has been revolutionized to the extent that any sense of technological continuity has been shattered within the lifetime of most of today's farmers. As a result agricultural entrepreneurship has followed the precepts of rationalization apparent in other industries, and farms have become bigger, more capital-intensive, and more specialized in their production. Farmers in turn have partaken in the gradual "disenchantment" of agriculture--the replacement of intuition by calculation and the progressive elimination of the mysteries of plant and animal husbandry by exposing them to scientific appraisal. Such changes have involved, to use the cliche often employed to summarize them, a move "from agriculture to agribusiness."

Without wishing to subscribe to any naive form of technological determinism, we believe it is nevertheless possible to trace a chain of causality from these transformations in farming technology and management to the significant social changes which have occurred in rural Britain since the war. One of us has attempted to explore some of these changes elsewhere (Newby, 1977, 1979a; Newby et al., 1978), and we do not wish to repeat those findings here except to make one relevant point. The economic exigencies of contemporary agriculture owe little to the workings of the free market in agricultural commodities. Individual farmers may indeed act as if they were governed by market rationality, but over the last three decades the state has intervened decisively and continuously as the midwife of technological change and the guarantor of profitability (Newby, 1979a,b).

The social consequences of this policy have not been considered seriously by any of the agencies involved in its formulation, for it was assumed that the vitality of British rural society could be measured by the prosperity of British farmers. The 1947 Agriculture Act therefore offered the single-minded pursuit of efficiency and stability (in the long term they amount to the same thing) by the Ministry of Agriculture while other departments, both locally and nationally, were left to mop up the social consequences among those who were relatively disadvantaged by this policy--small farmers, farm workers, unemployed rural school-leavers, and so on (see Newby, 1979b). The technological transformation of British agriculture, then, is not a product of the "hidden hand" of the market, but of quite deliberate policy decisions, consciously pursued and publicly encouraged up until the present day. This at least suggests why a technologically determinist account of social change in rural Britain is inadequate.

Nevertheless, changing agricultural technology has, together with state regulation, profoundly altered both the structure of the industry and the day-to-day nature of life and work in the countryside. The encouragement of fewer, larger, and more capital-intensive farms has resulted eventually in all of the catalog of social changes which are associated with rural British society today: the mechanization of agriculture, depopulation in the remoter rural areas, the urban middle-class invasion of most rural villages elsewhere, and widespread changes in the rural landscape and other environmental aspects of the countryside. These changes have not been the result of some immutable natural law, but of policy decisions in Whitehall or Brussels.

The Ministry of Agriculture, Food and Fisheries (MAFF), for example, has promoted technological change both directly through its grants and subsidies for farm capitalization and amalgamation, and indirectly through its complex manipulation of commodity price supports and guarantees which have protected farmers from the consequences of chronic overproduction.[2] MAFF has also provided direct assistance through its advisory service (ADAS) and its own research establishments. It also finances research in universities and other autonomous research centers and influences the priorities of the Agriculture

268

Research Council. A large and complex network of institutions has thus been erected in the public sector
in order to effect the technological transformation
that postwar agricultural policy has ordained. The
policy itself has remained entirely unconsidered.
MAFF, at least, adheres to the "technological fix" in
the drive towards cost-efficiency, and in this respect has followed many of the policies which are
familiar to American observers of the workings of the
U.S. Department of Agriculture.

These introductory remarks provide the context
for the main subject matter of this chapter. For the
increasingly capital-intensive nature of British agriculture has had one further effect which deserves
serious attention: it has made farmers more and more
dependent upon nonfarm inputs (machinery, agrochemicals, etc.) while also drawing them into the embrace of a much wider complex of industrial companies
involved in food marketing, processing, distribution,
and retailing. Agriculture is being slowly incorporated into sectors of the engineering, chemical, and
food-processing industries which collectively we may
call "agribusiness" (Davis, 1956). In Britain as in
the United States, the rise of agribusiness has im-
plied not only the increasing rationalization of agriculture, but the growth of a food-production
system, only a small proportion of which may actually
take place on farms.

Our purpose, then, is to describe the main features of this agribusiness system of food production
and to explore some of the implications of agribusiness in Britain for the structure of rural society.
In this respect, this paper may be seen as an extended footnote to previous work on farmers and farm
workers in East Anglia (Newby, 1977; Newby et al.,
1978). However, it may also be regarded as an exploration of some of the social implications of postwar agricultural policy which the policy makers
themselves so steadfastly ignore. For there is little doubt that in promoting a highly capitalized
farming industry, this policy has also promoted the
interests of agribusiness companies in British agriculture.

AGRIBUSINESS IN THE UNITED STATES --
A POSSIBLE FUTURE?

The term "agribusiness" was coined in the United
States to describe the vertical integration of certain companies to control the whole system of food

production from seeds to fast-food outlets. Although American agriculture is at a similar level of technological development as farming in Britain, it is organized institutionally in a very different way. Large corporations like Tenneco, Ralston Purina, Purex, and United Brands control most of the processes in the production of food, including seed manufacture, farming the land itself, storage and marketing, packaging, processing, wholesale distribution, retail sales, and even the ownership of restaurant chains and institutional food outlets.

Is this, one may ask, the shape of things to come in Britain? Viewed cross-nationally, British agriculture is certainly unusual in exhibiting a relatively low degree of vertical integration. With very few exceptions the major food-processing companies or agricultural suppliers have not directly involved themselves in farming and have preferred to deal on a contract basis with formally free farmers. However, a brief consideration of American experience allows some assessment to be made of how long British agriculture can remain structured in its traditional form--that is, consisting mostly of small, family-run businesses.

In a paper of this length it is impossible to offer a comprehensive and detailed account of American corporate agribusiness. Some scattered accounts are in any case already available (Hightower, 1973, 1975; Merrill, 1976; George, 1977; Perelman, 1977; Rodefeld et al., 1978; Morgan, 1979; Robbins, 1974). We are forced instead to take one example to illustrate some of the most prevalent trends in American agribusiness, and we have taken that of soybean production. This is admittedly an extreme case. But it shows vividly, even alarmingly, a possible scenario for the future organization of certain branches of British agriculture. It is also relevant for the following discussion, for Europe's largest agribusiness corporation, Unilever, holds a dominant position in the refining of vegetable oils in Britain and has enlarged its market share, not only of human food and vegetable oil, but in the crucial area of animal feedstuffs. Unilever is also involved in soybean production in the United States.

Soybeans and Agribusiness

The soybean has been described by one commentator (Rushton, 1973) as "the preeminent achievement of twentieth-century agriculture, a raw material with synthetic potentials for surpassing those of timber,

cotton, or peanuts--potentials surpassed only by petroleum." When soybeans are crushed and dissolved in
hexane, a petroleum-based solvent, they yield two
basic products: soy oil and soy meal. Soy oil is
the basic constituent of margarine and cooking oil.
It has helped to create the recent boom in quick-
service restaurants through its use as a cooking oil
for frozen french fries, chicken, pizzas, and do-
nuts. The chemical industry uses soy oils in soaps,
detergents, drying agents, paints, and printing
inks. With the increasing cost of petroleum, soy oil
is also becoming an important source for the manufacture of drugs and toilet goods, for urethane foams,
and for other derivatives of glycerine.

The enormous increase in demand for soy oil has,
perforce, created large quantities of soy meal as a
by-product. Soy meal makes an excellent animal feed,
accounting in the United States for over 90 percent
of pig and poultry food. It is also fed to cattle
and, in an extruded form, to humans as substitute
"meat." The latter has proved to be particularly
profitable in the so-called "institutional" market--
schools, canteens, airlines, hospitals, prisons,
etc. Ground and refined, soy flour is also used in
sausages, dog food, baby foods, baked "meat" pies,
convenience foods, whipped dessert topping, coffee
whiteners, and a variety of "cheese" and "milk" products. Ironically, not only is soy meal a main constituent of animal feed, it also provides the main
competition for animal and dairy products. Among the
many other social impacts, then, the control of soybean production grants at least the potential for
controlling many other areas of agriculture as well.

The United States controls 90 percent of the
world market for soybeans (Brazil is the only other
exporter of note), and 90 percent of U.S. production
takes place in the Mississippi River Valley, where
climatic conditions favor its growth. These conditions have favored the development of vertical integration among the corporate soybean producers. For
example, Cargill, one of the major American grain
distributors and the nation's second largest corporate contributor to the balance of payments, operates
fourteen soybean-processing plants, and export ter-
minals at sixty locations (Rushton, 1973:16). It
produces its own animal feeds, flour, and poultry.
Ralston Purina has diversified from animal-feed production into poultry, pet foods, Jack-in-the-Box
fast-food restaurants, tuna fish (packed in soy oil),
frozen food, and egg production.

Another conglomerate, Tenneco (Tennessee Gas
Pipeline Company), while not farming soybeans, is

closely involved in their processing and distribution. It has diversified from oil refining into agricultural machinery production, fruit and vegetable canning under its "Sun Giant" label, packaging (via its Packaging Corporation of America), shipbuilding, ship repair, engineering, fast-food outlets, gasoline stations, and supermarkets. Tenneco manufactures hexane, makes the farming equipment necessary for soybean planting and harvesting, and owns storage and packaging facilities. It even farms 1.4 million acres, mostly in California, but also in Kansas, Arizona, Michigan, and Texas. Tenneco's declared intention is "integration from seedling to supermarket."[3]

The geographical concentration of soybean production, allied to its extraordinary variety of uses, renders this branch of agriculture peculiarly susceptible to vertical integration and the growth of market oligarchy. But it is by no means exceptional--many other examples could be given, especially from fruit and vegetable production and from poultry and beef rearing. Many of the prominent agribusiness corporations in the United States are also familiar names in Britain--for example, Kellogg, General Foods, Del Monte, and Heinz--and are also heavily involved in agriculture in less developed countries (George, 1977; Tudge, 1977). They are frequently in the vanguard of multinational organization (the most notorious is arguably Coca-Cola) and, particularly in the Third World, pose acute problems of national sovereignty and market power (for example, in the "banana republics" of Central America).

Under these circumstances it becomes tempting to weave conspiracy theories around the exercise of oligarchical corporate power, and occasionally this is given credence by the United States' use of food exports in the realm of international diplomacy--"the food weapon," as Earl Butz, the Nixon administration's secretary for agriculture, once described it. But there is no need to invent conspiracy theories in order to discern the lack of public accountability embodied in the agribusiness conglomerates. They are actively involved in changing dietary habits and the structure of agriculture, food marketing, and retailing. They wield enormous market power--and yet remain impervious to control by politicians and consumers.

Sociologically, agribusiness corporations are of more than passing interest. Along with the state, they represent one of the most important agencies involved in the restructuring of rural society. The processes involved are often incremental and indirect but are nonetheless effective and far-reaching. A brief comparison between Britain and the United States readily indicates this. The agribusiness domination of certain sectors of American agriculture has produced a marked effect upon the social structure of those rural areas where they are concentrated--principally California, the Southwest, and Florida. Corporate control is manifested by absentee landownership, remote and bureaucratic decision making, and a local social structure consisting of a small group of managers and supervisors employed on a permanent basis juxtaposed with large numbers of migrant workers. This can be contrasted with, say, the British situation where few agribusiness corporations have attempted a restructuring of agriculture directly by farming land themselves, and where there is a virtual absence of migrant workers. The corporations have preferred instead to work their transformation by proxy, abjuring large-scale involvement in farming itself but controlling the conditions under which farmers operate. In Britain, the tendency is for farmers to become the outworkers of major agribusiness companies.

There are some plausible reasons why such a pattern of development is more appropriate in Britain than in the United States--and why, therefore, the American pattern of vertical integration may not be repeated. First, the historic cost of land has been much higher in Britain than in the United States, and rates of return on a year-by-year basis (i.e., yield) much lower. Agricultural production thus has to bear a much heavier burden of capital investment in Britain. Secondly, technological developments in food processing and marketing in Britain occurred when an already highly commercialized farming class was in existence, which could be relied upon to exercise quality control, ensure continuity of supply, etc., on a contractual basis. In the American "Sun Belt" this class was partially absent by the time that agribusiness was established: many processors had little choice other than to farm themselves. Thus in Britain the domination of the market has been assured by control of both farm inputs and outputs without actual involvement in farming itself. Indeed it is the realization of this factor which has led some American agribusiness corporations to withdraw from their farming operations (Cordtz, 1972). Finally, there are few economies of scale in farming (as opposed to processing) which are not attainable at a level well below that of agribusiness involvement and within striking distance of family proprietorships.

The importance of land and the vagaries of soil, topography, and weather ensure the constant readjustment of managerial decisions. Hence, personalized
forms of control become more necessary.

In Britain, then, agribusiness influence over
the structure of agriculture is likely to continue to
proceed indirectly, with agribusiness companies seeking out highly market-oriented "agribusinessmen"
farmers (Bell and Newby, 1974; Newby et al., 1978)
with whom to place contracts. Enough farmers have,
indeed, proved sufficiently flexible to the needs of
agribusiness companies for the latter not to feel the
necessity to vertically integrate and take up farming
themselves. This has enabled them to avoid the high
cost of purchasing managerial expertise in agriculture. It is, for example, surely not coincidental
that British agribusiness companies have been quite
willing to vertically integrate overseas (principally
in the ex-colonial parts of the Third World) where
these conditions do not, or have not, applied. In
Britain itself, contract farming has usually suf-
ficed.

In this manner, agribusiness companies have accelerated the trend towards the rationalization of
agriculture and the concentration of the industry on
fewer, larger farms. Smaller farmers, who do not
participate in such contractual arrangements, find
themselves becoming increasingly marginal, while the
larger farmers find their enterprise gradually transformed by the relentless "industrial" logic of agribusiness. Larger farmers are encouraged to become
more specialized in order to make the maximum possible use of their specialized technology and
skills. As a result, agriculture becomes organized
according to nonagricultural criteria, on the assumption that agriculture is merely a disguised form of
manufacture. This has numerous social implications,
not only for farming entrepreneurs, but also for farm
workers, the employees of food processors, and ultimately all of us as consumers.

The general public is largely unaware of these
trends--and, for that matter, rather uncaring. What
counts primarily to the consumer is the price of
food. Agribusiness companies themselves certainly
believe that they are performing a public service by
implementing the consumer demand for cheap food. The
changing pattern of consumer demand for food is also
encouraging the growth of agribusiness in Britain.
More of the food that we purchase is processed food
and, given current trends such as the increasing
proportion of working mothers, the demand for

convenience food is likely to increase, quite aside
from the encouragement given by the agribusiness companies' own advertising campaigns. Since the value
added from processing food is much greater than that
which is accrued from growing it, agribusiness domination of food production in Britain seems likely to
increase for the foreseeable future.

The following two sections of this chapter outline the current structure of agribusiness in Britain
in order to assess some of the implications of the
changing structure of food production in Britain--and
the changing role of farming within it. The first
section is concerned with farming inputs and the second with farming outputs. The conclusion offers some
speculative comments on the likely outcome of the
trend towards expanding agribusiness in Britain.

AGRIBUSINESS AND FARM INPUTS

Three industries--agro-engineering, agrochemicals, and feedstuffs--provide agriculture with its
major input requirements. A subsidiary area concerns
seed production, an area of increasing competition
between major agribusiness companies. Frequently,
seed production is carried out by firms also engaged
in feedstuffs and agrochemical production. This is
because new high-yielding hybrid varieties are often
vulnerable to disease and rely for success on applications of pesticides (Mooney, 1979). Information on
seed production is difficult to obtain, though it has
been a recent object of vertical integration in an
international market now worth £5 billion a year and
controlled by restrictive plant-breeding rights akin
to patents. In Britain alone, this market is worth
over £200 million per year.

Agro-engineering, agrochemicals, and feedstuffs
have all undergone massive growth since World War
II. The extent of technological change in agriculture has led to farmers' buying a far higher proportion of their inputs than was common under previous
house-and-hand technologies. Annual expenditure on
machinery is now greater than that on labor, and the
move to agricultural specialization away from mixed
farming systems has ensured that feedstuffs are the
greatest single item of expenditure for the contemporary farmer. During the 1970s, the rapid expansion
of the agro-engineering, agrochemicals, and feedstuffs sectors, characteristic of the previous two
decades, tailed off as market saturation was
reached.[4]

Different sectors adapted to the slackening of growth during the 1970s in different ways. In the feedstuffs sector, hundreds of small-scale manufacturers went out of business altogether, while the major producers integrated both horizontally and vertically by moving into livestock production. In the agro-engineering sector, the effects of the lack of growth in the domestic market have been mitigated by a switch into exports, which now accounts for 70 percent of production. Helped by the aid programs of many Western industrialized nations to the Third World, the less developed countries are regarded as the major target for market growth into the 1980s and 1990s. It is expected that demand for tractors, for example, will almost double among LDCs between 1976 and 1985, while demand in Europe and North America will actually decline slightly. By 1985 demand for tractors in Latin America will be greater than that in Europe (Massey-Ferguson, 1976). Whether because of these changes in the structure of the market or because of the vast sums required for research and development, each of the agro-input industries is dominated by a few giant, usually multinational, corporations.

Forward integration into agricultural production and food processing, and horizontal integration into other agro-input sectors, increasingly have been features of the activities of these corporations. Of the major companies in the three sectors supplying inputs in agriculture, only those engaged in agro-engineering have avoided integration into other agro-input or food-processing sectors in the U.K.[5] Within the agrochemical industry, for example, integration has tended to occur horizontally into processes which are technologically similar. Thus Imperial Chemical Industries (ICI) has moved from fertilizer production into pesticides and thence to the large-scale production of synthetic protein feedstuffs, enabling the construction of a technological package which combines well to facilitate research, development, and marketing. It has also moved into seed production via its subsidiary Scottish Agricultural Industries. Shell has followed a similar pattern, moving from the production of "Shellstar" fertilizer to pesticides and thence to seed production via Nickerson Seeds, owned by Shell, and Britain's largest marketing organization of agricultural seeds.[6]

As leading corporations diversify in this way, we are likely to see the emergence of distribution systems similar to those which have occurred on a larger scale in the United States, whereby company sales representatives or company-controlled merchants supply individual farmers with the bulk of their inputs and receive their output on contract. In some cases this occurs on a quid pro quo basis. This process is particularly apparent among the major companies in the feedstuffs industry, where integration has taken place more vertically into food processing (see table 18.1). The feedstuffs industry is particularly significant in Britain, both because of the importance of feedstuffs in farm expenditure and because the feedstuffs industry lies at the fulcrum of British agricultural production. Cereals grown in Britain are produced mainly for animal feed. Control of feedstuffs thus provides control of both of the main sectors of agriculture—the production of crops and the production of animal and dairy products.

The animal feedstuffs industry is a massive, though underresearched, sector. Today processed feedstuffs account for the entire diet of pigs and poultry, although cattle are the largest consumers, taking 45 percent of the output even though it constitutes only 20 percent of their feed. The ten to eleven million tons of feedstuffs supplied by this sector are also supplemented by seven to eight million tons produced by individual farmers' "home-mixing." Thanks to increases in output from domestic high-yielding cereal varieties, imports of "soft" grain for animal feed have declined by 15 percent over the last decade, but imports of soy meal (see preceding section) have increased dramatically in recent years. In 1977 soy meal made up 56.5 percent of the protein content of animal feeds, an increase of 55 percent in just six years.

According to a 1978 Price Commission report on this sector, there are some 235 manufacturers of feedstuff compounds and another 70 agricultural merchants who produce smaller quantities. However, just 7 manufacturers account for approximately 60 percent of output (and 5 for 50 percent), with the Unilever subsidiary BOCM-Silcock Ltd. (BOCMS) by far the largest producer, accounting for 21.4 percent of the British market. By contrast, production of farming cooperatives is estimated at 6 percent of total volume. Several socially significant changes have occurred in the enterprise structure of the industry. Since 1955 the total number of factories producing animal feeds has declined by more than half, from 1,050 in 1955 to 750 in 1969 and 480 in 1977—a decline mainly accounted for by the closure of factories producing less than twenty tons per week. The past twenty years has also seen a major shift in the

TABLE 18.1
Extent of Integration by Corporations with Major Agro-input Interests

Company	Seeds	Agricultural Machinery	Tractors	Pesticides	Fertilizers	Feedstuffs	Agriculture	Food Manufacturing	Wholesaling & Retailing
Imperial Chemical Industries (ICI)	x			x	x	x			
Fisons	x			x	x	x			
Shell	x			x	x	x	x		
Unilever						x	x	x	x
J. Bibby and Sons	x					x	x	x	
RankHovisMacDougall	x	x		x		x	x	x	x
Dalgety/Spillers	x			x	x	x	x		
Imperial Foods	x				x	x	x	x	x
Massey-Ferguson		x	x						
Int'l. Harvester		x	x						
Ford			x						
New Holland (Sperry Rand)		x							

Source: Original research by authors

locations of compound mills as manufacturers have established mills on inland sites.[7] This inland construction has led to a situation of overcapacity in the industry generally and has in turn led to the major companies seeking to protect themselves by vertically integrating along their distribution networks. Approximately 65 percent of manufactured feedstuffs are now sold direct to farmers by company salesmen. Many small, local, independent merchants have closed down.

AGRIBUSINESS AND FOOD PROCESSING

As indicated above, BOCM-Silcock Ltd. (BOCMS) is a subsidiary of the multinational combine, Unilever. Unilever also owns shipping lines (Norfolk Line, Palm Line), meat wholesalers and processors (Midland Poultry, Unox), paper mills (Thames Board Mills), and much, much more--812 companies in 75 countries manufacturing over 1,000 products.[8] Unilever is the most spectacular example of a vertically integrated, multinational agribusiness corporation, but it is by no means unique in controlling a proportion of both agricultural inputs (feedstuffs) and outputs. Farmers find that when it comes to marketing their produce (a notoriously weak aspect of British agriculture), they are drawn into the embrace of the food-processing industry, an industry also dominated by a few companies in most commodities and one which has seen rapid growth despite the volume of food expenditure having remained stable over recent decades.

The food-processing industry has promoted and prospered on the demand for "convenience" food--especially frozen foods, which increased by 250 percent between 1968 and 1975. A 1975 two-part study by the Director-General of Competition of the Commission of the European Economic Community (EEC) estimated that just 2.5 percent of the companies involved in food processing (or fifty-six companies) accounted for 78 percent of the British food-processing industry by output in 1968. Merger activity has been particularly pronounced in the frozen-food sector, so that by 1973 three companies--Unilever (Birds Eye), Nestle (Findus), and Imperial Tobacco (Ross)--controlled 90 percent of the market. Birds Eye alone accounts for 60 percent of the British market, while Unilever and Nestle between them control 70 percent of the market in Western Europe.[9]

These examples can be placed in a broader context by examining table 18.2, which shows the sales concentration ratios of the five largest enterprises in each of thirty-three product ranges. Thus in 1968, eighteen of the thirty-three product ranges recorded concentration ratios of 80 percent or more. However, table 18.2 gives no indication of the size of the five largest enterprises, so that the information must be combined with that in table 18.3, which gives the market shares of major food companies in selected products, in order to obtain some idea of market power. The size, in terms of turnover, of the

TABLE 18.2
Sales Concentration Ratios of Five Largest
Enterprises in Food Product Groups, 1963 and 1968

Food Product Group	1963	1968
Trades Showing an Increase		
in Concentration Ratio		
Meal and flour (white flour		
for breadmaking)	79.2	80.8
Bread (loaves or rolls)	71.4	77.3
Flour confectionery	51.0	60.1
Biscuits	65.5	71.0
Bacon and ham	47.4	56.9
Sausages and sausage meat	52.2	56.2
Sugar confectionery	35.9	43.5
Marmalade and jams	72.9	75.6
Other preserved fruit	37.7	45.7
Vegetables preserved in		
airtight containers	65.3	66.7
Vegetables (quick-frozen)	93.3	97.1
Pickles, sauces, and relishes	68.0	71.5
Vegetable and seed oils	82.3	84.3
Self-rising flour	88.0	91.7
Condensed and evaporated milk	93.4	94.4
Cocoa products	82.3	83.3
Margarine	92.8	93.8
Sugar	98.6	99.3
Fish and marine oils	92.8	92.9
Trades Showing a Decrease		
in Concentration Ratio		
Fish and fish products		
(quick-frozen)	91.7	91.1
Cheese and processed cheese	78.5	77.7
Meal and flour (excluding self-		
rising flour and semolina)	71.6	67.2

——————————————— Continued ———————————————

280

TABLE 18.2 (continued)

Cereal breakfast foods (for retail sale)	97.7	93.5
Butter	85.5	78.4
Milk powder	88.9	84.7
Ice cream and candy	93.1	91.2
Potato chips	91.6	83.3
Soups	92.5	90.4
Compound fat	84.8	82.6
Coffee, coffee and chicory extracts and essences	98.4	93.7

Trades with Concentration
Ratios for 1968 Only

Dressed poultry, carcass meat, and poultry (quick-frozen)	--	39.2
Heat-treated milk	--	44.2
Tea, blended	--	82.9

Source: Census of Production, 1968 (similar data not published since 1968).

top ten food-processing companies in the U.K. is also shown in table 18.4.

This picture of concentration within the food-processing industry is completed by considering the forward integration of these firms into wholesale and retail marketing. Here vertical integration has represented an alternative to merger activity as a means of protecting profit margins, minimizing costs, and securing an increased market share. Such forward integration has promoted and been accompanied by structural changes and social impacts in the retail food trade since the 1950s, most notably the gradual replacement of small-scale, independent, family grocery shops by supermarkets and chain stores. Seventy percent of the grocery market is now controlled by the ten largest chains, a development which has considerably altered the relationship between the food-processing and food-retailing sectors. Numerous food-processing companies have been forced to respond by securing marketing outlets, prompting a series of acquisitions and mergers, both offensive and defensive. Thus, two of the five leading food retailers, Allied Suppliers and Fine Fare, are owned by food

TABLE 18.3
Market Shares of Major Food Companies
in Selected Products, 1972

Product	Size of Retail Market (Million £)	Company	%Share
Breakfast cereals (ready to eat)	54	Kellogg	56
		Weetabix	21
		Nat'l Biscuit Co.	10
Bread	430	Assoc. Brit. Foods	26
		RankHovis MacDougall	25
		Spillers[a]	20
Biscuits	210	United Biscuits	40
		Assoc. Biscuits	20
Frozen fish	96	Unilever	63
		Nestle	18
		Imperial Group	7
Margarine	76	Unilever	70
Sugar	150	Tate and Lyle[b]	60
		British Sugar Corp.	25
		Manbre and Garton	11
Frozen vegetables	72	Unilever	74
		Nestle	20
Canned fruit	82	Del Monte	36
		Libby's	33
Canned soup	60	Heinz	63
		Crosse & Blackwell	14
Ice cream	115	Unilever	41
		Lyons Maid	43
Potato chips, puffs	72	Imperial Group	38
		General Mills	30
Tea	145	Brooke Bond	41
		Typhoo (Cadbury-Schweppes)	18

Source: Wardle, Christopher. Changing Food Habits in the U.K. London: Earth Resources Research Ltd., 1977.

[a]In April 1978 Spillers withdrew from the bread market.

[b]Since 1972, Tate and Lyle have acquired Manbre and Garton. Also, the relative market shares of Tate and Lyle and The British Sugar Corporation have altered considerably since Britain's entry into the EEC. Now these two companies have almost equal shares of approximately 98 percent of the total sugar market.

processors (Cavenham and ABF, respectively). The food distribution interests of leading food processors are shown in table 18.5.

The overall pattern of vertical integration in the food-processing sector is shown in table 18.6; this may be compared with table 18.1, which summarized integration among firms dealing with agricultural inputs. It should be emphasized, however, that the direct involvement of these companies in agriculture in the U.K. is much less than it may seem. Most of their farming operations in Britain involve research stations and demonstration farms. Fully commercial involvement in agriculture almost entirely takes place overseas, particularly in the less developed countries. Nevertheless, the extent of

TABLE 18.4
Size and Growth in Turnover of Ten Largest Companies in the Food-Processing Industry, 1972-1976

Company[a]	1972 Rank	Turnover[b] (Million £) 1972	1976	1976 Rank	Percent Increase
Unilever	1	1539	6760	1	339
Associated British Foods (ABF)	2	729	1301	3	78
Cavenham	3	462	1659	2	259
Rank Hovis MacDougall	4	441	921	5	99
Tate and Lyle	5	419	1274	4	204
Unigate	6	409	763	6	87
Union Int'l.	7	403	646	9	60
Cadbury Schweppes	8	349	667	7	91
Spillers	9	279	667	11	109
Brooke Bond Liebig	10	263	591	10	125
J. Lyons	11	259	651	8	251

Source: 1972 figures, European Office for Information study; 1976 figures, Institute of Grocery Distribution, Research Services Division Publication

[a]The Cooperative Wholesale Society, not included in company analysis, was the third largest food-sector concern in 1972, with a turnover of £596 million.

[b]Turnover figures for 1976 apply either to early 1976 or late 1975.

TABLE 18.5
Food Distribution Interests of
Leading Food Processors

Food Processors	Food/Retail/ Wholesale Interests	Type
Associated British Foods (ABF)	Fine Fare (incl. Melias) Allied Bakeries Group Alliance Wholesale Grocers	Grocers Bakers Wholesale grocers
Cavenham Group	Allied Suppliers	Grocers
Union Int'l.	J.H. Dewhurst T.W. Downs British Beef	Butchers Food Dists. Wholesale butchers
Brooke Bond Liebig	Baxters	Butchers
Fitch Lovell	Keymarkets (incl. D. Grieg) West Layton Lovell and Christmas	Grocers Meat Food wholesalers
Rank Hovis MacDougall	British Bakeries	Bakers
Spillers	Mead-Lonsdale Group	Meat wholesalers
Associated Dairies	Asda	Superstores
Booker McConnell	Budgen Holland and Barrett William Brothers Booker Belmont James Harper & Son (Edinburgh)	Grocers Health food shops Butchers Food wholesaling Food wholesaling
Barker & Dobson	Oakeshotts	Grocers

Source: Original research by authors

horizontal and vertical integration across large, multinational conglomerates is striking. Unilever, for example, is integrated horizontally via its use of animal and vegetable fats, oils, and solids in a range of products from margarine to deodorants. As far as vertical integration is concerned:

> At the lower end there are plantations, purchasing boards and trawler fleets which between them harvest materials as diverse as herrings, groundnuts and timber. At the next level there are the oil mills, slaughterhouses, factory

TABLE 18.6
Leading Food-Processing Concerns with Subsidiaries in Agricultural Production, Animal Feeds, Wholesaling, and Retailing

Company	Agri-cultural Production	Animal Feeds	Whole-saling	Re-tailing
Unilever	x	x		
Associated Brit. Foods				x
Cooperative Wholesale Society	x		x	x
Cavenham		x		x
Rank Hovis MacDougall	x	x	x	x
Tate & Lyle	x			
Unigate	x			
Union Int'l.	x		x	x
Cadbury-Schweppes	x			
Spillers	x	x	x	
Brooke Bond Liebig	x			
J. Lyons				x
Imperial Foods	x	x	x	x
Fitch Lovell	x		x	x
Fatstock Marketing Corp. (FMC)	x		x	
United Biscuits				x
H.J. Heinz	x			
J. Bibby	x	x		
Booker McConnell	x		x	x

Source: Original research by authors

ships and timber mills. At the third, the manufacturing operations: detergents, soap and margarine and container manufacture, food processing, freezing and canning, etc. At the fourth
level there is all the paraphernalia of selling,
from market research, advertising agencies, distribution depots and retail outlets to fish restaurants, industrial caterers and cleaners and
meat pie shops. (Counter Information Service,
1975)

Indeed, further integration within agribusiness occurs via interlocking directorships among many of the
leading companies.[10]

CONCLUSIONS

It is now possible to return to some of the sociological issues raised at the beginning of this paper and to reexamine them in the light of this brief
outline of agribusiness in the U.K. Clearly, the
growth of agribusiness raises important issues relating to social effects such as technology control,
dietary change, economic sovereignty, public accountability, and the concentration of economic power in
the production of a basic human need, food. However,
it is the implications of the rise of agribusiness
for the changing social structure of rural Britain
that we wish to concentrate on in these concluding
remarks.
At the outset it is important to make one obvious, though frequently overlooked, point: since the
war, agribusiness companies have become a major agent
in promoting social and economic change in rural
Britain. They have supplemented the state agencies
in setting up almost a parallel apparatus of advisory
and consultative services which aid selected farmers
in adopting new production technologies while assuring quality control over the finished product. All
animal-feedstuff companies, for example, provide a
comprehensive advisory service, exhorting the farmer
to introduce new methods employing their products.
Food processors also advise their contracted suppliers on husbandry techniques and hygiene precautions.
They offer credit and advice on the purchase of new
capital equipment, and may oversee the entire production process without intervening directly. In some
cases, this control is very tight indeed, reducing
the entrepreneurial autonomy of the farmer to that
almost of farm operator. The classic example is the

case of Birds Eye peas: the company employs fieldmen
who tell farmers when to sow the crop; who then inspect it, supervise spraying, and direct the harvesting operations.[11] As another example, Walls retains
considerable control over pig farmers (including pre-
scribing the feed to be used). The social implications are obvious to all concerned. As the former
chairman of Unilever, Ernest Woodroofe, remarked when
asked about what attracted him most about his job:

> It is the power to change things, the power not
> to have to accept things as they are. You can
> alter things. For instance, the agriculture of
> East Anglia has been altered by the operations
> of Birds Eye. (Counter Information Service,
> 1975)

"Factory farming" has also been facilitated by
the rise of agribusiness companies who can provide
the wherewithal of high capital investment, technological know-how, research and development facilities, and extensive marketing and advertising techniques which makes the assembly-line production of
food possible. These examples are, however, merely
the most direct and visible consequences of the rise
of agribusiness. Equally important though less quan-
tifiable results of encouraging agribusiness are the
rationalization of agriculture and the profit maximization of selected farmers, with implications for the
class relations of rural England (Newby, 1977; Newby
et al., 1978).

These changes continue. There are many more
technological innovations in the process of being
adopted in agriculture which will promote far-reaching changes in rural society. Perhaps two examples
will suffice to indicate this and provide a glimpse
of a possible future in certain sectors of British
agriculture. The first concerns the continuing expansion of factory farming. Having begun in poultry
and moved from there to pig and beef cattle production, the advance of factory farming was for long
stymied by the sheep. According to the logic of agribusiness, the sheep is nothing more than a woolly
pig and ought to be subject to similar techniques of
production. But sheep do not do well indoors, and
lose weight. So for over a decade the race has been
on to breed these disagreeable qualities out of sheep
and instigate the intensive production of sheep
(broiler lamb).

In 1978, it was announced that "Cambridge Sheep"
production had been achieved. Its qualities included

a high feed-conversion ratio, resistance to disease, and the ability to produce lambs at any time of the year. Although some technical difficulties still need to be overcome, it does not require much imagination to predict a situation in which one or more of the large food processors with interests in feedstuffs, meat processing, and retailing (Unilever? Imperial Tobacco?) will go ahead with the construction of integrated broiler-lamb factories (perhaps sited in development areas to take advantage of capital grants), selling the produce through their own supermarkets or on contract to others. And we will buy it because it will be cheaper. In twenty years' time we will have to rely upon folk memories of the time when sheep wandered around hillsides. What this will do to the economy and the social structure of upland farming areas need hardly be emphasized.

A second example returns us to the earlier consideration of that perfect agribusiness crop, the soybean. Unilever now serves the European market from just six oil mills, answering the huge increase in demand for soy meal associated with the rise of intensive livestock production. Leaving aside the complex issue of how far soybeans will replace meat as a source of protein in the human diet, the dramatic increase in soy-based animal feeds has threatened the main market of cereal producers in Britain and Europe and, in addition, the traditional mechanism of disposing of surplus dairy production, the feeding of skimmed or powdered milk to cattle. These two products are in chronic surplus within the European Economic Community, bringing the massive imports of soybeans into direct confrontation with the EEC's Common Agricultural Policy (CAP). Cheaper, oil-based animal feeds are ousting community-grown feedstuffs, contributing to the high cost of the CAP. Yet soybean imports represent the major breach in the Community's "tariff wall," and their volume continues to rise. With the CAP becoming a focus of political attention in Europe and with rising demands to eliminate the "inefficient" dairy producers as a result of the high cost of support policies, it will be interesting to see who gives way--Unilever (with its allies in the Mississippi Valley and the U.S. Department of Agriculture) or the small dairy farmers of Europe.

The "second agricultural revolution," then, is far from complete. Despite (indeed, because of) the energy crisis, agribusiness is not going to fade away. None of this is to suggest an apocalyptic vision of the future of British farming, for the

changes which will occur will largely be the extrap-
olation of existing trends. Surviving farmers are
likely to retain their nominal independence, but
their share of retail food prices seems destined to
decline further and they will find themselves even
more vulnerable to the agribusiness companies' marketing policies. So the British countryside of the
future will contain fewer farms, fewer people occu-
pied in agriculture, a more industrialized system of
production, and a rural social structure—and even a
rural landscape—which takes all of these factors
into account.

NOTES

1. It should be emphasized that the term "technology" is used in a very broad sense throughout this
paper. We use it to mean "techniques of production,"
which includes not merely implements of labor (new
machinery, etc.) but also forms of management. In
reality the two are virtually inseparable.
2. For details, see Self and Storing, 1962; Donaldson and Donaldson, 1972; Beresford, 1975.
3. Cited by Katz in Merrill (1976:42).
4. Only the market for pesticides is an exception. Here output doubled between 1963 and 1972,
aided by the husbandry requirements of the new high-
yielding cereal varieties referred to above. This
expansion seems likely to continue and has compensated for the more stagnant market in fertilizers for
the major agrochemical producers.
5. The American agribusiness corporation, Tenneco, has moved in the opposite direction by purchasing David Brown Tractors. The sectors where integration has been most extensive are agrochemicals and
feedstuffs. However, the types of integration entered into by these two sectors and the rationale
behind them have varied.
6. Nickerson Seeds also owns Rothwell Plant
Breeders, which, together with the government-backed
Plant Breeding Institute, dominates cereal breeding
in Britain. Rothwell and Rank Hovis MacDougall have
in turn formed a joint company, British Hybrid
Cereals, to commercially exploit new high-yielding
hybrids.
7. This move was to take advantage of increased
domestic supplies of cereals and other raw materials, to save on haulage costs, and to avoid port
congestion (Butterwick, 1969). Today only 30 percent of animal feeds are manufactured at the port

side, compared with 71 percent in 1959, and this has contributed to the deindustrialization of dockland areas in London, Liverpool, and Glasgow.

8. Among its products are Birds Eye frozen food; Vesta packaged meals; Batchelors canned vegetables and soups; Walls ice cream and meat products; Blue Band, Stork, Summer County, Flora, and Echo margarine; Spry and Cookeen lard; Crisp n' Dry cooking oil; and detergent and toilet preparations such as Lux, Persil, Omo, Comfort, Sunlight, Rexona, Breeze, Vim, Sunsilk, Twink, Harmony, Sure, Shield, Gibbs toothpaste, Close-Up, Signal, and Pepsodent. .

9. The frozen-food sector is an example of merger activity having been accompanied by market growth. However, the tendency towards monopoly is equally apparent elsewhere in sectors where demand is static or declining--for example, in bread manufacture.

10. See Newby and Utting (1984) for further details.

11. See Newby (1977:286-87) for a fuller description.

19
The Social Impacts of Biogenetic Technology in Agriculture: Past and Future

Jack Kloppenburg, Jr.

Since the rediscovery of Mendel's work in the late nineteenth century, plant and animal breeders have made far-reaching changes in economically important species. Yet social scientists have rarely addressed the profound social impacts of such "improvements." With the emergence of the new field of "biotechnology," agriculture is entering a new era of technological change. Kloppenburg's chapter represents an attempt to understand where we have been and where we are going as we enter what one writer has called an age of "synthetic biology." Kloppenburg suggests that an understanding of the development of hybrid corn can do much to illuminate the established structural forces which will materially shape the development and deployment of biotechnology. Drawing on Friedland's "projective" approach to social impact assessment, Kloppenburg delineates various analytic focuses which link observed historical patterns to future social impacts.

INTRODUCTION

Scholars and political analysts representing a wide variety of theoretical positions have recognized that technological advance is a principal factor contributing to structural change in United States

Jack Kloppenburg is currently a graduate student in the Department of Rural Sociology, Cornell University.

agriculture (e.g., Hightower, 1972; Perelman, 1977; Berry, 1977; Cochrane, 1979; Lu, 1979; Just et al., 1979; Goss et al., 1982). Considerable attention has been given to the labor displacing, environmental, and scale impacts of new mechanical and chemical technologies.

In contrast, the social consequences of the introduction of new biogenetic[1] technologies on American agriculture have been infrequently and inadequately addressed. When social-science research efforts have been applied to this area, they have been narrowly focused on a few highly visible cases closely connected with mechanization (for example, tomato breeding for mechanized harvest, Webb and Bruce, 1968; Friedland and Barton, 1976; Schrag, 1978), or on estimates of gross economic returns to genetic improvement of crops and their relation to agricultural research expenditures (for example, Griliches, 1957, 1958; Evenson and Kislev, 1975; Ruttan and Sundquist, 1982).

The general neglect of the social consequences of biogenetic technology in its American context differs sharply with social-science research orientations associated with the "Green Revolution." At the heart of the Green Revolution are new plant varieties with enhanced yield potential, the "miracle" rices and wheats developed by the international agricultural research centers (IARCs). Both supporters and critics of the Green Revolution recognize that the biogenetic component of the Green Revolution's package of innovations played a crucial role in fostering a whole series of far-reaching social and environmental changes. These include substantial yield increases in selected areas, regional inequalities, uneven adoption of the new technology, income inequalities at the farm level, increased scale and specialization of operation, labor displacement, mechanization, agrochemical dependence, depressed product prices, rising land prices, genetic erosion, pest-vulnerable monocultures, and environmental deterioration (Cleaver, 1972; Jennings, 1974; Perelman, 1977; Pearse, 1980; Plucknett and Smith, 1982). Plant-breeding programs in the United States are surely implicated in similar changes in American agriculture.

If the important role which biogenetic technology has played in changing the structure of agriculture in the United States has been too seldom addressed and too little appreciated, there has also been insufficient interest in projecting the social impacts of new agricultural technologies before they

are introduced. Some (e.g., Just et al., 1979:1280)
flatly assert that preparation of a meaningful impact
statement before a technology is ready for implementation is "virtually impossible." But to defer social assessment of innovations until they are ripe
for introduction is to forgo the opportunity to influence the actual development of the technology.
Friedland et al. (1981) have persuasively argued for
a "projective" rather than a "predictive" approach to
the study of the potential consequences of technical
innovation in agriculture. Such an approach emphasizes the historical and structural determinants of
technological change, and strives to project the
shape and direction of future social events rather
than to make highly particularistic and restricted
"point-estimate" predictions (Friedland et al.,
1981:27).

The recent emergence of the cluster of novel
biogenetic techniques popularly and generically referred to as "biotechnology"[2] makes the need to re-
dress these deficiencies a matter of substantial
contemporary importance. Biotechnology will bring
the biogenetic component of technological change in
agriculture to unprecedented prominence. The research orientations of social scientists need to be
adjusted accordingly. Moreover, if we are to guide
technical innovation into socially efficient and
equitable channels, we must make an effort to project, as Friedland urges, the social consequences of
deploying genetic engineering in the context of advanced capitalism.

This in turn implies the need to understand the
way that biogenetic technology has been introduced
and elaborated in the past. The emergent biotechnologies are no less amenable to social impact analysis
than any other technical form, but to understand the
trajectories associated with their deployment requires historical and comparative perspective. For
this purpose the case of hybrid corn is particularly
useful. The rise in productivity that resulted from
the introduction of hybrid corn represents a most
dramatic achievement of biogenetic technology in
agriculture. Moreover, the social changes catalyzed
by the development of hybrid corn were, like those
now emerging from biotechnology, "transformational"
rather than "incremental" in nature, having important
effects across many sectors. Thus, the experience of
hybrid corn provides analytic focuses (Friedland et
al., 1981:32) for looking at similar or parallel processes in the genesis and development of biotechnology.

This chapter has four principal objectives:

1. to draw the attention of social scientists to the vital role that biogenetic technology has played in generating social and structural change in agriculture;

2. using the example of the development of hybrid corn, to determine the historical range, nature, and direction of the social impacts generated by biogenetic technology;

3. to use the example of hybrid corn to put the development of biotechnology into historical and comparative context;

4. to identify a variety of areas which will reward detailed projective research into the social consequences of biotechnology in agriculture.

TECHNOLOGICAL CHANGE AND STRUCTURAL TRANSFORMATION IN AGRICULTURE

Over the last half-century, the direction of structural change in American agriculture has been unambiguous. While total cropland has remained virtually unchanged since the mid-1930s, farm numbers have fallen from a high of 6.8 million in 1935 to 2.7 million in 1978. During this period, average farm size nearly tripled and 10 percent of American farms now account for some 60 percent of total production (McDonald and Coffman, 1980:9). Parallel with this process of concentration and centralization at the farm level has been the rise to prominence of agribusiness. Between 1935 and 1977 the total volume of productive resources in farming changed little, but there was a complete reversal in the position of purchased and nonpurchased inputs (table 19.1). Currently, on-farm production processes account for only about 10 percent of the total value of finished agricultural products. About 40 percent of the value added derives from commercial inputs, and 50 percent is added in the post-farm stages of processing, transportation, and exchange (Lewontin, 1982:13). Those farmers surviving the continuous attrition to which operations are subject have become increasingly enmeshed in and dependent on factor and product markets dominated by large-scale, nonfarm capital.

The "technological treadmill" (Cochrane, 1979; Ruttan and Sundquist, 1982) constitutes a crucial

TABLE 19.1

Indexes of Total Farm Inputs, Major Input Subgroups, and Productivity,
United States, 1930-1977 (1967 = 100)

Year	Total Inputs	Nonpurchased Inputs	Purchased Inputs	Farm Labor	Machinery	Agro-chemicals	Farm Productivity
1930	101	176	50	326	39	10	51
1935	91	158	46	299	32	8	57
1940	100	159	58	293	42	13	60
1945	103	161	62	271	58	20	68
1950	104	150	70	217	84	29	71
1955	105	143	76	185	97	39	78
1960	101	119	86	145	97	49	90
1965	98	103	93	110	94	75	100
1970	100	97	102	89	100	115	102
1975	100	92	107	76	113	127	115
1977	103	88	118	71	116	151	118

Sources: U.S. Department of Agriculture, Changes in Farm Production and Efficiency,
1977. Statistical Bulletin No. 612, Economics, Statistics, and Cooperatives Service.
Washington, D.C.: U.S. Department of Agriculture, 1978, pp. 56-7. Cochrane, Willard W.,
The Development of American Agriculture. Minneapolis: University of Minnesota Press,
1979, Table 16.2.

linkage in the articulation of the structural transformations occurring at the farm and suprafarm levels. In the competitive-market model of the United
States farm economy, each farmer is an atomistic
"price taker." He or she has little hope of influencing the price at which produce is sold, and profitability of each operation is largely a function of
unit costs of production. New technology offers a
means of reducing these costs. Early adopters of innovations enjoy a temporary gain before other farmers
follow suit. Once the new technology is widely accepted, the cost curves for all adopters are once
again similar, but an increased supply of product
depresses prices and sets the stage for another round
of innovation. Those who fail or are unable to adopt
new technologies suffer economic loss; marginal producers are continually forced out of business, and
their operations are absorbed by more successful
operators. The effects of government price- and
income-support programs are ultimately negated by
this treadmill process.

Such a dynamic is an inevitable concomitant of
farming in a capitalist economy, and an important
source of social impacts. It encourages the canni-
balistic centralization of farm operations while
simultaneously ensuring a secure and expanding market
for the purveyors of new agricultural technologies.
The benefits of technological improvement in American
agriculture since 1930 have accrued principally to
agribusiness and to the small group of farm operators
in the technological vanguard. For the vast majority
of farmers, however, "technological advance has been
a nightmare" (Cochrane, 1979:352).

Machinery blueprints, breeding goals, and chemical research programs are social creations. Research objectives reflect the nature of and changes
in the social system in which they are embedded, and
tend to serve the purposes of the dominant interests
in that system. While private agricultural research
has unquestionably been designed to further capital
accumulation, publicly funded research has had a similar effect. Agribusiness frequently exerts direct
influence over the research agendas of the land-grant
universities and the state agricultural experiment
stations (Hightower, 1972), but for the most part
public research is in fact directly responsive to
farmer demands. The system of production and marketing in which farmers are enmeshed, however, ensures
that farmer "needs" involve additional purchased inputs (Buttel, 1981; Lewontin, 1982). Agricultural
research and technological innovation have been

principal mechanisms by which the conditions for the elimination of many farm operations have been created, even as surviving farmers are bound to and dominated by the upstream suppliers of inputs and the downstream purchasers of ever-increasing agricultural product. The example of hybrid corn provides ample justification for Lewontin's assertion that farmers are merely "the conduits through which the benefits of agricultural research flow to the large concentrations of capital" (Lewontin, 1982:14).

THE CASE OF HYBRID CORN

Corn (Zea mays) is the archetypically American crop. From the time when its adoption by the settlers of Plymouth Plantation allowed the survival of the colony, corn has held a prominent place in the economic and cultural life of the nation. Corn is planted on one of every three grain acres in the United States, and annual production accounts for about half of the world crop (Leath et al., 1982:1). Moreover, the development of hydrid corn[3] in the 1920s and its commercial availability in the mid-1930s set off a domestic precursor of the Green Revolution. Corn yields in the United States had actually been declining since 1870 (Cochrane, 1979:128). The introduction of hybrid corn reversed this trend and yields climbed sharply upward (figure 19.1). Adoption by farmers was extremely rapid and in the Corn Belt the transition from open-pollinated to hybrid varieties was completed within a decade. Despite a thirty-million acre reduction in the land on which grain-corn was harvested between 1930 and 1965, the volume of production increased by over 2.3 billion bushels and the proportion of acreage planted with hybrids climbed from 0.1 percent to over 95 percent (table 19.2).

Prior to the development of hybrid corn, the private seed industry was little more than a merchandiser for the "college-bred" varieties developed in public agricultural research institutions (Apfelbaum, 1956; Copeland, 1976). Since the seed from open-pollinated varieties could be saved and replanted, the market for seed was uncertain and volatile. Commercial seed prices could not deviate far from bulk grain prices, and there was little incentive for private research.

Hybrids, however, possess several characteristics which provided seed companies with an opportunity to break down the autonomy of the farmer, retain

298

the gains to proprietary research, and enlarge profit
margins. First, the offspring from the seed of a hybrid plant tend to revert to the character of the
grandparent inbred lines, with a consequent reduction
in yield. Grain of hybrid crops cannot be saved for
replanting, and new seed must be purchased each
year. Second, the use of inbreds as parent material
confers upon hybrids a "naturally" proprietary character since the particular combination of inbreds
used to produce any one hybrid can be kept secret and
cannot necessarily be duplicated by competitors.
Finally, the increased yield accruing to the users of
hybrid seed provided farmers with an incentive to
adopt it.
     Although hybridization held tremendous potential
for private capital, it was public research agencies
that undertook the lengthy and expensive research

FIGURE 19.1
U. S. Corn Yields, 1930-1980

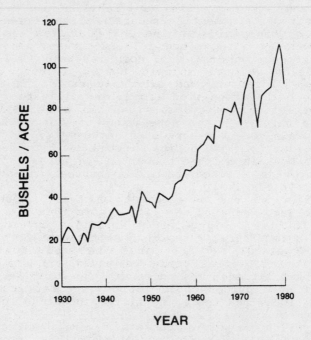

TABLE 19.2
Development of Grain-Corn Acreage, Yield, Production, Prices, and Selected Uses, United States, 1930-1980

Year	Acreage Harvested (Million Acres)	Yield per Harvested Acre (Bushels)	Production (Million Bushels)	Season Average Price per Bushel (Dollars)	Season Average Price per Bushel (Constant $ 1967)	Used for Feed (Million Bushels)	Exported (Million Bushels)	Corn Acres Planted to Hybrids (Approx. Percent)
1930	85.5	20.5	1,757	.60	1.00	NA	NA	00.1
1935	82.6	24.2	2,091	.66	NA	NA	NA	00.5
1940	76.4	28.9	2,206	.62	1.55	NA	NA	15.0
1945	77.9	33.1	2,577	1.23	1.48	NA	NA	53.0
1950	72.4	38.2	2,764	1.52	1.48	2,482	117	78.0
1955	68.5	42.0	2,873	1.35	1.45	2,366	120	87.0
1960	71.4	54.7	3,907	1.00	1.01	3,092	292	94.0
1965	55.4	74.1	4,103	1.16	1.13	3,362	687	95+
1970	57.4	72.4	4,152	1.33	1.33	3,570	517	95+
1975	67.5	86.3	5,829	2.55	1.27	3,570	1,711	95+
1977	70.0	90.8	6,357	2.02	1.05	3,744	1,948	95+
1980	NA	NA	NA	NA	NA	4,518	2,355	95+

Sources: Harvard Business School, Pioneer Hi-Bred International, Inc. Harvard Business School Case Study. Boston: Harvard Business School Case Services, 1978, p. 22. Leath, Mack N., Lynn H. Meyer, and Lowell D. Hall, U. S. Corn Industry. Agricultural Economic Report No. 479, Economic Research Service. Washington, D.C.: U. S. Department of Agriculture, 1982, p. 19. Sprague, G. F., "Agricultural production in the developing countries." Science 157 (18 August 1967):774-78.

program required to bring hybrid corn to commercial reality (Steele, 1978; Sprague, 1980).[4] Hybridization was by no means the only productive approach to corn improvement available, and the wholesale commitment of public resources to it was not a foregone conclusion. Agronomists of the time widely opposed the shifting research orientation (Crabb, 1947:174). Lewontin (1982) and Berlan (1982) have argued convincingly that yield gains similar to or better than those of hybrids could have been achieved in open-pollinated varieties via population-selection techniques.

Seed companies lobbied heavily in support of funds for hybrid research and offered their own farm facilities for field testing. They were aided greatly in the 1920s by then Secretary of Agriculture Henry C. Wallace, who engineered a number of important funding and research-personnel changes in the Agriculture Research Service of the U.S. Department of Agriculture (Crabb, 1947:99), and later by his son, Henry A. Wallace, founder of Pioneer Hi-Bred and Roosevelt's secretary of agriculture. Just as decisive was the ethic of client service with which the land-grant universities and state agricultural experiment stations were imbued. Since their "clientele" tended to be those aggressive, innovative farmers on the forefront of the technological treadmill (Hightower, 1973; Cochrane, 1979; Buttel, 1981), the public agencies responded to farmer demand for hybrids and their quick 15 to 20 percent yield increases. Tellingly, since 1940 virtually no research into open-pollinated corn varieties has been undertaken.

Hybrid corn varieties were rapidly adopted. Land planted to hybrids rose from 500,000 acres in 1935 to more than twenty-four million acres in 1939 (USDA, 1940:136). Dozens of seed firms, including industry leaders Pioneer Hi-Bred and DeKalb, were founded in the 1920s and 1930s in response to the commercial potential of the new hybrids. But the domination of the production and marketing of hybrids by large-scale capital was no more a foregone conclusion than was their development at the expense of open-pollinated varieties. The investment required to begin hybrid seed production was not excessive, and a number of state experiment stations and extension programs trained farmers to produce their own hybrid seeds (Steele, 1978; Sprague, 1980). The University of Wisconsin developed an administrative system and specialized machinery specifically designed to facilitate small-scale hybrid production (Crabb,

1947:206-7). However, the individual or small-scale
producer could not, of course, undertake the extensive and expensive research needed to develop
improved varieties of hybrid corn. Such producers
were thus crucially dependent on public breeding programs for the development of suitable commercial
varieties and for their supply of inbred parent lines
for those varieties.

In making individual and small-scale hybrid production feasible, public release of "finished" commercial varieties became a barrier to capital accumulation. Once public varieties had established the
profitability of hybrid corn, the private seed industry moved to eliminate this obstacle to their domination of the farmer. Arguing that product development
is rightfully the province of private industry and
that public/private competition is wasteful of resources, the large seed companies succeeded in displacing the public development of commercial corn
lines (Sprague, 1980; Eberhart, 1982). Public-sector
activity has been reoriented towards plant collection, germplasm evaluation and development, training,
and breeding-methods studies (Pardee et al., 1981;
Peterson, 1981; Eberhart, 1982). Circumscription of
public corn-breeding programs was accompanied by increasing private research expenditures devoted to the
development of proprietary inbred lines (Ruttan,
1982). With parent lines for finished commercial varieties no longer widely available from public agencies, small-scale hybrid production could not remain
competitive, and private research spending came to
constitute a significant barrier to entry for new
competitors (Harvard Business School, 1978:9).[5]

Publicly funded agricultural research has thus
come to effectively subsidize and serve private industry. Publicly developed inbreds were still used
in 72 percent of commercial hybrid corn lines in 1979
(Zuber and Darrah, 1980:241).   Indeed, public
research efforts sometimes serve no other purpose
than to enlarge the profit margins enjoyed by capital. An example is publicly developed "improvement"
of the efficiency of the hybridization process itself. A gene for cytoplasmic male sterility discovered in the 1950s was successfully incorporated into
female parent lines. This eliminated the need for
the expensive operation of detasseling plants by
hand, and meant the displacement of some 125,000 seasonal workers (Perelman, 1977:47).

The development of hybrid corn and the emascula-
tion of public breeding programs created an important

new space for the accumulation of capital in agriculture. The American seed industry is very much the
creation of hybrid corn. Between 1934 and 1944, hybrid corn sales went from virtually nothing to $70
million (Steele, 1978:29). Corn remains the life-
blood of today's seed industry, accounting for nearly
half of the $4 billion in seed sales generated by
American companies in 1981 (Davenport, 1981:9). Between 1967 and 1978, the price index for seed nearly
tripled, a jump higher than any other agricultural
input (Leibenluft, 1981:85), and in recent years the
industry has enjoyed pretax profits averaging more
than 20 percent (Harvard Business School, 1978:29).
Such profitability has not gone unnoticed. Since
1970 a wave of mergers and acquisitions has brought
much of the seed industry into the corporate folds of
transnational petrochemical and pharmaceutical corporations (see Fowler, 1980; Davenport, 1981). Of
the principal American seed firms, only Pioneer Hi-
Bred has maintained its independence. Such well-
known seed companies as Northrup King, Asgrow,
Trojan, and Funk have been acquired by, respectively,
Sandoz, Upjohn, Pfizer, and Ciba-Geigy. DeKalb
Agresearch has undertaken a joint venture with
Pfizer.

Hybrid corn was also instrumental in facilitating the expansion of other branches of the agro-
inputs sector. The noted corn breeder George Sprague
has observed that "the objective in plant breeding is
to develop, identify and propagate new genotypes
which will produce economic yield increases under
some specified management system [emphasis added]"
(Sprague, 1971:96). From the 1940s the "specified
management system" for which hybrid corn was being
bred presupposed mechanization and the application of
agrochemicals (Jones, 1949; Mangelsdorf, 1951).

The relationship between the introduction of
stiff-stalked, strong-rooted hybrid varieties and the
rapid expansion of machine harvest after 1930 is well
recognized (Sprague, 1955; Jenkins, 1955; Lu, 1979;
Just et al., 1979). Between 1930 and 1950 the number
of mechanical corn pickers and combines with corn
heads increased ninefold (Cochrane, 1979:198). But
changes in plant architecture did not just facilitate
mechanized harvest. New hybrids shaped to the machine had multiple ears and stiffer shanks connecting
the ear to the stalk. These features actually increased the difficulty and expense of hand harvest,
thereby encouraging mechanization. One can only assume that the total number of harvest workers displaced as a direct result of the introduction of

hybrid corn was substantial. Moreover, insofar as adoption of mechanized harvest was linked to hybrids, the benefits of the new seeds tended to flow to those farmers with the wherewithal to purchase machinery. Despite its "divisibility," biogenetic technology is not necessarily scale-neutral.

The volume of agrochemicals applied to corn (or any other crop) prior to 1940 was negligible (Irving and Wadleigh, 1972). But with nitrogen prices slashed by postwar surpluses, hybrids developed after 1945 were expressly bred for responsiveness to fertilizer (Steele, 1978:32). Nevertheless, yields leveled off between 1948 and 1955, just as hybrid-seed markets were reaching saturation. Breeders found a solution which assured expanding markets for both seeds and agrochemicals: they developed hybrids suited to higher plant populations and higher levels of fertilization.

Since the mid-1930s the planting rate for corn has climbed from 12,000 kernels per acre to 24,000 per acre in 1978, thus doubling the volume of seed-corn sales (Steele, 1978:39). Higher plant populations were subject to insect, disease, and weed build-up, and this in turn encouraged the use of insecticides, fungicides, and herbicides. Corn now accounts for a third of United States herbicide sales and a quarter of the market for insecticides (Farm Chemicals, 1981b:58). It has been a major contributor to the historical increase in the intensity of chemical use in American agriculture (table 19.1).

Table 19.2 illustrates additional facets of the impact of hybrid corn on industrial structure and organization. Much of the enlarged production resulting from the introduction of hybrid seed and associated cultural practices was absorbed by the rapidly growing livestock feed and fattening industry. Continuously increasing output kept corn prices low, facilitating the development of large feedlot operations (Simpson and Farris, 1982) and ultimately expanding markets for pork, beef, and poultry meat.[6] Also, corn exports increased some twentyfold between 1950 and 1980, providing the government with a "food weapon," as ex-Secretary of Agriculture Earl Butz put it, and creating massive accumulation opportunities for merchant capital involved in the international grain trade (Morgan, 1979).

If the development of hybrid corn has been important in undergirding the rise of agribusiness, it has proven to be powerfully destabilizing for many farmers. Hybrid corn was introduced just as the Roosevelt administration was trying to raise farm prices

by reducing production. Intensification of land use,
much of which can be attributed to the adoption of
hybrids, effectively nullified the effect of Agricultural Adjustment Administration production controls
on corn acreage (USDA, 1940; Paarlberg, 1964). Burgeoning yields and production[7] merely exacerbated en-
demic overproduction--the price of a bushel of corn
in constant dollars has actually fallen steadily
since 1940 (table 19.2).

The introduction of hybrid corn set the technological treadmill turning at an unprecedented pace.
Mechanization and chemical technology associated with
the new corn varieties further accelerated the vicious cycle of innovation/increased production/de-
pressed prices/further innovation. While farmers on
the treadmill's leading edge survived and even prospered, attrition rates were high. Between 1935 and
1960 the number of farms in the North Central region
(which encompasses the Corn Belt) declined by 35 percent. Tenants in particular were hard hit, and over
that period the number of tenant operations in the
North Central region was reduced by 62 percent (U.S.
Bureau of the Census, 1936 and 1961).

Just as hybrid corn had a differential impact on
farmers, it affected regions differently as well. It
is no accident that extensive commercial development
of hybrids occurred first in the Corn Belt, where
profit potential was highest. Hybrid seed entered
"good" areas before "poor" ones (Griliches,
1960:325). While Iowa had 90 percent of its corn
land planted to hybrids by 1936, Alabama had to wait
until 1948 before a hybrid variety adapted to its
climate was even available (Staub and Blase,
1971:120). Although corn is harvested for grain in
forty-one states, the Corn Belt now accounts for over
80 percent of United States corn production, with
half of that coming from Illinois and Iowa (Leath et
al., 1982:1).

Increasing regional specialization in corn production was reflected at the farm level as well.
Those farmers who survived each cycle of the technological treadmill absorbed their failed neighbors and
found that the growing scale and technical complexity
of their operation compelled them to specialize.
Many Corn Belt farmers eliminated their livestock operations and switched completely to cash-grain production. No longer requiring roughage for livestock,
such farmers replaced hay with soybeans in their crop
rotation with corn (DeGraff, 1966). Farmers also
found that, with heavy fertilization, continuous corn
production was possible. Fully 21 percent of corn

planted now follows a previous corn crop (Ruttan and Sundquist, 1982:83). The increased incidence of row crops has greatly exacerbated soil erosion (Batie and Healy, 1983).

Specialization has brought corn monocultures to vast acreages. While the practice of monoculture makes for efficiency in farming operations, it greatly increases susceptibility to pests and disease, especially at high plant populations. The threat of epidemic is further enhanced when the individual plants in the population are genetically uniform (Yarwood, 1970; Sprague, 1971), and this is precisely the case with regard to hybrid corn. Inbreeding is itself a process of genetic homogenization. Moreover, the pressures of competition frequently compel seed companies to utilize the same elite inbreds as parent material for their proprietary hybrids. In 1969 only six hybrids accounted for 71 percent of all acreage in the United States planted to corn (National Academy of Sciences, 1972:287).

The genetic vulnerability of the American corn crop was dramatically emphasized in 1970 when 15 percent of national corn production (1.02 million bushels) was destroyed by an epidemic of leaf blight (see National Academy of Sciences, 1972; Horsfall, 1975). The process of hybridization itself was directly implicated in this episode. The gene for cytoplasmic male sterility incorporated into hybrid corn lines to eliminate hand detasseling was the hereditary component susceptible to the blight. Since over 80 percent of all hybrids carried this cytoplasm, the epidemic swept cornfields from Miami to Minnesota, and would have been worse but for weather conditions unfavorable to the virus which caused the blight (Harlan, 1975). Though seed lacking the susceptible cytoplasm has been produced in subsequent years-- making hand or mechanical detasseling necessary again--the genetic base of hybrid corn remains dangerously narrow (Zuber and Darrah, 1980; Myers, 1983).

The development of hybrid corn has also materially influenced the goals and structure of public and private breeding programs in other crops. The achievement of hybridization has become a central objective of breeding research in most plant species. A wide variety of ingenious biogenetic strategies has been employed to regulate sexual expression so as to permit inbreeding and subsequent crosses.[8] But while hybrids have been developed for many vegetable species and for sorghum, sunflowers, and sugar beets, effective or economic hybridization has proven elusive in many of the most potentially lucrative crops--i.e., wheat, cotton, soybeans, alfalfa, rice.

Galvanized by the market control and profit potential accruing to "naturally" proprietary corn hybrids, seed corporations have, since the 1930s, lobbied for patent-like "breeder's rights" applicable to open-pollinated plant varieties. In 1970, despite the lack of evidence that public breeding had been anything but "remarkably effective" (Ruttan, 1982:25), a Plant Variety Protection Act (PVPA) institutionalizing breeders' rights became law.[9] Private capital would like, by legislative fiat, to repeat the experience of hybrid corn in those crops where public breeding is yet preeminent (table 19.3) and in which farmers still supply themselves and their neighbors with a large proportion of their yearly seed requirements (table 19.4).

The American hybrid bias in corn breeding has been transferred to other nations. The Food and Agriculture Organization of the United Nations (FAO) conducted a hybrid corn school in Italy in 1947 (Coffey, 1948:128), and 50 percent of all corn grown in that nation is still a combination of two lines developed by public agricultural research agencies in the United States (Johnson, 1982:157). Corn-breeding programs utilizing hybridization were begun in Mexico, Guatemala, El Salvador, Venezuela, Brazil, Uruguay, Argentina, Costa Rica, Cuba, Colombia, Peru, and Chile by 1951 (Mangelsdorf, 1951:46). In Kenya in 1956 the United States Agency for International Development and the Rockefeller Foundation funded a hybrid corn-breeding program under which purchasers of seed were obliged to buy fertilizer and agree to follow certain cultural practices (Sprague, 1967:777). Where commercial agriculture provides a market for hybrid corn, the large companies have established a presence. Pioneer, for example, markets its hybrid corn in over ninety foreign countries and has research centers in nine, including Egypt, India, the Philippines, and Thailand (Gregg, 1982).

In areas where extensive factor markets had yet to be created, the influence of hybrid corn was more subtle. But in shaping American breeding practices it also helped shape the nature of the Green Revolution. The Green Revolution was implemented largely by American scientists working in the Rockefeller and Ford Foundation-funded international agricultural research centers (IARCs). These centers are reminiscent of public agricultural research agencies in the United States not only in their institutional character, but in their "mission" orientation and

TABLE 19.3
Estimated Proportions of Privately and Publicly Developed Varieties in Farm Use in 1977, by Crop

Crop	Percent Private	Percent Public
Corn	85	15
Sorghum	82	18
Sugar Beets	71	29
Cotton	69	31
Tobacco	55	45
Alfalfa	42	58
Rye	16	84
Wheat	14	86
Oats	14	86
Soybeans	11	89
Rice	8	92
Barley	5	95
Peanuts	3	97

Source: Hanway, D. G., "Agricultural experiment stations and the Plant Variety Protection Act: Part 1." Crops and Soils Magazine 30 (February 1978):5-6.

TABLE 19.4
Percentage of the American Seed Market Supplied by Farmers Producing for Home Use or Local Sale, by Crop

Crop	Percent
Corn	5
Grain Sorghum	5
Alfalfa	5
Tobacco	10
Vegetables	15
Rye	25
Rice	30
Peanuts	30
Barley	50
Soybeans	65
Wheat	65
Oats	70

Source: Adapted from Leibenluft, Robert F., Competition in Farm Inputs: An Examination of Four Industries. Office of Policy Planning, Federal Trade Commission. Washington, D.C.: National Technical Information Service, 1981.

ideological commitment to client service. It is
therefore not surprising that the varieties developed
by the IARCs closely followed the pattern established
by the development of hybrid corn in the United
States: high response varieties with stiff stalks
bred for the best available lands, assuming the use
of fertilizer and other agrochemicals (Jennings,
1974; Plucknett and Smith, 1982). Nor should it sur-
prise us to find that the extensive social impacts of
Green Revolution biogenetic technology cited earlier
are closely paralleled by distinctly similar and
equally broad social impacts generated by the development and deployment of hybrid corn in the United
States.

BIOTECHNOLOGY AND THE NEED FOR PROJECTIVE RESEARCH

The sharp similarity observable in the social
impacts of the "corn revolution" and the Green Revolution raises an important point. Most of the principal consequences of the introduction of hybrid corn
were well developed prior to the inauguration of the
Green Revolution in the mid-1960s. Social scientists
could have, and perhaps should have, been in a position to observe the effects associated with the
introduction of hybrid corn and to subsequently anticipate, and possibly alleviate, certain negative
consequences stemming from the introduction of Green-
Revolution plant varieties.

Recent developments in the fields of molecular
and cell biology as well as biochemistry underline
the need for projective social impact analysis.
Since the 1950s scientists have known that the language of biology encoded in DNA is written in a four-
letter alphabet--conceptually simple but chemically
complex. In the last decade, researchers have made
scientific advances which have given them manipula-
tive access to the genetic code. Biotechnology takes
as its raw materials the building blocks of life itself. Alteration of the genetic or cellular integ-
rity of an organism in order to create novel life
forms designed for specific economic (or social) purposes will profoundly affect any production sector in
which biological processes or organic chemicals are
important--for example, the development and production of chemicals and pharmaceuticals, the management
of pollution and waste, the generation of energy, and
the production and processing of all agricultural
commodities.

Much effort has been devoted to the manipulation
of microorganisms to enable them to produce bulk

quantities of useful substances heretofore available only in small quantities (for example, interferons, insulins, vaccines, proteins, hormones). The "reprogramming" of microorganisms by the insertion of genetic material from plants, animals, and even humans is now a well-established practice. Human insulin produced by genetically engineered bacteria has been released for sale, and a wide variety of similarly manufactured chemical and pharmaceutical products--including a foot-and-mouth disease vaccine and bovine growth hormone--are currently undergoing clinical trials (Abelson, 1983:611).

The genetic complexity of the higher organisms makes interspecific transfer of hereditary material much more difficult than in the simpler life forms, but both public and private researchers are pursuing the development of bioengineered plant and animal varieties. Principal areas of research include nitrogen fixation, stress tolerance, enhanced photosynthetic activity, herbicide immunity, and hybridization. With the capacity to draw upon the entire range of genetic variation in the world biosphere, it should be possible to design plant and animal varieties whose attributes are precisely fitted to particular environmental conditions, production processes, and end uses. The government's Recombinant DNA Advisory Committee has recently relaxed its restrictions on field trials of plants containing foreign DNA in anticipation of a flood of requests for permission to make such tests (Budiansky, 1983:644).

So fundamental and powerful a new technical form as biotechnology will necessarily have far-reaching, and probably unprecedented, effects on the organization and social relations of production characteristic of American and world agriculture. In addressing this issue I accept the premise that "projective" study is an appropriate and useful tool for anticipating those effects. New technologies are not introduced into an historical vacuum but are developed within a particular set of social, economic, and ecological circumstances with established and knowable trajectories. The existing social formation thus conditions the manner in which biotechnology is being developed even as the formation itself is changing under the impact of the new technology. The social impacts deriving from biotechnology are not determined absolutely by the past, but they are materially shaped by it and can best be projected by analytic use of historical contexts.

If we could have anticipated many of the social effects of the Green Revolution with reference to the experience of hybrid corn, the same should be true of the emerging "gene revolution." Accordingly, the remainder of this paper is devoted to consideration of the manner in which various analytic focuses, discussed in the foregoing survey of the development of hybrid corn, illuminate the historical tendencies which are likely to influence the directions taken by biotechnology.

Structure of agribusiness. First, the development of hybrid corn contributed significantly to important changes in the structure of agribusiness. Biotechnology, too, promises to create a vast new space for the accumulation, concentration, and centralization of capital. Just as the hybridization of corn stimulated the formation of numerous seed companies in the 1930s and 1940s, over three hundred biotechnology research firms have been established by venture capitalists in response to the commercial possibilities of the new biogenetic technologies (for example, Agrigenetics, Calgene, DNA Plant Technologies, Genentech, Hybritech). Large, often transnational corporations whose interests are likely to be deeply affected by biotechnology have responded by purchasing over $840 million worth of equity in these new companies (Murray, 1983:249), and by establishing or enhancing their own research-and-development capabilities in biogenetic technology.

Many of the corporations investing heavily in biotechnology are those that have been active in acquiring seed companies over the last decade (see table 19.5). While the purchase of seed companies was initially motivated by rising world food demand and the passage of the PVPA, the rise of the biotechnology movement has greatly reinforced this trend, especially among the petrochemical and pharmaceutical transnationals which have important agrochemical interests. In biotechnology, plant breeding has found a common technical base with agricultural biochemistry (Geissbuhler et al., 1982). There are tremendous opportunities to coordinate and rationalize research, development, and marketing of the full range of genetic and chemical inputs.

Moreover, those agrochemical producers that have acquired seed companies and invested in biotechnology are well situated to dominate the gene revolution in agriculture. Apart from a few vegetatively propagated crops, there is no way to bring bioengineered plant varieties to market except via the seed. A plant-breeding capability, seed production and processing facilities, and distribution and marketing networks are critical to the rapid commercialization of biotechnology in the field-crops sector. These features are now enjoyed by the large petrochemical and pharmaceutical companies by virtue of their recent and continuing acquisitions of seed companies. Few of the remaining small, independent seed firms have either the human or financial resources to effectively pursue the avenues opened up by the new genetic technologies. As superior bioengineered crop varieties become available, the small companies still find themselves unable to compete with the research-and-development capabilities of the deep-pocket transnationals. These small companies will disappear or, as is more likely, be absorbed by larger firms desiring entry or expansion.

Also, in seeds (and this point applies equally well to animal germplasm) are encoded the genetic programs which control the biosynthetic processes by which plants grow and respond to the environment. To the extent that biotechnology will permit the reprogramming of those codes, the seed becomes a crucial nexus of control over the determination and shape of production processes in farming and food processing (Kloppenburg and Kenney, 1983). Seed companies, and by extension their transnational parents, are capable of setting their own breeding agendas according to their own criterion--profitability.

Structure of research. A second analytical focus for the assessment of the social impacts of biotechnology is the structure and control of scientific research. As in the case of hybrid corn, the knowledge of biological systems on which the new genetic technologies are based is the product of publicly funded research (Noble, 1983). And despite its promise, biotechnology is yet embryonic and faces many scientific obstacles which must be overcome if extensive commercialization of bioengineered products is to be achieved. Private enterprise is therefore interested in maintaining public research capabilities, but would like to shape them in support and subsidization of its own undertakings and, crucially, preclude the participation of public institutions in the commercialization of the products of biotechnology (Kenney and Kloppenburg, 1983). As occurred previously with hybrid corn, capital can be expected to generate a major restructuring of agricultural research as it seeks to establish control over the new technology.

One axis along which this transformation will occur is the elaboration of the public/private division of labor which accompanied the development of hybrid corn. With biotechnology introducing a determinant relationship between the seed and production

TABLE 19.5
Some Recent Seed-Company Acquisitions and Characteristics of Acquiring Firms

Acquiring Company	Seed Subsidiaries	In-house Biotech	Biotech Venture Firm Interests
ARCO	Desert Seed Company	X	IPRI Ingene Bioengineering Center
Celanese	Celpril, Incorporated Moran Seeds Joseph Harris Seed Company	X	
Ciba-Geigy	Ciba Geigy Seeds Funk Seeds Louisiana Seeds Hybridex	X	
FMC Corporation	Seed Research Associates	X	Centocor Immunorex
Monsanto	Farmers Hybrid Company Hybritech Jacob Hartz Seed Company	X	Genex Biogen Genentech Collagen
Occidental Petroleum	Ring Around Products Excel Hybrid Missouri Seeds Moss Seeds	X	

Parent	Subsidiary		
Pfizer	Trojan Seed Company	X	
	Jordan Wholesale Company		
	Clemens Seed Farms		
	Warwick Seeds		
Sandoz	Northrup King	X	Zoeon
	National N-K		
	McNair Seeds		
	Gallatin Valley		
	Rogers Brothers		
	Ladner Beta		
Shell	North American Plant Breeders	X	Cetus
	Nickerson Seed Company		
	Agripro, Incorporated		
	Tekseed Hybrid		
Stauffer	Stauffer Seeds	X	
	Blaney Farms		
	Prairie Valley		
Upjohn	Asgrow Seeds	X	
	Associated Seeds		

Source: Based in part on Fowler, Cary. "Sowing the seeds of destruction," Science for the People (September/October 1980):8-10.

processes, control over the introduction of plant and animal varieties into commercial circulation will be a matter of central importance. Public research-program administrators will be under continuous pressure to abandon activities which can profitably be undertaken by capital, and to fit their research agendas more closely to the needs of private enterprise (see, for example, the recommendations contained in Rockefeller Foundation, 1982).

Change along a second axis will be more fundamental. The development of hybrid corn compelled a restructuring of the relationships among a stable set of actors. Biotechnology has generated a new set of participants in agricultural research. The rapidity of scientific advance in biotechnology has meant that much of the expertise in the new technologies is located in academia. Corporations interested in biotechnology have responded by establishing unprecedented linkages with individual universities (Giamatti, 1982; Noble, 1983). Corporate-sponsored research into agricultural biotechnology is frequently contracted to institutions which are outside the traditional agricultural research community but at the cutting edge of molecular biology (table 19.6). The appearance of new actors (the biotechnology research firms and non-land-grant universities), in conjunction with an enlarged emphasis on corporate research, will compel a comprehensive restructuring of agricultural research and require the articulation of social relations between heretofore unconnected actors.

The nature of this restructuring is probably the single most important issue yet raised by the genesis of agricultural biotechnology. Unlike agrochemical and machine technologies, which primarily were developed by entrepreneurial capital (Lewontin, 1982:14), biogenetic research in agriculture has remained substantially a public-sector activity. True, hybrid corn and the Plant Variety Protection Act have contributed to the erosion of public preeminence in plant breeding, and public biogenetic research has in any case tended to benefit large-scale capital (Buttel, 1981). But this does not alter the fact that the land-grant universities, the state agricultural experiment stations, and the federal Agricultural Research Service are public institutions relatively autonomous from capital and therefore potentially contested terrain. To allow the further subordination of public agricultural research to the interests of capital is to lose an important institutional mechanism for the exertion of social control over the development and deployment of biotechnology.

TABLE 19.6
Major University/Industry Research
Contracts in Biotechnology

Company	Institution	(Million $)
Allied Chemical	California-Davis	2.5
Celanese	Yale University	1.0
Corning Glass Union Carbide Kodak	Cornell University	7.5
DuPont	Harvard University	6.0
Hoechst	Harvard (Massachusetts General Hospital)	50.0
Mallinckrodt	Washington University	4.0
Monsanto	Harvard University	24.0
Monsanto	Rockefeller University	4.0
Monsanto	Washington University	24.0
W. R. Grace	Massachusetts Institute of Technology	7.0

Source: Based in part on Murray, James R., "Patterns of investment in biotechnology," Bio/Technology 1 (May 1983):248-50.

In the absence of effective social control, capital will set both public and private research agendas according to the simple criterion of profitability. Research goals will be set for the express purpose of benefiting capital. Indeed, hybridization of pure-line crops from wheat to Douglas firs is a principal goal of the genetic engineers. Tissue culture has been used in an (as yet unsuccessful) attempt to isolate a male-sterile corn cytoplasm resistant to the leaf-blight virus that caused the 1970 epidemic and to eliminate once again the labor force needed for detasseling in the production of hybrid corn (Earle, 1982:185). Conversely, though socially desirable products may be perfectly feasible, private companies may not develop them if they are not sufficiently profitable.[10]

Agrochemical usage. A third analytical focus involves the utilization of agrochemicals. Recall that the development of hybridization preceded and materially facilitated the application of fertilizers and pesticides to the corn crop. Given the dominant position of the petrochemical and pharmaceutical

giants in biotechnology, it would be naive to think
that the new biogenetic techniques will not be used
to enhance capital accumulation via chemical sales.
Biotechnology introduces the possibility of designing
plants and animals in such a way that they are com-
plemented by, or even require, the application of
selected chemicals.[11] The first genetically engineered field-crop varieties to be commercialized are
expected to be types resistant to herbicides (Barton
and Brill, 1983). Like hybrid corn before it, biotechnology should stimulate an increase, rather than
a decrease, in the intensity of chemical usage in
agriculture.

Farmers' autonomy. In doing so it will also
follow the pattern set by hybrid corn in a fourth
analytical focus: the progressive erosion of the autonomy of the farmer and his increasing dependence on
factor markets. As plants and animals become increasingly "programmed," they will require sophisticated monitoring and management packages if their
productive potential is to be realized (Hanway,
1978b:5). This will certainly reinforce the trend to
on-farm utilization of electronic data evaluation and
processing techniques (Geissbuhler et al., 1982:505),
and such monitoring equipment may follow bioengineered crops and livestock as closely as the mechanical corn picker followed hybrid seed.

Acceleration of agrotechnology. Corollary to
this is a fifth point of comparison: biotechnology
parallels hybrid corn in its effect on the technological treadmill. Nearly all agricultural applications
of biotechnology that are currently contemplated contribute to increased yields. There can be little
doubt that biotechnology will enlarge the volume of
production and exacerbate the problem of agricultural
surpluses. A vivid illustration of this point is the
recent development of a bacterial strain genetically
engineered to produce large quantities of bovine
growth hormone (Bauman et al., 1982). Injection of
the hormone increases milk production in individual
cows by 10 to 40 percent with no additional inputs.
National milk production is currently about 10 percent in excess of consumption. While university and
corporate news releases trumpet the productivity
gains accruing to use of the hormone, no consideration is given to the impact on an already saturated
product market or to the consequences for milk producers.

Biotechnology may well set the stage for an especially rapid series of cycles on the technological
treadmill. At the farm level, biotechnology should

increase the reliance of the farmer on purchased inputs even as it accelerates the process of differentiation among farms and facilitates further concentration of operations (Kenney et al., 1982). The
myth of the yeoman farmer as a skilled craftsman may
persist, but the reality may be the "propertied laborer,"[12] given instructions by a home computer which
monitors the progress and needs of a crop grown from
genetically programmed seed provided by a corporation
to which the farmer is contractually bound and which
already owns the crop in the field.

Genetic diversity. A sixth area of impact is
the effect of biogenetic technology on genetic erosion and uniformity. Biotechnology contains an
enormous potential for both positive and negative impacts on genetic diversity in the global biosphere.
The entire stock of the world's genetic resources
suddenly becomes economically relevant (Myers,
1983). On the one hand, this creates an incentive
for conservation activities since lack of genetic diversity might prevent realization of the full potential of biotechnology. On the other hand, clonal
propagation and embryo-transfer techniques provide
the means to engineer a greater degree of genetic
uniformity in crops and livestock than ever before.
Biotechnology itself does not alter the nature of the
market forces in which it is embedded, and it is
these forces which constitute the root cause of
genetic uniformity (Kloppenburg and Kenney, 1983).
Hence Sprague (1971:103) is still correct in warning
that "the demands for new lines with higher productivity ensures a continual reworking of our existing
superior germplasm. This system almost guarantees
that we shall periodically be subject to serious
disease or insect problems." The conditions that
gave rise to the 1970 corn epidemic are still with
us.

International implications. Finally, biotechnology has international implications even more
striking than those of the Green Revolution or its
predecessor, the corn revolution. The potential of
bioengineering has excited those concerned with international agricultural development (Plucknett and
Smith, 1982; Brady, 1982; Swaminathan, 1982). Bioengineered crop varieties adapted to low levels of
fertility or tolerant of saline conditions could
raise food production in vast areas of the Third
World. For its part, transnational agribusiness
clearly views less developed countries (LDCs) as
lucrative markets for the products of biotechnology.
But it is also clear that no commercial seed firm is

interested in developing plant varieties for those who cannot pay for them (see note 10). There is a real and present danger that the new biotechnologies will benefit only the sophisticated, well-capitalized farmers of the world.

Differential access to the new technology will be reflected at the national level as well. Though some LDCs have established national biotechnology institutes, and the United Nations International Development Organization has called for the formation of an international center for genetic engineering and biotechnology (Zimmerman, 1983), Third-World programs may well suffer the same marginalization at the hands of capital that public agricultural research in the United States has experienced. The gene revolution in the Third World will probably involve the extraction of genetic resources from the LDCs, their incorporation into commercial plant and animal varieties in the corporate laboratories of the advanced industrial nations, and the reintroduction of these improved varieties into the LDCs via an expanding factor market. Once again, biotechnology may well reflect the historical experience of hybrid corn by generating not a reduction in regional disparities, but the intensification of existing inequities.

CONCLUSION

The example of hybrid corn clearly demonstrates that biogenetic technology has generated profound social change within the agricultural sector and beyond. There is no reason to assume that the influence of biogenetically based technological advance has been without similar, if less transformational, social effects in other commodities. The genetic improvement of both plant and animal species represents a rich lode of historical experience which has been mined only in a very preliminary fashion. Historically grounded social impact analyses of this process over the full range of agricultural commodities should prove extremely productive and will add a new dimension to our understanding of the nature and consequences of technological and structural change in agriculture.

Such analyses will not be of merely historical interest. The past contributes materially to the shape of the present, and an understanding of how a system is changing over time is the best indicator of its characteristics in the future. Modern genetic engineering represents a qualitative advance over the techniques of biogenetic technology which have been

available up to the present. Biotechnology can be
expected to generate social transformations of enormous importance on a global scale. It is vitally important that social scientists seriously address this
phenomenon before the new biogenetic technologies are
irretrievably deployed.

By using the example of hybrid corn, I have
tried to show how historical patterns can help us
come to grips with the future and to illuminate the
path ahead. My objective here has not been to provide a definitive projective analysis. Not only is
biotechnology still in its elemental phase, but the
vast scope of this new technical form and the scale
and diversity of its probable social impacts demand
the sort of comprehensive analysis which requires
much time and multiple studies. Rather, my aim has
been to define broad areas of importance in which
further and more detailed projective analysis can be
undertaken. The gene revolution is likely to involve
far more comprehensive social transformations than
did the Green Revolution. To move into the technical
era of genetic engineering as blindly as we did into
the Green Revolution would be both dangerous and
socially irresponsible.

NOTES

1. Biogenetic technology is defined as the manipulation of hereditary characteristics of a species
and/or the use of living organisms in production processes. The most prominent examples of biogenetic
technology are plant and animal breeding, but the
term also encompasses such diverse fields as fermen-
tation engineering and the inoculation of seeds with
nitrogen-fixing bacteria. In this paper I am, of
course, concerned exclusively with agricultural applications.

2. In this paper an important semantic distinction is maintained between "biogenetic technology"
and "biotechnology." Following current usage, the
term "biotechnology" refers to a cluster of highly
sophisticated, novel biogenetic techniques, developed
within the last decade as a result of major advances
in our understanding of molecular and cellular dynamics. The most prominent of these techniques are DNA
transfer ("gene splicing"), monoclonal antibodies,
protoplast fusion, and tissue culture ("cloning").
Thus "biotechnology" is a subset of "biogenetic technology," analytically distinguishable by its recent
vintage and its qualitatively superior potential for
directed alteration of living organisms. For

extended treatments of "biotechnology," see the special issues devoted to the subject in Scientific American (1981) and Science (1983), and the report of the Office of Technology Assessment (1981).

3. In open-pollinated corn, fertilization is not controlled. Hybrid corn is the product of a controlled cross between two or more "inbred" lines. Inbreeding is the process of self-fertilizing a variety over several generations so that particular characteristics may be isolated and retained while others are discarded. When inbred lines are crossed, the resulting hybrid seed exhibits heterosis, or "hybrid vigor," as it expresses the qualities of each parent line in synergistic combination. For an expanded account of hybrid corn breeding, see Walden (1978).

4. Social histories of the development of hybrid corn from popular, scientific, and industry perspectives include, respectively, A. R. Crabb's The Hybrid Corn-Makers: Prophets of Plenty (1947), H. K. Hayes's A Professor's Story of Hybrid Corn (1963), and H. A. Wallace and W. L. Brown's Corn and Its Early Fathers (1956).

5. It is now received wisdom among agricultural scientists that hybrid seed production is too complex and expensive a process to be undertaken by the individual farmer. Actually, there are farmers who now successfully produce hybrid seed for their own use, using what public inbreds are available and at a cost below that of commercial hybrid seed (see Krupicka, 1982).

6. Thus the principal impact of hybrid corn on the nutritional status of the American population has been, indirectly, greatly increased consumption of fats and oils. Corn that is used for human consumption has not improved in nutritional quality, and protein content may actually have declined since the elimination of open-pollinated varieties (Perelman, 1977:45). This is not to say that hybrids of improved food quality are not available. A number of hybrids with superior nutritional characteristics have been produced by public breeders concerned with world food problems (see Harpstead, 1971; Creech and Alexander, 1978). But such varieties do not yield as well as standard hybrids and present problems for machine harvest. Hence, farmers will not grow them and seed companies will not produce them.

7. With the widespread adoption and intensive use of agrochemicals after 1950, it has become increasingly difficult to partition yield gains into genetic, mechanical, and chemical components for the purpose of comparing relative contributions to productivity. Experiments comparing the performance of

open-pollinated varieties with hybrids widely grown
between 1930 and 1970 show that at least 40 percent
and possibly as much as 80 percent of the historical
yield increase in corn is attributable to genetic improvement (Russell, 1974; Duvick, 1977).

8. See Litzow and Osmun (1979) for a description
of methods used, by crop.

9. A substantial amount of controversy has accompanied passage of the Plant Variety Protection Act
and its later extension in coverage. See, for example, Mooney (1979), Fowler (1980), United States
Congress (1980), Kloppenburg and Kenney (1983.).

10. For a precedent, see Marshall (1983). The
biotechnology firm Genentech had been engaged in a
cooperative venture with New York University and the
World Health Organization. The objective of this
collaboration was the production of a malaria vaccine
via genetic engineering. Although technical obstacles had largely been overcome, Genentech withdrew
from the project because WHO refused to grant it an
exclusive license to market the vaccine.

11. Industry spokesmen are quite explicit regarding their strategic intentions. Dr. Klaus Saege-
barth, DuPont's director of agrichemicals research,
sees "the breadth of DuPont's line of crop protection
chemicals as literally representing a DuPont Crop
Management System" (Farm Chemicals, 1981a:21). Similarly, Dr. Wayne Johnson, venture manager for hybrid
crops with Rohm and Haas Company, has said, "We're
going all out to provide Rohm and Haas Company
licensed seed growers with a total package that includes proprietary hybrid parents, chemical and technical backup, the Hybrex service mark, and co-op
advertising support" (Seedsmen's Digest, 1982:22).
The president of Asgrow Seed Company (Upjohn) notes
that "the speculation that a variety could be developed that is dependent on a chemical for successful
use is definitely within the realm of possibility"
(Studebaker, 1982:27). Moreover, the seed itself becomes the ideal delivery system for chemical inputs.
Seed technologist Dr. Howard Potts (1983:47) foresees
planting the seed embryo "encapsulated with stored
food, insecticides, fungicides, safeners, and growth
hormones inside a plastic seed coat so that all
'seeds' have identical physical properties."

12. Here I follow Davis (1980) in using the term
"propertied laborer" to mean an individual who,
though owning means of production in land, is so dominated and controlled by off-farm capital (that is,
by means of contractual integration) that his position in actual relations of production is not qualitatively different from the propertyless laborer.

Part 4
Emerging Visions:
A Roundtable of
Sociological Opinion

20
Panel Discussion
Excerpts from the
1981 Annual Meeting of the
Rural Sociological Society

This edited panel discussion contains opinions expressed by several contributors to this book and by members of the Rural Sociological Society at the 1981 RSS meetings in Guelph, Ontario. Many questions related to social impact assessment (SIA) were addressed: Should formal environmental impact assessments--including social components--be required when agricultural technologies are developed with land-grant research assistance? How might equity concepts be included in social impact assessments of agricultural mechanization? And, of the many technologies studied in the rural sector over the last eighty years, which can be viewed as most socially "benign"?

Repeatedly, members of the audience cautioned against technological determinism and narrowly focused social impact assessment. The editors concur that technology is not merely tractors, fertilizers, and hybrid seed. Rather, it is a complex set of social forces conditioned by historical class relationships. Thus the social consequences of new agricultural technologies extend far beyond changes in the sex composition of the rural labor force and decreases in the numbers of migrant laborers employed in harvesting activities. Class relations determine--and are oftentimes strengthened by--the technology that is introduced. In the future, social scientists

must recognize this and accept the chal-
lenge of incorporating political economy
into social impact assessment.

Question 1: Based on research to date--that is, social impact assessments of agricultural mechaniza- tion--are some technologies more socially "benign" than others?

Jim Copp, Texas A&M University. Some people think there is bad technology and good technology. Perhaps. It "wonders me" (if I may use Pennsylvania talk) how so much technology can have unanticipated ramifications--how so much technology which appears to be good has ramifications that lead to consequen- ces we may not want. If I may take an extreme ex- ample and a somewhat unfair one, I learned this morn- ing at breakfast that the Mediterranean fruit fly appeared in California near or on an organic farm, an example of "good technology." Well, I do not think organic farming was to blame, but suppose it was. I do not think any technology, even alternative tech- nology, is necessarily blameless. With some technol- ogy, I am sure, it is easier to find more obvious unanticipated, undesirable consequences than in others. Technology perhaps is something like fire-- you can burn your hands working with it. Practically all technology has to be used with discretion--all technology may have this Pandora's box element in it.

Larry Busch, University of Kentucky. I guess I would take issue with Jim's fire analogy. Fire is a natural phenomenon, although it obviously can be used in social or antisocial ways, as the case may be. Technologies are not neutral in the sense that they just sit out there. They are only socially meaning- ful to the extent that they are used. When they are developed and when they are used, they are going to be used to benefit certain interests as opposed to other interests. They may be broader interests, they may be powerless interests, but I think it is impor- tant to note that technologies have that character.

Michael Perelman, California State University, Chico. I want to raise a subversive question. That is, might it not be a red herring to talk in terms of technology? Technology is a way of handling material resources within the context of a larger social ex- istence. When we look at a lettuce harvester, or a grape picker, or a particular chemical, we are really almost setting ourselves up for too narrow an interpretation. We must look at how a productive unit fits within a structure of other productive units and the social relations between the productive units, and insert that into the entire environmental system. I think if we start planning like that, then we might have a better sense for what we are getting ourselves into. Now that becomes subversive in another sense, of course, meaning that the market system, which is based on individualistic profits and incentives, is inappropriate to manage technology for purposes other than personal gain. So the question really comes down to the kind of social system you want. If you are going to have a capitalistic system in which everybody is more or less free to introduce any type of technology he or she wants, you are going to be having carbon copies of this discussion a hundred years from now--if we are lucky.

Sarah Elbert, Cornell University. I am puzzled because I assume that when you talk about technology, you are talking about it in a specifically agricultural context. This leads me to think that you are talking about the transformation of nature into products, which further leads me to think that you are essentially talking about a labor problem. Right? Technology is one of the means by which one controls labor. There are other means--family relationships or cooperative land or coercion or bureaucracy--these are just cataloguing devices. In any case, technology is clearly one means of controlling labor--using more labor or less labor, being more labor-intensive or less labor-intensive. I am interested in what the panel members think about the relationship between agricultural technology and labor control--control of the labor process. I do not necessarily mean that in a pejorative sense.

Bill Friedland, University of California, Santa Cruz. One of the things that was clearly revealed to us in our lettuce study was that one of the conditions under which the lettuce harvester would be used was if the labor supply were impeded, which was unlikely, or if the labor force got out of control. "Out of control" meant that it was organized at a level which management felt was no longer acceptable, in which there was a loss of managerial prerogatives and control over the actual production process. Now, in fact, there is a fair amount of organization amongst lettuce workers. But it is still one of the

most productive systems that exist, and the labor
costs are a relatively small fraction of the total
cost of production and distribution. What we have
here is a circumstance in which, if labor costs had
risen or if labor control had become problematic,
there would have been a shift to agricultural mechanization. That, I think, was clearly established.

Craig Harris, Michigan State University.   I
want to return to Michael Perelman's and Larry
Busch's comments. It seems to me that when question
one was asked, one could essentially build into the
question what the system is like at the moment. One
can say, "this is the current structure of the agricultural system for a particular commodity, these are
the resources of labor, control over land, or whatever; these are the people's motivations and incentives; this is why the different groups will probably
react to a particular technological development in a
certain way." All this does not say anything about
possible reactions to that technology in a totally
different system, granted. But I think one does have
to set those initial conditions and go on with the
SIA investigation.

Najwa Makhoul, Hebrew University.   I am an
agricultural researcher. I find it actually misleading to use the term "appropriate technology" because
it hides the real question that should be raised and
asked, which is: Under which social relations of production is a technology "appropriate" or "not appropriate?" It is the social relations of production
under which a particular technology is generated and
implemented that really matters. I am suggesting
that technology is not the relevant question.
      Technology is not neutral as such, and it is not
really fair to discuss it as though it were. For example, chemical pest-control methods will have detri-
mental social effects under conditions of either
socialist or capitalist production. However, some
technologies generated under capitalist conditions of
production are incompatible with those relations of
production and cannot be materialized under these relations. So, in a way, certain relations of production can generate a technology that is inappropriate
for these relations of production. So this becomes
the real question. It is very misleading, I think,
to talk in terms of alternative or appropriate technology without asking first what are the social relations in society, or what kinds of economic and
political domination and patterns of control over the
labor force exist in society.

Question 2: Under what circumstances should SIA in agricultural mechanization be performed? And who has primarily benefited from SIA in agricultural mechanization?

Gigi Berardi, Allegheny College. The obvious answer is that all technology should be susceptible to SIA. Every technology affects society. Every technology is embedded in a societal context and will have social impact, particularly with respect to who is in control of the technology and what are the prevailing social relations of production in the society where the technology is introduced. Many people would say this process should be monitored, possibly through SIA. In terms of who has benefited, I think the answer is very few people. We should ask: When an assessment is done, what happens to the assessment? Who is listening? Who is reading the assessment? What type of follow-up study is done on the assessment? If an impact is identified as being somewhat negative or mostly negative or completely negative, what does this mean? Does this mean that the technology is going to be discontinued? That alternatives are going to be explored? That alternatives are going to be adopted? And by whom? Are adjustments and compensations going to be made to the people who are negatively affected? I doubt it.

Even in tobacco, which has been intensively researched, it is likely that very little will be done to direct the mechanization process and/or facilitate the necessary adjustments resulting from labor displacement. The U.S. Department of Agriculture and the Department of Labor have subsidized considerable research on the impact of tobacco-harvest mechanization. Their agricultural scientists have been researching this for years. What has been done with their results and recommendations?

In the literature review I did [the review appears as chapter 2 in this volume], I looked at studies that were done on the impact of mechanization from the early 1900s until now. Nothing was done in the 1930s and 1940s when the federal administration was reasonably progressive and liberal, so I do not know what the future of SIAs for agricultural mechanization will be under the current administration.

Jim Copp. I would like to warn Gigi to be prepared for a lifetime of disappointments, since good research does not necessarily lead to wise decisions or to policy development. This is something which has always baffled me. Very often, policies are developed before good research has been done. The war on poverty is a good example. It was well-intentioned, but there was not adequate research to prepare for the war. On the other hand, when we do good research and when we have it ready, no one pays attention to our research. This is very frustrating for the social scientist. I was with the USDA in the Economic Research Service about the time they began thinking that they should be doing some research on the anticipated mechanization of tobacco harvesting and processing. They were already admitting that they had overlooked the impact assessment of mechanization of cotton production, which was quite an embarrassment. In the late 1960s and early 1970s, there was considerable enthusiasm in the Economic Research Service for starting work on tobacco mechanization before things began happening. In addition, they noticed that every year things were loosening up a little--the size of the allotments increased first, then it became possible to trade allotments, and so on.

Randy Ireson, Wilamette University. I would suggest, with regard to the whole SIA process, that a similar sort of development may have to occur that has already occurred with regard to environmental SIAs, i.e., that they become used in an adversarial process and as a tool for opponents and proponents of a particular kind of technology. In other words, they are no longer really value-neutral. This relates to the equity question and to the whole structure of society. Agricultural mechanization is not a scientific process, but rather a social, political and economic process, so perhaps we should look at SIAs in that light rather than in any other.

David James, University of Kansas. I want to respond to the possibility of modeling SIAs after environmental impact assessments. The process surrounding environmental impact assessments is certainly adversarial, but the resources that the adversaries bring to that process are very different. The typical outcome is that the side with the most resources wins the battle. At that same point, the process has served to legitimate the outcome, which has the same consequences as if it, perhaps, had not gone through an environmental impact assessment at all, except that the people have had their day in court and maybe have been able to submit a few things of importance. Perhaps there are some progressive outcomes from time to time, or some of the equity questions are solved, or if not solved, at least addressed in some minor way. I would guess

that the SIA process is having the same sort of effect. It serves the social purpose of legitimizing a
particular implementation of a particular technology. It also has a latent function of employing all
the people who do the SIA.

Larry Busch. I would like to make a couple of
brief comments. First of all, I think that it is
rather obvious from what you just said that having a
law passed that requires an SIA department in every
land-grant school in the United States and every agricultural college in Canada is likely to employ a
lot more sociologists, but it is not likely to have
an effect on much else. The reason for that, I
think, is that the people who are responsible for the
development of new technologies live in worlds which,
if you wish, are insulated from each other and insulated from the kind of information that an SIA is
trying to provide. To give an example, within entomology, the testing of toxicity of pest-control chemicals is reported in a journal which is separate from
the main entomological journals. This journal, the
Pesticides Monitoring Journal, is read exclusively by
toxicologists with intense interest in toxicity questions. If you look in any entomological journal
other than that one, you would have a difficult time
finding any article that discusses the toxicity of
any kind of agricultural chemical. There is something fundamentally fouled up here, and I think it
comes back to this question about control. Not only
does the technology control labor, but the organization of labor of scientists controls the kinds of
technologies that are developed as well.

**Question 3: What methodologies and data sources
are particularly relevant to agricultural-mechanization SIAs?**

Bill Friedland. I think David James's comment
about the relationship between SIA and environmental
impact assessment is quite correct. The client pays,
the client gets. That is what happened with environmental impact assessment. The problem, therefore,
becomes how do you do legitimate SIA, recognizing
that any assessment procedure is enmeshed in social
and political relationships. The concept of value
neutrality enables one to arrive at an objective
answer to an SIA. Perhaps the economists believe in
it, but if there are sociologists who still do,
they are out of date. There are ways in which one
can begin to build institutional structures to get
better social impact assessment through a series of

successive approximations. I am not in favor of leg-
islating a requirement for SIAs in everything, though
I did propose this in Production or Perish [Friedland
and Kappel, 1979] as a political strategy. The point
is that scientists are isolated from other groups of
scientists, not reading each other's journals and so
on.

At present we have no structural forces that
push people across disciplinary lines to any degree.
I would contend that one methodology which could be
used is a social impact methodology which is self-
correcting. That is to say, I am in favor of everyone in land-grant colleges who receives public funds
accounting for themselves in terms of the social impact of their work. I am well aware of the fact
that, if someone is doing basic research on genetics,
the social impact may not be apparent until fifty
years from now and that it is extremely hard to predict, in contrast to the work of an agricultural engineer who is making a cauliflower picker. Social
impacts will vary, but I would contend that, if the
different scientists were to write SIAs, and if we
could put these SIAs away in a file and take some out
every few years and do an evaluation study, over a
period of time we would be able to get better approximations as to what the social impacts are. SIA
methodologies must have the feedback loop built into
them.

Jim Copp. Your comment about accounting for
ourselves has made me shiver, Bill. Morally, we're
accountable to the general public, but in point of
fact the general public isn't listening. In Texas,
whom do we account to? Not to the general public.
We account to agribusiness and to the legislators who
are friendly towards agribusiness. To add to that
kind of accountability would be counterproductive.

**Question 4: How might equity concepts be in-
cluded in agricultural-mechanization SIAs (and should
they be included)?**

Charles Geisler, Cornell University. Let me
answer the two parts in reverse order. Should equity
considerations be included in agricultural-mechanization SIA, and how do we include it? First of all, if
sociologists do not respond to this challenge, who
will? It has been passed over by other disciplines
which, in the name of productivity and efficiency
priorities, have abjured this responsibility. It is
not just that early rural sociologists, many of whom

were religiously motivated, felt equity matters warranted humanitarian attention. Equity or distributional impacts must be evaluated lest key policy decisions always be done on efficiency terms. This is a real challenge for contemporary sociologists.

Secondly, and I think we should make no mistake about it, equity assessment is normative. As you have pointed out, however, so too is SIA and I do not think we should shrink from that reality. This is not to say that equity concerns need be "soft," nor casually studied. There are solid precedents for doing equity analysis, both in welfare economics and in the broad literature on distributive justice. This comes out of various philosophical traditions by people who have been deeply moved by questions of both temporal and intergenerational equity. Temporal equity means here current distributive fairness and equal exchange. Intergenerational equity argues for respecting the rights of future generations. In a more personal sense, I think we can't not do equity analyses. Inequity exists and can be reduced by social scientists confronting it. There is a difference between being neutral and being neuter. How can we, as sociologists who know the social world is teeming with norms and values, purport to be value-free, or use value neutrality as an excuse not to probe more deeply into equity issues? I think it was C. Wright Mills who said, "I have tried to be objective; I do not claim to be detached."

Jim Copp. Let me throw down a gauntlet: What is equity? Is it to each according to his or her needs, or to each according to his or her contribution?

Charles Geisler. That is a historically and geographically specific issue, one that is specific to a social formation. Different societies and different classes within these societies will answer that differently. What I think is important in SIA is to try to present alternative equity perspectives rather than just one definition—that of more and more efficiency. The distributional consequences of efficiency imperatives are usually fairly narrow for society. In the case of agricultural mechanization, we have seen historically that generating benefits is not the same thing as generating an equitable distribution of benefits.

Jim Copp. Would you agree that the system of equity we have now is "to each according to what he can take?"

334

Charles Geisler. I would say yes. And the mechanization of agriculture has not done much to change this. Still, it is important to bear in mind that efficiency and equity need not be opposed. This is often an unfortunate and unwarranted dichotomy. Part of our responsibility is to point out instances in which greater equity produces greater efficiency. Worker ownership of control has been or can be positively correlated with increased productivity. Redistributed land—one form of very real equity—can bolster efficiency and productivity. And municipally owned utilities, which I consider to be an "appropriate technology" from a productive relations standpoint, are resoundingly more efficient than narrowly distributed investor-owned utilities. So there are instances where they are complementary.

I mentioned two kinds of equity before. The first entails the labor-equity question. In the report several graduate students and I produced last year for the Congressional Office of Technology Assessment, at least one case study (the mechanization of cotton harvesting) looked at wages as well as labor displacement. Another equity dimension for labor is the suddenness of the introduction of a new mechanization process. A prolonged conversion allows time for readjustment, compensation, labor retraining, and other sorts of compensations society can come up with. Better yet, more time permits an intervention process whereby both labor and management have some say over new technologies in the workplace. Furthermore, the word similarity between equity as land tenure and equity as a social security and status is far from trivial. I reviewed the literature and found that there are often positive correlations between landownership and a number of characteristics which most people here would agree are positive things for individuals, for families, and for communities. Obviously, the dispossession of land means being pushed down the agricultural ladder towards wage-labor status on the bottom. Insofar as land dispossession was inherent in cotton-harvest automation, mechanization caused widespread deprivation, both material and psychological, among poor blacks and whites who had only recently attained a measure of economic security in owning land.

Larry Busch. I would like to come back to this appropriate-technologies point, though I am not sure what that means entirely. I think that as long as we have an agricultural technology which is essentially unidirectional—that is, development for the sake of efficiency--we are stuck with the dilemma. Technology serves as a kind of ideology. It can be argued by the various technical disciplines that the technologies that are being developed are the only ones that can be developed, through a "there is no choice" kind of argument. I think that's a fundamental problem. Unless somehow we start talking to people in the production sciences, and unless somehow people from the production sciences are able to relate to things outside of their own particular discipline, there is no way we can seriously consider a set of alternatives because there is not going to be any set of alternatives out there to consider.

Michael Perelman. I did not mean in my earlier statement that the only possibility for an authentic SIA would be in a socialist or a communist society, but I would like to point out that the term is a bit ambiguous. The "social" can be what we assess or it can refer to what class interests are behind the assessing; that is the very real politics of SIA.

Greg Hooks, University of Wisconsin. I am going to be repeating some of the themes from the previous comments. In much of this discussion, we have commented that the technologies are not neutral and that society and social relations are implicit in the technologies. I think this is so. The question posed is whether politics render SIA dysfunctional. Are the dealings we have with SIA unfortunately reformist, and are we legitimizing a system that we would like to change in doing SIA? I think this is an unfortunate conclusion and an unfortunate dismissal of SIAs because it leaves us with a largely irrelevant political discourse. In terms of agricultural mechanization, it leaves us with nothing to do but to throw a few stones at a passing tomato harvester. Equity is part of the existing political discourse and we cannot dismiss it because we do not like the context. It is part of the arena in which we are involved if, as sociologists, we are going to participate in state policy formation and in social movements outside of the state that might transform state policies. If the neo-marxist position is substantially correct, then the main people who benefit from mechanization would be the producers, and not all producers either, but rather those who survive the mechanization process. We should be able to consistently identify who it is that benefits. In doing that, I think we have the potential of using that evidence, that argumentation, to form the SIA procedures Bill Friedland described. I would suggest that we follow this course of action and that we not dismiss SIAs for their lack of productivity vis-à-vis environmental issues.

Bill Friedland. There is no question in my mind that this is a complex issue which involves far more than, let us say, the institution of an administrative procedure in the agricultural experiment station in the state of California, Kentucky, or anywhere else. I think that anyone who thinks about this process as an administrative change either does not know what is going on or is trying to "dehorn," to use an old Wobbly expression, that basic idea which exists behind some of the proposals that have been made here today.

We can establish a required SIA in the whole land-grant system and it will not mean a thing unless there is some kind of serious transformation which occurs in social relationships. Otherwise, all that will happen is what happened to all of the other great ideas in the past--like the land-grant system itself. It was a great idea which was essentially put forward as a way of trying to deal with the problem of rural inequality vis-à-vis urban inequality, the income distribution problem. It was an equity problem. People were fleeing the land and something had to be done. Fundamentally, there was a certain validity to it, but look what came out--the system which probably contributed more than any other factor to the absolute annihilation of the population in agriculture. It was incredibly successful in raising productivity and eliminating the agricultural population. If you want to think about the problem, you have to think in terms of social relationshhips, relationships in production. There is simply no escape from that process. Unless we start thinking in terms of how you make a transition from the kind of rampant, private incentives which exist in our society and how they can be brought under control--under population control--and routed back towards the grass roots with genuine popular participation, SIA turns into the same thing as environmental impact assessment. As I said previously, the client that pays for it gets the results. It will happen with SIA, too. In this case, I think the right client is the people, not the people's representatives, because we know what happens with the representatives of the people. We have to become the political process and we have to draw the whole population into the political decision-making process on a continuing basis. The only way, of course, you can do that is by changing material, social, and political relationships.

Integrated Reference List

Abel, Theodore. 1948. The operation called verstehen. American Journal of Sociology 54:211-18.

Abelson, P. H. 1983. Biotechnology: An overview. Science 219 (11 February):611-13.

Adelman, L., and Durant, B. 1973. Who Are These Men?: A Study of the Tramps of Downtown Stockton (and the Agencies that Serve Them). Research Monograph No. 10. Davis, California: University of California.

Allgood, James G., et al. 1971. Planning for Profit--Field Crops. Circular No. 519. Raleigh, North Carolina: North Carolina Agricultural Extension Service.

Allison, F. E. 1973. Soil Organic Matter and Its Role in Crop Production. New York: Elsevier Scientific Publishing Co.

Anderson, A. H. 1961. The 'Expanding' Rural Community: Adjustment Problems and Opportunities. Bulletin No. 464. Lincoln, Nebraska: Nebraska Agricultural Experiment Station.

Anderson, A. H., and Miller, C. J. 1953. The Changing Role of the Small Town in Farm Areas: A Study of Adams, Nebraska. Bulletin No. 419. Lincoln, Nebraska: Nebraska Agricultural Experiment Station.

Apfelbaum, R. S. 1956. Taking research to the farmer. In Proceedings of the First Annual Farm Seed Industry-Research Conference. Washington, D.C.: American Seed Trade Association.

Babb, E. M.; Belden, S. A.; and Saathoff, C. R. 1969. Analysis of cooperative bargaining in the processing tomato industry. American Journal of Agricultural Economics 51 (February):13-25.

References for all chapters are combined in this list. Inadequate citations were improved whenever possible, but some references remain incomplete.

Bagdikian, B. H. 1967. The black immigrants. Saturday
    Evening Post (15 July):25-29, 64-68.
Bainer, R. 1977. Commentary on the mechanization of
    American agriculture. Pp. 317-21 in Agricultural
    Literature: Proud History, Future Promise.
    Washington, D.C.: Graduate School Press, U.S.
    Department of Agriculture.
Ball, A. G., and Heady, E. O. 1972. Trends in farm and
    enterprise size and scale. Pp. 40-58 in A. G. Ball
    and E. O. Heady (eds.), Size, Structure and Future
    of Farms. Ames, Iowa: Iowa State University Press.
Barlow, Frank D., and Fenske, Leo J. 1945. Tractors on
    Upland Farms in North Louisiana. Bulletin No. 399.
    Baton Rouge, Louisiana: Louisiana Agricultural
    Experiment Station.
_____. 1947. Cost and Utilization of Power and
    Equipment on Farms in the Mississippi River Delta
    Cotton Area of Louisiana. Bulletin No. 417. Baton
    Rouge, Louisiana: Louisiana Agricultural Experiment
    Station.
Barnes, R. F. 1967. The California Migrant Farm
    Worker, His Family, and the Rural Community.
    Research Monograph No. 6. Davis, California:
    University of California.
_____. 1969. Conflicts of Cultural Transition: A
    Review of Dilemmas Faced by the Mexican-American
    Farm Worker and His Family. (Reference
    incomplete.)
Barnett, P. 1975. Lettuce harvester could displace
    Salinas farm workers. Cal Aggie. Davis,
    California: University of California.
Barton, K. A., and Brill, W. J. 1983. Prospects in
    plant genetic engineering. Science 219
    (11 February):671-75.
Batie, Sandra S., and Healy, Robert G. 1983. The
    future of American agriculture. Scientific
    American 248 (February):45-53.
Bauman, D. E.; DeGeeter, N. J.; Peel, C. J.; Lanza,
    G. M.; Gorewit, R. C.; and Hammond, R. W. 1982.
    Effect of recombinantly derived bovine growth
    hormone (bGH) on lactational performance of high
    yielding dairy cows. Paper presented at the 77th
    Annual Meeting of the American Dairy Association,
    University Park, Pennsylvania, June 27-30.
Bawden, L. D. 1973. The neglected human factor
    (invited address). In Proceedings, American
    Journal of Agricultural Economics 55
    (December):879-87.
Beale, Calvin E. 1972. Impact on changing tobacco
    demand and technology on population and

migration. In A. Frank Bordeaux and Russell H. Brannon (eds.), <u>Social and Economic Issues Confronting the Tobacco Industry in the Seventies.</u> Lexington, Kentucky: University of Kentucky.

Becket, J. 1966. <u>The Domestic Farm Laborer: A Study of Yolo County Tomato Pickers.</u> (Reference incomplete.)

Becket, J. W. 1967. Labor efficiency and utilization. <u>California Citrograph</u> 52 (June):318-27.

Beegle, J. A. 1961. Sociological aspects of changes in farm labor force. In Center for Agricultural and Economic Adjustment, <u>Labor Mobility and Population in Agriculture</u>. Ames, Iowa: Iowa State University Press.

Belden, J., and Forte, G. 1976. <u>Toward a National Food Policy</u>. Washington, D.C.: Exploratory Project for Economic Alternatives.

Bell, Colin, and Newby, Howard. 1974. Capitalist farmers in the British class structure. <u>Sociologia Ruralis</u> 14 (1/2):3-21.

Bennett, Charles A. 1938. The relation of mechanical harvesting to the production of high grade cotton. <u>Agricultural Engineering</u> 19 (September).

Berardi, G. M. 1976. Environmental impact and economic viability of alternative methods of wheat production: A study of New York and Pennsylvania farmers. Master's thesis, Cornell University, Ithaca, New York.

_____. 1977. An energy and economic analysis of conventional and organic wheat farming. In <u>Food, Fertilizers and Agricultural Residues</u>. Ann Arbor, Michigan: Ann Arbor Science Publishers.

_____. 1978. Organic and conventional wheat production: Examination of energy and economics. <u>Agro-Ecosystems</u> 4:367-76.

_____. 1979a. Energy use and drainage development on dairy farms in northern New York. Ph.D. dissertation, Cornell University, Ithaca, New York.

_____. 1979b. <u>Mechanization of Flue-Cured Tobacco Production and Impact on Agricultural Labor: A Study of Employment and Locational Adjustments by Tobacco Growers, Seasonal Labor, and Farm Communities</u>. Baltimore, Maryland: Department of Geography, University of Maryland, Baltimore County.

Bereano, P. 1974. <u>Technology as a Social and Political Institution</u>. New York: John Wiley.

Beresford, Tristram J. 1975. <u>We Plough the Fields</u>. Harmondsworth, England: Penguin.

Bergland, Bob. 1980. The federal role in agricultural research. Remarks prepared for delivery before

340

administrators and program staff people from all
units of the U.S. Department of Agriculture's
Science and Education Administration, Sheraton
Conference Center, Reston, Virginia. Washington,
D.C.: Office of the Secretary, U.S. Department of
Agriculture, January 31.

Berlan, Jean-Pierre. 1982. Réexamen de l'analyse
économique du changement technique: le cas du
mais hybride. Unpublished paper. Université de
Marseilles.

Berry, Wendell. 1977. The Unsettling of America:
Culture and Agriculture. San Francisco: Sierra
Club Books.

Bertrand, A. L. 1948. The social processes and the
mechanization of southern agricultural systems.
Rural Sociology 13 (1):31-39.

_____. 1950. Some social implications of the
mechanization of southern agriculture.
Southwestern Social Science Quarterly 31:121.

_____. 1951. Agricultural Mechanization and
Social Change in Rural Louisiana. Bulletin No.
458. Baton Rouge, Louisiana: Louisiana Agricultural Experiment Station.

_____. 1958. Agricultural technology and rural
social change. Chapter 26 in A. Bertrand (ed.),
Rural Sociology: An Analysis of Contemporary Rural
Life. New York: McGraw-Hill.

Bertrand, A. J.; Charlton, L.; Pederson, H. A.;
Skrabanek, R. L.; and Tarver, J. D. 1956. Factors
Associated with Agricultural Mechanization in the
Southwest Region. Bulletin No. 567. Fayetteville,
Arkansas: Arkansas Agricultural Experiment Station.

Bills, N. L., and Barkley, P. W. 1973. Public
Investments and Population Changes in Three Rural
Washington State Towns. Agricultural Economic
Report No. 236. Washington, D.C.: U.S. Department
of Agriculture, Economic Research Service.

Binswanger, Hans P., and Ruttan, Vernon W. 1978.
Induced Innovation: Technology, Institutions and
Development. Baltimore: Johns Hopkins University
Press.

Bishop, C. E. 1967a. The urbanization of rural
America: Implications for agricultural economics.
American Journal of Agricultural Economics 49
(December):999-1008.

Bishop, C. E., ed. 1967b. Farm Labor in the United
States. New York: Columbia University Press.

Black Economic Research Center. 1973. Only Six Million
Acres: The Decline of Black-Owned Land in the
Rural South. Report sponsored by Clark College,
prepared under the direction of Robert S. Browne,
New York.

341

Bonnen, C. A., and Magee, A. C. 1938. Some tech-
    nological changes in the high plains cotton area of
    Texas. Journal of Farm Economics 20
    (August):605-15.
Bonnen, C. A., and Magee, A. C. 1939. An Economic
    Study of Farm Organization in the High Plains
    Cotton Farming Area of Texas. Bulletin No. 568.
    College Station, Brazos County, Texas: Texas
    Agricultural Experiment Station.
_____. n.d. A Study to Determine the Social and
    Economic Effects on Farms of a Definitely Planned
    Program of Soil Conservation. (Reference
    incomplete.)
Bonnen, J. T. 1969. The absence of knowledge of
    distributional impacts: An obstacle to effective
    program analysis and decisions. Vol. 1, pp. 419-49
    in United States Congress, Joint Economic
    Committee, The Analysis and Evaluation of Public
    Expenditures: The PPB System.
Booster, Dean E.; Varseveld, George W.; and Putnam,
    Teryl B. 1970. Progress in Mechanization of
    Strawberry Harvesting. Special Report 305.
    Columbus, Ohio: Ohio State University
    Agricultural Experiment Station.
Bossung, Kenneth. 1976. Pioneering appropriate
    technology. People and Energy 2 (March):1-2.
Bowen, H. R., and Mangum, G. L. 1966. Automation and
    Economic Progress. Englewood Cliffs, New Jersey:
    Prentice-Hall.
Bowers, Wendell, and Rider, Allen R. 1974. Hay
    handling and harvesting. Agricultural Engineering
    55:12-18.
Brady, Nyle C. 1982. Chemistry and world food
    supplies. Science 218 (26 November):847-53.
Brake, J., ed. 1970. Emerging and Projected Trends
    Likely to Influence the Structure of Midwestern
    Agriculture, 1970-1985. Monograph No. 11.
    University of Iowa College of Law.
Breimyer, H. F., and Barr, W. 1972. Issues in
    concentration versus dispersion. In Who Will
    Control U.S. Agriculture? Special Publication 27.
    Urbana-Champaign, Illinois: University of Illinois,
    College of Agriculture, Cooperative Extension
    Service.
Brewster, J. M. 1958. Technological advance and the
    future of the family farm. Journal of Farm Ecology
    40 (December):1596-1608.
Brunn, S. D. 1968. Changes in the service structure of
    rural trade centers. Rural Sociology 33 (June):
    200-06.

342

Bryant, E. S., and Leung, K. M. 1967. Mississippi Farm
Trends 1950-1964. Bulletin No. 754. State
College, Mississippi: Mississippi Agricultural
Experiment Station.

Buchele, Wesley F. 1982. A short history of the round
baler. Agricultural Engineering 63(4):18-20.

Budiansky, Stephen. 1983. Green light for plant
field-trials. Nature 302 (21 April):644.

Buttel, Frederick H. 1980. The political economy of
agriculture in advanced industrial societies:
Some observations from the United States. Paper
presented at the Annual Meeting of the Canadian
Sociology and Anthropology Association, Montreal,
June.

_____. 1981. American Agriculture and Rural
America: Challenges for Progressive Politics.
Bulletin No. 120. Ithaca, New York: Cornell
University, Department of Rural Sociology.

Buttel, Frederick H., and Gertler, Michael E. 1982.
Agricultural structure, agricultural policy and
environmental quality: Some observations on the
context of research in North America. Agriculture
and Environment 7:101-19.

Butterwick, Michael W. 1969. Vertical Integration and
the Role of the Co-operatives. Oxford, England:
Central Council for Agricultural and Horticultural
Co-operation.

Butz, E. 1975. Bountiful harvest: The hope for peace.
Address before the Economic Club of Chicago,
Chicago, Illinois, December 9.

California Agrarian Action Project. 1978. No hands
touch the land: Automating California farms.
Science for the People 10 (January-February):20-28.

Campbell, A., and Converse, P., eds. 1972. The Human
Meaning of Social Change. New York: Russell Sage
Foundation.

Campbell, J. S.; Sahid, J.; and Stang, D. 1971. Law
and Order Reconsidered. Report of the U.S. Task
Force on Law and Law Enforcement to the National
Commission on the Causes and Prevention of
Violence. New York: Praeger.

Cargill, B. F., and Garrett, R. E. 1975. The 'big
picture' of lettuce handling. Transactions of the
American Society of Agricultural Engineers 18:7-9.

Cargill, B. F., and Rossmiller, G. E. 1969. Fruit
and Vegetable Harvest Mechanization: Manpower
Implications. Report No. 17. East Lansing,
Michigan: Michigan State University, Rural Manpower
Center.

Cargill, B. F., and Rossmiller, G. E., eds. 1970.
Fruit and Vegetable Harvest Mechanization:
Technological Implications; Manpower Implications;

Public Policy Implications. East Lansing, Michigan: Michigan State University, Rural Manpower Center.

Carleton, W. M. 1963. Trends in fruit and vegetable harvesting. Agricultural Engineering 44 (March):139.

Carleton, W. M., and Vanden Berg, G. E. 1970. That hidden migration: History now. Agricultural Engineering 51 (October):596-97.

Carter, H. O., and Johnston, W. E. 1978. Agricultural productivity and technological change: Some concepts, measures, and implications. Pp. 73-122 in Technological Change, Farm Mechanization and Agricultural Employment. University of California Publications 4085.

Carter, H. O., and Youde, J. G. 1974. Some impacts of the changing energy situation on U.S. agriculture. American Journal of Agricultural Economics 56 (December):878-87.

Carter, L. J. 1977. Soil erosion: The problem persists despite the billions spent on it. Science 196 (April):409-11.

Castle and Cooke, Inc. 1977. Annual Report to Shareholders.

Center for Rural Affairs. 1976. Wheels of Fortune: A Report on the Impact of Center-Pivot Irrigation on the Ownership of Land in Nebraska. Walthill, Nebraska: Center for Rural Affairs.

Chittick, D. 1955. Growth and Decline of South Dakota Trade Centers, 1901-1951. Bulletin No. 448. Brookings, South Dakota: South Dakota Agricultural Experiment Station.

Choi, H., and Coughenour, C. M. 1978. Socioeconomic Aspects of No-Tillage Agriculture: A Case Study of Farmers in Christian County, Kentucky. Lexington, Kentucky: University of Kentucky, Department of Sociology.

Clark, W. 1975a. Competition and the price of food. Pp. 107-09 in Catherine Lerza and Michael Jacobson (eds.), Food for People, Not for Profit. New York: Random House.

_____. 1975b. U.S. agriculture is growing trouble as well as crops. Smithsonian 5 (10 January): 59-65.

Cleaver, Harry M., Jr. 1972. Contradictions of the green revolution. Monthly Review (June):80-111.

Cochrane, Willard W. 1979. The Development of American Agriculture. Minneapolis: University of Minnesota Press.

Coffey, W. C. 1948. A challenge to the hybrid seed corn industry. In Proceedings of the Third Annual

344

Hybrid Corn Industry-Research Conference.
Washington, D.C.: American Seed Trade Association.
Commoner, B. 1971. The Closing Circle: Nature, Man,
and Technology. New York: Knopf.
Constandse, A. K. 1969. Social implications of
mechanization of agriculture. Sociologia Ruralis
9:333-39.
Constandse, A. K.; Hernandez, P. F.; and Bertrand, A. L.
1968. Social Implications of Increasing Farm
Technology in Rural Louisiana. Bulletin No. 628.
Baton Rouge, Louisiana: Louisiana Agricultural
Experiment Station.
Consumer Reports. 1973. Why tomatoes you buy this
winter may be tough, tasteless and costly.
Consumer Reports 38 (January):68-9.
_____. 1975. Competition and the price of food.
Pp. 107-09 in C. Lerza and M. Jacobson (eds.), Food
for People, Not for Profit. New York: Random
House.
Cooper, Morton; Barton, Glen T.; and Brodell, Albert P.
1947. Progress of Farm Mechanization.
Miscellaneous Publication No. 630. Washington,
D.C.: U.S. Department of Agriculture.
Copeland, Lawrence O. 1976. Principles of Seed Science
and Technology. Minneapolis, Minnesota: Burgess
Publishing Company.
Cordtz, Dan. 1972. Corporate farming: A tough row to
hoe. Fortune 86 (August):134-39, 172-75.
Cottrell, F. 1955. Energy and Society. New York:
McGraw-Hill.
Council for Agricultural Science and Technology (CAST).
1980. Organic and Conventional Farming Compared.
Ames, Iowa: Council for Agricultural Science and
Technology.
Council on Environmental Quality. 1978. Environmental
Quality: Ninth Annual Report. Washington, D.C.:
U.S. Government Printing Office.
Counter Information Service. 1975. Unilever's World.
Anti Report No. 11. Nottingham, England: Russell
Press.
CRA. 1973. U.S. Department of Agriculture and the
National Research Council. Report of the Committee
on Research Advisory to the USDA. Springfield,
Virginia: National Technical Information Service.
Crabb, A. Richard. 1947. The Hybrid Corn-Makers:
Prophets of Plenty. New Brunswick, New Jersey:
Rutgers University Press.
Creech, R. G., and Alexander, D. E. 1978. Breeding for
industrial and nutritional quality in maize. In
D. B. Walden (ed.), Maize Breeding and Genetics.
New York: Wiley-Interscience.

Crosson, Pierre. 1979. Agricultural land use: A
    technological and energy perspective. In Max
    Schnepf (ed.), Farmland, Food and Our Future.
    Ankeny, Iowa: Soil Conservation Service of America.
Currie, J. M.; Murphy, J. A.; and Schmitz, A. 1971.
    The concept of economic surplus and its use in
    economic analysis. Economic Journal (December):
    741-99.
Data Probe, Inc. 1980. The New Farm Subscriber Survey.
    Emmaus, Pennsylvania: Rodale Press.
Davenport, Caroline. 1981. Sowing the seeds--Research,
    development flourish at DeKalb and Pioneer
    Hi-Bred. Barron's 61:9-10,33.
Davis, John Emmeus. 1980. Capitalist agriculturalist
    development and the exploitation of the propertied
    laborer. In F. Buttel and H. Newby (eds.), The
    Rural Sociology of the Advanced Societies.
    Montclair, New Jersey: Allenheld, Osmun and Co.
Davis, John H. 1956. From agriculture to
    agribusiness. Harvard Business Review 34
    (January/February):107-15.
Davis, V. W. 1969. Labor or capital--the road ahead.
    Pp. 113-52 in B. F. Cargill and G. E. Rossmiller
    (eds.), Fruit and Vegetable Harvest Mechanization:
    Manpower Implications. Report No. 17. East
    Lansing, Michigan: Michigan State University,
    Rural Manpower Center.
Day, R. H. 1967. The economics of technological change
    and the demise of the share-cropper. American
    Economic Review 57 (May):427-49.
DeGraff, Herrell. 1966. Livestock production in the
    United States. In Proceedings of the 15th Annual
    Meeting of the Agricultural Research Institute.
    Washington, D.C.: National Academy of Sciences,
    National Research Council.
Dickman, A. I. 1976. Oral history of the processing
    tomato harvester. Project funded by a grant from
    the California Tomato Growers Association through
    the University Library at the University of
    California, Davis. A. I. Dickman, interviewer
    and director of the project.
Diehl, W. D. 1966. Farm-nonfarm migration in the
    southeast: A costs-returns analysis. Journal
    of Farm Economics 48 (February):1-11.
Dillingham, H. C., and Sly, D. F. 1966. The mechanical
    cotton-picker, Negro migration, and the integration
    movement. Human Organizations 25 (Winter):344-51.
Doering, O. C., III. 1978. Appropriate technology for
    U.S. agriculture: Are small farms the coming thing?
    American Journal of Agricultural Economics 60
    (May):293-94.

Donaldson, F. G., and McInerney, J. P. 1973. Changing machinery technology and agricultural adjustment. American Journal of Agricultural Economics 55 (December):829-39.

Donaldson, John G. S., and Donaldson, Frances. 1972. Farming in Britain Today. Prepared for Commission of the European Communities by Development Analysts Limited. Baltimore, Maryland: Penguin.

Dorner, Peter. 1971. Needed redirections in economic analyses for agricultural development policy. American Journal of Agricultural Economics 53 (February):8-16.

_____. 1977. Transformation of U.S. Agriculture: The Past Forty Years. Agricultural Economics Staff Paper No. 126. Madison, Wisconsin: University of Wisconsin.

Drucker, P. F. 1946. Exit king cotton. Harper's (May).

Duncan, Otis Durant. 1940. The Theory and Consequences of Mobility of Farm Population. Circular No. 88. Stillwater: Oklahoma Agricultural Experiment Station.

Durant, B. 1970. Housing Sacramento's Invisible Man: Farm Workers, Hustlers, and Misfits. Research Monograph No. 9. Davis, California: University of California.

Durost, Donald D., and Black, Evelyn T. 1977. Changes in Farm Production and Efficiency, 1977. Statistical Bulletin No. 581. Washington, D.C.: U.S. Department of Agriculture, Economic Research Service.

Duvick, D. N. 1977. Genetic rates of gain in hybrid maize yields during the past 40 years. Maydica 22:187-96.

Earle, Elizabeth D. 1982. Application of genetic engineering to corn improvement. In Proceedings of the 36th Annual Corn and Sorghum Research Conference. Washington, D.C.: American Seed Trade Association.

Eberhart, S. A. 1982. Relationship between public and private breeding research as viewed by a privately supported research program director. In Pioneer Hi-Bred International, Report of the 1982 Plant Breeding Research Forum. Des Moines, Iowa: Pioneer Hi-Bred International.

Eckstein, Otto. 1961. Water-Resource Development. Cambridge, Massachusetts: Harvard University Press.

Economic Research Service. 1969. Potential Mechanization in the Flue-Cured Tobacco Industry with Emphasis on Human Resource Adjustments. Agricultural Economic Report No. 169. Washington, D.C.: U.S.

Department of Agriculture, Economic Research
Service.

Economics, Statistics, and Cooperatives Service (ESCS).
1978. Technological Changes in the Production of
Flue-Cured Tobacco: Anticipated Socio-Economic
Consequences--An Executive Summary and Annotated
Bibliography. Washington, D.C.: U.S. Department
of Agriculture, Economics, Statistics, and
Cooperatives Service, Development Strategies
Project Research Team.
_____. 1980. Outlook for U.S. Agricultural
Exports. Washington, D.C.: U.S. Department of
Agriculture.

Emerick, C. F. 1896. Agricultural discontent.
Political Science Quarterly 11:433-63.

Erickson, E. P.; Erickson, J. A.; and Hostetler, J. A.
1980. The cultivation of the soil as a moral
directive: Population growth, family ties, and
the maintenance of community among the Old Order
Amish. Rural Sociology 45 (Spring):49-68.

European Economic Community (E.E.C.). 1975. A Study of
the Evolution of Concentration in the Food Industry
for the United Kingdom. Parts I and II. Brussels:
Commission of the European Communities,
Directorate-General, Competition.

Evenson, Robert E., and Yoav Kislev. 1975.
Agricultural Research and Productivity. New Haven,
Connecticut: Yale University Press.

Farm Chemicals. 1981a. The DuPont agrichemicals
story. Farm Chemicals 144 (March):13-35.
_____. 1981b. A look at world pesticide markets.
Farm Chemicals (September):55-60.

Farm Implement News. 1938. Farm implement manufacturers' income. Farm Implement News (14 July).

Farm Management Extension. 1965. A Cost and Return
Guide for Selected Field Crops in North Carolina.
Circular No. 462. Raleigh: North Carolina
Agricultural Extension Service.

Faulkner, E. H. 1943. Plowman's Folly. Norman,
Oklahoma: University of Oklahoma.

Field, D. R., and Dimit, R. M. 1970. Population Change
in South Dakota Small Towns and Cities, 1949-1960.
Bulletin No. 571. Brookings, South Dakota: South
Dakota Agriculture Experiment Station.

Fineberg, R. 1971. Green Card Workers in Farm Labor
Disputes. New York: Knopf.

Finsterbusch, Kurt, and Wolf, C. P. 1977. Methodology
of Social Impact Assessment. Stroudsburg,
Pennsylania: Dowden, Hutchinson and Ross.

Flinn, W. L., and Buttel, F. H. 1980. Sociological
aspects of farm size: Ideological and social

consequences of scale in agriculture. Paper
presented at the Annual Meeting of the American
Agricultural Economics Association, University of
Illinois at Urbana-Champaign, July 28.

Flora, J., and Rodefeld, R. D. 1978. The nature and
magnitude of changes in agricultural technology.
In R. D. Rodefeld et al. (eds.), Change in Rural
America: Causes, Consequences and Alternatives.
St. Louis, Missouri: C. V. Mosby Company.

Folse, C. L., and Riffe, W. W. 1969. Changing patterns
of business services and population in Illinois
rural villages. Illinois Agricultural Economics 9
(1):26-32.

Ford, Arthur M. 1973. The Political Economics of Rural
Poverty in the South. New York: Ballinger.

Fowler, Cary. 1980. Sowing the seeds of destruction.
Science for the People (September/October):8-10.

Franta, Harry. 1975. Antle enters pre-cut lettuce
business. The Packer 18 October:1,6.

Fredricks, Anne. 1979. Agribusiness in the lettuce
fields. Food Monitor No. 10 (May/June):12-15.

Fridley, R., and Holtzman, J. 1974. Predicting the
socio-economic implications of mechanization by
systems analysis. Transactions of the American
Society of Agricultural Engineers 17(5):821-25.

Friedland, William H. 1969. Making sociology relevant:
A teaching-research program for undergraduates.
American Sociologist 4 (May):104-10.

_____. 1973a. The social impact of technology.
Paper presented at the First National Land Reform
Conference, San Francisco, California, April 25-28.

_____. 1973b. Social Sleepwalkers: Scientific and
Technological Research in California Agriculture.
Research Monograph No. 13. Davis, California:
Department of Applied Behavioral Sciences,
University of California.

_____. 1974. State politics and public interest.
Society 11:54-62.

_____. 1979. Who killed rural sociology? A case
study in the political economy of knowledge production. Paper presented at the Annual Meetings of
the American Sociological Association.

_____. 1982. The end of rural society and the
future of rural sociology. Rural Sociology 47
(December):589-608.

Friedland, W., and Barton, A. 1975. Destalking the
Wily Tomato: A Case Study in Social Consequences
in California Agricultural Research. Research
Monograph No. 15. Davis, California: University
of California.

_____. 1976. Tomato technology. Society 13 (September/October):34-42.

Friedland, William H.; Barton, A., and Thomas, R. J. 1978. Manufacturing Green Gold: The Conditions and Social Consequences of Lettuce Harvest Mechanization. Davis, California: Department of Applied Behavioral Sciences, California Agricultural Policy Seminar, University of California.

_____. 1979. Conditions and consequences of lettuce mechanization. HortScience 14:110-13.

_____. 1981. Manufacturing Green Gold: Capital, Labor and Technology in the Lettuce Industry. New York: Cambridge.

Friedland, William H., and Kappel, Tim. 1979. Production or Perish: Changing the Inequities of Agricultural Research Priorities. Santa Cruz, California: University of California, Santa Cruz, Project on Social Impact Assessment and Values.

Friedland, W. H., and Nelkin D. 1972. Technological trends and the organization of migrant farm workers. Social Problems 19 (4):509-21.

Friends of the Land. 1943. Does plowing hurt the soil?: A symposium on Faulkner's book. LAND 3 (Summer).

Frundt, H. J. 1975. American agribusiness and U.S. foreign agricultural policy. Ph.D. dissertation, Rutgers University, New Brunswick, New Jersey.

Fuguitt, G. V., and Deeley, N. A. 1966. Retail service patterns and small town population change: A replication of Hassinger's study. Rural Sociology 31 (March):53-63.

Fujimoto, I. 1969. Mechanization and farm labor: Inequities and social consequences. In B. F. Cargill and G. E. Rossmiller (eds.), Fruit and Vegetable Harvest Mechanization: Manpower Implications. Report No. 17. East Lansing, Michigan: Michigan State University, Rural Manpower Center.

Fulco, L. J. 1969. How mechanization of harvesting is affecting jobs. Missouri Labor Relations 92 (March):26-32.

Fuller, Varden. n.d. Rural Worker Adjustment to Urban Life. Policy Paper in Human Resources and Industrial Relations No. 15. Ann Arbor, Michigan: University of Michigan, Institute of Labor and Industrial Relations.

_____. 1969. Political pressures and income distribution in agriculture. Pp. 255-63 in V. W. Ruttan, A. D. Waldo, and J. P. Houck (eds.), Agricultural Policy in an Affluent Society. New York: Norton & Company.

Fuller, V., and Mason, B. 1977. Farm Labor. Giannini
    Foundation Research Paper No. 437. Berkeley,
    California: University of California.
Fusfield, D. 1970. The basic economics of the urban
    and racial crises. Review of Black Political
    Economy 1 (March):63.
Gallup Organization, Inc. 1979. 1979 National
    Gardening Survey. Burlington, Vermont: National
    Association for Gardening.
Gardner, B. D., and Pope, R. D. 1978. How is scale
    and structure determined in agriculture? American
    Journal of Agricultural Economics 60 (May):295-302.
Garoyan, Leon. 1974. Some economic considerations of
    the California iceberg lettuce industry.
    Unpublished paper. University of California,
    Davis, Department of Agricultural Economics.
Gates, P. W. 1960. The Farmer's Age: Agriculture
    1815-1860. New York: Holt, Rinehart and Winston.
Geisler, Charles C.; Cowan, J. Tadlock; Hattery, Michael
    R.; and Jacobs, Harvey M. 1981. Sustained Land
    Productivity: Equity Consequences of Alternative
    Agricultural Technologies. Bulletin No. 119.
    Ithaca: Cornell University, Department of Rural
    Sociology.
Geissbuhler, Hans; Brenneison, Paul; and Fischer,
    Hans-Peter. 1982. Frontiers in crop production:
    Chemical research objectives. Science 217
    (6 August):505-10.
Genovese, E. 1967. The Political Economy of Slavery.
    New York: Pantheon.
George, Susan. 1977. How the Other Half Dies: The Real
    Reasons for World Hunger. Montclair, New Jersey:
    Allanheld, Osmun and Co.
Giamatti, A. Bartlett. 1982. The university, industry,
    and cooperative research. Science 218 (24 Decem-
    ber):1278-80.
Giedion, Siegfried. 1969 [1948]. Mechanization Takes
    Command. New York: W. W. Norton, Inc.
Glass, Judith Chanin. 1966. Conditions which facili-
    tate unionization of agricultural workers: A case
    study of the Salinas Valley lettuce industry.
    Ph.D. dissertation, University of California, Los
    Angeles.
Goldschmidt, W. 1946. Small Business and the
    Community: A Study in Central Valley of California
    on Effects of Scale of Farm Operations. Report to
    the Special Committee to Study Problems of American
    Small Business, United States Senate, December 23.
    _____. 1978. As You Sow: Three Studies in the
    Social Consequences of Agribusiness. Montclair,
    New Jersey: Allanheld, Osmun and Co.

Goss, K. F. 1979. Review essay. Rural Sociology 44 (Winter):802-06.

Goss, K. F., and Rodefeld, R. D. 1977. Consequences of mechanization in U.S. agriculture, 1935-1975. Paper presented at the Rural Sociological Society Annual Meeting, Madison, Wisconsin, September.

Goss, K. F.; Rodefeld, R. D.; and Buttel, F. H. 1979. The Political Economy of Class Structure in U.S. Agriculture: A Theoretical Outline. AE & RS 144. University Park, Pennsylvania: Pennsylvania State University, Department of Agricultural Economics and Rural Sociology.

_____. 1982. The political economy of class structure in U.S. agriculture: A theoretical outline. In F. H. Buttel and H. Newby (eds.), The Rural Sociology of the Advanced Industrial Societies. Montclair, New Jersey: Allanheld, Osmun and Co.

Gray, L. C. 1937. Agricultural machinery. Encyclopedia of the Social Sciences, Volume 1. New York: Macmillan.

Gregg, Elizabeth. 1982. The Seed Industry: Perspective and Prospects. Research paper. New York: Drexel Burnham Lambert, Inc.

Gregor, H. F. 1963. Regional hierarchies in California agricultural production: 1939-1954. Annals of the Association of American Geographers 53 (March): 27-37.

_____. 1964. A map of agricultural adjustment. Professional Geographers 16 (January):16-19.

_____. 1970. The large industrialized American crop farm: A mid-latitude plantation variant. Geographical Review 60 (April):151-75.

_____. 1979a. The large farm as a stereotype: A look at the Pacific Southwest. Economic Geography 55 (January):71-87.

_____. 1979b. The regional assessment of U.S. agricultural industrialization. Paper presented at the 75th Anniversary Meeting of the Association of American Geographers, Philadelphia, Pennsylvania, 22-25 April.

Griliches, Zvi. 1957. Hybrid corn: An exploration in the economics of technological change. Econometrica 25 (October):501-22.

_____. 1958. Research costs and social returns: Hybrid corn and related innovations. Journal of Political Economy 66 (October):419-31.

_____. 1960. Hybrid corn and the economics of innovation. Science 132 (29 July):275-80.

352

_____. 1968. Agricultural productivity and technology. International Encyclopedia of Social Sciences 1:241-45.

Grise, Vernon N.; Shugors, Owen K.; Givan, William D.; and Hoff, Frederick L. 1975. Structural Characteristics of Flue-Cured Tobacco Farms and Prospects for Harvest Mechanization. Agricultural Economics Report No. 227. Washington, D.C.: U.S. Department of Agriculture, Economic Research Service.

Guither, H. D. 1963. Factors influencing farm operators to leave farming. Journal of Farm Ecology 45 (3):567-76.

Guither, H. D., ed. 1972. Who Will Control U.S. Agriculture? Publication No. 32. Urbana, Illinois: North Central Regional Extension.

Hahn, C. T. 1971. Movements of pesticides by runoff and erosion. Transactions of the American Society of Agricultural Engineering 14:445.

Hall, C. W. 1968. Bibliography on Mechanization and Labor in Agriculture. Special Paper No. 6. East Lansing, Michigan: Michigan State University, Rural Manpower Center.

Hambidge, G. 1940. Farmers in a changing world--A summary. In G. Hambidge (ed.), Yearbook of Agriculture, 1940. Washington, D.C.: U.S. Government Printing Office.

_____. 1978. American agriculture--The first 300 years. In R. D. Rodefeld et al. (eds.), Change in Rural America. St. Louis, Missouri: C. V. Mosby Co.

Hamilton, C. Horace. 1937. Population Changes in Texas, 1937. Mimeo. College Station, Texas: Texas A & M College Agricultural Experiment Station, Division of Farm and Ranch Economics.

_____. 1939. The social effect of recent trends in the mechanization of agriculture. Rural Sociology 4 (March):3-19.

Hanway, D. G. 1978a. Agricultural experiment stations and the Plant Variety Protection Act: Part 1. Crops and Soils Magazine 30 (February):5-6.

_____. 1978b. Agricultural experiment stations and the Plant Variety Protection Act: Part 2. Crops and Soils Magazine 30 (March):5-7.

Hargood, Margaret Jarman. 1947. Farm Operator Family Level of Living Indexes for Counties of the United States, 1940 and 1945. Washington, D.C.: U.S. Department of Agriculture, Bureau of Agricultural Economics.

Harlan, Jack. 1975. Our vanishing genetic resources. Science 188 (9 May):618-21.

Harold, L. L. 1972. Soil erosion by water as
    affected by reduced tillage systems. Proceedings
    of No-Tillage Systems Symposium. Columbus, Ohio:
    Center for Tomorrow.
Harpstead, Dale D. 1971. High lysine corn. Scientific
    American 225 (August):42.
Harris, Louis, and Associates, Inc. 1980. Outline for
    press briefing on a survey of the public's
    attitudes toward soil, water and renewable
    resources conservation policy. New York: Louis
    Harris and Associates, Inc.
Hart, John Fraser, and Chestang, Ennis L. 1978. Rural
    revolution in east Carolina. Geographical Review:
    435-58.
Hartman, Paul Theodore. 1966. Work rules and
    productivity in the Pacific coast longshore
    industry. Ph.D. dissertation, University of
    California, Berkeley.
Harvard Business School. 1978. Pioneer Hi-Bred
    International, Inc. Harvard Business School Case
    Study. Boston: Harvard Business School Case
    Services.
Hatch, E. 1975. Stratification in a rural California
    community. Agricultural History 49 (January):
    21-38.
Hawley, E. 1966. The politics of the Mexican labor
    issue. Agricultural History 40:157-76.
Hayes, Herbert K. 1963. A Professor's Story of Hybrid
    Corn. Minneapolis: Burgess Publishing Co.
Hayes, S. E. 1978. Farm and nonfarm wages and
    benefits, 1948-1977. Pp. 33-72 in Technological
    Change, Farm Mechanization and Agricultural
    Employment. Publication 4085. Davis, California:
    University of California.
Hayes, S., and Mamer, J. 1977. Pressures on
    Agriculture: Farm Labor--Current Issues. Leaflet
    No. 2960. Davis, California: University of
    California Division of Agricultural Sciences.
Hays, Virgil W.; Bard, Robert C.; Brokken, Ray F.;
    Edgar, S. A.; Elliott, Wayne T.; Finland, Maxwell;
    Heffernan, W. D.; Lassiter, Charles A.; Moon,
    Harley W.; Naqi, Syed A.; Paulsen, Arnold A.;
    Shutze, John V.; Teague, Howard S.; Vinson, Ralph;
    Visek, Willard J.; Vocke, Gary; Wallace, Harold D.;
    White-Stevens, Robert H.; Wolf, Dean. 1981.
    Antiobiotics in Animal Feeds. Report No. 88.
    Ames, Iowa: Council for Agricultural Science and
    Technology.
Headley, J. C. 1972. Agricultural productivity,
    technology and environmental quality. American
    Journal of Agricultural Economics 54 (5):749-56.

354

Heady, E. O. 1960. Extent and conditions of agricultural mechanization in the United States. Chapter 3 in J. L. Meij (ed.), Mechanization in Agriculture. Chicago, Illinois: Quadrangle.

_____. 1974. Rural development and rural communities of the future. From Rural Industrialization: Problems and Potentials. Ames, Iowa: North Central Regional Center for Rural Development.

Heady, Earl O., and Sonka, Steven T. 1974. Farm size, rural community income and consumer welfare. American Journal of Agricultural Economics 56:534-42.

Heffernan, W. 1972. Sociological dimensions of agricultural structures in the United States. Sociologia Ruralis 12 (August):481-99.

Hennessey, W. J. 1970. The hidden migration. Agricultural Engineering 51 (October):596-99.

Heringer, Lester. 1964. Need for mechanization more evident. California Tomato Grower 7 (January): 1-11.

Hernandez, Manuel, and Costa, Alan. 1977. Effect of Mechanical Harvesting Technology on Farm Employment for 10 Selected Crops of California. Sacramento, California: Assembly Office of Research.

Hertford, Reed, and Schmitz, Andrew. 1977. Measuring economic returns to agricultural research. Pp. 148-76 in Arndt, Dalrymple, and Rutten (eds.), Resource Allocation and Productivity in National and International Agricultural Research. Minneapolis, Minnesota: University of Minnesota.

Higgins, F. Hal. 1958. John M. Horner and the development of the combined harvester. Agricultural History 32 (January):14-24.

Hightower, Jim. 1972. Hard Tomatoes, Hard Times: The Failure of the Land Grant College Complex. Washington, D.C.: Agribusiness Accountability Project.

_____. 1973. Hard Tomatoes, Hard Times. Cambridge, Massachusetts: Schenkman Publishing Company.

_____. 1975. Eat Your Heart Out: How Food Profiteers Victimize the Consumer. New York: Random House (Vintage).

Hill, L. D. 1962. Characteristics of the farmers leaving agriculture in an Iowa county. Journal of Farming Economics 44 (May):419-26.

Hoff, Frederic L.; Givan, William D.; Shugors, Owen K.; and Grise, Vernon N. 1977. Flue-cured tobacco mechanization and labor: Impact of alternative production levels. Agricultural Economics Report No. 638. Washington, D.C.: U.S. Department of Agriculture, Economic Research Service.

Holmes, Roy H. 1932. Rural Sociology. New York: McGraw-Hill Book Company, Inc.

Holt, J. 1970. The impact of industrialization of the hired farm work force upon the agricultural economy. American Journal of Agricultural Economics 52:780-87.

Holtman, J. B.; Hansen, C. M.; and Pierson, T. 1977. Michigan mechanical strawberry harvest feasibility studies. Paper presented at meetings of the American Society of Agricultural Engineers, St. Joseph, Michigan, June 26-29.

Hoover, D. M. 1976. Foreword in R. A. Kramer, Impact of Mechanization on Farm Labor Markets: A Short Bibliographic Guide to the Literature. Report No. ERS-38. Raleigh, North Carolina: North Carolina State University, Department of Economics.

Hoover, Dale M., and Perkinson, Leon B. 1977a. An Executive Summary of Flue-Cured Tobacco Harvest Labor: Its Characteristics and Vulnerability to Mechanization. Economics Special Report No. 46. Raleigh: North Carolina State University, Department of Economics and Business.

_____. 1977b. Flue-Cured Tobacco Harvest Labor: Its Characteristics and Vulnerability to Mechanization. Economics Research Report No. 38. Raleigh: North Carolina State University, Department of Economics and Business.

Hoover, Dale M., and Pugh, Charles R. 1973. Probable Location of Flue-Cured Tobacco Production under Modified Lease-and-Transfer Programs. Circular No. 557. Raleigh: North Carolina Agricultural Extension Service.

Hopkins, John A. 1941. Changing Technology and Employment in Agriculture. Washington, D.C.: U.S. Department of Agriculture, Bureau of Agricultural Economics (U.S. Government Printing Office).

Horne, Roman L., and McKibben, Eugene G. 1938. Changes in Technology and Labor Requirements in Crop Production: Mechanical Cotton Picker. National Research Project Report A-2. Philadelphia: Works Progress Administration.

Horsfall, James G. 1975. The fire brigade stops a raging corn epidemic. In That We May Eat: Yearbook of Agriculture, 1975. Washington, D.C.: U.S. Department of Agriculture.

Hull, Carolyn. 1972. Antle: From lettuce trimmer to champion. The Packer (12 August).

Hurst, W. M., and Church, L. M. 1933. Power and Machinery in Agriculture. Miscellaneous Publication No. 157. Washington, D.C.: U.S. Department of Agriculture.

Hussen, Ahmed M. 1978. Economic feasibility of
    mechanical strawberry harvesting in Oregon:
    Estimated private and social benefits and costs.
    Ph.D. dissertation, Oregon State University,
    Corvallis, Oregon.
Irving, George W., and Wadleigh, Cecil H. 1972.
    Environmental impacts of increased production
    efficiency. In Proceedings of the 21st Annual
    Meeting of the Agricultural Research Institute.
    Washington, D.C.: National Academy of Sciences-
    National Research Council.
Jacobs, Harvey M. 1980. Equity in agricultural land
    retention: A social and political assessment of
    local and state policies. Master's thesis, Cornell
    University, Department of City and Regional
    Planning, Ithaca, New York.
Jasny, N. 1938. Research Methods on Farm Use of
    Tractors. New York: Columbia University Press.
Jenkins, Merle T. 1955. Corn agronomy. In Proceedings
    of the 4th Annual Meeting of the Agricultural
    Research Institute. Washington, D.C.: National
    Academy of Sciences-National Research Council.
Jennings, Peter R. 1974. Rice breeding and world food
    production. Science 185 (20 December):1085-88.
Johnson, H. G. 1962. The social policy of an opulent
    society. Pp. 180-95 in Money, Trade, and Economic
    Growth. Cambridge, Massachusetts: Harvard
    University Press.
Johnson, S. S., and Zahara, M. 1976. Prospective
    lettuce harvest mechanization: Impact on labor.
    Journal of the American Society for Horticultural
    Science 101 (August):378-81.
Johnson, V. A. 1982. Relationship between public and
    private breeding research as viewed by a publicly
    supported research program director. In Pioneer
    Hi-Bred International, Report of the 1982 Plant
    Breeding Research Forum. Des Moines, Iowa: Pioneer
    Hi-Bred International.
Johnston, E. A. 1938. The evolution of the mechanical
    cotton harvester. Agricultural Engineering 19
    (September).
Johnston, P. E., and Willis, J. E. 1933. Horse and
    Tractor Power on Illinois Farms. Bulletin No.
    395. Urbana, Illinois: Illinois Experiment
    Station.
Jones, Donald F. 1949. Changes in hybrid seed corn
    production in the future. In Proceedings of the
    4th Annual Hybrid Corn Research Conference.
    Washington, D.C.: American Seed Trade Association.
Just, Richard E.; Schmitz, Andrew; and Silberman,
    David. 1979. Technological change in
    agriculture. Science 206 (14 December):1277-80.

Kellogg, Charles E., and Knapp, D. C. 1966. The College of Agriculture: Science in the Public Service. New York: McGraw-Hill.

Kelly, C. 1967. Mechanical harvesting. Scientific American 217(1):50-59.

Kendrick, J. W. 1964. The gains and losses from technological change. Journal of Farm Ecology 46:1065-72.

Kenney, Martin; Buttel, Frederick H.; Cowan, J. Tadlock; and Kloppenburg, Jack, Jr. 1982. Genetic Engineering in Agriculture. Bulletin No. 125. Ithaca, New York: Cornell University, Department of Rural Sociology.

Kenney, Martin, and Kloppenburg, Jack, Jr. 1983. The American agricultural research system: An obsolete structure? Agricultural Administration 14:1-10.

Klepper, Robert, et al. 1977. Economic performance and energy intensiveness on organic and conventional farms in the corn belt: A preliminary comparison. American Journal of Agricultural Economics 59:1-12.

Kloppenburg, Jack, Jr., and Kenney, Martin. 1983. Biotechnology, seeds, and the restructuring of agriculture. Insurgent Sociologist 12(2).

Knetch, J. L.; Haveman, R. H.; Howe, C. H.; Krutilla, J. V.; and Brewer, M. F. 1969. Federal Natural Resources Development: Basic Issues in Benefit and Cost Measurement. Washington, D.C.: George Washington University, Natural Resource Policy Center.

Kolb, J. H. 1959. Emerging Rural Communities: Group Relations in Rural Society: A Review of Wisconsin Research in Action. Madison, Wisconsin: University of Wisconsin Press.

Kramer, R. A. 1976. Impact of Mechanization on Farm Labor Markets: A Short Bibliographic Guide to the Literature. ESR-38. Raleigh, North Carolina: North Carolina State University, Department of Economics.

Krause, K. R., and Kyle, L. R. 1970. Economic factors underlying the incidence of large farming units: The current situation and probable trends. American Journal of Agricultural Economics 52 (December):748-63.

Krupicka, Ron. 1982. Beating DeKalb at its own game. Prairie Sentinel 1 (December/January):4-5.

Kumar, Ramesh; Chancellor, William; and Garrett, Roger. 1977. Estimate of the Impact of Agricultural Mechanization Developments on In-Field Labor Requirements for California Crops. Davis, California: University of California, Department of Agricultural Engineering.

358

Kyle, L. R.; Sundquist, W. B.; and Guither, H. D.
    1972. Who controls agriculture now? The trends
    underway. In North Central Public Policy Education
    Committee, Who Controls U.S. Agriculture? Special
    Bulletin No. 27. Urbana-Champaign, Illinois:
    University of Illinois, College of Agriculture,
    Cooperative Extension Service.
Langsford, E. L., and Thibodeaux, Ben H. 1939. Plan-
    tation Organization and Operation in the Yazoo
    Mississippi Delta Area. U.S. Department of Agri-
    culture Technical Bulletin No. 682. Washington,
    D.C.: U.S. Government Printing Office.
Lawrence, Francis J. 1975. Strawberry Breeding and
    Evaluation for Mechanical Harvesting. Bulletin
    No. 131. Columbus, Ohio: Ohio State University
    Agricultural Experiment Station.
Leath, Mack N.; Meyer, Lynn H.; and Hall, Lowell D.
    1982. U.S. Corn Industry. Agricultural Economic
    Report No. 479. Washington, D.C.: U.S. Department
    of Agriculture, Economic Research Service.
Leibenluft, Robert F. 1981. Competition in Farm
    Inputs: An Examination of Four Industries. Office
    of Policy Planning, Federal Trade Commission.
    Washington, D.C.: National Technical Information
    Service.
LeRay, Nelson, and Crowe, G. B. 1959. Labor and
    Technology on Selected Cotton Plantations in the
    Delta Area of Mississippi, 1953-54. Bulletin No.
    575. State College, Mississippi: Mississippi
    Agricultural Extension Service.
Lester, Jerry. 1961. Enter Teamsters. California
    Farmer (17 June):573.
LeVeen, P. 1978. The prospects for small-scale farming
    in an industrial society: A critical appraisal of
    Small Is Beautiful. In R. C. Dorf and Y. L. Hunter
    (eds.), Appropriate Visions. San Francisco,
    California: Boyd and Fraser.
Levitan, S. 1973. Work Is Here to Stay, Alas. Salt
    Lake City, Utah: Olympus Publishing Company.
Lewontin, Richard. 1982. Agricultural research and the
    penetration of capital. Science for the People
    (January/February):12-17.
Lianos, T. P., and Paris, Q. 1972. American
    agriculture and the prophecy of increasing misery.
    American Journal of Agricultural Economics 54
    (November):570-77.
Linfield, Michael. 1977. Agricultural mechanization
    in California: A background paper. United Farm
    Workers. (August). Sacramento Bee.
Little, I. M. D. 1950. A Critique of Welfare
    Economics. Oxford: Clarendon Press.

Litzow, Margaret E., and Ozmun, J. L. 1979.
Seventy-five years of research on growth and
development of vegetable crops. HortScience 14
(June):350-54.

Lockeretz, William; Shearer, George; and Kohl, Daniel H.
1981. Organic farming in the corn belt. Science
211 (6 February): 540-47.

Loftsgard, L. D., and Voelker, S. W. 1963. Changing
rural life in the Great Plains. Journal of Farm
Ecology 45 (5):1110-18.

Long, Larry H., and Hansen, Kristen A. 1977.
Selectivity of black return migration to the
south. Rural Sociology 42 (3):317-31.

Lorenzen, C., and Fridley, R. B. 1966. Mechanizing
specialized crops. Agricultural Engineering
47:336-37.

Lorenzen, C., and Hanna, G. C. 1962. Mechanical
harvesting of tomatoes. Agricultural Engineering
43:16-19.

Los Angeles Times. 1978. How UC's machines short-
changed California farm workers. Los Angeles Times
(2 April).

Lu, Yao-Chi. 1979. Technological change and
structure. In U.S. Department of Agriculture,
Structure Issues of American Agriculture.
Agricultural Economic Report No. 438. Washington,
D.C.: U.S. Department of Agriculture, Economics,
Statistics and Cooperatives Service.

Lucier, Gary, and Smith, Allen. 1982. Farm income
update. Pp. 11-13 in Agricultural Outlook
(September). Washington, D.C.: U.S. Department of
Agriculture, Economic Research Service.

Lynch, Duke. 1968. The revolution of California
tomatoes. Canner/Packer, Western Edition,
137(4):10A-10F.

Madden, J. P. 1978. Agricultural mechanization, farm
size and community development. Agricultural
Engineering 59 (8):12-15.

Madden, J. Patrick, and Baker, Heather Tischbein.
1981. An Agenda for Small Farms Research.
Washington, D.C.: National Rural Center.

Madden, J. Patrick, and Partenheimer, Earl J. 1972.
Evidence of economies and diseconomies of farm
size. Pp. 91-107 in A. Gordon Ball and Earl O.
Heady (eds.), Size, Structure, and Future of
Farms. Ames, Iowa: Iowa State University Press.

Mahaffey, Doris, and Doty, Mercer M. 1979. Which Way
Now? Economic Development and Industrialization in
North Carolina. Raleigh, North Carolina: North
Carolina Center for Public Policy Research, Inc.

360

Mangelsdorf, Paul C. 1951. Hybrid corn. Scientific American 185 (August):39-47.

Mangum, G. L. 1967. Contributions and Costs of Manpower Development and Training. Policy Papers in Human Resources and Industrial Relations, No. 5. Ann Arbor, Michigan: University of Michigan, Institute of Labor and Industrial Relations.

Mangum, G., and Walsh, J. 1973. A Decade of Manpower Development and Training. Salt Lake City, Utah: Olympus Publishing Company.

Mann, Charles Kellogg. 1975. Tobacco: The Ants and the Elephants. Salt Lake City, Utah: Olympus Publishing Company.

Manning, Helen. 1977. Man outworks lettuce machine. Salinas Californian (25 August):1.

Marshall, Eliot. 1983. New York University's malaria vaccine: Orphan at birth? Science 219 (4 February):466-67.

Martin, Lloyd W. 1976. A field-scale technical and economic evaluation of strawberry mechanical harvest, handling and processing. Proposal submitted to the North Regional Commission, Corvallis, Oregon.

Martin, Philip, and Hall, Candice. 1978. Labor displacement and public policy. Pg. 34 in Technological Change, Farm Mechanization and Agricultural Employment. Publication 4985. Berkeley: University of California, Division of Agricultural Sciences.

Martin, P. L., and Johnson, J. S. 1978. Tobacco technology and tobacco labor. American Journal of Agricultural Economics 60(4):655-61.

Martinson, O. B., and Campbell, G. R. 1980. Betwixt and between: Farmers and the marketing of agricultural inputs and outputs. In Frederick Buttel and Howard Newby (eds.), The Rural Sociology of the Advanced Societies. Montclair, New Jersey: Allanheld, Osmun and Co.

Marx, Leo. 1964. The Machine in the Garden. New York: Oxford University Press.

Mason, John E. 1942. Cotton allotments in the Mississippi Delta New-Ground area. Journal of Land and Public Utility Economics 18:448-57.

Massey-Ferguson. 1976. Free World Demand for Tractors. London: Massey-Ferguson, Ltd.

McConnell, G. 1953. The Decline of Agrarian Democracy. Berkeley: University of California.

McCrory, S. H.; Hendrickson, R. F.; and Committee. 1937. Technological Trends and National Policy. National Resources Committee, Section on Agriculture. Report of the Subcommittee on Technology to

the National Resources Committee. Series: United
States, 75th Congress, 1st Session, House Document
No. 360.

McDonald, Thomas, and Coffman, George. 1980. Fewer and
Larger Farms by Year 2000--And Some Consequences.
Agriculture Information Bulletin No. 439.
Washington, D.C.: U.S. Department of Agriculture,
Economics and Statistics Service.

McElroy, R. C. 1969. Manpower implications of trends
in the tobacco industry. Talk given at the Association for Public Program Analysis Conference,
U.S. Civil Service Commission, Washington, D.C.,
June 16.

McGibben, E. G., and Griffin, R. A. 1938. Changes in
Power and Equipment--Tractors, Trucks and
Automobiles. WPA Report A-9. Philadelphia: Works
Progress Administration.

McMaster, John Bach. 1883. History of the People of
the United States. New York: D. Appleton and Co.

McMillan, Robert I. 1949. Social Aspects of Farm Mechanization in Oklahoma. Bulletin No. B-339. Stillwater, Oklahoma: Agricultural Experiment Station.

McWilliams, C. 1971. Factories in the Fields. Santa
Barbara, California: Peregrine Press.

Meij, J. L. 1960. Mechanization in Agriculture.
Amsterdam: North-Holland Publishing Company.

Meister, D., and Loftis, A. 1977. A Long Time Coming:
The Struggle to Unionize America's Farm Workers.
New York: MacMillan.

Mellor, J. W. 1954. The economics of mechanization in
agriculture: A study of resource substitution.
Ph.D. dissertation, Cornell University, Ithaca,
New York.

Merrill, Richard, ed. 1976. Radical Agriculture. New
York: Harper.

Metzler, W. H. 1964. The Farm Worker in Changing
Agriculture. Giannini Foundation Research Report
No. 277. Davis, California: University of
California.

Meyerhoff, Al. 1980. Big farming's angry harvest.
Newsweek (3 March):11.

Milk, R. G. 1972. The new agriculture in the U.S.: A
dissenter's view. Land Economics 48 (3):228-35.

Miller, J. E. 1975. Automatic harvesters mechanize
North Carolina's tobacco industry: The effect on
the tobacco farmer. Raleigh, North Carolina:
University of North Carolina (25 February):11.

Miller, Thomas A.; Rodenald, Gordon E.; and McElroy,
Robert G. 1981. Economies of Size in U.S. Field
Crop Farming. ESS Staff Report No. AGESS810224.
Washington, D.C.: U.S. Department of Agriculture,
Economics and Statistics Service.

362

Mishan, E. J. 1960. A survey of welfare economics, 1939-1959. Economics Journal 70 (June):197-264.
_____. 1969. Welfare Economics: Ten Introductory Essays. 2d ed. New York: Random House.
Mooney, Pat R. 1979. Seeds of the Earth: A Private or Public Resource. London: International Coalition for Development Action.
Morgan, Dan. 1979. Merchants of Grain. New York: Viking Press.
Morrison, P. 1972. The Impact and Significance of Rural-Urban Migration in the U.S. Rand Corporation.
Motheral, J. R. 1953. Do tenure practices retard machine harvesting of cotton? The Agricultural Situation. Bureau of Agricultural Economics. Washington, D.C.: U.S. Department of Agriculture.
Muckleston, Keith W., and Highsmith, Richard M., Jr. 1978. Center pivot irrigation in the Columbia Basin of Washington and Oregon: Dynamics and implications. Water Resources Bulletin 14:1121.
Murray, James. 1983. Patterns of investment in biotechnology. Bio/Technology 1 (May):248-50.
Musgrave, R. A. 1969. Cost-benefit analysis and the theory of public finance. Journal of Economics Literature 7 (September):797-806.
Myers, Norman. 1983. A Wealth of Wild Species. Boulder, Colorado: Westview Press.
National Academy of Sciences. 1972. Genetic Vulnerability of Major Crops. Washington, D.C.: National Academy of Sciences.
_____. 1975. Agricultural Production Efficiency. Washington, D.C.: National Academy of Sciences.
National Planning Association. 1970. Policies for Rural People in the 1970s. Washington, D.C.: U.S. Government Printing Office.
National Resources Committee. 1937. Technological Trends and National Policy. 75th Congress, House Document 360 (June).
National Rural Health Council. 1980. Pesticides and You. Washington, D.C.: Rural America.
Nelson, Peter, and Eden, Ada B. 1942. Labor skill requirements vary with type of farming. Current Farm Economics 15:185-88. (Publication of Oklahoma A & M College, Oklahoma.)
New Land Review. 1980. Environmental impact statements should be required on USDA Cooperative Research Service sponsored projects. New Land Review (Spring):10.
Newby, Howard. 1977. The Deferential Worker. London: Allen Lane.
_____. 1979a. Green and Pleasant Land?: Social Change in Rural England. London: Hutchinson.

_____. 1979b. Urbanism and the rural class structure: Reflections on a case study. British Journal of Sociology 30 (December):475-99.

Newby, Howard; Bell, Colin; Rose, David; and Saunders, Peter. 1978. Property, Paternalism and Power. London: Hutchinson.

Newby, Howard, and Utting, Peter. 1984. Agribusiness in Britain. London: Hutchinson. Forthcoming.

Newsweek. 1961. Bud in bloom. Newsweek (23 October): 80-82.

Nicholson, Joseph Shield. 1892. Effects of Machinery on Wages. London: S. Sonnenschein.

Noble, David. 1983. Academia incorporated: Selling the tree of knowledge. Science for the People 15 (January/February):7-11, 50-52.

North Carolina Department of Agriculture. 1979. North Carolina Tobacco Report No. 235. Raleigh: North Carolina Department of Agriculture, Tobacco Affairs Section, Division of Marketing.

Oelhaf, R. C. 1978. Organic Agriculture: Economic and Ecological Comparisons with Conventional Methods. Montclair, New Jersey: Allanheld, Osmun and Co.

Office of Technology Assessment, U.S. Congress. 1981. Impacts of Applied Genetics. Washington, D.C.: U.S. Government Printing Office.

_____. 1982. Impacts of Technology on U.S. Cropland and Rangeland Productivity. Washington, D.C.: U.S. Government Printing Office.

Ogburn, William F., and Nimkoff, Meyer F. 1950. Sociology. 2nd ed. New York: Houghton-Mifflin Company.

Olson, Kent D.; Langley, James; and Heady, Earl O. 1982. Widespread adoption of organic farming practices: Estimated impacts on U.S. agriculture. Journal of Soil and Water Conservation 37 (January/February):1-21.

Paarlberg, Don F. 1964. American Farm Policy. New York: Wiley.

Padfield, Harland, and Martin, William E. 1965. Farmers, Workers and Machines: Technological and Social Change in the Farm Industries of Arizona. Tucson, Arizona: University of Arizona Press.

Pardee, William; Phillipson, David; Billings, James; and Kalton, Robert. 1981. Panel discussion--public vs. private research. In Proceedings of the 27th Annual Farm Seed Conference. Washington, D.C.: American Seed Trade Association.

Parsons, F. L. 1963. Discussion--changing rural life in the Great Plains. Journal of Farm Ecology 45 (December):1117-18.

Parsons, K. H., and Owen, W. F. 1951. Implications of
    trends in farm size and organization. Journal of
    Farm Economics. Proceedings of the Annual Meeting
    of American Agricultural Economics Association,
    November.
Parsons, Philip S. 1966. Costs of Mechanical Tomato
    Harvesting Compared to Hand Harvesting. Bulletin
    No. AXT224 (May). Davis, California: University of
    California Agricultural Extension Service.
Pearce, Andrew. 1980. Seeds of Plenty, Seeds of Want.
    New York: Oxford University Press.
Pederson, H. A. 1952. Attitudes relating to mech-
    anization and farm labor changes in the Yazoo-
    Mississippi delta. Land Economics 28 (4):353-61.
_____. 1954. Mechanized agriculture and the farm
    laborer. Rural Sociology 19:143-51.
Perelman, M. J. 1972. Farming with petroleum.
    Environment 14 (October):8-13.
_____. 1973. Mechanization and the division of
    labor in agriculture. American Journal of
    Agricultural Economics 55 (August):523-26.
_____. 1976. Efficiency in agriculture: The
    economics of energy. Pp. 64-86 in R. Merrill
    (ed.), Radical Agriculture. New York: Harper.
_____. 1977. Farming for Profit in a Hungry
    World: Capital and Crisis in Agriculture.
    Montclair, New Jersey: Allanheld, Osmun and Co.
Perkinson, Leon. 1979. Migration into a North Carolina
    Rural Area, 1970-74. Economics Information Report
    No. 57. Raleigh: North Carolina State University,
    Department of Business and Economics.
Peters, Edward T. 1885. Some Economic and Social
    Effects of Machinery. Salem, Massachusetts: Salem
    Press.
Peterson, C. E. 1981. We need them both. Seedsmen's
    Digest 32 (March):24-29, 46-48.
Peterson, Willis L. 1967. Return to poultry research
    in the United States. Journal of Farm Economics 49
    (3):656-69.
Pfeffer, Max J. 1980. The social relations of subcon-
    tracting: The case of contract vegetable production
    in Wisconsin. Unpublished paper. University of
    Wisconsin, Madison, Department of Rural Sociology.
Phelps, Charles S. 1902. Is there a decadence of New
    England agriculture? New England Magazine 25
    (October):374-83.
Phillips, R. E.; Blevins, R. L.; et al. 1980.
    No-tillage agriculture. Science 208:1108.
Phillips, S. H., and Young, H. M. 1973. No-tillage
    Farming. Milwaukee, Wisconsin: Reiman Associates.
Pierce, Walter H., and Pugh, Charles R. 1956. Cost
    of Producing Farm Products in North Carolina.

Agricultural Economics Information Services
Bulletin No. 52. Raleigh: North Carolina State
University, Department of Agricultural Economics.

Pimentel, D.; Dritschilo, W.; Krummel, J.; and Kutzman,
J. 1975. Energy and land constraints in food
production. Science 190:754-61.

Pimentel, D.; Hurd, L. E.; Belloti, A. C.; Forster,
M. J.; Oku, I. N.; Sholes, O. D.; and Whitman, R.
J. 1973. Food production and the energy crisis.
Science 182 (October):443-49.

Pimentel, D.; Lynn, W.; MacReynolds, W. K.; Heines, M.;
and Ruch, S. 1974. Workshop on research
methodologies for studies of energy, food, man and
the environment, phase 1. Cornell University,
Ithaca, New York.

Pimentel, D., and Pimentel, M. 1979. Food, Energy and
Society. New York: Halsted Press.

Pimentel, D.; Terhune, E. C.; Dyson-Hudson, D.;
Rochereau, S.; Samis, R.; Smith, E. A.; Denman, D.;
Reifschneider, S.; and Shepard, M. 1976. Land
degradation: Effects on food and energy resources.
Science 194:149-55.

Plucknett, Donald L., and Smith, Nigel J. H. 1982.
Agricultural research and Third World food
production. Science 217 (16 July):215-20.

Ponder, H. 1971. Prospects for black farmers in the
years ahead. American Journal of Agricultural
Economics 53 (May):297-301.

Potts, Howard C. 1983. Strengthening exercises for
seedsmen. Seedsmen's Digest 34 (June):
16,20,24,25,47.

President's National Advisory Commission on Rural
Poverty. 1967. The People Left Behind.
Washington, D.C.: U.S. Government Printing Office.

Prest, A. R., and Turvey, R. 1965. Cost-benefit
analysis: A survey. Economics Journal 75
(December):683-736.

Price Commission. 1978. Prices, Costs and Margins in
the Production and Distribution of Compound Feeding
Stuffs for Cattle, Pigs and Poultry. London: Her
Majesty's Stationery Office.

Produce Marketing. 1961. Antle goes all out for field
wrap. Produce Marketing (November):17-19.

Pugh, Charles R. 1978. Provisions of the Tobacco
Program, Consequences of Their Elimination and
Alternatives. Raleigh: North Carolina State
University.

Quaintance, H. W. 1904. The Influence of Farm
Machinery on Production and Labor. Publication
of the American Economic Association. New York:
Macmillan.

Raper, Arthur. 1946. The role of agricultural
     technology in Southern social change. Social Focus
     25:21-30.
Rasmussen, W. D. 1962. The impact of technological
     change on American agriculture, 1862-1962. Journal
     of Economic History 22 (December):578-99.
_____. 1968. Advances in American agriculture:
     The mechanical tomato-harvester as a case study.
     Technology and Culture 9 (October):531-43.
_____. 1975. A postscript: Twenty-five years of
     change in farm productivity. Agricultural History
     49 (January):84-86.
_____. 1977. The mechanization of American
     agriculture. Pp. 295-315 in Agriculture
     Literature: Proud History, Future Promise.
     Washington, D.C.: U.S. Department of Agriculture.
Raup, P. 1961. Economic aspects of population decline
     in rural communities. In Center for Agricultural
     and Economic Adjustment, Labor Mobility and
     Population in Agriculture. Ames, Iowa: Iowa State
     University Press.
_____. 1978. Some questions of value and scale
     in American agriculture. American Journal of
     Agricultural Economics 60(2):303-08.
Razee, Don. 1976. The advantages of transplanting
     lettuce. California Farmer (20 November):6.
Reeder, W. W., and LeRay, L. N. 1970. Farm Families
     under Stress. Bulletin No. 1027. Ithaca, New
     York: Cornell University, Agricultural Experiment
     Station.
Rees, A. 1966. Economic expansion and persisting
     unemployment: An overview. Pp. 327-49 in R. A.
     Gordon and M. S. Gordon (eds.), Prosperity and
     Unemployment. New York: Wiley.
Report of the Industrial Commission. Vol. 10. 1901.
     Washington, D.C: U.S. Government Printing Office.
Research and Planning Services. 1979. North Carolina
     State Government Statistical Abstract. Raleigh,
     North Carolina: Division of State Budget and
     Management.
Robbins, W. 1974. The American Food Scandal. New
     York: William Morrow.
Robinson, E. A. G. 1958. The Structure of Competitive
     Industry. Chicago: University of Chicago Press.
The Rockefeller Foundation and The Office of Science and
     Technology Policy. 1982. Science for Agriculture:
     Report of a Workshop on Critical Issues in American
     Agriculture. New York: The Rockefeller Foundation.
Rodale, Robert. 1980a. The Cornucopia Project.
     Emmaus, Pennsylvania: Rodale Press.

_____. 1980b. Organic paths to food security. Speech given at Ohio State University, Columbus, Ohio, October.

Rodefeld, R. D. 1974. The changing organizational and occupational structure of farming and the implications for farm work force individuals, families and communities. Ph.D. dissertation, University of Wisconsin, Madison, Wisconsin.

_____. 1975. Evidence, issues and conclusions on the current status and trends in U.S. farm types. Paper presented at the Annual Meeting of the Rural Sociological Society, San Francisco, California.

_____. 1979. The Family-Type Farm and Structural Differentiation: Trends, Causes and Consequences of Change, Research Needs. Staff Paper 24. University Park, Pennsylvania: Pennsylvania State University, Department of Agricultural Economics and Rural Sociology.

Rodefeld, R. D.; Flora, J.; Voth, D.; Fujimoto, I.; and Converse, J., eds. 1978. Change in Rural America: Causes, Consequences, and Alternatives. St. Louis, Missouri: C. V. Mosby Company.

Rogers, E., and Burdge, R. 1972. Social Change in Rural Societies. 2nd ed. New York: Appleton-Century-Crofts.

Rogers, James Edwin Thorold. 1866. History of Agriculture and Prices in England. Vol. I. Oxford: Clarendon Press.

Rohrlich, G., ed. 1970. Social Economics for the 1970's. New York: Dunellen Company.

Rushton, Bill. 1973. South coast conspiracy. Southern Exposure 2(2/3):4-21.

Russell, W. A. 1974. Comparative performance for maize hybrids representing different eras of maize breeding. In Proceedings of the 29th Annual Corn and Sorghum Research Conference. Washington, D.C.: American Seed Trade Association.

Ruttan, Vernon W. 1982. Changing role of public and private sectors in agricultural research. Science 216 (2 April):23-29.

Ruttan, Vernon W., and Sundquist, W. Burt. 1982. Agricultural research as an investment: Past experience and future opportunities. In Pioneer Hi-Bred International, Report of the 1982 Plant Breeding Research Forum. Des Moines, Iowa: Pioneer Hi-Bred International.

St. John, E. 1974. The Plight of Unemployed Single Farmworkers. Research Monograph No. 14. Davis, California: University of California.

Salinas Californian. 1961a. Antle, Teamsters sign field contract. Salinas Californian (5 May):1,3.

368

_____. 1961b. Bud Antle Inc. resigns from grower
group. Salinas Californian (8 May):1-2.
_____. 1972. Bud Antle dies. Salinas
Californian (2 August):1-2.
Sanderson, Dwight. 1937. Research Memorandum on
Rural Life in the Depression. Bulletin No. 34.
New York: Social Science Research Council.
Santa Cruz Sentinel. 1975. Lettuce growers develop
mechanical harvester. Santa Cruz (California)
Sentinel (20 July):8.
Saville, R. J. 1941. Trends in mechanization and
tenure changes in the Southeast. In The People,
the Land and the Church in the Rural South.
Chicago: Farm Foundation.
Scheiffer, J. C., and Fujimoto, I. 1969. The Social
Implications of Agricultural Mechanization: A
Bibliography. Davis, California: University of
California, Department of Applied Behavioral
Sciences.
Schmidt, F. 1964. After the Bracero. Los Angeles,
California: University of California, Los Angeles,
Institute of Industrial Relations.
Schmitz, A., and Seckler, D. 1970. Mechanized agri-
culture and social welfare: The case of the tomato
harvester. American Journal of Agricultural
Economics 54 (November):569-77.
Schrag, Peter. 1978. Rubber tomatoes: The unsavory
partnership of research and agribusiness. Harper's
256 (June):24-25, 27-29.
Schultz, T. W. 1953. The Economic Organization of
Agriculture. New York: McGraw-Hill Book Co.
_____. 1961. A policy to redistribute losses from
economic progress. Journal of Farm Economics 43:
554-65.
_____. 1968. Institutions and the rising economic
value of man. American Journal of Agricultural
Economics 50:1113-22.
Schumacher, E. F. 1973. Small Is Beautiful. New York:
Harper & Row.
Science. 1983. Special issue on biotechnology.
Science 219 (11 February).
Scientific American. 1981. Special issue on industrial
microbiology. Scientific American 245 (September).
Scientific American Supplement. 1900. Farming by
machinery. Scientific American 50 (21 July):20528.
Seedsmen's Digest. 1982. Hibrex hybrid wheat program
accelerates. Seedsmen's Digest 33 (October):22-24.
Segur, Hub. 1974. Lettuce: From seed to supermarket.
Unpublished paper. University of California,
Davis, Department of Applied Behavioral Sciences.
Self, Peter, and Storing, Herbert J. 1962. The State
and the Farmer. London: Allen and Unwin.

Servin, William. 1979. Irrigation dries up small
    farms. In These Times (22-28 August).

Shea, K. P. 1966. American agriculture: Who stole the
    revolution? Environment 18 (October):28-38.

Shear, G. M. 1968. The development of the no-tillage
    concept in the U.S. Outlook on Agriculture 5:247.

Sheffield, Leslie F. 1977. The economics of
    irrigation. Irrigation Journal 27:18.

Showalter, Ralph. 1973. Tobacco Farm Mechanization
    Project, Phase II. Raleigh, North Carolina:
    Social Development Corporation.

Simpson, James R., and Farris, Donald E. 1982. The
    World's Beef Business. Ames, Iowa: Iowa State
    University Press.

Sinclair, S. 1958. Discussion--Technological advance
    and the future of the family farm. Journal of Farm
    Economics 40 (February):1609-12.

Sisler, D. G. 1977. The World Food Situation: What Is
    the U.S. Role? Ithaca, New York: Cornell
    University, Department of Agricultural Economics.

Sjaastad, L. A. 1962. The costs and returns of human
    migration. Journal of Political Economy 70
    (October):80-93.

Smith, E. J. 1975. Employment Changes in the Flue-
    Cured Tobacco Area, 1969-1970. Agricultural
    Economic Report No. 309. Washington, D.C.: U.S.
    Department of Agriculture, Economic Research
    Service.

Smith, Helen Everston. 1900. Colonial Days and Ways.
    New York: Ungar.

Smith, H. P. 1938. Progress in mechanical harvesting
    of cotton. Agricultural Engineering 19
    (September).

Smith, Roger. 1977. Lettuce picker may renew UFW,
    growers' battle. Part III. Los Angeles Times
    (22 August):9-10.

Smith, T. Lynn. 1947. Sociology of Rural Life.
    Revised edition. New York: Harper and Brothers.

_____. 1974. Studies of the Great Rural Tap Roots
    of Urban Poverty in the United States. New York:
    Carlton Press.

Solis, F. 1971. Socioeconomic and cultural conditions
    of migrant workers. Social Casework 52 (1):308-15.

Sorokin, P. A.; Zimmerman, C. C.; and Galpin, C. J.
    1930. A Systematic Source Book in Rural
    Sociology. Minneapolis, Minnesota: University
    of Minnesota Press.

Splinter, William E. 1977. Center pivot irrigation.
    Scientific American 234:90.

_____. 1979a. Energy and the center pivot.
    Irrigation Journal 29:42.

_____. 1979b. Agricultural mechanization -- A credibility problem. Agricultural Engineering 60:42-43.

Sprague, G. F. 1955. Corn genetics. In Proceedings of the 4th Annual Meeting of the Agricultural Research Institute. Washington, D.C.: National Academy of Sciences, National Research Council.

_____. 1967. Agricultural production in the developing countries. Science 157 (18 August): 774-78.

_____. 1971. Genetic vulnerability in corn and sorghum. In Proceedings of the 26th Annual Hybrid Corn Industry Research Conference. Washington, D.C.: American Seed Trade Association.

_____. 1980. The changing role of the private and public sectors in corn breeding. In Proceedings of the 35th Annual Corn and Sorghum Research Conference. Washington, D.C.: American Seed Trade Association.

Staub, William J., and Blase, Melvin G. 1971. Genetic technology and agricultural development. Science 173 (9 July):119-23.

Steele, Leon. 1978. The hybrid corn industry in the United States. In D. B. Walden (ed.), Maize Breeding and Genetics. New York: Wiley-Interscience.

Steinhart, J. S., and Steinhart, C. E. 1974. Energy use in the U.S. food system. Science 184 (April):307-16.

Stewart, Robert E. 1979. Seven Decades that Changed America: A History of the American Society of Agricultural Engineers. St. Joseph, Michigan: American Society of Agricultural Engineers.

Stockdale, J. D. 1969. Social implications of technologic change in agriculture. Paper presented at the Annual Meeting of the Rural Sociological Society, San Francisco, August 29.

_____. 1977. Technology and change in United States agriculture: Model or warning? Sociologia Ruralis 17 (1/2):43-58.

Stoltzfus, V. 1973. Amish agriculture: Adaptive strategies for economic survival of community life. Rural Sociology 38 (Summer):196-206.

Stone, Marvin D. 1977. Effects of center pivot irrigation on land use, land tenure, and settlement patterns on a selected Great Plains landscape, the Holt table portion of Holt County, Nebraska. Ph.D. dissertation, University of Kansas, Department of Geography and Meteorology, Manhattan, Kansas.

Street, James H. 1946. The tractor revolution. Atlantic Monthly 177:111-15.

_____. 1957. The New Revolution in the Cotton
Economy. Chapel Hill, North Carolina: University
of North Carolina Press.

_____. 1966. Mechanizing the cotton harvest.
Agricultural History 40:157-76.

Studebaker, John A. 1982. Fifty years with breeder's
rights. Seedsmen's Digest 33 (May):22-27.

Suggs, C. W. 1972. The mechanical harvesting of flue-
cured tobacco. Part 1: Leaf removing device.
Tobacco Science 16.

_____. 1974. Mechanical harvesting of flue-cured
tobacco. Part 5: Factors affecting rate. of
adoption. Tobacco Science 18.

Swaminathan, M. S. 1982. Biotechnology research and
Third World agriculture. Science 218 (3 December):
967-72.

Taylor, P. S. 1938. Power farming and labor displacement in the cotton belt, 1937. Monthly Labor
Review 46 (March):595-607.

Technology on the Farm. 1940. Special report by an
Interbureau Committee and the Bureau of Agricul-
tural Economics of the United States Department of
Agriculture. Washington, D.C.: U.S. Government
Printing Office.

Thomas, Robert J. 1980. Citizenship and labor supply:
The social organization of industrial agriculture.
Ph.D. dissertation, Northwestern University,
Evanston, Illinois.

Tolley, G. S., and Farmer, B. M. 1967. Farm labor
adjustment to changing technology. Pp. 41-52 in
C. E. Bishop (ed.), Farm Labor in the United
States. New York: Columbia University Press.

Triplett, G. B., and Van Doren, D. M. 1977. Agriculture without tillage. Scientific American 236
(1):28.

Truog, E. 1944. Plowman's folly refuted. Harper's
189:173.

Tudge, Colin. 1977. The Famine Business. London:
Faber.

Tweeten, L. G. 1965. The income structure of farms by
economic class. Journal of Farm Economics 47
(2):207-21.

Tweeten, Luther, and Huffman, W. 1980. Structural
change: An overview. Pp. 1-98 in L. Tweeten, W.
Huffman, S. Sonka, and R. D. Rodefeld, Structure of
Agriculture and Information Needs Regarding Small
Farms. National Rural Center Small Farms Project,
Paper VII. Washington, D.C.: National Rural
Center.

Uhl, J. N. 1969. The industrialization process.
1969. Pp. 83-97 in B. F. Cargill and G. E.
Rossmiller (eds.), Fruit and Vegetable Harvest

372

Mechanization: Manpower Implications. Report No.
17. East Lansing, Michigan: Michigan State
University, Rural Manpower Center.
United States Bureau of the Census. 1936. United
States Census of Agriculture, 1935. Vol. 1, Table
3, p. xx.
_____. 1961. United States Census of Agriculture,
1959. Vol. 2, Table 24, pp. 1124-28.
_____. 1972. Census of Population: 1970,
Employment Profiles of Selected Low-Income Areas,
Selected Rural Counties in North Carolina. Final
Report PAC(3)-74. Washington, D.C.: U.S.
Government Printing Office.
United States Congress, House of Representatives.
1980. Plant Variety Protection Act Amendments.
Hearings before the Subcommittee on Department
Investigations, Oversight, and Research of the
Committee on Agriculture. Ninety-sixth Congress.
Washington, D.C.: U.S. Government Printing Office.
United States Department of Agriculture (USDA). 1940.
Technology on the Farm. Special report by an
Interbureau Committee and the Bureau of Agricul-
tural Economics, U.S. Department of Agriculture.
Washington, D.C.: U.S. Government Printing Office.
_____. 1948. 1949 Agricultural Outlook Chart.
Washington, D.C.: U.S. Government Printing Office.
_____. 1963. Soil Survey of Dundy County,
Nebraska. Washington, D.C.: U.S. Department of
Agriculture, Soil Conservation Service.
_____. 1968. Vegetable Processing--Annual
Summary: Acreage, Production, and Value of
Principal Commercial Crops by States with
Comparisons, 1961-1968. Washington, D.C.: U.S.
Department of Agriculture, Statistical Reporting
Service.
_____. 1969. Potential Mechanization in the
Flue-Cured Tobacco Industry with Emphasis on Human
Resource Adjustment. Agricultural Economics Report
No. 169. Washington, D.C.: U.S. Department of
Agriculture.
_____. 1975a. Minimum Tillage: A Preliminary
Technology Assessment. Washington, D.C.: U.S.
Department of Agriculture, Office of Planning and
Evaluation.
_____. 1975b. That We May Eat. Washington, D.C.:
U.S. Government Printing Office.
_____. 1975c. Structural Characteristics of
Flue-Cured Tobacco Farms and Prospects for
Mechanization. Agricultural Economic Report No.
309. Washington, D.C.: U.S. Department of
Agriculture, Economic Research Service.

_____. 1977a. Flue-Cured Tobacco Mechanization and Labor: Impacts of Alternative Production Levels. Agricultural Economic Report No. 368. Washington, D.C.: U.S. Department of Agriculture, Economic Research Service.

_____. 1977b. Agricultural Statistics 1976. Tables 614 and 626. Washington, D.C.: U.S. Department of Agriculture.

_____. 1978. Changes in Farm Production and Efficiency, 1977. Statistical Bulletin No. 612. Washington, D.C.: U.S. Department of Agriculture, Economics, Statistics, and Cooperatives Service.

_____. 1979. Natural Resources Capital in U.S. Agriculture. Unpublished ESCS staff paper, U.S. Department of Agriculture, Economics, Statistics and Cooperatives Service.

_____. 1980a. Agricultural Statistics 1980. Washington, D.C.: U.S. Government Printing Office.

_____. 1980b. Report and Recommendations on Organic Farming. Washington, D.C.: U.S. Department of Agriculture.

_____. 1982. Economic Indicators of the Farm Sector: Income and Balance Sheet Statistics, 1981. Report ECIFS 1-1. Washington, D.C.: U.S. Department of Agriculture, Economic Research Service.

United States Department of Agriculture and the National Research Council. 1973. Report of the Committee on Research Advisory to the USDA. Springfield, Virginia: National Technical Information Service.

United States Government. 1938. A Study of Farm Mechanization and Farm Labor Changes. 1938. Texas AES, WPA, and FSA joint study. (Reference incomplete.)

United States Senate. 1975. The flue-cured tobacco industry--changes and adjustments. Pp. 295-302 in Ninety-third Congress, 2nd session, Senate Committee on Agriculture and Forestry, United States Agricultural Outlook. Washington, D.C.: U.S. Government Printing Office.

_____. 1978. Priorities in Agricultural Research of the United States Department of Agriculture: A Summary Report of the Hearings. Washington, D.C.: U.S. Government Printing Office.

University of California. 1974. A Century of Service, University of California 1874-1974. Berkeley, California: University of California, Division of Agricultural Sciences.

University of Iowa, State University Center for Agricultural and Economic Adjustment. 1961. Labor Mobility and Population in Agriculture. Ames, Iowa: Iowa State University Press.

USDA. See United States Department of Agriculture.

374

Valvano, Vincent M. 1981. Concentration and centralization in U.S. citrus production: A political-economic approach. Paper presented to the Conference on the Political Economy of Food and Agriculture in Advanced Industrial Societies, Guelph, Ontario, Canada.

Vance, Rupert. 1945. All These People. Chapel Hill, North Carolina: University of North Carolina Press.

_____. 1946. Wanted: The South's Future for the Nation. Atlanta, Georgia: Southern Regional Council.

Vandiver, J. S. 1966. The changing realm of king cotton. Trans-Action 3(November):24-30.

Vincent, A. F. 1969. The agricultural labor market in Arizona. Pp. 223-44 in B. F. Cargill and G. E. Rossmiller (eds.), Fruit and Vegetable Harvest Mechanization: Manpower Implications. Report No. 17. East Lansing, Michigan: Michigan State University, Rural Manpower Center.

Wade, N. 1973. Agriculture: Social sciences oppressed and poverty stricken. Science 180 (May):719.

_____. 1975. Agriculture: Academy group suggests major shakeup to President Ford. Science 190 (December):959.

Walden, D. B. 1978. Maize Breeding and Genetics. New York: Wiley-Interscience.

Wallace, Henry A., and Brown, William L. 1956. Corn and Its Early Fathers. East Lansing, Michigan: Michigan State University Press.

Walsh, George E. 1900. Machinery in agriculture. Cassiers Magazine 19 (December):137-48.

_____. 1901. Steam power for agricultural purposes. Harper's Weekly 45 (June):567.

Wardle, Christopher. 1977. Changing Food Habits in the U.K. London: Earth Resources Research, Ltd.

Watkins, Rupert. 1979. Tobacco Information. North Carolina Extension Bulletin AG-187 67-78. Raleigh, North Carolina: University of North Carolina.

Webb, Raymond E., and Bruce, W. M. 1968. Redesigning the tomato for mechanized production. In Science for Better Living: Yearbook of Agriculture, 1968. Washington, D.C.: U.S. Department of Agriculture.

Wells, David A. 1898. Recent Economic Changes and Their Effect on Distribution of Wealth and Well-being of Society. New York: D. Appleton and Company.

Wernick, Sarah, and Lockeretz, William. 1977. Motivation and practice of organic farmers. Compost Science 18.

West, Quentin M. 1976. Why ERS should expand work in technology assessment. Pp. 1-3 in Economic

Research Service, U.S. Department of Agriculture, Technology Assessment: Proceedings of an ERS Workshop, 20-22 April.

Western Growers and Shippers Association. 1961. Mechanical harvesting: Progress report. Newport Beach, California: Western Grower and Shipper (April):14-15.

White, Henry. 1903. The problem of machinery. American Federationist 10 (February):83-86.

White, T. K., and Irwin, G. D. 1972. Farm size and specialization. In A. G. Ball and E. O. Heady (eds.), Size, Structure, and Future of Farms. Ames, Iowa: Iowa State University Press.

Whittelsey, N. K., et al. 1976. Benefits and Costs of Irrigation Development in Washington. Vol. II: Final Report. Prepared for the House of Representatives and the Legislative Transportation Committee. Department of Agricultural Economics, Washington State University, and the Washington State Legislature.

Williams, B. O. 1939. The impact of mechanization of agriculture on the farm population of the south. Rural Sociology 4 (September):300-13.

Winslow, Marj. 1976a. Revolution likely in lettuce fields. The Packer (10 April):19c.

_____. 1976b. Revolution hits California fields: Green army changes techniques. The Packer (15 May):12b-13b.

Woolf, W. F. 1971. The economics of a reduced labor supply on cotton farms. Louisiana Agriculture 14(2):10-11.

Yarwood, C. E. 1970. Man-made plant diseases. Science 168 (10 April):218-20.

Yeager, L. B., and Tuerck, D. C. 1969. Trade Policy and the Price System. Scranton, Pennsylvania: International Textbook Company.

Zahara, M., and Johnson, S. 1979. Status of harvest mechanization of fruits, nuts, and vegetables. HortScience 14:578-82.

Zahara, M.; Johnson, S.; and Garrett, R. E. 1974. Labor requirements, harvest costs, and the potential for mechanical harvest of lettuce. Journal of the American Society of Horticultural Science 99 (November):535-37.

Zimmerman, Burke K. 1983. Conflicts pervade Third World biotech proposal. Bio/Technology 1 (March):131-32.

Zobel, Melvin P., and Parsons, Philip S. 1965. Tomato Costs, 1965: Hand Harvest, Yolo County. Mimeo. Davis, California: California Agricultural Extension Service.

376

_____. 1969. <u>Tomato Costs of Production: Yolo County--1969</u>. Mimeo. Davis, California: California Agricultural Extension Service.

Zuber, M. S., and Darrah, L. L. 1980. 1979 U.S. corn germplasm base. In <u>Proceedings of the 35th Annual Corn and Sorghum Research Conference</u>. Washington, D.C.: American Seed Trade Association.